Stewart Granger's talent for writing is as exciting as his talent for acting – and living. Funny, heart-breaking, hair-raising and always completely candid, this autobiography discusses openly his tempestuous private life and presents a vivid insider's view of movie-making.

He is best known for his starring roles in: *The Man in Grey*, *Madonna of the Seven Moons*, *Waterloo Road*, *Saraband for Dead Lovers*, *Adam and Evelyne*, *King Solomon's Mines*, *Scaramouche*, *Young Bess*, *The Prisoner of Zenda*, *Beau Brummell*, *Bhowani Junction* and *Harry Black and the Tiger*.

Man is born unto trouble, as the sparks fly upward.

Job 5:7

STEWART GRANGER

Sparks Fly Upward

A PANTHER BOOK

GRANADA
London Toronto Sydney New York

Published in paperback by Granada Publishing Limited in 1982

ISBN 0 586 05599 1

First published in Great Britain by
Granada Publishing Limited 1981
Copyright © Stewart Granger 1981

Granada Publishing Limited
Frogmore, St Albans, Herts AL2 2NF
and
36 Golden Square, London W1R 4AH
866 United Nations Plaza, New York, NY 10017, USA
117 York Street, Sydney, NSW 2000, Australia
100 Skyway Avenue, Rexdale, Ontario, M9W 3A6, Canada
61 Beach Road, Auckland, New Zealand

Printed and bound in Great Britain by
Cox & Wyman Ltd, Reading
Set in Baskerville

Granada ®
Granada Publishing ®

For my darling daughter Lindsay who hid me away in her little house and saw that I kept writing, and for my dear friend Kitty Black without whom I would have found it impossible.

Prelude

Mrs Perryman lived out in North London in one of a row of semi-detached houses, all identical, all ugly, with geraniums in window boxes and an aspidistra in the parlour. She was one of the most famous clairvoyants in England and my mother and I had been visiting her regularly for many months. My mother had recently lost the man she had adored for twenty years. She couldn't accept the fact of his death and had got in touch with Mrs Perryman in order to give her hope that he wasn't lost to her for ever, so I would sit with her as she spoke to her beloved Victor. It was uncanny and rather frightening to see my mother holding long conversations with a voice coming from Mrs Perryman who had gone into a trance. She was convinced that she was speaking to Victor and after each seance would ask me anxiously for reassurance. 'That was Victor who came through, wasn't it? You could feel it too, couldn't you?' And I would always agree, but I didn't feel it, not really, not at all. There was something, of course. How could that woman have described him so vividly? How could she have known that his pet name for my mother had been 'Freddy', her real name being Frederica; that he used to drive a yellow car, loved his meerschaum pipe that my mother had given him for Christmas? How could she have known all these things unless there was something. But at the age of twenty I was sceptical and only attended these seances to keep my mother company.

Mrs Perryman always told me that she was glad I was there as I was very psychic and gave out a lot of 'ectoplasm', whatever that was, which helped her in her work. One day she told me that she would like to tell my fortune as I had a very interesting aura.

'He's a Taurus, isn't he, Mrs Stewart?' she asked. 'What hour was he born?' My mother told her that I'd been born at 2 a.m. 'Ah, a triple Taurus. I knew there was something interesting. A very strong sign indeed, very strong.' My mother gave me a look as much as to say 'how right she is'. I just smiled back.

'Now give me your hands.' Mrs Perryman examined the palms, pressed them and smoothed them as she muttered to herself. Then she took a velvet cloth off something on the table, revealing a crystal ball. Oh no, I thought to myself, not a crystal ball! Soon she'll be asking me to cross her palm with silver. Then she started to mutter to herself again and seemed to be going into one of her trances, suddenly in a deeper voice she said, 'Trouble, trouble, boil and bubble.'

I couldn't help correcting her. 'It's "bubble, bubble, toil and trouble," Mrs Perryman.'

'That's as may be, my dear, but I see much more trouble in your life than bubble.' That shut me up. 'You're going to be very successful in your chosen career. You'll be a fine stage actor.' She knew I was enjoying myself as a poorly paid film extra and I suppose thought that this prediction would cheer me up.

'I have no intention of being an actor, Mrs Perryman, no intention at all. I'm just a film extra and like it that way.'

'Well, that's what you think, my dear. I'm just telling you what I see here. Yes, you'll be very successful, it'll take time and there'll be lots of hard work but you'll get there in the end, you'll succeed if. . .' and then she paused as a worried look came over her face.

'Mrs Stewart, would you leave us for a moment. I think I could work better with your son alone.' My mother reluctantly left the room. 'I didn't want to say this in front of her, she's suffered enough, poor lady.' A cold shiver went down my spine. What was she going to tell me that might make my mother suffer? She was gazing intently into that crystal ball. 'I see a fork here when you're twenty-nine.' She looked up at me searchingly. 'If you survive that fork. . .'

'You mean I might die when I'm twenty-nine,' I asked rather anxiously. After all, that was only nine years off and I was really beginning to enjoy my life.

'I'm not sure, my dear. I see so much suffering and death but nothing is certain or the rest of your life wouldn't be so clear.' Then her face brightened. 'If you survive, I see such success, fame, money. You'll become a film star, the biggest film star in England.'

Now I began to feel better. This was absolute rubbish and so her warning about my imminent death was rubbish too, but I still wanted her to go on as there's something fascinating when a fortune teller weaves fantasies about your future triumphs. You know it's all nonsense but you still want to hear it.

'You'll be married to a lovely girl and have two children.' Then she looked a bit sad. 'Oh dear, I see a divorce but then you'll cross the sea and become a world-famous film star – world-famous, dear.' She became very excited as if she was partly responsible for this fantastic achievement. 'Oh, I wish I could be there to see it but I shan't,' she said sadly. I was to learn later that she had terminal cancer at the time and knew it. 'You'll marry again, another famous film star and have a daughter and much success and happiness for you both.'

Her face changed again as she worriedly looked into that crystal. 'Oh dear, I see another fork when you're forty-seven.' That was a long way off so it didn't give me the same feeling of dread that the earlier prediction had. 'Please, dear, do remember what I say. Do take care when you're forty-seven, won't you?' I'm going to take care the whole bloody time, I thought. 'If you survive this fork there'll be another divorce, I'm afraid. How sad for your daughter.' She brightened up again. 'You'll cross the water, back to England. Your success will continue and I see another marriage. Another marriage, dear, won't that be nice. But with all your success there'll be trouble, lots of trouble, but you're a fighter, you're strong, you'll succeed. Don't worry, dear, you'll succeed. I'm tired now, can't go on any more. Was it interesting?' She asked as if she hadn't been sure what she'd said and then I realized all this time I'd been speaking to her 'control'.

'Yes,' I replied. 'Fascinating. Thank you so much, Mrs Perryman. I hope some of the things come true. How much do I owe you?'

'Nothing, dear, nothing at all.'

I left her still gazing into that crystal ball. I collected my mother and we started off towards the car. She could see I was rather preoccupied. 'What did she tell you?'

'Oh, nothing much.'

'But she must have told you something.'

I looked at her a moment. 'Well, darling, she told me I was going to be a film star, a world-famous film star. How about that?' I thought she'd find the idea as ridiculous as I did, but she didn't.

'Well, why not? I always thought you'd be something special.' Of course, after all, she'd produced me, hadn't she!

1

I was born on 6 May 1913 in a flat in the Old Brompton Road, London, and christened James Lablache in the little church in The Boltons: James after my father, the eighth eldest son in a direct line, all of whom had been christened James, and Lablache after my mother's great-grandfather Luigi Lablache, the world-famous *basso profondo*.

My father, Major James Stewart, RE, OBE, was a Scot, the eldest of thirteen, seven boys and six girls. All the boys were big, their average height being six foot one, but my grandmother was tiny and my father used to tell me how, when she was really angry, he and his brothers would lift her on to the enormous drawing-room mantelpiece and keep her there until she'd promised they wouldn't be punished. He always spoke of his family with great love. He was an army man in a long line of army men, a great athlete, as all the silver cups on the Welsh dresser in the dining-room testified, and seemed to have won every trophy for track events at Cheltenham College. He passed first out of Woolwich (no mean feat back in the 1880s), showing he had great academic brilliance, something I didn't inherit. He was fifty-five when I was born, a confirmed bachelor until he met my mother and just lost his head over her. He had spent most of his youth in the Indian Army and was a typical product; everything by the book. If it wasn't, he was rather lost and I, apparently, was not 'by the book'. He always seemed to be rather shocked at what he'd sired. He was a very gentle man, and I never saw him lose his temper or swear. I wish he had. I wanted to love him but I was never able to get close to him. He was a sort of ghost in our home; he was there, but he never asserted himself. Like all young children I could sense when something wasn't normal and there was certainly something not normal in his relationship with my mother. To start with, the sleeping arrangements were so odd. I was in one room with my nanny, my sister Iris and my mother in another, and my father had a small monkish bedroom to himself. I never saw him cuddle my mother, or kiss her, except on the cheek when he said goodnight, and I noticed how she always turned her head away. Of course, I never saw them in bed together.

My mother was a famous beauty. Her father was an actor and her mother, Jane Emmerson, had been a member of Henry Irving's company. When she told Irving she was going to marry my grandfather he replied, 'If you marry that bloody foreigner, you'll never work for me again.' Well, she did and she didn't.

Mother fell in love very young with an Honourable Fitz – Herbert or William, I can never remember which. They eloped when she was eighteen and lived much of the time in Monte Carlo where they were very social, going to parties every night, although my mother knew that her husband was very ill. She would beg him to rest but he wouldn't listen and a year later he died in her arms of tuberculosis, so poor Mummy had to come crawling back to my grandmother who was an absolute bitch and made her life hell. So here was my beautiful mother, dying to get away from home and here was my poor bachelor father. They met and that was it. After a brief courtship they married. My father was the happiest man in the world and my mother was able to leave home.

But now comes trouble. First, an actor; young, good-looking, hot-blooded. My father, a big man, remember, chases him round London with a riding crop. End of first trouble. Then a politician; young, good-looking, hot-blooded, etc. My father meets him and tells him that if he doesn't lay off, his career will be ruined, as my father has political influence. End of second trouble. There seems to have been a pause here and a certain amount of connubial tranquillity as my sister is born, and a year later my mother becomes pregnant with me. Finally the third trouble arrives, in the shape of the new GP, Dr V.A.L.E. Corbold, after which my poor father gave up. And here's an odd thing. My mother's grandfather taught Queen Victoria and her children to sing and Corbold's father taught them to paint. That's why the poor man had all those names: Victor after Her Majesty, Albert after her husband, Louis after Princess Louise, his godmother, and Edward after the Prince of Wales. To please my mother, and also because I loved him too, my wife and I named our son James after my father and Vale in memory of Uncle Victor. I don't think young James has ever forgiven me.

As a child I had Latin good looks and a strong character, meaning I had black hair and a hell of a temper. My sister Iris was plain, quiet and deadly and war was declared between us at a very early age. She was a Scorpio and if I was a triple Taurus, she was a quadruple Scorpio, if that's possible. Of course, my Nanny, who was a trouble-making cow, would fill my ears with choice bits like, 'Your Mummy sleeps with your sister because she loves her more than she loves you, and you can see how much more attention she gets than you do', which didn't help my attitude towards my sister or my mother.

At a very early age I remember wanting to attract the attention of the men of the family, my father and, as I thought at the time, my uncle, but they didn't seem to want to know. Much later I understood why. One was completely emasculated and the other was just plain guilty, but try explaining that to a four year old. I simply couldn't understand why I was only disciplined by my mother or by Nanny.

Holidays were spent in our house in Polperro, Cornwall. Actually it was Uncle's house but I didn't know that at the time. We also had a 30 ft motor launch with a dinghy so there were lovely outings when we'd take picnic hampers and fish on the way to the coves, then row ashore to bathe and play on the white sandy beaches. In those days there were no tourists and I remember my fury once when some other picnickers were on *our* beach.

I was about three when I first tried to see how much I could get away with. All was ready for one of our outings: lovely hampers of food and drink, the dinghy at the wharf to take us aboard, when I announced that I didn't want to go. Instead of my father or Uncle picking me up by the seat of my pants and throwing me into the boat, they looked rather embarrassed and slightly disgusted, which merely added to my fury. Then Mummy, Nanny and my sister started pleading with me. The more they pleaded the more adamant I became, sneaking looks at my father to try and get some response from him, and then at my uncle. Nothing. Just icy disapproval. The outcome was we didn't go. Instead of a bloody good hiding all I had were a lot of females fussing around me.

At home the women never left me alone to discover things for myself so, on those trips to Cornwall, I spent as much time as possible with the fishermen and the farmers. I adored them. I tried to speak like them and copy their lovely soft dialect. I remember one day, after an outing with my fishermen friends, I had been given an enormous conger eel and a pollock to take home. I arrived at the kitchen, covered in fish scales and stinking to high heaven, announcing 'Look, mother, look 'ere. Look at this bloody pollock – must weigh ten fookin' pound – and look at this conger: bloody boogger must weigh a ton.'

My mother showed no visible signs of acute shock. Later she told me there'd been a conference about this problem and the adults had decided that if they drew my attention to my language and forbade me to use it, I would realize just what I was saying and do it on purpose, but if they ignored it I'd eventually grow out of it. I never did.

But those holidays were a dream for a small boy, living

14

and mixing with those giants, the fishermen. The kid getting in the way but always being treated gently and sympathetically. And then there were the farmers with their understanding of animals, and willing to share the excitement of harvesting with me. First we'd go to the local baker to collect our Cornish pasties. Delicious. A mixture of onions, potatoes and beef rolled inside pastry and baked. Nobody in the village had their own ovens. We did, of course, but we were the gentry and I didn't want my pasty to be cooked at home. So our Cornish cook would prepare my pasty and I'd rush off and line up with the others, then hand over my pasty to the baker, who would mark it, and pop it in with the rest. The smells that came out of that oven! My mouth would water and I couldn't wait to take my first big bite. The remainder would then be wrapped in greaseproof paper and shoved in my pocket for later consumption after the morning's work in the field. We would all meet at an appointed place. There'd be a large flat bed cart, drawn by two horses, and the farmer, his help and the wives would all jump on among the bales of hay and we'd start off for the fields. The harvesting would begin. I'd ride on the harvester, always getting in the way, but thinking I was helping. The women had already begun to prepare the lunch. Then there would be the excited cries of the whippets as rabbits bolted out of the corn: the smell of the wild flowers mingling with the sea breeze, seagulls flying over looking for scraps, and then lunch. Out would come my pasty. The women would have brought a fruit pie and of course that great invention, Cornish clotted cream. The men would drink rough homemade cider from a barrel, but for me it was only lemonade. However, once I was allowed a glass of cider, and went home stoned out of my tiny mind. Wonderful days! And I behaved myself because my instinct told me that, if I didn't, I wouldn't be invited again.

My uncle taught me to swim when I was about three. He rigged up a harness on the end of a fishing rod and when we were out at sea I would go over the side with a strap round my chest. I was then told to dog-paddle and kick out with my legs, and splashed around happily because I knew I couldn't sink. This continued for a few days, ten minutes at a time, until I was told I could swim and Uncle released the pressure on the line. Of course, once he told me what he was going to do, down I went. Later he caught on and didn't tell me. I would go on swimming thinking I was being supported until I'd hear a quiet voice saying, 'Jimmy, I'm not supporting you. You're swimming', and down I'd go. But after a while I gained confidence. By the time I was four I was a pretty good swimmer and at five I was a fish. The sea never held any fear for me and I would spend hours diving off those ragged Cornish rocks, exploring all the underwater caves, shrimping and lobstering. It's strange, but I never suffered from vertigo if the sea was beneath me. I would scramble fearlessly up the most dangerous cliffs as long as there was water below, but when I saw the ground beneath me, I would get dizzy and be paralysed with fear.

I remember being appalled when Barrett, our boatman, told me he couldn't swim, that none of the fishermen swam. They wore heavy hobnailed sea boots that came up to their knees, thick serge trousers and woollen pullovers and, in cold weather, heavy reefer jackets. He explained that, if they fell in with all that clobber, there wasn't a hope, they were going to drown. If they could swim, maybe they could put off the final moment for two or three minutes, but in the end they would go down and they'd sooner get it over as quickly as possible. I was so upset I started to cry – my wonderful fishermen friends not able to swim! I could see them thrashing hopelessly about in the water and then going under. It gave me nightmares for years.

2

As well as those wonderful holidays, the most vivid memory of my childhood, apart from the unpleasantness of school, was being taken to the cinema. My mother was fascinated by the 'movies' and an ardent fan of all the great stars of that silent era, Ramon Navarro, Lewis Stone, Douglas Fairbanks and of course, Rudolf Valentino. She would never go anywhere alone and as Uncle was busy with his practice and my father occupied at the Ministry of Works, she used to take me. Great excitement. There was one drawback, however. I had been born with a nervous stomach, not helped by the vast amounts the Stewarts used to eat, especially in Cornwall, and I would get so worked up by some of the epic films like *Scaramouche, Ben-Hur,* or *The Prisoner of Zenda* that I would rush out during the film, throw up in the loo, rush back to my seat and, to much shushing from our neighbours, my mother would tell me what I'd missed. I'll never forget how we sat riveted to our seats through the exciting parts and crying our eyes out at the sad bits, but it never entered my head that I might one day become an actor. I was quite happy being an ardent admirer of all those super special creatures I saw on the screen.

School. Oh God, how I hated schools, all of them, except the first, the kindergarten, the School of the Holy Family. That was fun. We were looked after by a lot of nuns and I don't remember any bullying or unpleasantness. Maybe that was because it was a mixed school and you just don't bully little girls. Perhaps a pull at a pigtail or two, but that didn't count.

But my first prep school! Awful. I don't know what happens to boys when they get in a bunch. Individually they are quite nice but in a gang – well, they become a gang. And if you are at all individualistic, look out. I wasn't used to boys. I was neat and tidy, so of course I got ink squirted over my new collar, or treacle on the chair just before I sat down, or some other damn foolery. Whenever I attacked one of the bullies I would be set on by about five others, which scared the hell out of me. I was afraid and, not understanding, thought I was a coward. I couldn't go to my father and explain my feelings as I felt too ashamed and also I didn't have that kind of relationship with him. Had I done so, he could have explained that feeling fear isn't necessarily a sign of cowardice. To be brave is simply to conquer fear. I didn't understand this and was constantly trying to prove to myself that I wasn't a coward, so I went looking for trouble. This apparent belligerent attitude affected my whole life. Because of this I took up boxing, much as I loathed it, as I thought this would be another way of proving myself. I was quick on my feet. I didn't like being hit so I used to dance round my bewildered opponent, only stopping every now and then to slug him. He wouldn't be able to lay a glove on me to his fury and frustration but that was okay by me. I became champion boxer of the school at ten against boys of at least two years older, so I must have been pretty good. The best thing about this prep school was their method of punishing for bad behaviour. You weren't kept in to write a hundred lines or do some dreary essay. You were sentenced to so many minutes of hard exercise in the gym under the supervision of Sergeant Moja, an ex-Guards drill instructor. I spent practically every afternoon after school doing physical jerks under the close scrutiny of the sergeant, and this way developed a very good physique. Thank you, sergeant. I hated you at the time but I've lived to be grateful.

Then it was time for me to go to my first boarding school, Uncle's college, Epsom. Doctors' sons had special terms and you could start studying for your first MB there which put you a little ahead of the other students when you went on to university or hospital. I got in through Uncle's influence. I didn't want to follow my father in the family tradition of the army as I couldn't accept the idea that anyone who'd been commissioned before you could give you orders simply because he was your senior. I also had to admit to myself that I loved my uncle more than my father. He was warmer and funnier and Mummy seemed to like him more; this didn't seem disloyal to me because I believed he was my father's brother.

My life at home must have been happy as my first day at boarding school was a nightmare. I developed a violent attack of homesickness the moment I saw my mother and Uncle driving off and leaving me alone with all those noisy monsters. There were other new boys too. They had the same lost look and frightened eyes filling with tears at the least provocation.

There was one new boy with bright carroty red hair. Just because he looked different, the gang picked on him. Carrots was terrified and started to cry openly, which only made things worse for him, as they were now jeering as well as ragging him. I had to interfere, to prove to myself I wasn't as scared as I felt. I slugged a couple of them and started dancing around in my famous boxing style, which didn't meet with their approval at all. Who's this bloody new kid interfering with our sport? It did have one good effect. Carrots was forgotten and all their attention was centred on me. In the middle of trying to take on five or six boys at once, my homesickness suddenly got the better of me and I started crying myself. So I got jeered at too and all my good and noble intentions went for nothing. But I'd made a fatal mistake. I had drawn attention to myself and I was going to live to regret it. I also remember that Carrots didn't even sympathize, he avoided me like the plague. That should have been a lesson, but I didn't learn it.

I really blotted my copybook during the sadistic initiation known as 'the new boys concert'. All the older boys sat around tables, eating baked beans or eggs or whatever, which they had cooked up themselves, and on the side they had prepared lumps of soggy bread dipped in some horrible concoction which smelt and stuck and oozed when it was thrown at the new boys – *us*. We had to stand on a table, recite a poem, tell a joke and sing a song. Naturally the victims would recite some dreary verse, tell an awful flat joke and sing quaveringly and off-key. The worse they were, the more the audience would enjoy it and pelt them with their specially prepared ammunition.

Well, I was going to be different. I got up on the table and said, 'Poem'.

> Cold. Cold. Cold. Cold as a frog in a pool,
> Cold as the tip of an Eskimo's tool.
> Cold, cold, gloomy and glum,
> Like the fringe of the hairs round a Polar bear's bum.
> Cold as charity – and that's pretty chilly,
> But not as cold as poor dear Willy. He's dead,
> Poor bastard, he's dead.

Shocked silence. No laughter. No bread throwing. Nothing.

Then I told a fairly funny joke. Not a titter. Not a laugh. But still no bread. Having a good treble voice I sang a popular song in tune and got all the words right.

Again silence from the rabble in front, but I noticed that some of the more senior boys were looking at me with a sort of amused admiration. I thanked them politely and got out of there as quickly as I could. I never lived it down. The cocky new boy who tried to be clever. So I thought to myself, sod the lot of you. Who needs you? But I did need them. I was very lonely.

Religion should have coloured my life at this period, but I'm afraid it didn't. At Polperro on Sundays I would go with my family to church or chapel, but not to hear the word of the Lord. We went to hear the Cornish sing. Lovely voices, and everybody would be there so I could make dates to go rabbiting or fishing or crabbing. I think what influences a child with regard to religion is how God is represented in your church, and our representative at school, the clergyman, wasn't very inspiring, in fact he was a crashing bore.

The one thing he did have going for him, though, was a very pretty plump daughter, who was my first crush! She used to sit with the masters in a special pew facing the choir, so in order to get a better look at my love I became a chorister. As our choirmaster knew about my famous ancestor, Luigi Lablache, he welcomed me. The only drawback was choir practice in the evenings, when I could have been in the gym, or on the playing fields. What one suffers for love! But it was worth it, because when I wasn't singing, I was eyeing her and, when her father went up into the pulpit and started one of his interminably boring sermons, instead of going to sleep like all the rest, I pretended close attention to every word to impress his daughter. I'm sure she wasn't aware of this, but I would imagine I'd caught her eye at certain moments and that a flash of understanding of my passion had come into hers. Actually she looked as bored with her father's sermons as we all were, and she'd often stifle a yawn. Tragic in a way, because we had proof, one Sunday, of what church could have been.

Occasionally the Headmaster would invite a special member of the ministry to come and give a sermon, and one day our guest was a Franciscan monk. Why a Catholic was preaching in a Protestant chapel I don't know, but there he was. He was a very impressive man, tall, good-looking, with a tonsure and flowing dark brown habit with a white cord round his waist. When he spoke he had a beautiful voice, but the astonishing thing was that he told a funny story. There was a shocked silence. Then he said, 'I've just told you what I think is a very funny story and you didn't laugh. Why? Do you think you mustn't laugh in God's house? Do you think that He doesn't like to hear laughter? Of course He does. I'll tell it again.' And he did. This time we fell about and after that we listened fascinated to what he said. He didn't preach or sermonize or intone or listen to his own voice. He spoke quietly, simply and, much more important, interestingly. If he'd been my teacher, I would have had an awareness and love for religion and perhaps I'd have had a faith and belief in something which is sadly lacking in my life today.

At half term and special weekends my mother and Uncle would come down and take me into the town for tea. It was always the same meal for me: three poached eggs on toast, followed by two or three chocolate éclairs. Indigestible but filling. But on one occasion my mother seemed rather strained and Uncle left us alone on some pretext. My mother started rather nervously by asking if I missed Nanny? She was no longer my Nanny as, ever since I was about eight, she had helped in the home and with the cooking, etc. I replied 'Not particularly.' My mother, rather surprised, but also rather relieved, then proceeded to tell me that they had had to let her go as there really wasn't room in the flat for her.

'Good, high time,' I said. My mother looked aghast at this seemingly cold-blooded response.

'But I thought you loved her,' she said.

I told her I only loved the family, Daddy and Uncle, Iris and her.

'And now there's something else.' She looked at me for a long time. 'About Uncle. You see, darling, he's not really your uncle.'

I was stunned.

'What d'you mean, he's not my uncle? You mean he's not Daddy's brother?'

'No. Only a very special friend.'

I remember starting to cry, suddenly feeling confused and guilty about my father.

'But why didn't you tell me before,' I asked.

'Oh, I don't know. I really didn't think about it. Lots of

children call special friends of their parents, Uncle. It was only because you started asking me about Daddy's other brothers and sisters that I decided you had to be told. It doesn't change anything, darling. You can still call him Uncle and it doesn't alter the fact that he is very fond of you.'

'You don't understand,' I mumbled. 'May I go back to school?'

This was the first time I'd ever asked to go back to school one second before I had to.

'All right,' she said and out we went to look for the car where Uncle was sitting waiting. It was unreal. I'd loved this man all my life but suddenly I couldn't look at him. He was somehow different. He'd taught me to swim, taught me his love of the sea, of gardening, of medicine. He, not my father, and now he wasn't my real uncle. Somehow he had betrayed me. We drove back to school in silence. I jumped out of the car with hardly a goodbye and rushed down to the lavatory, the only place at school where you could be alone, locked myself in and cried my heart out.

Of course I had really known for ages. It was so obvious that my mother didn't love Daddy and so obvious that she did love Uncle. Christmas, for instance. Waking in the morning, rushing into Mummy's room, jumping into bed with her: me on one side and my sister on the other, and opening the stockings, one present at a time. The excitement, the screaming and shouting and laughter and happiness. Then my father would come in, kiss my sister and me and wish us a happy Christmas, rather nervously and shyly. Then he would go and the uproar would start again. After a time the phone would ring and a look would come over my mother's face as she answered and it would be Uncle. And it was always the same game. He would tell her something and she would rush out and look in some place where he'd hidden a present the day before. Then back to the phone and another short talk and Mummy would rush off to another place for another present. They had been hidden all over the house and I'll never forget the happiness on my mother's face and the love! Of course I had known. Now I had to admit it to myself and it hurt. It was years before my mother referred to it again.

Unlike my father, I was no good at track events, at least I never won anything, but swimming, rugby and shooting were my specialities. Boxing I avoided like the plague. I was a bloody good boxer, but I hated the smell of the locker room, sweat, feet, BO and blood-stained gloves. Being big, strong and fast, I was good at rugger and could get rid of my aggression on the field in a positive way. I got my colours for rugby and swimming and in my last two years in college both teams had an unbeaten record.

When I was sixteen and a half, having passed my matriculation, A levels or whatever you call it now, my father summoned me to his study and told me he'd had a financial upset. He'd made some bad investment and lost a lot of money. He explained that he could afford to send me to university and hospital, but after that I'd be on my own. In other words, I couldn't specialize as I had planned but would have to be a General Practitioner. I could tell from the way he spoke that even sending me to university would be a strain on the budget and I asked him if I couldn't just leave school and look around for a job, as I wasn't sure now that I wanted to be a doctor under those circumstances. The look of relief on his face made up for my disappointment. I would have liked to have been a doctor. I think I might have been a good one.

3

My first employment was with the Bell Punch Company, at about thirty shillings a week. I got the job through the influence of one of my sister's beaux, but I hated it and the less said about it the better. I was fired eventually, after which I didn't quite know what to do with my life. One day in a coffee shop I ran into a friend who asked me if I had a car. I told him I had an Overland Whippet which was a car of sorts, bright red, nicknamed The Fire Engine and the pride of my life. He then asked if I had a decent wardrobe? Did I have a dinner jacket and tails? I told him I did, though not very smart as I'd bought them second-hand.

'Then be a film extra. You get a guinea a day and the best crumpet in the world.'

Now my initiation into crumpet had only recently taken place and I wasn't averse to sampling more. My baptism occurred when I went to Paris with a rugby club team to play the French police and the French army. It was a very exciting trip as I'd never been out of England before and, although all expenses were paid by the club, it was my father's generosity that gave me the opportunity to sample some of the Paris night life, as he had slipped me ten pounds the day before we took off, the equivalent of about 1,500 French francs in those days.

On our first evening we all trooped out to a night spot called the Bal Tabarin in Montmartre. I was standing at the bar sipping an Alexander, a very sickly but potent mixture of cognac, crème de Cacao and cream, when I suddenly felt a tug at my arm. I looked down and there was a tiny, extremely dishy young lady smiling up at me. I remember she had an urchin cut hair-style, rare in those days, and looked quite adorable. I could manage a little school French and understood she was asking if I would like to go somewhere with her. I asked my friends rather nervously what they thought I should do? I got a quick answer, with a reminder that the match started at two the following afternoon. Promising not to let them down, I shyly followed my tiny companion into the night.

She took my hand and walked me determinedly round the corner to a place called Le Paradis. She told me to give the rather evil-looking old crone at the door one hundred francs and in return I was handed a key. We climbed the stairs, my little friend obviously knowing the terrain well, and came to a door which she unlocked, ushering me into a small room containing only one piece of furniture: a very ample circular bed covered with cushions. At that moment a girl appeared at the door and asked what we would like. 'Champagne,' said my companion quickly and told me to give the girl another hundred francs. By now I was beginning to wonder how many of my remaining notes I'd be expected to peel off.

The champagne arrived and I gulped down a glass to give me courage as this was the first time I'd ever been face to face with an attractive female who was starting to take off her clothes and was obviously expecting me to do the same. Nervously I admitted that I was a virgin. This seemed to turn her on as with shrieks of delight she started ripping off my clothes and pouring more champagne down my throat. After the Alexanders I was starting to feel no pain and began my initiation into the secrets of love-making enthusiastically if somewhat clumsily. It's not easy, this thing called sex, and I needed a good deal of coaching from my partner, but luckily she was a born teacher. A virgin was a novelty for her and she was so gentle and understanding that it wasn't in any way sordid. I knew by this time that she was a professional and wasn't teaching me for love, but she did it with humour and tenderness and I shall always be grateful to her.

I had very little sleep that night but next day, after promising to return, I played excellent rugby, threw French

26

policemen all over the field and felt great.

That night my initiation continued, after a dinner consisting of two enormous steaks washed down with a bottle of red wine, which cost me another two hundred francs. The next morning it was time to say goodbye and I didn't quite know how to bring up the subject of payment. I needn't have worried. Josette, as she was called, asked me how much I had and, when I turned out my pockets, she divided the amount – so much for her, so much for me. She cried when we said goodbye, so perhaps I hadn't been so bad after all. In fact, I don't think I was ever as good again in my life. I played rugby very badly that afternoon.

So, remembering Josette, I eagerly asked my friend how one went about becoming a film extra. 'Easy. Just register with an agent and leave it to him.'

I remember they put 'young upper-class playboy type' on my index card. Playboy, eh?

I got a call for my first job and turned up at the studio at the ungodly hour of 6.30 in the morning. On arrival I was told to report for wardrobe and make-up. It was a costume epic and of course nothing fitted, including the wig. On the first day of my film career I discovered two allergies: one to the spirit gum used to stick on wigs, and the other to second assistant directors who treated extras like dirt.

Next I was told, 'Go and make yourself up.' I was pushed into a large changing-room with mirrors right along the wall. I took a seat next to a very good-looking young fellow and was given a stick of bright orange grease-paint, essential in those days because of the blinding white light of the arc lamps. As I was smearing this disgusting stuff on my face I turned to my neighbour and asked him if he'd done this often?

'No', he said. 'This is my first time.'

'Me too', I replied. 'By the way, why are you doing it?'

'Because you get a guinea a day and the best crumpet in the world.' We were buddies from then on. His name was Michael Wilding.

Dear Mike. We had great times together and neither of us had any intention of becoming actors. We were just doing it for the fun, the money and the birds. Later we were destined to marry two of the most beautiful girls in the world, and had to take our responsibilities rather more seriously. But, looking back, those were among the happiest years of my life. Not a care in the world – enough money to have a good time – girls in abundance. Mike was a very talented artist. He had studied at the Slade School of Art, and one day intended to make art his career, but personally I was quite content to continue as a film extra for the rest of my life. The only thing that might stop this was the fact that I wasn't the most popular fellow with the second assistants.

It was understood that you would kick back twenty per cent of your wages, and then maybe they'd put you on call the next day or ask for you on the next picture. I've never liked bribery and blackmail. I consider that if you do your job well that should be enough. Naive, maybe, but that's how I saw it. I refused to kick back and so didn't get as much work as I might have done. Also I dislike intensely being treated like dirt and yelled at. Ask me nicely and I'll do anything you want; yell at me and I'm a mule. Typical Taurus.

Mike was much more easy going and consequently worked more. I was very nearly banned from one studio, but luckily for me the head boy was my type of man. I had told an assistant director to go and screw himself so I was reported to the studio manager, Joe Grosmith. He called me in and said, 'Now listen, Jim, using bad language is fuckin' awful. I mean, you've got to have respect for a fuckin' second assistant. You know, they've got their job to do. Now, Jim, don't let me hear any more of this, right?'

'Yes, sir.'

'All right. Be a good lad and piss off.'

And I pissed off thankfully.

It was at this time my mother asked if I'd mind giving up my room and sleeping in the cook's room, as Uncle had fallen on hard times and was forced to give up his London home. He was ill, his practice had become smaller and smaller and he just couldn't make ends meet. My father, bless him, suggested he should come and live with us, not only because he was genuinely fond of Uncle but, much more important, he knew it would make my mother happy. So I moved into the maid's room and Uncle moved into my room. But his health was failing and after a long illness, with my mother nursing him herself day and night, he died. I remember early one morning I was lying in bed reading when I heard my mother calling frantically.

'Jimmy! Jim, come quickly. Help me – help me!'

I rushed into Uncle's room but I knew I could do nothing. I felt so helpless as my mother pleaded with me to do something. She couldn't believe he was dead. I tried to comfort her, but what could I say? What can anyone say at a time like that? I was in pretty bad shape myself as it was the first time I'd experienced death, let alone the death of somebody I loved.

My father tried to comfort my mother, but he was as upset as anyone. My sister arrived, then the undertaker, we had to choose a coffin, then the vicar appeared to discuss when the funeral should take place; letters, cards with black borders, all the legal details – death can be a traumatic experience. My poor mother wanted to be left alone in her grief so it fell to me to handle everything. At last the flowers were thrown into the grave, the earth rattled down on the coffin, tips were handed to the gravediggers (it wasn't so streamlined in those days) and we went back to the apartment to face life without Uncle. My mother was inconsolable and I was very worried about her health. She just couldn't accept the fact that Uncle was dead. That was when she took up spiritualism. We were very close at that time and she would tell me of her guilt complex over her treatment of my father.

'Don't think I didn't suffer,' she told me. 'But I thought it was the best way. He didn't want me to leave him and I couldn't give up Uncle. Please try and understand.'

'Of course I do,' I told her, not understanding my father's behaviour at all.

'Do you know what Daddy said to me when Uncle died?'

'No,' I said, not really wanting to know.

He said, well, my darling, after all these years, at last I've got you to myself. I felt so awful, Jimmy. What I'd put this poor man through!'

I thought to myself, poor Daddy. He hasn't really got her to himself even now.

Although I had my room back, I felt uneasy and guilty when my mother came in to see me. I'd have given anything if she could have found Uncle there in my place. But I was young and it quickly became my room again; the meeting place for Mike and our other friends and, of course, numerous girls.

Once I had an experience that didn't include my room, or for that matter, a girl. I was working as an extra on a film starring Henry Kendall. He was very friendly and would make a point of coming over and talking to me whenever he got the chance. Naturally I was very flattered that he should pick me out – I was pretty bloody naive in those days. We would talk about sport and training, and he asked me if I would care for the job of training him, as he had to get fit for his next film. He suggested Margate, a famous seaside resort, and asked me if I would chauffeur him down – all expenses paid and two pounds a day wages? I jumped at the chance.

I duly reported to his flat and, after putting his bags in the car we drove off, me at the wheel. Henry was a very funny man and was breaking me up with laughter at all his stories and experiences until we had cleared London and were on the coast road to Margate. Suddenly I felt his hand on my thigh and heard him say how much he had looked forward to being alone with me and what a wonderful time we were going to have together. My mouth went dry and I began to sweat. Oh, my God, I thought, why hadn't I realized?

Whoever got a job like this for nothing? I felt a complete fool, which of course I was. Miserably I drew the car into the side of the road and switched off.

'What's the matter?' he asked.

Nervously I tried to explain that I wasn't one of those.

'Then why the hell did you come?' he asked. 'You don't really think I asked you just to show me all those beastly exercises?'

'Yes,' I confessed. 'I did.'

'Well, you're a prick,' he said.

We both stared moodily out of the car.

'With all those beautiful young men around I had to choose a square!' he muttered.

'Shall I drive you back?' I offered.

'No,' he said. 'We're more than half-way there and I've made the bookings. So we may as well go on. But on one condition. I won't make a pass at you, but for Christ's sake, promise that you won't try to train me. I hate exercise.'

'Are you sure?' I asked nervously.

'Yes, yes, of course. You've nothing to worry about.'

And I hadn't. It was a marvellous holiday and he was a delightful companion. He never referred to the subject again, bless him. But he was right. I was a prick.

Then something happened that was to change everything and give me some direction in my life. I had cut a finger which had become infected and I had to visit our new doctor. While I was sitting in his waiting room, his wife came in. She was Susan Richmond, an actress who taught at the Webber Douglas Academy of Dramatic Art, and told me how interested she was to learn that I was an actor. I laughed and told her I was only a film extra and had no intention of ever being an actor.

'Oh, but it's in your blood,' she said. 'Your grandfather and grandmother were on the stage, and your great-great-grandfather was a world-famous singer. Why don't you give it a try? The head of the drama classes at the Webber Douglas is a lady called Ellen O'Malley and she used to act with your grandfather. Why don't you come along with me and try for a scholarship?'

So, when my finger had been lanced and bandaged, Susan and I set out for the Webber Douglas. Ellen O'Malley turned out to be a delightful old lady with the most beautiful eyes and shining gold hair.

'Oh,' she said, as I entered with Susan. 'You're so like your grandfather and your voice is exactly the same. He had a lovely voice, you know.'

I didn't think I had a lovely voice. I just spoke. Ellen handed me a book of Shakespeare and asked me to read something.

'Fine,' she said when I had finished. 'Fine. You have a natural talent for projecting. You don't mutter like most students. I think I might arrange a scholarship for you. Would you like that?'

'Very much,' I told her. 'How much does it pay?'

'It doesn't pay anything,' Susan said rather sharply, 'but it means you can study here for nothing.'

'I'm sorry,' I said, 'but I have to earn my living.'

Ellen seemed genuinely disappointed and told me that, if I changed my mind, I should come and see her and she would arrange everything. Apparently she had been very fond of my grandfather. As we were leaving I saw two lists pinned to a notice board, one with about fifty names and the other with only about eight. I was beginning to get an idea.

'What are those lists?' I asked Susan innocently.

'Oh,' she said, 'those are the female students' – pointing to the long list. 'And those are the male students' – pointing to that very short list. Fifty females and only eight males, I thought, those are the kind of odds for me.

'Susan,' I said. 'I've changed my mind. I'll take that scholarship.'

And that's how I became an actor. I realized that it was neither my voice nor my talent for projecting that had got me the scholarship. They were just hard up for male students. So now they had nine!

My first weeks at drama school consisted mainly of mastering stage technique. Something you'd do automatically in normal life became enormously complicated up on that stage in front of a lot of other students, all hoping you would make an ass of yourself. I didn't disappoint them.

'Come through the door, shut it behind you with one hand, facing the audience, move across stage, sit down, cross the left leg over the right, pick up the phone with the right hand, pass it over to the left, at the same time picking up a cigarette and lighting it before dialling', was one of my instructions. Simple. No problem. But on the stage something else again. It was amazing how difficult it was to do the most ordinary things 'naturally', when you were trying to follow directions, but my confidence gradually increased as I realized the other students were as clumsy as I was. And then the first speaking part. The first experience of 'drying up' when you not only forget the lines but even where you are and what your name is. But it was all great fun and very competitive and, by God, we acted. Over-acted to a degree that must have embarrassed our teachers.

In my last term I played Charles Surface in *The School for Scandal* which gave me the chance to take snuff and wave a handkerchief around. I don't think any actor has ever taken so much snuff and waved that handkerchief around so much before or since. I rather fancied myself in the part, but I could hardly get the lines out as my nose was clogged up with fuller's earth, substituted for snuff. What a performance.

I was busy learning to be an actor and doing odd bits of 'extra' work for pocket money, but I do remember a Christmas dinner when my father took us all completely by surprise. He shyly asked if he might tell a story that he'd recently heard at his club. We groaned inwardly and said, 'Of course, Daddy, go ahead.' He cleared his throat and began nervously, 'There were these friends who were going to a Lord Mayor's banquet and they had a bet as to who would be the first to say arsehole three times.' Our jaws dropped. My father continued calmly: 'The men were seated at the banqueting table when the first course was served. Sole. "Ah, soles," one of the competitors triumphantly announced. "My favourite fish are soles," he continued, holding up two fingers, and then got carried away. "These are arseholes, aren't they?" '

We all collapsed with laughter. My father went rather pink as we clapped and cheered and asked him if he knew any more. My mother was looking at him as if she'd never seen him before, and suddenly it was clear to me. My dear father, a mouse in his own home, was a man at his club among his army chums, laughing and telling jokes and being what he should have been at home. What a waste of a good man.

I remember another occasion when my mother had unwittingly shown her complete indifference to him. I must have been about seven. The 1914-18 war was over, my father had finally retired from the army and was putting his uniform away in moth-balls. He thought he would show himself in full dress for the last time. I was reading in the drawing-room and my mother was dusting, or something, when suddenly my father appeared, stood in the doorway, gave her a salute, and said, 'How do I look?' My mother hardly glanced at him.

'Very nice, dear, very nice,' she said and continued dusting. I can still see the crestfallen look on my father's face.

'I think you look absolutely great, Daddy,' I said. He thanked me but he didn't really want praise from me. He turned quietly and went out. My impulse was to rush after him and tell him that I loved him and not to take any notice of my mother as women didn't understand these things, but I just stood there and said nothing. Now here he was, embarrassed and blushing, but delighted he'd made his children and their friends laugh and that we'd all thought it was a great joke. I thought it was. I still do.

4

After about two years of what you might laughingly call study came the end of term shows. A few minor agents and producers from some of the smaller repertory companies came to see if there was any talent going. I can't remember what I played but evidently it served its purpose as a Mr Andrew Osborne came round and asked if I would like to play second lead at the Hull Repertory Theatre at three pounds a week. I said, 'Sure, I'd love to.' So I was told to report to Hull at such and such an address on such and such a date. Again butterflies in the stomach. Packing up to go to school again, only this time it was to determine whether or not I'd make it as an actor, and whether I could really earn my living, if you can call three pounds a week living.

So at the age of twenty-two I turned up in that cold, dreary city on the east coast of England, Hull. The building was huge, draughty and very ugly, but it was a professional theatre, and people actually paid to go in. I was given the address of some theatrical digs, which turned out to be the home of a delightful old Yorkshire lady with five daughters. I never once saw another man in that house. I suppose the thought of living permanently with six women was too much for most men, but for me it was heaven. I was looked after, mothered, sistered, waited on and fed. They darned my socks, ironed my shirts, pressed my trousers, fed me three times a day, all for twenty-five bob a week.

I was very happy there, but for one thing – that bed. It had an enormous sag in the middle, so the springs and mattress bulged inwards and downwards, which meant I could never sleep on my side, only on my back and in a semi-upright position. But, after giving my all in the theatre and eating one of their home-cooked Yorkshire dinners, I always slept like a log.

There was a zany actress in the cast called Ambrosine Phillpotts and two very good juvenile character actors: William Mervyn and Maurice Denham, all three of whom went on to much bigger and better things. The rest I can't remember, except for our leading man, a very pompous actor, who horrified me by peeing in the wash basin. He said it was too cold to go down the corridor to the lavatory. Disgusting. Later I peed in the basin too. That corridor really was a bitch in winter.

The work went well and I seemed to be doing all right as I was soon cast in leading parts. So I thought to myself, Hell, leading parts for only three pounds a week? I should get a raise. So I reported to the manager's office and told him that I should get more money. He didn't share my view and told me I was lucky to be in work at all. So of course I lost my temper, gave a month's notice and told him I was off to the Birmingham Rep. He laughed sarcastically and gave as his opinion that I'd as much chance of getting into the Birmingham Rep as he had of being Queen of England.

As I closed the door I was already beginning to agree with him. Christ, what a fool, to have boasted like that. What a conceited, arrogant idiot. I had a week off so I tore down to London to see my benefactress, Susan Richmond, and once again she came through. She knew the manager of the Birmingham Rep who, by a miracle, happened to be looking for a new leading man. I went along to see him, exaggerated my experience a little, rather intimating that I'd played in a great many films but had decided to forgo this lucrative career in order to become a serious actor, and he fell for it. I got the job. Imagine my new-found pride when I marched into the Hull manager's office and told him 'I'm the new leading man at the Birmingham Rep at seven pounds a week.' To give him his due he congratulated me and said he'd miss me.

Ambrosine told me she had a good friend in the Birmingham Rep called Elspeth March, who would help me find digs and generally steer me right. She, Ambrosine, would give me a letter of introduction, so clutching this letter, I reported to the stage door of Sir Barry Jackson's Birmingham Repertory Theatre, the most prestigious repertory company in England at that time.

The actors came streaming off the stage at the end of rehearsals and I looked nervously for the lady Ambrosine had described, 'a tall, statuesque, beautiful girl, with thick black hair', and there she was! The description fitted. She also had a beautiful voice and lovely delicate hands. I introduced myself and handed over Ambrosine's letter of introduction. Elspeth read it, gave me a glance and started to laugh.

'What are you laughing at,' I said haughtily.

'Do you want to know what she says?' Elspeth asked.

'Well, what does she say,' I ventured, rather uncertainly.

'That you're a good actor, but not to tell you so, as you think rather a lot of yourself already. Also she thinks you're sexy as hell.'

With that Elspeth gave me a cool look. Obviously she didn't agree or wasn't going to let on even if she did.

Three years later we were married.

The Birmingham Rep wasn't a weekly rep, as I had been used to at Hull, but two-weekly. We would play at night, rehearse the next play in the mornings, and map out a third play in the afternoon. This meant having three parts in our heads at the same time. Wonderful training, but my God, the work! I literally used to put a wet towel round my head at night while I desperately tried to study the lines, all of them long parts, as I was mostly playing leading roles. But it was an exciting experience and with the confidence of youth, I felt nothing was impossible.

The great advantage of the Birmingham Rep was that

every summer the theatre would close and the whole company moved to Malvern, to take part in the Festival there. For us, this meant a different play every night for six nights; usually three Bernard Shaw plays, two eighteenth-century Restoration comedies and one modern play. Malvern was not far from Stratford-upon-Avon, so theatre enthusiasts from all over the world would come first to Malvern, to see their Shaw and Sheridan and then move on to Stratford for Shakespeare.

Now I was to learn that there are four entirely different styles of acting: the modern, Shavian, Restoration and Shakespearean, which is why Britain produces so many superb character actors and actresses, and why practically every one of them is at home in costume. So very early on I got my training in three styles and a little later I joined the Old Vic and experienced the fourth – Shakespearean.

At Malvern, G.B.S., as Shaw was known, would always attend the final rehearsals and, of course, change everything the producer had planned. Shaw was very gentle and understanding but with a wounding wit and we were all overawed and rather terrified of him. On learning that my grandfather, Luigi Lablache, had been in the original cast of some of his plays, he said to me by way of a compliment, 'Oh yes, Lablache, good-looking man. Always remembered his lines.' Coming from G.B.S., this was the highest praise. How he had acted was not so important. He had remembered the master's lines.

One of the characters I was playing that year was Magnus in *The Apple Cart,* who has a speech which goes on for about ten minutes; one of the longest in any play, a feat of memory in itself. Among the first-night audience were the originator of the character, Cedric Hardwicke, the author, G.B.S., and all the London critics. This didn't faze me and, although terrified, I sailed through the big speech without a fault. Shaw congratulated me afterwards on my memory and told me in that lilting Irish that I had a good voice but didn't know how to use it. He said nothing about my performance. When I was sitting rather dejectedly in my dressing-room, I was told by the producer that Shaw's coming round to see me at all meant he'd approved and that he wasn't known to throw compliments around. I felt a little better.

At that festival, in addition to Magnus, I played Dunois in *Saint Joan,* Charles Surface in *The School for Scandal* (taking much less snuff this time), Glumdalca, a singing and dancing giantess in an eighteenth-century pantomime, *Tom Thumb the Great,* and Anderson in Shaw's *The Devil's Disciple.* If I were asked to repeat that programme today I'd run a mile, but in those days I was young, enthusiastic and desperately keen to be a good actor.

The theatre at Malvern was beautifully set in its own grounds with a lovely garden of flowering shrubs and rare trees and Elspeth had the honour of being one of the actresses photographed with G.B.S. on his eightieth birthday when a tree was planted in his honour.

Another famous personality who had graced the boards the year before I was there was a young actor named Errol Flynn. Elspeth told me about this fantastic looking young man who, although only playing very small parts, had taken the whole festival by storm, not by his acting, but by his diving and swimming. There was a pool at the bottom of the garden and while the tourists were taking lunch Errol would dazzle his captive audience. Apparently he taught Elspeth to play poker and when I asked her where, she replied 'in his bedroom'. I asked if that was all he'd taught her to which she haughtily replied, 'Well, you should know better than anyone.' She was right, of course, as she was a virgin when I met her.

But as she was a very attractive lady I wasn't the only man in her life. She had a boy friend at Stratford and would shoot off to see him at the drop of a hat. I would show my disapproval on these occasions by trying to screw her up as much as possible on the stage. For example, when we were playing one of the pairs of lovers in *A Midsummer Night's Dream* and Oberon put us to sleep, we had to lie on a very uncomfortable draughty stage for about ten minutes while Oberon and Titania and Puck carried on. I used to relieve Elspeth's discomfort somewhat by throwing my cloak over her. But when she had been visiting this other fella I let her freeze her behind. Gradually her trips to Stratford became fewer and fewer, and finally stopped altogether.

Elspeth was a very good actress, a joy to work with and very popular with the whole company. That was another thing that irritated the hell out of me.

'Don't you dislike anyone?' I would ask her.

'No, not really,' she'd reply.

I didn't either, actually, but a lot of the company would get up my nose with their petty jealousies and tricks on the stage, but all this left Elspeth unmoved. She liked everyone and everyone liked her.

Apparently my efforts in *The Apple Cart,* for which I had received very good write-ups, had not gone unnoticed, as an agent called John Gliddon, who was later to handle Vivien Leigh, turned up and asked if he could represent me. I signed up with him and not very much later he arranged a contract for me with Basil Dean, a very successful theatre impresario and film director. I was to be paid thirty pounds a week – riches in those days, as my salary at the Birmingham Rep was only ten pounds a week. He also arranged a contract for Elspeth with Dean, as she had made a great success at Malvern, so we both arrived in London thinking we were going to take the town by storm, which of course we didn't. We had both been big fish in a small pond. Now we were tiddlers in a very big ocean.

5

Elspeth went into a play with Flora Robson and Jack Hawkins and I began rehearsing for a mammoth production at Drury Lane called *The Sun Never Sets*, a dramatic, semi-musical version of 'Sanders of the River' with Leslie Banks and Edna Best. I played the juvenile lead – more juvenile than leading. Basil Dean had the reputation of being the rudest, most sadistic and sarcastic producer in the business and, by God, he lived up to his reputation. Once when I became very upset by his attacks, Leslie Banks tried to console me by telling me Dean wasn't just picking on *me* – he did it to everyone. After a verbal thrashing during rehearsals one day, Leslie had become so angry that he had fainted. The whole cast was horrified, but Dean simply walked up on to the stage, nudged Leslie with his foot and said, 'Break for lunch.' This made me feel a little better, but not much.

I became terribly depressed when I learned that my father was desperately ill with cancer. He had suffered a lot of pain during the last year or two but had put it down to indigestion and wouldn't go to a specialist. Now it had been diagnosed and it was too late to operate as he was seventy-seven and unlikely to survive surgery. He refused to go to hospital and lay in his small monklike bedroom, but he wasn't alone now as my mother nursed him with the same care and devotion she had given Uncle, and my sister and I spent as much time with him as possible. I begged the doctor to arrange that Daddy shouldn't suffer too much, and he assured me he would feel no pain as he was giving him large injections of morphia.

Every time I went to rehearsal, to be sworn at and ridiculed by Dean, I dreaded coming back to find him gone. Then one morning he looked terribly feeble and scarcely seemed to know me. I pleaded with Dean to let me go early only to be told I should be a professional and not allow personal problems to interfere with my work. The bastard kept me to the last moment and, even though I rushed home, I was too late. My mother told me that the morning paper had carried a publicity photo of Leslie Banks and announced the opening of *The Sun Never Sets* with the cast list, myself included. In his semi-conscious state my father had thought the photo was of me. He had whispered to my mother, 'He's made a success, hasn't he, our Jimmy. I'm so proud of him.' He died holding the paper.

When I was alone with him I knelt and asked him to forgive me for my selfishness and lack of understanding. I like to think that at the end he knew we all loved him and, being the kind of man he was, that he understood and forgave us.

Again those awful burial arrangements. At least I was let off rehearsals to go to the funeral. I think Dean realized I was going anyway so graciously gave his consent.

We were now approaching opening night and the dress rehearsals were interminable, as this was an extravaganza with witch doctors especially imported from Africa, a plane crash on stage, human sacrifices with cannibals yelling and screaming, singing, dancing and very little acting. Anything that could go wrong went wrong. In fact, a complete balls up.

The shortest appearance of a stage star in any play on our opening night merits an entry in the *Guinness Book of Records*. Leslie Banks and I were tied up to the torture posts with screaming natives jabbing and flicking us with fly whisks when Edna Best was carried past on the head of an enormous negro. They disappeared off stage and suddenly, instead of Edna reappearing, her understudy came on. Leslie and I looked at each other in amazement. Apparently this negro had turned too suddenly and cracked Edna's head open on a piece of scenery. She never returned to the play as it was off in three weeks. *The Sun* set very quickly and disastrously, I'm afraid.

Elspeth and I were officially engaged by this time and the marriage had been planned. We had found a delightful maisonette in the Kings Road, Chelsea, and were picking up odds and ends of furniture, and decorating it. We felt now was the time as we were both working and our combined salaries were a colossal fifty pounds a week. Long before the wedding day, my play was off and Elspeth was out of work as well. Dean had to go on paying me as I had a contract, so he immediately pushed me into another play with a small, very unshowy part. I wasn't exactly taking London by storm as I had planned.

And then I heard on the grapevine that my hero, Laurence Olivier, was going to direct a play called *Serena Blandish,* starring Vivien Leigh, at the tiny Gate Theatre. The part of Lord Ivor Cream was still uncast. I got away from Dean's rehearsal, rushed down to the Gate and asked to see the director. I was shown in and came face to face for the first time with my idol, the man who had been the cause of my giving some pretty devastatingly bad performances in rep. I thought that Larry was the most exciting, virile, inventive, beautiful actor in the theatre, and certainly I wasn't alone in this opinion. I used to rush down to London whenever I had a week off to see him at the Old Vic. What was worse, I used to try and copy him and I'm no Larry Olivier. Now here was my idol, actually talking to me. I stammered out that I would like to read for the part of Lord Ivor if it wasn't cast. He told me it wasn't and would I like to run through a scene with Vivien Leigh right away? I was then introduced to this ravishing beauty and shakily tried to give a performance in a part I'd read only a moment before. I was awful. But Larry was charming and helpful and I gradually calmed down and gave a reasonable reading. A short conference between Larry and Vivien followed. Larry then came over and told me I'd got the part, but did I understand it only paid three pounds a week? I told him I understood (thinking to myself, shades of the Hull Rep), but there was a slight detail which had to be straightened out.

'I'm under contract to Basil Dean,' I explained, but if they could hold the part for two hours I was sure I could arrange everything. Larry gave me a grin and wished me good luck. I tore back to the theatre, saw Dean's manager and explained the situation, adding that I was sure Mr Dean wouldn't want to pay me that huge salary just to play this bit part and, if he wished, I would release him from the contract. At this I expected an outburst and a lecture on what great things Dean had planned for me, but instead, after a ten-second conversation with Dean, the manager returned and told me Dean thought it a brilliant idea. I signed a piece of paper, he signed a piece of paper, and that was that.

Then an awful feeling! Elspeth! I hadn't discussed it with Elspeth. I had just thrown away a year's contract at thirty pounds a week for a four-week engagement at three pounds a week, and we were about to be married. I rang her and she said, 'If that's what you want, go ahead. In fact, it's a good start for a marriage, because we can't very well go any lower.'

I rushed back to the Gate, gave Larry the good news and we had a drink to seal the bargain. I needed that drink badly because by now I wasn't so sure I'd done the right thing.

I got to know Vivien while working with her and she impressed me as very hard-working and certainly very ambitious. She had two passions, her love for Larry and her determination to play Scarlett O'Hara in *Gone with the Wind*. We all thought she was nuts to think she had a ghost of a chance, but look how it turned out! That was in 1938.

All preparations were now complete and the day of my wedding arrived. We were married in the little church in The Boltons where I'd been christened, and Elspeth looked divine. She came down the aisle rather nervously and as she took her place beside me, she started whispering something about a sweep. I couldn't understand and thought maybe she had changed her mind and wanted to call it off. However, she quietened down and we were married. After signing the register I asked her what she had been trying to say and she explained that coming to the church with her father she had seen a chimney-sweep which meant good luck, and she was trying to tell me, to cheer me up. We went on to the reception where Elspeth accused me of paying more attention to Larry and Vivien than to her.

'But darling, that's Larry Olivier.'

'Well, to hell with him,' she said. 'I'm your bride. This is meant to be my day.'

During the reception we made our escape amid the best wishes of all our friends and relations, had the usual rice thrown over us and drove off on what everyone thought was our honeymoon but which in effect was a short journey to our new home. There we unpacked, made enthusiastic but hurried love, and I shot off to the Gate Theatre for the evening performance. Poor Elspeth. She never did get a honeymoon.

One thing I regretted bitterly was that my father couldn't have been there. He adored Elspeth and was really responsible for my deciding to marry her. I had been rather selfishly going on with my life, with Elspeth always there, but frankly no thought of marriage. I was only twenty-four at the time and liked the arrangement very much. Typical male, I suppose. I remember my father saying to me one evening, 'When are you going to announce your engagement to Elspeth? She's a very special person. Don't let her get away, my boy!' Christ, I'd never thought of that possibility so I immediately asked her to marry me.

'And about time too,' she said. She always knew what was good for me.

The Gate Theatre engagement had come to an end and now there we were, newly married, in a new home with the furnishings not paid for and nothing coming in. Luckily Elspeth's family friends had been thoughtful enough to send cheques instead of the usual toast racks and silver spoons, so

45

we survived on those. Then my agent got me a part in a film called *So This Is London*.

By this time it had been decided that I should change my name. There happened to be a young fella in America getting to be quite well known, also called James Stewart, which might lead to confusion. So I took the name Granger which I think was my Scottish grandmother's maiden name, though my friends continued to call me Jimmy, much to the bewilderment of my newer acquaintances. When I eventually met James Stewart in Hollywood, I asked him if that was his real name as I hated to think it might have been Joe Bloggs and I had given up my family name for nothing. Jimmy assured me seriously that there had been no deception on his part, and I felt better. But even so there was often confusion.

So, having become Stewart Granger, I was ready for my first film part. I hated it: the waiting about; the lights; the camera making you feel self-conscious; the close-ups when you are looking past the camera to someone off screen, but are so conscious of that lens glaring at you – the very opposite of stage work when you have those blessed footlights to blot out the audience; shooting the script out of sequence – having to pick up a scene in the morning that you'd half finished the night before; the boredom of the crew who always seemed to be picking their noses during your best scenes. This is not for me, give me the theatre anytime, I thought. This view seemed to be shared by the producers and critics as there wasn't an abundance of offers coming my way.

Luckily something did materialize and Elspeth and I were asked to do a season of plays at the lovely old theatre in Aberdeen. To my amazement I got a call at the same time from Tyrone Guthrie, the administrator of the Old Vic, to come and discuss the possibility of joining the company for the new season. The leading man was to be Robert Donat, another of my idols. I think he was the only actor who was so outstanding that on two occasions his performance caused me to see a film through twice. Once was in *Goodbye, Mr Chips* for which he won an Oscar and the other was in *The Citadel*. Naturally I jumped at the chance. The leading actress was to be a very dishy American lady called Constance Cummings, married to Benn Levy, a successful English playwright, one of the few American actresses who could play Shakespeare and Shaw with authority. She made a wonderful St Joan and I thoroughly enjoyed playing Dunois opposite her, and her Juliet was enchanting.

When discussing Donat's choice of parts, Guthrie said how lucky he was to have an actor who could play all the great Shakespearean roles.

'All of them,' said Guthrie, 'except of course Romeo. But who wants to play Romeo?'

Donat looked at him for a moment and then asked, 'Why do you think I can't play Romeo?'

He could have been a wonderful Macbeth, Othello, Lear, Shylock or Leontes, but Romeo was the part he had to choose. Disaster. Robert was no longer boyish, he looked wrong in the costume, his legs were too short. But Guthrie had made a mistake – he should never have said 'except Romeo'.

Rehearsals were not due to start for two months, so I had time to go to Aberdeen with Elspeth where we had a marvellous time playing the leads in ten of our favourite plays. The juveniles in the company were a pair who later made a big name for themselves, Dulcie Gray and Michael Denison. Aberdeen was the town where the Gordon Highlanders were stationed, with their barracks at the Brig of Don. The Colonel and his lady often came to the theatre, and little did I think as I drank Scotches with them that soon he would be my commanding officer. War was imminent.

This was early 1939, and I don't think that anyone in their right minds really believed Chamberlain's bit of paper would halt that raving lunatic across the Channel. But we were in the theatre, and the show must go on.

I had to leave Elspeth and report to the Old Vic for

rehearsals. Very exciting, but in the middle war broke out. What to do? Was I to rush off and join up? No, I was told. Entertainment is vital at this time. The Old Vic is a national institution and must carry on. We were to open in Buxton and do a short provincial tour before coming back to London. I wired Elspeth to join me and we were both overjoyed to see each other again. Like everyone else in England at that time, we had both been expecting the bombings to start immediately, but there seemed to be an uncanny lull. Nothing was happening.

The tour was a success but difficult, owing to the black-out and travel restrictions, and eventually Guthrie decided to put all the productions into moth-balls and reopen when the war was over – probably by Christmas. They remained in moth-balls. We never did reopen as the war took slightly longer than everyone expected.

My new agent, Jack Dunfee, then suggested that I go into a play his company was producing, again with Leslie Banks and Edna Best, but I felt strongly that I should enlist as things were beginning to hot up and we were getting hell knocked out of us in France. Jack insisted that I would be more useful in entertainment than serving as a private in the army, so we started rehearsals. I just couldn't concentrate when every day I read about the setbacks in France and so I quit and joined up in the Gordon Highlanders. There was about a month to go before I had to report to Aberdeen, so we decided to move out of the flat. We couldn't afford it anyway. Elspeth would live near Windsor where she could get work in the rep. She was now the breadwinner because I would be earning a mere two shillings and sixpence a day plus seventeen shillings a week for her. Not really enough to live on, even in those days.

To give some idea of the present runaway inflation: during the year Elspeth and I were first married, between us we had been earning about twenty-eight pounds a week. Out of that we had clothed and fed ourselves, paid the rent, run a small car and occasionally given a party. The other day I took my car into a filling station in Spain. The cost of a full tank of petrol was four thousand pesetas – about twenty-eight pounds.

While we were rushing around packing and looking for a place for Elspeth to live, with typical woman's logic she announced that she wanted a baby. I looked at her in amazement.

'Are you mad?' I asked. 'Here am I going into the army; we've no money; you've got to earn your living and on top of that I don't want to have to worry about your being pregnant as well as me getting my arse shot off.'

'Typical,' snapped Elspeth. 'Typical man, just thinking of yourself. What about me? Supposing you don't come back?'

We looked at each other for a second and Elspeth burst into tears.

'Oh God, I didn't mean that,' she said. 'Don't you understand, darling. I love you. If anything happened I'd have nothing – nothing of you.'

So it was decided, but we'd only got a month so it meant a lot of hard work. Looking back on it, the work wasn't really all that hard. Then came the awful parting and the dreary train journey to Aberdeen where only six months before we'd been the toast of the town. Now I was returning as a private, the lowest form of animal life in the British army.

Christ, those first days. The horrified amazement on the sergeant-major's face when he took in the nervous shuffling group of recruits lined up before him. I had been at the OTC at college so I knew something about drill. Also, being an actor, I could assume the impression of confidence and Gungho which I was far from feeling. But some of the others literally didn't know left from right and on the command – Attenshun! Right dress! – there was utter confusion. The sergeant let out an audible groan and addressed us in broad Scots.

'Ye've joined the Brigade of Heelanders, and Heelanders ye'll be if it kills me, but I've the feeling it might kill ye furst.' With that cheering thought we were marched off to get our uniforms, rifles – no ammunition, of course – mess tin, knife, spoon, fork and bedding. We were then detailed to different barracks – twenty-eight to a hut. That night as I lay dazed in bed I was more homesick and scared than I'd ever been in any of my schools. The black-out boards were up, so no air could enter the room, and the smell of unwashed bodies soon became overwhelming. And the noises! The different types of snoring, the muttering and groaning, the farting and belching. Oh Jesus! But eventually, overcome by exhaustion, I slept.

A loud voice with the command: 'Rise and Shite' and a banging on the foot of the bed woke us. We groggily tried to put on our new uniforms and make the beds under the instruction of several lance-corporals. We were then paraded outside and marched into an enormous mess hall where we tucked into a pretty substantial breakfast of eggs with mounds of bread and butter. Tea was ladled out of a huge urn which we drank out of our mess tins, not easy to start with as it ran out of the square corners, but we soon learned not to drink but to suck it up. The outlook was improving. At least we weren't going to starve and to a Stewart that's half the battle.

Then we were marched back to barracks and told we had half an hour to shave, shit, shower and be ready for parade. There was a sudden rush to the three lavatories – called bogs – and queues formed at the two basins. I was one of the last to finish shaving and then went into a bog to do the usual. I was appalled. It was everywhere. I could maybe understand it being on the seat, even on the floor, but how in Christ's name could they get it on the ceiling? But there it was.

I have nothing especially new or interesting to say about army life, but some moments do stand out in my memory, such as the day I met my first Nazi. The Aberdeen fishermen were not very fond of the German Luftwaffe, as they had a habit of machine-gunning defenceless fishing boats out at sea. So, when any plane was shot down, there was a mad race between the Navy and the fishermen to get at the surviving crew: the Navy to hold them for interrogation and the fishermen to hold them under water. On one occasion the Navy managed to get there first and rescued the crew of a light bomber. They were brought to our barracks until they could be moved under guard to the interrogation centre.

The sergeant airgunner was an ordinary frightened little man, the bomb aimer and co-pilot the same, but the pilot – he was something else: an arrogant swaggering son of a bitch. He was under guard in the sergeants' quarters and I, by this time risen to the dizzy ranks of a provisional lance-corporal, unpaid, was in charge of the detail to bring his breakfast. This we did very smartly, and placed a lovely plate of eggs, bacon, sausages and fried bread in front of this arsehole. *We* never got sausages *and* bacon. With a defiant gesture this brute swept this meal, plus a mug of priceless coffee, onto the floor. The sergeant gave him a look and ordered us to bring another helping. After a lot of swearing from the mess cook we returned and delivered the second offering, but this time, as we put it on the table, the sergeant ordered us to about turn. Behind us we heard a sort of stifled gurgle, the sound of a plate smashing, and odds and ends hitting the floor. On the order to about turn again, to our joy we saw this arrogant bastard with sausages sticking out of his collar and fried egg all over his face.

'He tripped,' our sergeant told us. 'He's not hungry now, are you ducks?'

This sergeant wasn't the fellow to pick a quarrel with if you were a German. His father had been killed on the Somme in the First World War and he himself had been wounded on the beaches at Dunkirk.

Then there was the time I went into action against the enemy, a heroic performance. The Luftwaffe had bombed a large freighter near the coast and blown a hole in her side. She was able to beach herself, and salvage and repair work were going on as we could ill afford to lose one of our precious ships. The Germans had other ideas and at dawn and dusk they would send a Stuka divebomber over to try and knock her out. Our job was to protect her. We used to mount a beach patrol of about five men and a Bren gun, together with one magazine of ammo. Ammunition was scarce at this moment, in fact it was almost non-existent. Now, north-east Scotland in late winter is cold, and I mean cold. The wind that came off the North Sea could penetrate anything. I used to put on long underwear, pyjamas, battledress trousers, woollen vest and shirt, sweater, jacket, overcoat, scarf and balaclava. Tying all this down would be our equipment and gas mask. We used to mount the patrol at eight in the evening and were relieved at eight next morning. It was a long night!

We'd take turns trying to find protection against the wind among the concrete blocks studded along the beach against invasion. One morning, having passed a miserable freezing night, we'd managed to brew up some tea. What a mistake! In a matter of minutes I was dying to go. Now this was no easy matter as it took quite a time to get my trousers down. I left a chap in charge of the gun, disappeared behind a block and started to take off the gas mask, the equipment, unbutton the coat, take down my trousers, pyjama trousers, long johns and with a freezing arse was just about to start when along came a Stuka, making that awful screaming noise as it dived. I hobbled out from behind the block, tripping over my layers of pants, grabbed the gun, blazed away at the plane, and the bloody thing dived into the sea. I was so overcome with my prowess I forgot all about my trousers and was dancing about being congratulated by my comrades when we saw a Spitfire doing a Victory roll. He was the killer, not me. Well, maybe one of my bullets had found the mark too.

Just about this time I received a letter from Elspeth telling me all that hard work had paid off and she was pregnant. She sounded ecstatic and was already demanding a list of my favourite names should it be a girl. If it was a boy he would automatically be called James. Tradition. She then told me she had talked to our mothers and they'd agreed to give her an allowance so she could come up to Aberdeen to be near me. I was thrilled at the idea as I was missing her terribly. It seemed that I was going to be stationed there for eternity as my papers were lost at the War Office. I'd been marked PO, potential officer, owing to my previous OTC training, but on my papers my mother's maiden name of Frederica Lablache had aroused suspicion; a spy; a bleeding Italian in their ranks. They found out eventually that I was only one-thirty-second Italian, but in the meantime my papers were mislaid. So there I remained, a provisional lance-corporal, unpaid, while all my mates were sent off to fighting battalions.

Elspeth arrived and I found her a nice room with a family just outside the barracks. It was so cold we'd get into bed to keep warm and on a tiny cooker I'd brew up baked beans and poached eggs which we'd eat under the blankets. But going back to barracks was pretty depressing – that awful smell and knowing Elspeth was so near made the separation even worse.

Suddenly orders came to go up to Cruden Bay as an attack from Norway was expected and that part of the coast was undefended. Luckily there was a hotel there for Elspeth. We did our training and were shown the positions to take up should there be an invasion, but the weapons were a joke. Old Lee-Enfield rifles from the First World War with about ten rounds of ammo each, worn-out Bren guns with one magazine and about four 3-inch mortars with six shells to a mortar. Hardly enough to stem the might of a German Panzer division. Luckily they didn't come.

Elspeth was now well past her seventh month and one evening we were having supper in the restaurant, discussing plans for her to go south to have the baby, when she said, 'Oh God! I've wet myself.'

We started to laugh and looked round self-consciously to see if anyone had noticed and then she went ashen.

'Oh Jimmy. It's begun. The pains are starting.'

I was completely panic stricken. I didn't know what the hell to do. There was no hospital, no doctor, nothing. I told her to get some things packed and, with the help of a woman there, she managed. I rushed back to the barracks to try and find someone in authority who could give me compassionate leave, but there was no one about – all the officers were away somewhere and there were no senior NCOs around either. So, thinking to myself, to hell with it, I grabbed my shaving things and took off. Luckily I found a man at a garage who agreed to drive us to Aberdeen for a special price. Meanwhile Elspeth had telephoned a friend who knew of a nursing home in Aberdeen and gave her the address.

It was a nightmare journey. I remember saying to Elspeth when she told me she wanted a baby that I didn't want to be anywhere near during the actual birth as I had a complex about the cries, the pain and the blood. I was abnormally sensitive to this as a result, I think, of my horror at seeing calves being pulled out of their mothers' bodies in Cornwall. When I said that, someone must have heard me and decided otherwise. It took us three hours to get to Aberdeen and poor Elspeth, in horrible pain, was in labour all the way. We couldn't drive fast because of the black-out and there was only a small beam of light from the masked headlamps – we nearly ended up in a ditch about three times. Eventually we arrived and Elspeth was rushed to a room where a doctor was waiting and the door was closed in my face. I paced about in the hall, nearly out of my mind with worry and was told by a nurse to keep still as my army boots were making an awful clatter. It was then about two in the morning and the other patients were trying to sleep.

After what seemed like hours the doctor came out, followed by a nurse carrying something wrapped up in a blanket. They told me it was a boy and alive, but very weak with only a fifty-fifty chance of survival, as they had no incubator available. I asked about Elspeth and was told she'd had a very bad time but had been given an injection and was now all right and asleep. Seeing the relief on my face he added that it wouldn't be a bad idea if I had a bit of sleep too. So I bedded down somewhere and passed out. Next morning a nurse brought me a cup of tea and asked whether I'd like to see my baby. When I saw him he seemed so tiny and so still. He weighed about three and a half pounds and there was a needle in his arm through which he was being fed.

I asked to see Elspeth and we hugged each other, cried a bit and she asked if I'd seen our son. They'd brought him to her that morning just for a moment. I told her I had and wasn't he beautiful and all the things I could think of to try and make her feel better. She asked me anxiously if I was sure he'd be all right, and I told her of course. But I'd seen the look of pity on the nurse's face when she'd shown him to me. He died the next morning. There was one moment when I'd felt a ray of hope as his tiny hand gripped my finger, but a few hours later he was dead. Elspeth, of course, was inconsolable. Poor darling, she'd had such a hell of a time and been so brave and now – nothing. I had to leave her as I had gone AWOL for two days and that's no joke during a war.

Miserably I turned myself over to the MPs and was taken back to Cruden Bay under arrest. I spent a day or two in the guard house with some other wrongdoers and then I was brought up in front of the Colonel. This was the man with whom I'd downed quite a few Scotches in my theatre dressing-room only a year before but now we weren't quite so social. However, I got off with only a severe reprimand. The Colonel's wife was a friend of Elspeth's and I think the girls had had a get-together.

Apparently the threat of invasion had fizzled out and we returned to Aberdeen. Elspeth went back to London to recuperate and work in the theatre to take her mind off things.

At last my orders came through and at the beginning of 1941 I moved to an Officers Training Camp at Morecambe Bay. Somehow during this time I must have had some leave because Elspeth was in the family way again and very happy. Towards the end of my training she arrived on a visit and immediately became bosom friends with the commanding officer's wife. Elspeth has this gift – people love her. The training went on, the time approached for our final exams and we were asked to choose what regiments we would like to be commissioned into. Nothing was guaranteed but we could at least state a preference. I didn't put down the Gordons as, having been a private there so long, with so many of the NCOs as mates, I didn't fancy going back and ordering them about. I chose the Black Watch and to my astonishment was accepted.

Then one morning I was told to report to my CO. He looked rather grim and told me my wife had been taken off to the local hospital and to get there as quickly as possible. Oh God! I thought to myself. Not again!

When I got to the hospital I was told to wait. I was still dressed as a jock, a private, and privates didn't get any privileged treatment, but eventually after pleading with any nurse whose attention I could attract, I was allowed to see Elspeth. It was all over. She'd had another miscarriage. While I was holding her hand and trying to comfort her she suddenly went chalk white and passed out. I couldn't rouse her and thought she was dying. I raced out of the ward, grabbed the first nurse I saw and asked where the doctor was.

'They're all having their tea and can't be disturbed.' When I asked where, she pointed to a door and added, 'But you can't go in.'

Like hell, I thought. I stormed in and asked which doctor was looking after my wife as she was desperately ill. A man looked up and said I had no right to barge in. He would visit my wife when he was ready. I grabbed hold of him and, lifting him out of his chair, told him he'd better be ready then and there. He went rather white and when I put him down, followed me reluctantly. When he saw Elspeth he shouted for a nurse and shoved me out of the room. After a while he reappeared, told me she'd been haemorrhaging badly and I was quite right to come and fetch him. She was okay now, and he assured me that in future he would keep a special eye on her. I thanked him, mumbling an insincere apology and went in to see her. She was amazingly brave and said she was sorry for messing things up. She apologized to me. I told her that if I heard any more of that kind of nonsense, ill as she was, I'd smack her bottom, which at least drew a faint smile.

Having got my uniform together I reported to the Black Watch depot at Perth. The commanding officer was a formidable gentleman called Colonel Vesey Holt, DSO, MC and Bar, who made it very plain at my first meal in the mess what he thought of newly arrived 2nd lieutenants. His voice suddenly boomed out during a lull in the conversation.

'Stewart. I hear you used to be an actor.'

'Yes, sir.'

'Strange. I thought all actors were either conscientious objectors or pansies.'

All the other officers were waiting to see how the new boy would take it.

'Apparently not, sir,' I replied. 'Just one of those war-time rumours.'

A shocked silence and a glare from the adjutant.

'Another thing,' the Colonel continued. 'Wasn't your father a regular army officer?'

Christ, I thought. He's really done his homework.

'Yes, sir,' I answered politely, waiting for the shaft.

'Wasn't he shocked when his son became an actor,' he asked with a smile, but with the utmost contempt on the word 'actor'...

Here goes, I thought to myself. I'm not taking any more

of this shit. I'm twenty-seven years old and I didn't join up to be baited by regular army types.

'Yes, I think he was rather shocked,' I answered sweetly. 'You see, at twenty-two I was earning three times more as an actor than he was getting after forty years in the army.'

Slight exaggeration, but I had made my point. Silence. The Colonel gave me an appreciative smile as he said 'Interesting', and started a conversation with a major on his left. But the adjutant's glare had become really ferocious, though I noticed that another major, who had had an eye shot out at Dunkirk and wore a patch, gave me a broad wink with what remained. I had one sympathizer anyway. Next morning I was given hell by this twenty-two-year-old adjutant, a territorial who had never been through the ranks. I answered that if my behaviour was so insufferable in the mess would he kindly see that I was posted to a fighting battalion as soon as possible? He said he would, with pleasure.

And in no time at all I was posted to the 6th Battalion, a very famous unit whose officers and men all displayed the Croix de Guerre ribbon as shoulder flashes. Apparently during the First World War, this battalion, while occupying a well-known wine château, had drunk the entire contents of the cellars. Next day they'd gone into action, roaring drunk, and wiped the floor with the Germans. The French general in command had been undecided whether to court martial the lot or award them all the Croix de Guerre. As the regiment was suffering from a monumental collective hangover he considered they had been punished enough and settled for the decoration. At the time I joined them they were just waiting for orders to be posted overseas, and we were told to expect a visit from our Colonel-in-Chief which caused tremendous excitement. Our Colonel-in-Chief was the Queen herself, now the Queen Mother, and she took the salute as the whole battalion marched past. Afterwards she addressed us.

'My highlanders,' she began. A spontaneous roar went up

from the ranks and I found myself waving wildly with the rest. We would all have died for her then and there. After her speech I had the honour to be among the officers who lunched with her in the mess. Looking at her lovely face, with that radiant smile, I remember thinking to myself, 'At this moment, in this mess, here is someone really worth fighting to protect.' But I never got round to it. The combination of hard training, army cooked meals, forced route marches and sleeping in ditches, combined with the worry about Elspeth, had proved too much for that nervous stomach. I developed an ulcer and was sent off to hospital.

In spite of a diet of citrate of milk, I was eventually invalided out of the army and found myself, with very mixed feelings, on a train heading for London. On the one hand I had to admit I was overjoyed to be rejoining Elspeth, on the other I felt both guilty and a failure. All that training, all that square bashing and route marching, and for what? To be invalided out with a bloody ulcer. The sense of shame remained with me for a long time, especially when I heard that my battalion had gone into action in North Africa with a hundred per cent casualties. I received this news in a letter from one of my corporals who had survived; although badly wounded he gave me the details of the tragedy and said I could be proud of my men. Proud of them? Of course I was proud of them. But I felt I should have been there. Suddenly I remembered the clairvoyant. I was twenty-nine when I was invalided out and so missed being killed with the rest of my company. I remembered her words, 'You're going to be a successful actor', at a time when I had no intention of going on the stage and again, 'Do take care, dear, when you're twenty-nine.' Well, I had become an actor and I had unwittingly 'taken care' when I was twenty-nine. I didn't have long to wait to see whether any more of her predictions would come true.

6

Elspeth and I started our new life together in her aunt's house at Windsor. Elspeth was the leading lady in the rep and for almost the first time in my working life I became a kept man. It wasn't really that bad. Elspeth's aunt and her cook fussed over me and fed me whatever delicacies rationing would allow and gradually my health came back. But I felt I must start working again.

Robert Donat, who had been exempt from army service because of his asthma, heard I was convalescing and offered me a part in an interesting play he was starring in called *To Dream Again*, which was to go on tour, prior to opening in London. In spite of the bombings and burnings, the terror and deaths, the black-out and petrol rationing, people were still going to the theatre. In fact, the theatres and cinemas were booming.

The play was a flop and didn't reach London, so I was out of work again. Then Binkie Beaumont, London's top impresario, offered me the job of taking over the lead in *Rebecca* which had been running at the Strand Theatre for over a year and, soon after I opened in the part, I received a call from my agent to report to Gainsborough Studios to test for a film being made there called *The Man in Grey*, starring James Mason, Phyllis Calvert and Margaret Lockwood. Later I learned that they were stuck for the fourth leading part and that Robert Donat, who was working for them on another picture, had suggested they try me. The agent claimed he got me the job which would eventually lead to stardom. Rubbish. Robert Donat got me the chance. I got the job. The agent used the phone and for this call would get ten per cent of my earnings for the next fourteen years.

I arrived at the studio and Ted Black, the producer, took me on to a set where the director, Leslie Arliss, was in the middle of shooting. A script was shoved into my hands and I was told to study a certain scene. When I thought I had the lines more or less pat I indicated to an assistant that I was ready and the director told me to run the lines through with Margaret Lockwood, the lady with whom I was to test. She was very understanding and patient, but the scene must have looked ridiculous. Margaret was dressed in eighteenth-century costume with a very elaborate make-up and hairdo and I was in sports jacket and grey flannels. Naturally I was shaking with nerves but she was completely calm as she was already in the film and not on trial like myself. Then those dreadful words came that I was to hear so often in the future.

'Quiet, everyone, quiet. All right with the cameras?' from the first assistant.

'Speed,' from the cameraman.

The clapper boy snaps the clappers in my face.

'Scene 1. Take 1.'

'Action,' from the director.

I started. My voice seemed all wrong in that deathly stillness. It was too loud. I was used to projecting for the theatre, not speaking conversationally as one does in films.

'Cut,' shouted the director. 'All right, Stewart. Once more. Relax, nothing to worry about, it's fine, just a little more natural.'

The secret of good film technique – you act but you mustn't seem to act. Be natural. The hardest thing in the world to do. My knees were shaking, I had a dry mouth and I was sweating, but I must be natural. Once more I heard 'action', and off I went. Quieter this time, but just as nervous. I got through the scene and heard 'Cut, print,' and then Ted Black said, 'No, don't print,' and moved off into a corner with the director.

'I've blown it,' I thought miserably. 'They're not even

bothering to print it.' I looked anxiously at Margaret who smiled back encouragingly and moved off to her dressing-room. I was alone. The crew were busy setting up the cameras and lights for the next scene in the film and nobody was paying the slightest attention to me. I started walking towards the exit when I heard Ted Black call out.

'Where do you think you're going? Come over here. I want to talk to you.'

I went over to him and he asked me if I would go and get my hair bleached. I looked at him in amazement. Bleach my hair just for a test?

'Not a test,' he said. 'For the film. You've got the part.'

I was staggered. I thought I'd been terrible and everybody had been embarrassed. Apparently not. They'd all thought I'd done well. This was their way of telling me not to get a big head. English reticence. I went down to make-up to discuss this bleaching and Ted explained that it was very important to the film as Mason the villain and Margaret the villainess had dark hair, while Phyllis, who played the heroine, was blonde, so I, as the hero, had to be blond too. I nearly said, 'No, to hell with it. I'm dark and have dark skin and eyes and would look ridiculous blond,' but I reluctantly agreed and the bleaching started. This was a ghastly affair and, surprisingly enough, very painful. I had thick black hair in those days and it obstinately refused to change colour. More and more peroxide was poured on, stinging my scalp, and eventually I turned a sort of orangey yellow. Horrible. I loathed the sight of myself. Then the head make-up man started studying my face.

'Hm,' he said to himself. 'Eyes too close together – ears stick out – nose crooked. Lips too full. Hmmm.'

Then he stepped back and studied me again, shaking his head as much as to say, 'Well, I don't know how I'm going to make him presentable.' It really built up my confidence. I knew I had faults but, Jesus, was I that bad? Then he spoke.

'We'll pluck your eyebrows in the centre, that'll open out

the eyes a bit. I can stick the ears back with tape and wax and paint out the mouth. I'll shade the nose to straighten it. How did you get it bent like that?'

I looked at him a moment.

'I had a fight with a fellow for criticizing my looks,' I said. 'I knocked his nose off altogether.'

He got the message and laughed.

Then I was taken to be fitted for costume and, while this was going on, a script was thrust into my hands by a second assistant who told me to stand by at home and he'd call me when I was needed. What about the contract, I thought to myself? How much am I going to get? How many days work? What billing? I asked Ted Black this before I left and was told it would all be worked out with my agent. On the bus going home I read the script. It was great. Big, romantic, melodramatic, with a wonderful part for me. I couldn't believe my luck. Elspeth and I had rented a little maisonette in Chelsea again and by the time I got home I was so excited I could hardly get a word out, but after a big slug of Scotch I said quietly, 'Elspeth! If I manage to play this part well, and I know I can, I'll be a star. I know it, darling. I'll be a star. Our troubles are over.' Little did I know.

My agent, Dunfee, rang me the next day to tell me he had fixed a good contract for me. I was to get the princely sum of one thousand pounds for twelve weeks work. I thanked him dutifully, asking myself why hadn't he called me and asked my opinion before settling everything? But actually, looking back, I'd have played the part for nothing. It was such a chance.

The call came and I reported for my first day's work at six in the morning, as the make-up man said he needed two hours to complete the transformation. In later years I was to get this down to ten minutes flat. The ears were the problem. He would stick them back. I would pull a face or laugh and one would pop out again. He told me seriously that if I didn't grimace or smile everything would be all right. Rather a difficult undertaking since I was to play a laughing, swashbuckling roustabout at the beginning of the film. I then realized he wasn't interested in what happened on the set. He was only interested in how I looked when I left his department. He had painfully plucked away my eyebrows in the centre, which gave me a rather startled look, and painted over my upper lip to make it less rosebuddy. I thanked him and, as I made my way to the set, wiped the colour off my mouth and pulled the tape and wax away from behind my ears. Nobody seemed to notice or care.

As I entered there was a very different atmosphere to the time only a few days before when I had nervously tested for the part. I was greeted by the assistant director and led to a chair which had my name on it, placed next to a chair with 'Phyllis Calvert' stencilled on its back. This was the lady I was to play opposite but whom I hadn't so far met. I hoped to God we'd get on as we had to play some pretty lurid love scenes together. At that moment she made her entrance surrounded by her make-up man, hairdresser, wardrobe women, stand-in and publicity man. She was a strikingly beautiful reddish blonde and, as we were introduced, I noted her eyeing me rather warily. She'd already heard about my Rabelaisian shouts of protest at having to have my hair bleached to match hers and my surly reaction to the make-up man's criticism of my facial defects.

This was my first experience of the make-up department 'grapevine'. Apparently I hadn't treated them all with the appropriate deference due to their illustrious position and had already been labelled as embarrassingly outspoken and 'difficult'. After all, at 5.30 in the morning, the normal hour for the ladies to report for hairdressing, make-up and wardrobe, there isn't very much intellectual conversation going on, just gossip, and apparently I had been the hot topic every morning before my arrival. It was a strange and rather nerve-racking experience to be eyed speculatively by a leading lady who knew she had to play violent love scenes with a man she'd only met that morning, wondering how he would kiss, whether he'd try to take advantage of those embraces, whether he had BO or bad breath. I could see it all going through her mind as we started to rehearse.

Playing love scenes in the movies is much more demanding than in the theatre. Not every actor likes the actress he's playing opposite and vice versa, in fact some have been known to cordially detest each other, but nobody in a theatre audience is aware of this animosity. Unlike the camera, they can't see the expression in the eyes, only see the movement and hear the dialogue, but the camera sees everything, right into the mind of the actor. You really have to feel love at the moment you are being photographed otherwise that camera picks it up immediately. Eventually I got over this tricky situation by thinking of someone I really loved as I gazed adoringly into the face of someone I wasn't so mad about. However, quite soon there were a couple of scenes in the can with Miss Calvert and the director not seeming too dissatisfied.

I got on fine with Margaret Lockwood who, although having patrician beauty, also had the raucous laugh of a truck driver, an endearing combination. Oddly enough, my first scene with her was the one in which I had tested, but this time, of course, we had to play it to the end, when I had to slap her across the face. In those days a man striking a woman was practically unheard of in the cinema and the fact that the man was the hero made it even more daring. I'd had no experience of hitting women and asked Margaret whether I shouldn't fake it?

'Hell, no. Hit me, but try and do it in one take, eh?'

I assured her I would do my best. The cameras rolled, we spoke the dialogue and I clouted the beautiful Miss Lockwood across the chops. I was so horrified at the noise of the blow and the stricken look on her face as her eyes started to fill with tears that I froze and couldn't continue the scene, so of course it had to be done again. Margaret was marvellous and assured me that it hadn't hurt at all and her reaction had been just her good acting.

'Oh darling, I'm so sorry. I'll do better next time, I promise.'

Again we started the scene. Again I clouted her and again that terrible stricken look came over her face as the sound of the slap echoed around the silent studio. I couldn't stand it, and hugging her to me started to comfort her.

'You silly twit. Stop being such a gentleman and finish the bloody scene.' Margaret was quite right. Of course I was being a 'silly twit' but I seemed quite incapable of saying the few lines after the blow that would mean the scene could be printed. Eventually I nerved myself not to be affected by Margaret's stricken look, hit her, said my lines and walked out of shot.

'Print,' shouted the relieved director.

'Thank God,' muttered Margaret, gingerly nursing her swollen jaw.

As I was sitting rather dejectedly in my chair trying not to feel too much of a fool one of the 'Sparks' came up to me.

'Have a few pints before the next time, Jim. I always do before I clout my old woman on Saturday nights. It's easy, mate.' I know he was just trying to make me feel better but, thank God, in my whole film career, I never had to hit a woman again. Strangely, that unpleasant scene became the high spot in the film and was partly responsible for my future success. The women in the audience loved it.

James Mason was a joy to work with. Absolutely professional and, although far too good an actor for my comfort, he gave me confidence and much needed help. He had been on the stage too, so we had our love of the theatre in common but I only had two scenes with him, more's the pity.

Binkie Beaumont had refused to release me from the play and the effort of rushing to the theatre after working all day in the studios was beginning to tell. On one occasion I was doing a difficult scene in the film where I had to play Othello and began fluffing the lines. Time was running out, as I had to leave to get to the theatre and, desperately tired, the next time I fluffed I let out a stream of four, five and six letter words. Shocked silence.

Now, everyone on the set had heard those words before, but I had forgotten that I was the centre of attention with the lights focused on me, the camera and crew concentrating on me, the men on the gantry looking down and the usual hush when a scene is being played. I had really let rip and there were ladies present... Oh dear, oh dear. I apologized and eventually managed to get the scene right and rushed off to the theatre. But I was often to forget how vulnerable the film actor is whilst working. Every gesture, every word, any arguments, any show of temperament is magnified and exaggerated because everybody is looking at you, you are the centre of attention, so it pays to behave at all times. How often I forgot this!

Of course all the time I was filming the war was still going on: bombings at night, the sound of the sirens, the ack-ack pounding away, the shouts of the air-raid wardens telling us to fix our black-out, the glow of the fires, thankfully in the distance. Lying awake at night with Elspeth clutched in my arms thinking, I must get some sleep, I have to get up early, and finally forgetting everything in making love. Fear and despair are great aphrodisiacs. I managed to keep my mouth shut when certain members of the crew started complaining about the tea and buns being late, or being asked to work extra hours for which they would be paid overtime. But I thought to myself, 'you ought to be a private in the Gordons, mate. You'd have more to worry about than overtime.' The transition from lowly 2nd lieutenant to budding film star had been too sudden. I couldn't take it in.

My first leading part in films came to an end, but I already had another offer to appear in a film called *The Lamp Still*

Burns, produced by Leslie Howard. He wanted to make it to show his appreciation for the nursing profession. A beautiful French girl he was deeply in love with had died very suddenly of an infection, as she had an allergy to the antibiotics in use at the time. Like my mother, he had become interested in spiritualism and apparently a message had come through from the other side saying he should make this story. Was it merely a coincidence that the lady who introduced him to the clairvoyant just happened to have a script handy and that her husband, Maurice Elvey, was a director? Naturally Elvey directed the film.

Leslie was a dear man, very gentle and easy-going on the surface, but no fool. He realized, I think, that Elvey wasn't directing the film as he wanted and, before he left for Lisbon on a special mission, he assured Rosamund John, who was playing the lead, and myself that on his return he would get rid of Elvey and direct the film himself. We were both very relieved as Elvey was a disaster in every way. But it was not to be. Mysteriously, Leslie's plane was shot down on his return flight and he was never heard of again. Elvey took over complete control and when the picture was released, it was a disappointment.

During the filming I hadn't been inattentive and Elspeth was well into her sixth month.

There was great excitement as the gynaecologist had diagnosed twins. But again it was not to be. I came home from work one evening and on the floor outside Elspeth's room I saw two small lifeless objects. The doctor had been right. Twins, a boy and a girl. It seemed that Elspeth was never to be a mother. For my part I was quite happy with a family of one, her! If it hadn't been for her desperate longing to have a child, I'd have dissuaded her long before. But now we both agreed that enough was enough and for the moment we'd concentrate on each other. She joined the American Red Cross as a driver and looked cute as hell in her uniform.

My agent was on the phone again, wanting to see me

urgently, as he had great news. He had managed to persuade Gainsborough Studios to offer me a seven-year contract. But I remembered Robert Donat telling me never to agree to a long-term commitment if I wanted to amount to anything as a serious actor. When I told Dunfee this, he said I should jump at the chance as long-term contracts were very hard to get: the war would be over some day and all those potential film stars would come pouring out of the services and then where the hell would I be? This speech from a man who was supposed to have faith in me! I argued that the part in *The Man In Grey* had been immensely showy, and that the film might be a great success. Why didn't we wait and see? To my surprise he lost his temper and told me not to be so ungrateful after all the work he had done on my behalf.

'You actors', he said, 'always think with one part you're going to jump to stardom. It takes years and years and you might never make it. But with this studio behind you, you'll have a chance.'

All the work he'd done, indeed. He hadn't even bothered to read the script, hadn't asked to see any of the rushes or even a rough cut. I tried to convince him that if I was right, we could made any deal we wanted – there might even be a chance for me to produce or direct one day.

'And if you're wrong,' he said, 'what then? You've got a wife to support. You should think seriously of the future.'

I leafed miserably through the interminable pages of whereases and wherefores and fifth year, seventh year, etc., but I wasn't really taking it in. I knew I shouldn't sign. Knew I wasn't the type to take orders for seven years, with no say in the choice of parts; or the right to return to the theatre. I knew I'd rebel and there'd be problems. But I also had to consider seriously that maybe he was right. I did have Elspeth and the future to think of, and after two and a half years in the army I was penniless – in fact, I owed money. It was at this time more than any other that I needed an agent who had confidence in me. Someone to say, 'They must think you're good or they wouldn't offer you this contract', because by this time it was quite obvious that the studios were trying to persuade my agent to get me to sign and not the other way round.

There was silence for a moment while I tried to think clearly. I still wasn't happy, but I suddenly remembered Mrs Perryman. She'd said I would be a star if I survived that fork when I was twenty-nine. Well, I was now thirty.

'Okay, Jack,' I said. 'I'll sign. But on one condition: that they double everything. Whatever money they've offered, double, or I'm not interested.' Silence.

'My deah fellow,' he drawled. 'They'll never agree to that. It's just a waste of time my asking them. Now look here, Jimmy. Listen to me. You sign that contract now or you'll regret it.'

I walked out of the office before he could persuade me because I was beginning to waver. I went home, told Elspeth what I'd done and, being the kind of person she is, she backed me.

'It'll be all right, darling, I know it. Don't forget what you told me. If I play this part well, it'll make me a star. Remember?'

Yes, I remembered. I had been showing off a bit and now didn't feel nearly as confident as I had then. I heard nothing for a week and then Jack was on the line. He sounded jubilant, as if the whole thing had been his idea.

'They went for it, Jimmy. I managed to persuade them.'

Persuade them my arse, I thought, and when I signed the contract I remembered Donat's warning again.

'Seven years,' I thought. 'Oh shit.'

The Man In Grey was a smash hit and I became a star overnight.

7

Owing to the success of the partnership, I was cast again opposite Phyllis Calvert in a Victorian melodrama called *Fanny By Gaslight*, with James Mason as the villain, lucky chap. Villains are so much more interesting to play and for me so much easier. A hero has to smile and be charming, but a villain who scowls and snarls would, considering my feelings at the time, have taken far less effort. Again, unfortunately, I had very few scenes with James but the ones I did have were fun. He was very generous to me in many ways. He was married to my boss's niece, Pamela Ostrer, who was not exactly penniless. Her uncle, Maurice Ostrer, always known as Bill, ran the studios and on a suggestion from Pam and James I had had the foresight to have Bill written into my contract. In other words, if Ostrer were to retire, I was free. This small clause was to lead to a minor melodrama in the not too distant future.

Most of my scenes with James were on location and we used to have lunch together. He always arrived with baskets of goodies packed by Pam: eggs, tinned salmon, tinned sardines, butter, chocolate, all very scarce in those days, but James or Pam seemed to be able to find them and he would always share them with his consistently starving friend Granger. I had neither the contacts nor the money for these delicacies and lunch was always a high spot in my working day with him.

At the end of the film there was a duel between the hero and the villain. The villain, of course, is a crack shot and the poor young hero needs a lot of luck if he is to survive. Well, I thought, I'll have the audience pulling for me and, at last, maybe I might steal a scene from my friend James. As they set the camera up on James's close-up my heart sank. He had thought up a brilliant piece of business. He wore a rose in his buttonhole and, as he turned up the collar of his jacket to lessen the target area, he took the rose, sniffed it and with a wistful smile threw it away. With this small gesture, in spite of playing a bastard all through the film, he got the total sympathy of the audience. So, although I won the duel, I lost out in the picture. Anyway, those salmon sandwiches were great.

In 1943 our armies had eventually been victorious in North Africa and the newly formed 51st Highland Division, under the command of General Ritchie, had distinguished itself. The cinemas were full of newsreels of the victory march in Tunis in which the massed bands of the Highland regiments had thrilled the audiences. John Drummond of Megginch Castle, who had befriended me whilst I was stationed at Perth, was a good friend of General Ritchie and was given fascinating accounts of this action. I decided to write a film script combining some of these incidents with my experiences as a private and officer in Highland regiments.

During one of my leaves, John Drummond had taken me on a visit to the home of the Earl of Dumfries, one of Britain's largest landowners, and I had been most impressed when I had accompanied him and his twelve-year-old son on a tour round some of his tenants. The boy addressed the crofters and farmers very respectfully, calling them 'sir', asking after their families and enquiring about any problems they might have. On the way home I overheard the Earl telling his son never to forget that these people didn't work for him, he, his son, worked for them. They were his responsibility. I based the leading character in my script on this man, who commands the attack in Africa and, having everything to live for, gives up his life for his country. I hoped to play this part myself.

When I was a private the kilt was not issued and had to be

purchased out of our own money. The first to buy one had been a Cockney who had no idea how to put it on. We all gave him different advice and he reported to the guardroom with the kilt the wrong way round, wearing a Glengarry instead of a bonnet and with his hose flashes in front instead of at the side. We all listened gleefully to the roars of the inspecting sergeant. The little Cockney was an endearing East Londoner, typical of his kind and in my script he would distinguish himself in battle. I hoped this part would be played by Johnny Mills.

Another character in my barracks was a real Highlander, the only one there, who had been a poacher in Civvy Street. He had been quite unable to hit the target on the range when spread out in the position required by army instructions but, when curled up in his own unique firing style, put five consecutive shots in the bull's-eye in as many seconds. This man, being a true Highlander from the Outer Isles, had the gift of second sight and in North Africa foretold his own death. The adjutant who was censoring the mail before the big attack had asked him why he had told his wife he was going to die and was wishing her goodbye. From General Ritchie I heard that this character had described the manner of his death in precise detail. There would be a dead piper on one side, a burning tank on the other, and over a small hillock he would be lying dead. The adjutant thought this was nonsense, because no pipers were used in action, but what he didn't know was that the Captain commanding that particular company carried his pipes with him and, on being pinned down, ordered his batman to pipe his men into the attack. After the action was over the adjutant went back to take the names of the casualties and there the Highlander lay, exactly as he had described it, with the burning tank on one side and the dead piper on the other.

Another character was a Glaswegian tearaway who used to sew razor blades into the back of his bonnet so that in a brawl he would just whip it off and disfigure his opponent.

Charming fellow. He was a complete rebel, hating any form of discipline and despising all the traditional trappings of Highland regiments. When the regimental band in full dress beat retreat, with the whole battalion standing watching in admiration, he lay sprawled on the grass refusing to get up and show any respect. This man had his legs smashed up in action, but when he heard his regimental band marching past in the streets of Tunis as he lay in hospital, implored the nurses to hold him up so that he could stand to attention. He had won the MM and proved himself an outstanding soldier. I had a young Scottish actor named Gordon Jackson in mind for this part.

Our sergeant had had one ambition in life and that was to whip his father when he had taken sufficient beer to give him courage. I'll always remember his pride when he returned from leave and told us that the old bastard had kicked the hell out of him again. He adored his father and the men in his platoon adored him. He was killed in action and so would never know whether he could have beaten his 'Da'.

Then there was the huge gentle giant from Nottingham who had worked in a lace factory and become more Highland than any of us, even trying to imitate the singsong dialect. When his friend was killed beside him he had gone berserk and grabbing a Bren gun as if it were a toy, rushed into a hail of bullets and wiped out the machinegun nest that had killed his friend. He was posthumously awarded the MM.

These were to be my leading characters. I had seen the documentary *Desert Victory* and registered the audience's reaction when they heard the bagpipes. Everyone had cheered. My film would have a background of this thrilling music, and I decided to call it *The Ladies From Hell*. This was the name given to the Highlanders by the Germans in the 1914-18 war. The story goes that when these Jocks took up their position in the trenches they would lob a package over into No Man's Land. On recovering it, the Germans would unwrap a piece of paper on which was written 'We take no

74

prisoners, do you?' When the Jocks came over the top with bayonets fixed and their kilts swirling, the Germans ran, knowing better than to try to surrender. The theme of the script was that, although hardly any of us who had joined up had been Highlanders, through training and tradition we had become part of a crack Highland regiment and helped regain the honour of the 51st Highland Division who had surrendered at the beginning of the war at St Valéry. Excitedly I took my script along to Bill Ostrer.

I explained that with my experience in the Gordons and Black Watch I would love the chance to co-produce with him. The next day Bill told me he didn't like it as it had no women in it, no love interest. I pointed out that this was a story about men. You met the wives and girl friends when they went on leave and surely that was enough? But Bill had been used to films starring Phyllis Calvert, Margaret Lockwood, Jean Kent or Patricia Roc with myself and James Mason and wanted to stick to this formula. Sadly I put my script away. A year later Carol Reed, one of our top producer/directors, came out with a film called *The Way Ahead*. It was a smash hit and there wasn't a woman in it. It was practically the same story as mine, but without the Scots regiments and the bagpipes and without the fascinating characters I had described, based on real people. When I complained to Bill Ostrer, he told me that everyone made mistakes and the next time he'd listen to me more carefully. But anyway I had proved one thing. I did have a good story sense and I might be a good producer one day and not just a dreary film actor having to interpret other people's ideas.

My next epic was a film called *Love Story,* shot on location in my beloved Cornwall. On the train I shared a compartment with the director who asked me what I thought of the script. Not knowing he'd written it, I told him it was the biggest load of crap I'd ever read. Apparently later he told the story around town. 'Here's this young actor I directed in *The Man In Grey* and made into a star and he tells me my script is crap. Ungrateful bastard.'

But it was crap. I played a man going blind. The villagers dislike me as they think I should be in the army. Why don't I tell them I'm going blind? Margaret Lockwood is dying of some unnamed disease. We meet. I don't tell her I'm going blind. She doesn't tell me she's dying. The audience knows all this but we don't. We fall in love. Great stuff! She is a pianist/composer and writes the Cornish Rhapsody – best thing in the film, incidentally – and so it goes on. I was wrong, of course. It was a smash hit and there wasn't a dry eye in the house.

While I was preparing for this epic, Elspeth had met another doctor to whom she'd poured out her troubles. This man came up with a bizarre suggestion. Perhaps it had all been my fault. Perhaps I had what was termed degenerate sperm. I hotly denied there was anything degenerate about my sperm since I only had to hang my trousers over the bedhead and she got pregnant. Did that imply degeneracy, I demanded haughtily. You don't understand, she said. It had nothing to do with potency, but with the way I impregnated the egg. She'd lost me there. Anyway, not wanting to seem unco-operative, I went to see this doctor who asked me to do it in a test tube.

'Do what?' I asked innocently.

He explained he had to have a sample of my sperm in order to make the necessary tests. I looked at him aghast.

'In that?' I asked. 'It's so small and I'm not that good a shot.'

He looked at me impatiently as if it was the most natural thing in the world for a man to masturbate into a small test tube at eleven o'clock on a cold winter's morning. I looked across at the nurse, thinking she might help, but she didn't seem at all co-operative. I asked the doctor how much time there was between the act and his testing and he explained that if I was to put white of egg in the test tube first and then my possibly degenerate sperm, everything would be hunky-dory for about an hour or so. I was beginning to feel slightly nauseated, but determined that Elspeth should participate in this orgy.

I got a taxi and clutching the test tube arrived home and asked Elspeth if she had an egg. They were still rationed, and this little experiment was going to cost us one of our two weekly eggs. When I explained to her what was needed, she collapsed on the floor in hysterics. I told her sternly that laughing was going to get us nowhere and to please co-operate as the taxi was ticking up outside and I didn't want to waste the egg. I don't know how we managed but I was soon back in the taxi and on my way to deliver the precious results. Of course I wasn't degenerate, or at least, my sperm wasn't. The very idea.

Now that the ball had been thrown back into her court, Elspeth decided she'd like to have another try. My heart sank. Oh God, not again. I tried to persuade her to adopt a child but she was adamant. Our child or nothing. One day she came home flushed with excitement and poured out the story of her meeting with a Dr Roy Saunders, a gynaecologist. He had been recommended by her friend Mary, the wife of the actor John Mills. Mary had told her that if anyone could arrange for her to have a child this man could as, in her opinion, he was the greatest authority on childbirth existing. Elspeth had just been to see him and this was why she was so excited. After giving her a very extensive examination he had asked if she really wanted a baby? She had replied, 'No, no, of course not. I just had all those miscarriages for fun. Don't be ridiculous. Of course I want a baby.'

Roy Saunders then told her that he hadn't asked the question lightly as what she would have to do was not easy. Not every woman would be prepared to make the sacrifice.

'What do I have to do?' Elspeth asked. 'I'll do anything.'

He then explained that her problem was a tilted cervix.

Whenever the baby reached a certain weight the cervix collapsed and a miscarriage followed. The remedy entailed lying flat on her back for seven months. As soon as she was two months pregnant, she must be prepared to go to bed and stay there. Without any hesitation Elspeth had agreed.

What a prospect, I thought. My wife seven months an invalid! Not being able to move for fear of losing the baby! What would happen if there was an air-raid? Bombs were falling practically every night. But I didn't have the heart to share my fears, she was so excited. However, I did insist that we move into the country where the bombing might not be so concentrated. Only a few days previously, while an air-raid alert was on, we had been walking along the Kings Road on our way home when we heard the terrifying sound of a falling bomb. I threw Elspeth on the ground and covered her with my body. After the bomb had exploded a little way away we picked ourselves up and Elspeth was furious with me because she had laddered one of her precious nylon stockings. So much for my heroism. How could I go off to work, knowing she was helpless in bed? So she agreed and started looking for a house just outside London.

We found one near Stoke Poges, only a hundred yards from the spot where Thomas Gray wrote his famous 'Elegy in a country churchyard'. Beautiful, peaceful countryside, an hour from London and within easy reach of Denham Studios where I was to work. And now a strange thing happened. On cleaning up this home, called Monkseaton, I came across a bundle of papers that had been pushed away to the back of a drawer. They consisted of a collection of poems by various poets, all relating to the subject of death and the hereafter. One of the poems was signed by Leslie Howard. We discovered that this was the house he had been living in when his French girl friend had died. We gave the poems to his daughter, and I believe she had them bound and kept them. But of all the houses that we had seen, to have chosen this one seemed extraordinary.

Now I began to experience what it meant to be under contract. When we returned from Cornwall, having finished the location work on *Love Story,* my boss, Bill Ostrer, asked to see me. He told me that they were doing a film called *Waterloo Road* starring John Mills and that he would very much like me to play the part of a Cockney spiv. However, there was one snag. They would be shooting it at the same time as *Love Story* and would I mind doing both simultaneously? The schedules could be worked out and if it was all right with me he would consider it a great favour. Now, when you are under contract, being paid by the week, and your boss asks you to do him a favour, it's best to agree. Otherwise the favour turns into an order and, if you refuse that, you are suspended. So I played the game and said I would be very pleased to do him this favour and I hoped one day he might do one for me. Of course, my boss answered, I was just to ask.

Adjusting to those two parts wasn't exactly easy. One was a romantic heroic lover and the other a very unromantic, unheroic shit with a broad Cockney accent. I am six foot two inches and about fifteen stone, and had to allow myself to be beaten up by Johnny who stands at about five foot eight and weighs in under eleven stone – no easy feat. Surprisingly, the fight turned out very well and we did all the stunts ourselves as we were both useful boxers and in very good shape. But that's not really the way to build up a star. The public doesn't like its favourites to be versatile. The hero must always be heroic and the bastard must always be a shit. You would never accept Gary Cooper shooting a man in the back and then running off with his wife, whereas if Bogart did it you would cheer.

John had just been invalided out of the army with the same problem as I had. Ulcers. We used to exchange pills and powders and give each other advice about what not to eat, and of course agreed that the worst thing was cigarettes. We both smoked like chimneys. Happily I received good notices for this effort and it was one of the few villains I was allowed to play in my film career. But if I have to be absolutely honest, I hated being beaten by John Mills. It was against all my sporting instincts. Incidentally, in this particular film I wasn't allowed to use any bad language. I'm not talking about four letter words – I wasn't even allowed to say damn, God or Christ. How we used to portray brutality in those days without using those words, I don't know. But we did and it seemed to work.

I found it very difficult to adjust my entire life to being a film star and all that that entailed. I couldn't go anywhere without being stared at, pointed at and sometimes mobbed. I couldn't adjust. I'd always been something of a loner, now I was expected to share with the world my views on sex, marriage, politics and home cooking. I'm afraid I wasn't exactly respectful to the various journalists, or rather gossip columnists, who interviewed me. I couldn't take them seriously. I couldn't believe that any one would really be interested in what my favourite colour was, or music, painting, poem, politician, position, author, actress, seaside resort, food, drink, dog, cigarette – Christ, the infantile questions I was asked. My embarrassment made me seem churlish and of course the press quickly dubbed me difficult, but apparently I was good copy as I could always be relied on for controversial repartee.

The saying that all publicity is good publicity as long as your name is spelt correctly isn't true. Not in my case, anyway. If I was questioned about my work, naturally I would try and answer truthfully and as interestingly as possible, but where my private life was concerned, I would become unco-operative and abrasive. I longed to tell them to get stuffed and occasionally couldn't resist the temptation. Not good public relations, I'm afraid, but there was a war on and to me it all seemed so unimportant. My studio also thought I was unco-operative as I was often asked to appear at cinemas where one of my pictures was showing and I hated doing it, partly from nerves, partly from a complex that I imagined the audiences would be asking themselves why this six foot two inch, appparently healthy, hunk of man wasn't in the army. Besides I always felt I would be a disappointment. How could I compete with that romantic image on the screen?

About this time two characters entered the film industry who were to revolutionize it and be partly responsible for its destruction. J. Arthur Rank was a rich North-country flour miller. John Davis, who was to become his right-hand man, was a brilliant accountant. Rank used to teach at Methodist Sunday schools and had films made to illustrate his teaching. He found that making these films through outside studios was becoming too expensive, so he bought a studio. Then it became obvious that he couldn't employ this studio economically with Biblical films only so he started making commercial pictures. It seemed to him that the obvious way to guarantee showing time for these films was to own the cinemas, so he bought a chain. Then he bought a distribution company, followed by his own laboratories and in a very short time he was the biggest and most influential film maker in Europe. Of course it was more complicated than this but that in effect was how it happened and all with the help and connivance of John Davis. It was only a question of time before he bought Gainsborough Studios to which I was under contract.

The Hungarian director, Gabriel Pascal, who had conned G.B.S. into giving him the film rights of all his plays, had had a great critical and financial success with the film of *Pygmalion,* starring Leslie Howard and Wendy Hiller. Pascal persuaded Rank that he should make a blockbuster film and that he, Pascal, had the very subject: Shaw's *Caesar and Cleopatra.* He promised that it would be the most star-studded, expensive, prestigious film made in the history of the British cinema. Unfortunately Rank fell for it. Claude

Rains was cast as Caesar and Vivien Leigh, fresh from her triumph as Scarlett O'Hara, was to play Cleopatra. I was to play Apollodorus, a character that completely confused me as I think Shaw meant him to be queer, which was not exactly my scene.

During all the hectic preparations, Elspeth was installed in bed in our new home, the doctor having confirmed that she was pregnant. There was only one catch – this house which was supposed to give her security from the bombings lay directly in the flight path of the new menace from Hitler's Germany – the dreaded V1, better known as the 'Doodlebug'. These unmanned miniature planes were fired from launching pads on the French and Belgian coasts and their route to London passed directly over our house. The area became thick with batteries of anti-aircraft guns desperately trying to shoot the missiles down before they reached London, with terrifying results for us. Not only had we the fear of a direct hit, but also the fear of being hit by unexploded doodles, unexploded ack-ack shells and the usual debris resulting from concentrated shell fire. It became a nightmare, as I knew Elspeth wasn't going to move from that bed for anything, her baby coming before a few falling bombs, so every evening after work I would come home half expecting to see the house a wreck, but thank God the worst that happened was a fire in the garden caused by part of a falling doodlebug.

The picture dragged on interminably. I think Pascal must have had a row with Rank's minions and decided to bankrupt him in retaliation. He really took his time. The film was scheduled to take four months. It took over a year and every morning I had to be dressed and made up with hair suitably curled, as Pascal never knew what scene he was going to shoot next.

There were many attractive girls on the set and other films were also being shot at Denham, so every evening after work the actors would congregate in a pub close by and plans would be made for a party. But not with me. I went home every evening after one drink as I felt guilty enjoying myself when Elspeth was lying helpless alone in bed. Not entirely alone, of course, as she had friends who would come over during the day and we had acquired a living-in cook and a daily. Nevertheless I felt it my duty to be with her. Elspeth had one advantage over me. At least she had this growing child inside her to give her comfort and a sense of accomplishment. Normally Elspeth was great company, amusing, funny, clever, always interesting and what was more important, interested in me. But now her whole mind seemed to be centred on her stomach. The conversation was always about when the baby had moved, how it was growing, the fear she had from an unexplained pain. And of course there was no sex. I was thirty at that time, a film star, not unattractive to the ladies and I received many invitations which I always turned down. But selfishly I began to resent it. I began to feel stifled by this constant state of pregnancy, the shattering disappointments, the sad look of unfulfilment on my wife's face. As a male chauvinist pig, naturally I thought that she should be fulfilled by the very fact that she had me. It wasn't my happiest time, but I did my best not to let Elspeth know, and I hope I succeeded. It wasn't so difficult, really, as I loved her dearly, but unfortunately I was no longer in love with her.

On the set the conversation was also about pregnancy, as Vivien, who had always wanted Larry's child, was in the family way and apparently efforts were being made to complete the film quickly to give her time to rest. But I don't think Pascal gave a damn. Nothing was going to hurry him. On one fateful day he insisted that Vivien play a difficult and strenuous scene that could easily have been shot with a double. It entailed rushing over a slippery marble floor and flogging a slave. She slipped and fell heavily. Two days later she miscarried. She never forgave Pascal for this and from then on was constantly trying to have him replaced by another director, but without success.

There were lighter moments, of course. The production manager was a man called Pinky Green who was not endowed with an over-abundance of charm and was cordially loathed by all of us. One day the scene called for one of Vivien's ladies-in-waiting to lead in a baby leopard. The girl was absolutely terrified and production was held up while everyone gave her advice on how to handle it. Then on to the set came Pinky Green, wanting to know what the hell was holding everything up and, on being told it was the baby leopard, contemptuously said he'd show the girl how to do it. The leopard fastened its teeth in his hand. Pandemonium broke out with people trying to detach the leopard from the now screaming and terrified Pinky, while the rest of us were trying to hide our glee. Eventually the leopard was hauled off and Pinky was given an anti-tetanus shot. Who was to know the poor bugger was allergic to the stuff? He turned blue. Our assistant director was an Aussie named Bluey Hill and for days all action would stop and the cast and crew would gather round Bluey while he made his daily telephone call to Pinky's house.

'Hullo, Mrs Green? This is Bluey. How's Pinky? Still green, oh dear. Well, tell him Bluey called and we all hope he'll soon be back in the pink.' It helped cheer us up.

Pascal also had his moments when he would enchant us with his outrageous sadistic genius. The main set of Cleopatra's palace was gigantic with about ten larger than life-size nude male statues. Attached to our crew was a very repressed, humourless lady who was the Technicolor adviser and had to pass judgment on all costumes, make up, sets, etc. This lady was obviously a virgin who had never seen a naked male body. One day, in front of the whole cast and crew, Pascal started studying the private parts of these huge nude statues and sent for Phyllis. In a loud voice, in front of everyone, Pascal began, 'Phyllis, my darling, you know about these things. Tell me, aren't those men's cocks too small.' She fainted with embarrassment.

Another gigantic set was the Pharos, built on the back lot around a lake. At a certain moment, Apollodorus (me) delivers Cleopatra wrapped in a carpet to Caesar. This entailed using a huge crane and lifting me and a dummy Vivien from the boat on to the Pharos which towered about a hundred feet above. I had to place one foot on a gigantic hook and, clutching the chain with my hands, be swept about 150 feet into the air before being lowered on to the set above. As an acute sufferer from vertigo I was absolutely terrified. I asked that they shoot it without rehearsal as I wanted to get it over with. The cameras turned, the crane started to winch me up and when I had reached the highest part, a doodlebug was heard coming towards us. Panic. Everyone rushed off to take cover. I was left dangling in the air, knowing that if I fell I wouldn't land in the water, but on to the spiky scaffolding directly beneath me. I hung on desperately. The bomb went off about 200 yards away and the whole construction started to sway. I yelled out in terror and suddenly some of the men realized what had happened.

'Christ, it's old Jim. We've forgotten the poor bugger. All right Jim, hang on, mate, we'll get you down.'

Slowly the crane deposited me on solid ground. I started to breathe again but I couldn't let go of the chain.

'You're all right now, mate,' the men told me. 'You can let go now.'

But I couldn't. The terror had made me clutch the chain so hard that my fingers were frozen on to it. They had to be forcibly opened one by one.

The great day came and Elspeth was rushed off to the Princess Christian Maternity Home in nearby Windsor. My sister came down to keep me company, as she knew how nervous I was and we paced up and down outside for hours.

The doctor would send a nurse out periodically to report progress. Apparently Elspeth was having some difficulty and it might be necessary to perform a Caesarean. It was well past midnight when suddenly we heard a doodlebug coming. The engine cut out and we knew it was coming down. We both crouched against a wall and the bloody thing went off about a hundred yards away. In the stillness, after that terrible crash, I heard the cry of a baby. Apparently the impact had had the desired effect and popped the baby out. A few minutes later the doctor called to us from an upstairs window and told me to come and see my son. When I walked into the room, Elspeth was radiant with pride and joy and, when the nurse placed the bundle in my arms, I nearly dropped it with excitement. So this was what it was all about. He looked so strong and fit compared with the tiny creature we had lost in Aberdeen. I swore to myself then that I would be a good father, that he wouldn't make the mistakes I'd made, that I would guide his life and love, advise and protect him.

It was then about four in the morning and I had to report for make-up at seven. It didn't seem worth going home, so my sister and I tucked into bacon and eggs at an all-night restaurant and I went straight on to the studio. I was having my hair curled when the assistant director told me to report to the set as Pascal would like to discuss the next scene. I staggered down, beginning to feel the effects of lack of sleep and duly reported on the set. Nobody there. As I was looking around suddenly everybody came streaming in, cheering, and Vivien appeared with a doll dressed in swaddling clothes and placed it in my arms. Bless them. We all had champagne and luckily Pascal decided he could work without me and I was sent home. After ringing the hospital to check that everything was okay I slept for twenty-four hours. Having a baby is very exhausting for the father.

8

Caesar and Cleopatra went on interminably and we were all getting bored and irritable. One day a friend of mine who was working on another picture asked me if I'd make up a fourth, as a young actress named Glynis Johns, whom I'd known since she was a child actress, had developed a crush on me and had been pestering him to ask me for weeks. He himself was taking the star of his film, a devastatingly beautiful young lady whom I'd seen around the studio but never met. I told him I would like to very much. The thought of going out on the town with two lovely ladies after nine months of celibacy and husbandly devotion attracted me very much. Of course I was asking for trouble and it came. With Elspeth's, 'Go out and enjoy yourself, you deserve it', ringing in my ears, we took off.

It was years since I'd worn a dinner jacket, except to a film première, so it felt like a real occasion, escorting two beautiful sexy young girls who looked absolutely irresistible. My male companion, Roland Culver, was older and not really the swashbuckling type, so it was up to me to do most of the dancing while he sat at the table and saw that the drinks kept coming. Eventually at about two in the morning, slightly inebriated, we reluctantly made our way home. We all lived out in the country and as the chauffeur-driven car was mine, I had to drop my companions off one by one. Roly was first and so I was alone in the back seat with those two gorgeous ladies.

It was very dark with the black-out and only the faint glow of the headlights, and I was contentedly thinking about my dancing with the ravishing film star. I had to admit she'd excited me when I held her in my arms.

Then suddenly a voice said very clearly, 'Well, are you going to kiss him or aren't you?' I think Glynis was as surprised as I was and didn't react immediately.

'All right,' the voice continued. 'I gave you your chance and if you won't, I will.'

With that two arms surrounded me and a very passionate kiss ensued. I was by no means reluctant as I'd been dying to do just that all evening, but coming so suddenly and in front of Glynis, I was completely tongue-tied and couldn't come up with any glib response. We sat in embarrassed silence until it was time to drop off Glynis. I kissed her goodnight, told her I hoped the evening had helped her get over her crush and got back into the car, with Glynis's reply that she most certainly had contributing to my embarrassment. The car moved off with me huddled away in one corner, and the lady in the other.

'Were you shocked?' she asked. I mumbled something about not really, a little surprised perhaps.

'Why surprised? You must have known I've been dying to do that all evening.'

How can you tell the most beautiful girl in England you really had no idea she felt like that, without seeming to be a complete clot? I remained silent.

'Didn't you like it?' she continued.

'Very much,' I replied. 'Very much indeed.'

'Well, what are you doing over there? Come over here.'

As only a few feet separated us it didn't take me long to get 'there' and I was lost. I'd never felt anything like this in my life! I had had to push sex away into the background for so long and now – 'Oh Christ', I thought, 'this has got to stop. It's mad.' We arrived at where she lived and I saw her to the door.

'I'm sorry. I'm not normally so obvious about the way I feel,' she said. 'I just couldn't help it.'

I tried to sound sophisticated and calm as I answered with all the usual clichés about the dancing and the music and the champagne being responsible. But as we looked at each other I knew, and I think she did too, that it had nothing to do with that. Something much more serious had happened.

'Goodnight, darling. I must go home to my wife and child,' I said, rather to hurt myself than to hurt her.

'Oh, my God,' she said quietly and went inside.

I stood at the door for a long time and then slowly went back to the car. What the chauffeur thought I had no idea and cared less, but my thoughts were something else. The first time I had been let out I'd disgraced myself. Just once and I had blown it. I'd fallen in love.

Next morning I made some excuse to get out of the house as I couldn't face Elspeth and walked for miles. I couldn't get the lady out of my thoughts. And I had to work in the same studio. How was I going to avoid her? And what was worse, how could I bear not to see her again?

We both tried, for a long time. We would pass in the corridors and say a light 'hi, there' to each other, but every time I felt as if I'd been kicked in the stomach. I couldn't concentrate. I couldn't remember my lines, which Vivien noticed and commented on. And then of course the inevitable happened.

'Let's have a drink at the pub,' someone suggested.

'Okay,' I answered, 'just one.'

And there she was. We both knew it was wrong and couldn't last, but we simply couldn't resist it. We were desperately in love. Desperate because, as well as the joy and excitement of being together, we both felt guilty. When I was home I tried to behave as naturally as possible, making excuses for my lack of ardour, putting it down to nervous exhaustion from the film, but really it was because I couldn't sleep. When I looked at my son I remembered my promises to him when he was born and thought bitterly, 'What a hell of a way to keep them.'

Those months were the most exhilarating as well as the unhappiest I've spent. We tried to be discreet but we were both so easily recognizable. It had its funny side at times when we'd arrange a meeting and suddenly run into a friend and have to pretend we'd met accidentally. We'd rush off with a muttered 'see you outside the Empire Cinema in half an hour', only to find another mutual friend outside the Empire and we'd have to go into the whole absurd routine all over again. I never realized we had so many friends or that London was so small. We thought nobody knew. Apparently our secret was shared by half the profession.

This became clear one day on the set when I appeared more muddled and confused than usual in a scene with Vivien. She eventually became exasperated and told me in the waspish voice she sometimes used, to try and concentrate more on my work and less on Deborah Kerr! My God, she'd mentioned the lady's name out loud in front of everyone. I went white with shock and then red with fury. I told Vivien that such a remark, coming from her of all people, was in the height of bad taste and marched off to my dressing-room. Vivien followed, apologized and said she hadn't realized how serious it was and of course, she should have understood my position. I told Vivien that what had shocked me most was that nobody else had seemed surprised.

'Are we being so obvious?' I asked her.

'Yes, darling,' she said. 'Very obvious. I think the only person who doesn't know is your wife.'

That's when I decided to tell Elspeth and take the consequence, as I hated the idea of her being the centre of all this gossip and being made to look ridiculous. When I did her reaction was extraordinary, as I should have expected.

'Poor old boy,' she said with a smile. 'I knew something was very wrong. You've been far too quiet lately. You haven't lost your temper for ages.'

I tried to explain how it happened, that I hadn't meant to hurt her, that neither of us realized what was happening until it was too late.

'What the hell do you want me to do?' I asked. 'You know

I love you, but I don't seem able to handle it.'

Eventually we both decided I should move to a hotel and try and get myself straightened out. For the sake of her child, who completely filled her every moment, Elspeth didn't want a divorce and felt we should do everything we could to save our marriage. I moved out, feeling a complete failure as a husband and as a father. What a God-awful time to fall in love.

While this was going on, David Henley, Rank's representative, approached me about a new contract to run for five years. I was surprised, as the current contract had over four years to run and yet here he was, offering money, for a six months extension. Why this generosity? Then the penny dropped. Of course. Rank was going to buy Gainsborough Studios, which meant that Ostrer would go and I'd be free. I told Henley my suspicions but he hotly denied them, swearing that Rank was incapable of such dishonesty. I went straight to Bill Ostrer and asked him outright if it was true that Rank was buying him out? Bill wouldn't answer. I realized that I was part of the Gainsborough package and that Rank didn't only want to buy the bricks and mortar – he wanted the writers, directors and actors under contract, which included me. Rank must have known about the Ostrer clause in my contract, which was why I was so generously being offered a new one.

'Bill,' I said. 'Do you remember when I did those two films simultaneously? You promised me a favour. Well, here's the favour. Tell me whether you are going to leave.'

Again he refused to answer. I met Henley and worked out a deal whereby I'd get some tax free money, and with both his and my agent's guarantee that Ostrer was not leaving, I signed the new contract. Rank bought Gainsborough Studios and Ostrer left very soon after. If he'd returned the favour as promised or if Henley's word had been good, I'd have been free. And after that sort of treatment they expected me to be co-operative?

My part in *Caesar and Cleopatra* eventually came to an end and I was shunted into another costume epic, *Caravan*, in which I played a rich English gent who goes off to Spain, is kidnapped, rescued by a gypsy lady and loses his memory. I'd already lost my mind trying to play the part, so that bit wasn't difficult. It ended up with my flogging the villain into the swamps where he sinks into the quicksands. Although I had been shot in the shoulder during this exercise, I managed to grasp my loved one without any painful effects, my loved one of course being a girl from England. I don't remember what happened to the gypsy heroine – she probably sank in the quicksands too. I hated every moment of the picture but it made a lot of money.

Then there was *Madonna of the Seven Moons*. This time I played a Sicilian gangster, the lover of a lady (Phyllis Calvert, of course), who suffered from schizophrenia: half the time she was a duchess living in splendour, the other half she was my mistress, living in squalor but making up for it by being screwed by me. The director thought that by having my still plucked eyebrows thickened, my black hair curled, my lips painted red and by wearing pin-striped, shoulder-padded suits, I'd become a Sicilian. Wrong. I became embarrassed. To make matters worse I had to sing and accompany myself on the guitar, as apparently all Sicilian gangsters sing and play the guitar. I sang quite well, but apparently not well enough for the producer. I was dubbed. I'm a bass. The man who dubbed me was a falsetto tenor. Oh dear, I knew I should never have signed that contract. All my serious theatre training wasted on having to play these ridiculous and totally unreal characters. The fact that all those films made money, and that I had become one of Britain's top box office stars, wasn't that important to me. An actor always likes praise from his fellow actors and, appearing in this kind of junk, I certainly wasn't getting any. But as a friend once reminded me when I was moaning about my sad fate, 'It's better than digging ditches, mate.

Don't ever forget that.'

To my amazement *Madonna* made a fortune. I suppose it was what the public wanted at that time, complete escapism, but I had to sit back and let my friends in the profession send me up rotten because of my Sicilian gangster characterization, especially the falsetto singing.

As far as my love affair was concerned, I soon discovered that nothing can survive the feeling of guilt, the incessant gossip and the necessity of having to avoid one's friends. Neither Deborah nor I could remain insensitive to this atmosphere and so unhappily we ended it, and I went back to Elspeth.

Although London was still under fire from the V1 and V2 rockets, the end of the war seemed to be in sight, so now that my financial position was slightly better, I decided to buy our first home in the country. We found a lovely Elizabethan house with fifteen acres of woodland and garden near Haslemere, which was only about an hour's drive from London.

We moved in and were lucky to find the most marvellous group of help. Humphrey was our head gardener (if he had a first name I never knew it), and an absolute gem. After days in the studios making rubbish, it was such a pleasure to walk round the grounds with him, planning our orchard and kitchen garden, the chicken runs and pig sties. I became totally immersed in being a country squire. There were stables at the far end of the property so of course I bought a couple of horses and naturally needed a groom. Bill Rushton appeared as if from nowhere and proved to be another gem. He had worked for Lord something or other and so was able to guide me in the proper way of running a stable with all the necessary tack. These two men became my good friends, and I'd spend hours listening to their experiences and plans for our property.

Humphrey loved to shoot and, for that matter, so did I, so I rented 2000 acres, which in turn necessitated a couple of gamekeepers. There were two other men who worked with Humphrey. One, a dear old boy, we inherited with the property, and the other a newcomer that Humphrey found, named Pip Phillips. Pip had a lovely red-headed wife and a little boy called Robin, and I moved this family into a spare cottage on the estate. Robin had free run of the gardens and the house, as his mother helped indoors and, apparently young Robin's connection with people from the theatre who visited us coloured his whole life. He became a very well-known leading man but eventually gave up acting to become an even more famous theatrical producer, and made a great success at the Shakespeare Theatre, Stratford, Ontario, in Canada.

On the domestic side, Elspeth had found a wonderful nanny for Jamie and was as busy as I, arranging the nursery. We had advertised for a cook and one day a Hungarian lady, called Esther, turned up and, having inspected the house and inmates, announced that we would be her family. Apparently she had adopted us. Within a week she informed us that to make her family complete we should also employ a friend of hers, Louisa, who was almost as good a cook as she was, and therefore she wouldn't have to worry about us on her day off. From the moment Esther and Louisa entered our lives, our problems were over. Although they both insisted on calling me Mr Sir, they were each as bossy as hell and ordered us all about, but it was a pleasure to obey them. They were both absolute geniuses in the kitchen and never before or since have I eaten such food. I remember one day having asked for *apfel strudel*. Elspeth told me to go into the kitchen and look at the pastry. I went in – asking permission first – and could see nothing. I reported this to Elspeth who told me it was on the kitchen table. I went back and could still see nothing, except a new transparent tablecloth. Eventually it dawned on me that that was the pastry. It had been rolled so fine that it was transparent and hung over the large table on all sides. Incredible.

I had also found another treasure: Wendy Adshead, who became my secretary and whom I nicknamed 'the Cog'.

What a darling girl. She was to stay with me until I left for America and I wish I could have taken her with me. So our little family consisted of three gardeners, a groom, two cooks, two maids, a private secretary, a nanny, two game-keepers and a chauffeur, because I now had a pre-war Rolls-Royce. Although wages were much lower in those days, this was a pretty large overhead and I had to work like mad just to support it all. I certainly couldn't afford a suspension from my bosses. Naturally they encouraged my extravagance as they loved their stars to be in debt, because this made them more amenable. But it was worth it to me. My life in the country kept me sane. Here was privacy and contentment. Here I wasn't a film star, just the boss, and, I hope, a friend.

To my horror I learned that my next film was to be the life of Paganini, the world-famous violinist. I rushed into the producer's office and held out my hands.

'Look at them,' I said. 'These aren't the hands of a violinist – they're the hands of a boxer. How the hell am I going to convince anyone I can play a violin – let alone be the greatest violinist the world has ever known?'

The producer replied calmly that I had nothing to worry about as Yehudi Menuhin was recording the music. I nearly burst a blood-vessel. How could anyone be such a clot?

'I'm not suggesting you're expecting me actually to play the bloody violin,' I exploded. 'But you're expecting me to *look* as if I'm playing it, aren't you?'

'No, no, we've got it all worked out,' the clot informed me. 'You'll have one violinist bowing and another doing the finger work – all you'll have to do is learn how to hold the violin under your chin and pull the appropriate faces.'

There was a silence.

'This I would like to see,' I said. 'Show me.'

So a rehearsal was arranged with two violinists playing a piece that would be in the film. The man doing the finger work was crouched at my feet, reaching up and unable to see the strings: the one doing the bowing was behind me with his head down so as not to be in the shot and couldn't see what he was doing either. I stuck the violin under my chin and made faces. We rolled some film and the next day met in the projection room to see the result. It was fantastic. It looked like somebody making faces while two hands were doing strange and unco-ordinated things to a violin but not in time to the playback. The lights came up and I saw the clot looking a little sheepish.

'So you've got it all worked out,' I said. 'What do you suggest now?'

'Well, Jimmy, it looks as if you'll have to learn to play the violin, doesn't it?' He smiled at me brightly. 'You've got two clear months – that should give you time, if you work hard.'

I gave up. In two months I was expected to learn to play an instrument that takes any musician years. But it was a challenge and I thought to myself, 'I'll show them. In spite of these hands I'll bloody well look as though I'm playing the violin.'

I was given a coach, the first violinist of the Philharmonic, a dear man called David McCallum, who should have played the part as he looked exactly as I had pictured Paganini: large piercing black eyes, high forehead, emaciated features, slim body and wonderful hands with long tapering fingers. Not exactly a description of me. But this man had something else. He had enthusiasm and dedication and, what was most important, he communicated them to me. I would listen to him for hours as he told me the fascinating story of the two geniuses, Stradivarius and Guarnerius who, born in the same street in the same small town of Cremona in Italy, created the most fantastic violins, violas, cellos, whose incredible tonal properties have never since been reproduced. David was the proud owner of a Strad and, as an incentive, promised me that I could use it in the film. Dear man.

The day came when I was invited to watch Menuhin recording the pieces I was to play so that I could study the style and facial expressions a musical genius employs. I was expecting him to use theatrical gymnastics while he was playing these difficult and dramatic works, but he seemed to do absolutely nothing. He just produced the most exquisite sound with his eyes closed and with practically no facial expression or movement at all. I decided my Paganini would have to be a bit more athletic if I was going to disguise the fact that I couldn't play.

Menuhin was using a very famous Strad, I think it was called 'The Emperor', as the makers gave their special instruments names and the violinists in the orchestra used to cluster round him after a recording and ask to touch it. He was so charming with them. He would ask if they would permit him to try one of their violins and, after playing it, would congratulate them on possessing such a fine instrument. Of course Menuhin could make any violin sound like a Strad, but the look of pride on their faces when they heard this was very moving. When I confessed my fears of making a fool of myself, he told me I couldn't possibly make a bigger fool of myself than he already had. Apparently he had been tested to see whether he could play the part, with disastrous results. He couldn't get a word out. When the cameras rolled, he told me, he just froze.

Once the recordings were made, the hard work with David started. I would have to use a greased bow so there wouldn't be any scratchy noises during a take, which made it doubly difficult. It's hard enough to get a good bowing action when the hair is really gripping the strings, but with greased hairs it's practically impossible. We worked for hours, days, weeks. Awkwardly I tried to make my clumsy fingers move over the strings, even attempting to simulate a vibrato. Eventually David told me he thought I was ready.

The script wasn't about the real Paganini at all, just a romantic story in which the leading man happened to play the violin. Menuhin's recordings were wonderful, which made the film worth seeing and, to my amazement, I received many letters from violinists all over the country, congratulating me on my impersonation. They knew how bloody hard it was and this praise made it all worthwhile.

During the filming I played a practical joke on David which I much regretted afterwards. At rehearsals I would use some cheap mock-up fiddle and, when David thought I was ready for a take, he'd hand me his treasured Strad and I'd hand the fake over to the property man. David knew I used to get mad sometimes when I couldn't get the fingering right, and had seen me smash a couple of fake violins on the floor. One day I arranged a little trick with the prop men. David handed me his violin and, as he turned away, I quickly exchanged it with the fake. David was standing by the camera to see that my timing was right as this was a very difficult and complicated piece. The cameras rolled. I started playing and pretended to get into a fury at messing it up. I smashed the apparently irreplaceable Strad down on the table, and it disintegrated. David gave a low moan and fainted. I never thought he'd believe I'd do a thing like that. I was sure he'd realize it was a joke and join in the laughter. I rushed up and started patting his face and yelling to the props to bring the violin. As he stirred in my arms I kept repeating that it was all right. It had been a joke. His beautiful Strad was safe. He didn't seem to take it in. He looked up at me with tears in his eyes and said, 'Oh Jimmy, how could you? How could you?' When he finally realized it had all been a joke, although a very stupid one, he showed his friendship for me by handing back his violin and telling me to play the piece the way we had rehearsed it. I tried to give a specially good performance for his benefit.

During the filming two momentous things happened. The war ended and, six months later, Elspeth gave birth to our daughter Lindsay. This time she'd only had to lie in bed for five months and could get up to take a bath and go to the loo, so it wasn't quite so frightful. Also, thank God, there had been no bombing. It had been a strain again for both of us, but was well worth it when Lindsay came into the world. Daughters are always rather special to their fathers and this one was no exception. She was and is an angel.

9

About this time, as it was possible to travel abroad again, the Rank Organisation suggested I made a personal appearance tour of Holland and Belgium. Apparently my films were showing there and they wanted me to appear in about ten different cinemas. The idea appalled me but the inducement offered was that, if I co-operated, my expenses would include a trip to Paris and the South of France. Who could resist that kind of offer, and the thought of visiting Paris again was delightful. I had last seen that lovely city in 1944 when it had been liberated by the Americans and I was entertaining the troops with a thriller called *Gaslight*.

I remember one bizarre incident that took place in the little hotel behind the Opéra where we actors were billeted. This hotel and the British Officers' Club were then the only two buildings in Paris off-bounds to the American troops who were, quite rightly, after their victorious and bloody campaign, having a high old time. One evening, when we were quietly having dinner, a very large and very drunken Texan soldier burst in and wanted to make whoopee with two of our attractive ladies, Deborah Kerr and Nan Hopkins, another luscious blonde. The owner of the hotel was present and should have handled the situation but, oddly enough, he disappeared and it was left to me to sort out this raving giant. I led him out into the hallway and was tactfully explaining to him that he was off-bounds when he told me that if he wasn't going to get 'a piece of ass', as he delicately described it, he was going to kick the shit out of me. Here we go again, I thought. Why couldn't I have kept quiet and left him to one or two of the other members of the cast to handle? But of course I'd had to show off, and here I was facing a specimen that only Texas can produce; about six foot five, rangy, with a jaw that seemed carved out of granite and fists like hams.

I went into my dancing routine, hoping to make him dizzy and thinking to myself that I'd better make the first punch a telling one or he'd kill me, when in burst two US MPs. To my astonishment they didn't grab him, they grabbed me, and it was only the pleading of the drunken Texan that stopped them beating me over the head with their clubs. Apparently I had become the Texan's buddy and we were having a little work out to pass the time. With that all three staggered out, as both the MPs were also slightly pissed.

I returned to my companions and was explaining grandly that I had handled the situation and there was nothing more to fear, when the hotel owner timidly put his face round the door. I thanked him sarcastically for his help, but he explained that he had to get rid of his pistol in case of a search, as carrying arms was against the law. When I enquired why he went around armed, he told me that it was in order to protect his women. Apparently there were many like him who objected to the advances the conquering American soldiers were making to their womenfolk. When I asked if he had carried a pistol during the German occupation, he informed me that there had been no necessity as the Germans had behaved like gentlemen. Shee-it, as they say in Texas!

Anyway, the thought of seeing Paris again with not quite so many Americans around was attractive and I was told when I got there to contact a certain lady who would see to everything for me. Elspeth wouldn't leave her young family so I took a friend of mine, David Hamilton, with me, and we duly embarked my old Rolls on the ferry and took off. Paris in 1946 was a dream city. The natives were charming and co-operative and really seemed pleased to see us. We were even charged the same prices as the French, which doesn't seem to be the case today. We moved into the Meurice and I quickly phoned my contact, a lady called Suzanne Roquere, and made a rendezvous at the George V bar. On arrival this charming Parisienne asked me what she could do for me as she had been instructed to make my stay in Paris memorable. Thinking she was an employee of the vast Rank empire, I started giving instructions as only big-headed film stars can and was quickly brought down to earth on learning that she was merely a friend who was doing Rank a favour. I humbly apologized and she roared with laughter, telling me she adored being ordered about and please not to stop. She turned out to be an amazing lady and fast became my companion's girl friend, he being a very attractive chap.

I dutifully did my personal appearances, even making a speech at the cinemas in Holland in phonetic Dutch, not an easy language, to roars of laughter from the audience who all spoke English. Suzanne was waiting for us in Paris and had arranged the itinerary for our trip to the Hotel du Cap, Eden Roc, so we duly started off, all three sitting in front, with me chauffeuring the lovers. Half way there, as it was very hot, I was driving in an open-neck shirt when Suzanne suddenly told me to hold still as there was some 'animal' on my neck. Instead of flicking it off she triumphantly crushed it, at which moment the 'animal', a wasp, stung me. Apart from an allergy to heights, spirit gum, movie acting, the Press and J. Arthur Rank, I am allergic to wasps. My neck started to swell until I was permanently in the position of looking over my left shoulder. My two lovesick friends thought it hilarious until I nearly hit a truck and as David wouldn't leave his Suzanne alone and take the wheel I pulled over at the next roadside bar. We all ordered long, iced alcoholic drinks and took it in turns to take the ice out and apply it to my neck. As the ice melted rapidly it meant ordering quite a few drinks but, whether from the alcohol or the ice, the swelling did go down. But now another problem arose. I could look straight ahead but I couldn't see too well as I was completely pissed, so we all had to sleep it off in the car.

Eventually we all arrived at that wonderful hotel and

booked a suite each. The price at that time was ten pounds a day for all three, including meals. Today it's more like ten pounds for breakfast. The short holiday was glorious, the French being the greatest hoteliers and restaurateurs in the world, and the clear Mediterranean sea made me determined to have a boat and one day spend my holidays there.

All too soon I had to return to start work on my next epic, *Captain Boycott*. This was a film set in Ireland in which I played a rebellious Irishman surrounded by members of the Irish Abbey Theatre players. It is said that no actor can survive playing opposite a child actor or a dog. Let me add here that it is just as lethal playing with the Abbey Players. Apart from being able to act you off the screen they can also drink you under the table. Enough said about that film, except that it had one other Englishman in it, my dear friend Robert Donat, and he could survive dogs, children, and all the Abbey Players put together.

During the studio work on this film, which was shot at Pinewood, I stayed at The Savoy as commuting was too tiring. During one weekend at home, Elspeth had entertained a very attractive French lady to tea. She was to be responsible for a not very admirable incident in my life.

One evening, after the usual tiring battle with my Irish colleagues, I was taking a shower in my suite when the phone rang. The concierge told me there was a Madame something or other wishing to speak to me. This turned out to be Elspeth's French friend who wished to see me on a very personal matter. Slightly intrigued I invited her up, hastily drying myself, put on a dressing-gown and welcomed her at the door. Having offered her a drink, I asked what this personal matter was? She calmly put down her glass, started untying my dressing-gown and told me she wanted to make love to me, only she used a more abbreviated expression. Now my only excuse is that I was tired and weak and she was decidedly attractive and determined. I was raped.

About two weeks later I began to get ominous sensations and pains in that part of my body that had so interested her. I visited the family doctor and after the usual tests he told me in a rather shocked voice that I had contracted a virulent dose of clap. Dear God, I thought, what kind of friends does Elspeth have? To make matters worse the lady in question had been undergoing treatment which meant that the usual shots of penicillin wouldn't be sufficient and I would have to undergo a series of six-hourly shots over a three-day period. Antibiotics were scarce in those days and this little exercise was going to cost a bomb. Elspeth and I had arranged to take our son down to my mother's for the weekend and I couldn't possibly cancel the visit. When I explained this to the doctor, he told me he would work something out and he certainly did.

He now seemed very embarrassed and said he had to ask a very personal question. I told him to go ahead as we were being pretty damn personal already. He enquired if I'd had intercourse – a lovely expression – with my wife since contracting this social disease? As it had been two weeks since the episode I told him it was pretty certain I had. He then announced that he would have to examine Elspeth as she might also be infected. Oh no, oh God, no! That meant I'd have to tell her everything. He explained that there was no other way and I'd better face up to it. It was all right for him, I thought. How would he like to go and confess to his wife that he had screwed one of her friends and contracted the clap? And it had to be done right away. Gloomily I drove home and, having fortified myself with a couple of Scotches, I faced Elspeth.

'What are you doing taking Scotch at this hour?' she asked. 'You never drink at lunch-time.'

'I think the occasion merits it,' I told her. 'You'd better sit down.'

I had already decided that attack was the best defence and

so in an outraged voice I told her how I had been raped by her French lady friend. I must have made it sound funny, as she screamed with laughter and asked me if it was good?

'Good?' I yelled. 'Good? On top of raping me she gave me the clap.'

Elspeth seemed to find this even more hilarious and told me that it served me right. I told her if she thought that was funny, wait for the next bit. On hearing the news that she would have to be tested herself, her mood changed to outrage.

'Disgusting,' she hissed at me. 'Disgusting. To think that you could give your wife the clap.'

'I didn't,' I hissed back. 'Your French friend did.'

By now we were both in hysterics, not from anger, but from laughter. Elspeth, bless her, could always see the funny side of everything. Thank God she was all right but, as she came out of the doctor's surgery, she had a strangely triumphant smile on her face. He had certainly worked something out. Elspeth was to give me the shots.

I will never forget that weekend at my mother's. Every six hours Elspeth would remind me of her duty, and my mother was slightly bewildered at our frequent disappearances. I also think Elspeth had arranged with the doctor to use the longest needle possible, and with every jab she would enquire sweetly whether it had been worth it.

10

Blanche Fury, my next film, was a melodrama. I approached this assignment with a certain amount of trepidation as the character I was to portray was so contrived that I knew there was nothing I could do to make it believable. It was very nice being top box office, but it would also be nice, once in a while, to receive a little encouragement from the critics. Having been very generous over my first few films, they now seemed determined to belittle everything I did.

'Granger gives his usual performance,' they'd say. 'What happened to that unusual talent he showed earlier in his career?'

The studio heads, of course, were very unsympathetic to my complaints. What the hell does it matter what the critics say as long as there are queues at the box office? But it does matter to the actor. He starts to lose confidence and enthusiasm. Instead of his work being an exciting challenge it becomes a chore.

About this time I began to realize that I was also allergic to being a film star. I loved the industry as I still found film-making fascinating, but the other side of the camera was beginning to interest me much more – choosing the story, developing the script, planning the production, casting each part perfectly, the excitement of experimenting with new camera techniques, new sound-effects and editing ideas intrigued me so much more than just acting. Besides, we actors were entirely in the hands of the scriptwriter, the producer, director and cutter. Often I'd go to see a film that I had sweated over six months before, only to find my favourite scene had been cut, my carefully worked-out reaction in close-up had been transposed to another situation. Maddening and frustrating. Rarely were the critics knowledgeable enough to discern the difference between an actor's fine performance in a bad part and a mediocre performance in a great part. If the part was bad you were bad, and vice versa. However, I didn't forget that it was still better than digging ditches.

At home the great day was fast approaching for my first big shoot. I'd gone to great lengths with my two gamekeepers to raise about a thousand pheasants, in addition to the 500 or so wild birds that were already on the land, so I looked forward to a pretty substantial bag. Raising pheasants from eggs was no easy task, and bloody expensive. First I had to find about a hundred broody hens, very difficult at that time. Then I had to construct housing for them while they were sitting. The location picked out in the woods had to be wired against predators, and the hens had to be fed and watered. When the eggs hatched, the chicks had to be cared for; later, when they didn't need their foster mothers, they had to be moved to specially located runs. My friends and I got pretty fed up with eating boiled chicken, but some use had to be found for the hundred superfluous broody hens, and that's a lot of boiled chicken!

Eventually the great day arrived and my guests, Michael Wilding, John Mills and one or two locals, took up their positions. Mike didn't really know how to shoot so I told him to point the gun away from the rest of us, pull the trigger and hope for the best. Humphrey had hired beaters and together with the seemingly confident gamekeepers, the beat started. We could hear them in the distance and the guns were nervously waiting for the explosion of birds as they were flushed from the woods. We waited. Nothing came. The beaters were approaching when suddenly a lone pigeon soared out of the woods and flew leisurely across the line of guns who dutifully blazed away. The pigeon disappeared contentedly in the distance, completely unscathed, but that was only a pigeon; wait for those pheasants and then there'd be some action. We waited.

The beaters came closer. Then a pheasant and a pigeon flew out, straight over Mike who, aiming at the pheasant, shot the pigeon. I managed to bring the pheasant down with a shot up the behind. Things were looking up. The beaters were almost on us when two more pheasants flew out and were blown to pieces as all of us, thoroughly impatient by this time, had let off together. The beaters appeared, and the gamekeepers (looking slightly shifty, I thought), asked how the sport had been. I told them that it might have been better, as one and a half brace of pheasant and one pigeon among six guns wasn't overwhelming. Exchanging knowing looks, the keepers assured me that the next drive would really produce the goods. It didn't. In fact during the whole season we shot about fifty pheasant – fifty out of a potential 1,500 isn't very good and, on making a quick calculation, I worked out that each pheasant had cost me £250. It transpired that my trusty keepers had been knocking the roosting pheasants on the head and selling them in a town nearby at five pounds a brace. Bastards. I quickly gave up rearing pheasants.

At home I'm afraid things weren't going well. Elspeth and I were starting to quarrel and accusations were hurled around about my being away too much and her being glued to the nursery. She had tried so hard for this family and now, having achieved it, seemed to feel she had no further challenge. The reaction to all that suffering and disappointment had set in for us both. She took solace in the bottle, I in rushing around frenetically trying to discover why I was so unhappy. Elspeth was beginning to find this domesticity as stifling as I did. She was a fine actress and loved the theatre and she now resented my continually working while she was tied to the house. It's very difficult to explain our feelings at that time. All of us in England were going through a reaction to the long years of war. While we had lived with bombings and death, we'd all been united. In a strange way we'd been happy. We'd all taken pride in the way we had survived the seemingly overwhelming odds and had faced life with a sense of humour and camaraderie. Now the challenge had gone, people were beginning to get snappy with each other, tempers flaring at the least thing. I suppose it was a natural reaction, but it was not an easy time.

We decided on a trial separation. Elspeth started acting again and went into a Noel Coward play. I moved into a small flat in Reeves Mews behind Grosvenor House. The children were well looked after, as the whole household revolved around their comfort. Elspeth commuted from London as she loved to drive and I would come down at weekends to see my two adorable babies. I loved them dearly and it was only the thought of their future that had kept us together until now, but I remembered the effect my mother's misguided loyalty to my father had had on all of us and was determined our family life wouldn't follow that unnatural pattern. The one difference was that Elspeth and I had nobody else in our lives. But once I moved into my tiny flat I knew the trial separation would probably become a permanent one.

To take my mind off these problems I threw myself into converting an air-sea rescue pinnace that Mike Wilding and I had bought. He too was having marital problems and he and his wife, Kay Young, a very beautiful show girl, were getting a divorce. It was easier for Mike as he had no children but he was just as miserable and confused as I was. The boat we had found was a naval surplus vessel which we had picked up cheaply and we thought we could convert it at a reasonable price. However, we quickly learnt that, once in the hands of a marine architect and a boatyard, nothing's cheap. Most of the time Mike and I didn't understand a word the architect was saying with his abaft the starboard bulkhead and the galley forrard of the cuddy, with a sponson amidships, port and starboard. When we asked what would get us ashore we were told we could choose what we preferred – jolly boat, bumboat, fly boat, cock boat, skiff, scow, dinghy, coble or punk. Mike and I enquired whether it wouldn't be easier just to take a taxi? But it was great fun and we used to picnic in the boat while she was being rebuilt, much to the confusion of the shipyard men. We would arrive in a Rolls – Mike had one too by now – and Rushton would get out the hamper and booze and we'd all splice the mainbrace.

One day Rushton, who was working as my groom, came to me, very white-faced and shaking, and said he wanted to leave. This was a shock as I thought he had been happy. The great thing about our home was that everyone got on so well and seemed happy in their work. Then he told me the real reason. Apparently one of my horses, although fairly quiet to ride, was an absolute terror in the stables. Rushton had been blown up in the war and his nerve had gone, so he felt he couldn't do his job properly. I told him not to be an ass and that if anyone was leaving it would be the horse, but I gathered he was slightly disenchanted with all horses by now and so he became my chauffeur. I remember when he first came, he asked me if I'd had much experience with horses, and how we laughed when I told him the extent of my equestrian abilities.

I was seventeen when I first climbed into the saddle and was doing it to impress a very horsy lady I had a crush on. Our locale was the New Forest and I was the only male in a group of learners. When we were well into the depths of the forest I realized I desperately needed to pee. It had been hard enough to mount this animal and I knew that even if I could get down I'd never get up again unaided. I was too shy to ask my horsy instructress in front of all those girls to help me down from my horse to pee, so I gradually hung back, letting the others go on ahead, and tried to do it from the saddle. My riding breeches had a flap, which meant I had to pull it out over the top – quite a feat in itself. Just as I started to let go the bloody horse bolted, I lost my hold and it slipped back into my breeches. With all my thoughts concentrated on trying to stop this crazy animal I had forgotten to stop peeing, and the rest of the ride was a nightmare. The girls looked at me very strangely as I squelched away. I didn't turn up for my second lesson, but under Rushton's patient tutelage I became a very proficient horseman, which stood me in good stead later in my film career.

There was one very successful studio outside the Rank Group run by an extremely shrewd film-maker, Michael Balcon. He specialized in low-budget domestic comedy films which, although highly successful in Britain, didn't have much international appeal and at this time all our film-makers were trying to break into the American market. In Britain films had to be highly successful to make any profit at all, and usually just managed to break even, so Michael Balcon at Ealing Studios decided he'd make a film with a wider appeal. He chose *Saraband for Dead Lovers*, the romantic historical drama of the love affair between Sophia Dorothea, married to George of Hanover, and the Swedish adventurer Koenigsmark. The script fascinated me as I'd had no idea this love affair was the reason why the wife of George I of England, the mother of George II, spent the last thirty years of her life a prisoner in the castle at Ahlden.

Rank had apparently been persuaded to loan me out to Ealing to play the part of Koenigsmark, and for once I enthusiastically agreed, as I loved the story and the character I was to portray. Michael Balcon and his team of producers and directors weren't used to employing highly paid and as they thought 'troublesome' film stars – to them stars automatically spelt trouble. Stars had to have decent dressing-rooms, had to be treated with some respect, had fixed hours of work, in other words, had to be treated as any good artist should, whether he was a star or not. But not at Ealing. Oh, dear me, no. At Ealing the producers were God;

next in order of divine importance came the writers, then the directors, then the technicians, and a long way after them came the actors. If they could have made their films with puppets they'd have been much happier because to them actors were a bloody nuisance: they might answer back sometimes, arrive late, have a headache, forget their lines – in other words, they were human.

I very quickly picked up those vibes on my first visit to discuss costumes and hairstyles, as it was necessary to wear a wig for the part. I immediately encountered resistance when I asked that the wig should be attached as a fall and not as a complete wig, as I was allergic to spirit gum. This request was greeted with looks of outrage, and arguments ensued between the producer, head of make-up and the wig department. They tried to convince me that it was impossible, and just the kind of stupid request a star would make, as if to imply that I had only developed this allergy since reaching stardom. The fact that I had suffered tortures as a very lowly repertory actor in the theatre whenever wigs or beards had to be employed was neither here nor there. Also, it was much easier in the theatre to cover up the sores the spirit gum created, but I didn't think it would help the film much if blood was seen to trickle down my forehead in the close-ups. I suggested they get an actor who didn't have my allergies and left, hoping I wouldn't be suspended as my imminent divorce wasn't going to be cheap. Next day I received a call asking politely if I would please come to the wig department. When I arrived the lady in charge told me confidentially that my idea was a good one anyway, as it would look much more natural and save time trying to mask the hairline, but she implored me not to tell the producer that she'd said so. I had at least one friend.

The film started on location at Blenheim Palace and had been in progress for some days before I reported for work. I turned up in my Rolls with Rushton at the wheel and learned later that this had caused great offence and my fellow actors had been warned to look out as they had to work with a 'star'. I could sense the atmosphere immediately and at the beginning it was one of sufferance. All this due to the fact that I had an allergy to spirit gum and was known to speak my mind – unpardonable, as stars were not supposed to have minds. As we drove through the splendid grounds of Blenheim, I could see the crew working on a scene in the distance. Suddenly a figure on horseback detached itself and came galloping towards us. Rushton and I had both got out of the car by then, and realized something was wrong. The period hat and wig had fallen off and the bald-headed rider was sawing frantically at the reins. Rushton and I went to the rescue, grabbing the bridle and bringing the obviously terrified horse to a stop. The animal wasn't nearly as terrified as its rider, who very clumsily but thankfully leapt to the ground. He and I looked at each other in silence a moment, and then I held out my hand.

'You're Peter Bull, aren't you? I'm Stewart Granger. What happened?'

When Peter had calmed down a bit he explained that in order to get the part he'd had to say he could ride a horse, but it was clear he had a bigger allergy to horses than I to spirit gum. In the scene he had just played, the director had asked him to say his line and move past camera, but the horse had other ideas. This story enchanted me, as anybody putting one over on the studios immediately finds a soft spot in my heart, and we became friends. I'm happy to say this friendship has lasted to this day.

Peter is a very rare human being; one of the few truly gentle and kind men I know. He has an enormous sense of humour, great wit and has endeared himself to millions with his book on Teddy Bears.

So thanks to assurances that I was quite a decent chap from Peter Bull and Michael Gough, who had been in *Blanche Fury* with me, the actors were won over. These included my leading lady, Joan Greenwood, a green-eyed, gravel-voiced enchantress, and Balcon's daughter, Jill. The five of us became inseparable. Now only the studio brass had to be convinced. The director, Basil Dearden, was no problem and we became good friends, but the producer, Michael Relph, was a very supercilious gentleman and quite impervious to my charms. He showed his contempt for actors by having all the scenes sketched on a board with our positions marked and instructions on when we should move.

My first scene in the studio was with a very formidable French star named Françoise Rosay. When, having consulted the drawings, Basil gave her instructions as to where and on which line she should move, to my joy she rebelled and for once I wasn't the one who had to head the insurrection. I backed her up and suggested it might be a good idea if we could have five minutes rehearsal to work out the moves with the director and to everyone's satisfaction. The board of drawings disappeared and so did the producer. It was a very happy unit and with a cast like Françoise, Frederick Valk, Flora Robson, Anthony Quayle, Peter and Joan, the film turned out very successfully and was one of the few I've always been proud of.

Elspeth and I had decided that in order to avoid headlines in the papers we would be divorced under the name of Stewart and not Granger. At that time the divorce courts would not accept incompatibility as sufficient grounds, so it would have to be adultery or nothing. Naturally I had to provide the grounds and, having arranged everything with our lawyers, took off for Paris where the dastardly deed was to be done. Suzanne and David, who were living together in Paris, decided that I shouldn't have to use a professional co-respondent, as Suzanne would do the job herself. We all booked rooms at a hotel, having arranged that Elspeth's private detective would arrive next morning and collect the evidence. David and Suzanne took one room and I took another on a floor below. At 7.30 in the morning it was

113

agreed that Suzanne would join me in my bed and await the arrival of the private eye, all very amusing but still somewhat degrading.

Suzanne arrived punctually. We waited, laughing and joking, sitting up in bed as far from each other as possible. Luckily it was a double bed. The 'eye' didn't arrive, and Suzanne started to get madly self-conscious; after all, she was David's girl friend and what the hell was she doing in my bed? It didn't seem so funny by eight o'clock, so we decided to order coffee, which arrived together with the private eye. He took out his notebook and asked us our names. I gave him mine, Suzanne gave a fictitious one, and he solemnly jotted them down. There was a pause and I asked him if he was waiting to see us perform? He had the grace to blush and assured me that wouldn't be necessary. We invited him to join us for coffee but he told us he had to dash off as there was another couple waiting. David came down after a call from us, and we all enjoyed breakfast together, the tension now broken; but we were relieved that the sordid business was over.

11

At last our boat was ready and, thinking it a good idea to make myself scarce in England, Mike and I decided to take her down through the canals to the South of France. We hired a captain and his wife as crew and set off to cross the Channel. Before setting off, we'd had a very drunken dinner party on board with our friends and, feeling no pain, I sent the skipper below and decided to take her across myself. The Channel can be very unfriendly and, not being a good sailor, the rolling and tossing of the boat was having its effect on me, so with detailed instructions to Mike on what course to steer, I slumped into a seat in the wheelhouse and dozed off in misery.

A little later a peculiar movement of the boat woke me up and I looked around. Things didn't seem quite right. The swell seemed to be coming from a different direction so I studied the binnacle and discovered that Mike had unwittingly allowed the boat to swing round 180 degrees and we were now heading back the way we came. When I scathingly criticized Mike's seamanship his excuse was that I may have been feeling seasick but he had been feeling drunk. I couldn't argue with that and, setting a new course, we finally made Le Havre. I hoped to God the skipper hadn't noticed our balls-up as I didn't want a mutiny so early on in the voyage.

Going through the canals with their interminable series of locks can be peaceful and soothing but it can also be a bloody bore. The boat was sixty-five feet long with three Perkins diesels and a shallow draft which enabled her to enter these locks. It was difficult to navigate her as she was steered by the engines and, when one of these gave up the ghost early on, life wasn't quite so peaceful. When we arrived in Paris

Mike and I decided to stay there and, hiring another hand, wished the skipper good luck and told him we'd join him at Marseilles. We moved into the George V.

The next evening we were in that famous bar checking the action, when we spotted a film agent neither of us cared for very much. He was talking to friends and, although studiously trying to avoid his glance, we couldn't help overhearing him discussing Hedy Lamarr. Immediately he became a lot more attractive and we hailed him as a long lost friend and invited him to our table. He refused politely, telling us he had to join Miss Lamarr in her suite as he was accompanying her on her trip. He casually asked if we'd like to meet her as she was giving a small cocktail party? Would we like to meet Miss Lamarr? Would we not! Many years before Mike and I had sat in the stalls drooling over this luscious lady, and the chance of actually seeing her in the flesh was irresistible.

We both accepted graciously and were soon ushered into her presence. She turned out to be very beautiful still but extremely bossy and in some strange way not at all feminine. There were several of her friends present and, while they dutifully listened to her views on everything from French fashions to French pancakes, Michael and I exchanged disappointed looks. Suddenly Miss Lamarr noticed the two late arrivals and gave me a very appraising look. While continuing her unending harangue she kept darting these looks at me like a cat savouring a bowl of cream. Mike and I finished our drinks and were edging towards the door when I received instructions from the agent to remain. As Miss Lamarr was ushering the others out, including Mike, she hissed at me, 'You stay!' Now I was alone with her and didn't quite know what was expected of me. I looked at her with a rather vacant smile and received a look of astounded outrage.

'My God, I don't believe you want to!' she said.

'Want to what, Miss Lamarr?' I asked nervously.

'You know very well. Kings want to. Heads of studios want to. Presidents want to. Why don't you want to?'

'Oh, but I do want to, Miss Lamarr.'

'Then go and get your clothes off,' she snapped.

Obediently I went into the bathroom and miserably started to take my clothes off.

'Hurry up. I've got an appointment at the hairdresser,' I heard through the door.

I entered the bedroom where the lady was already lying naked and dutifully took up my position. If only she'd shut up and stopped giving orders, the ordeal might have been consummated with some pleasure as she was still very attractive and, in spite of the thought of all those kings, presidents and heads of studios possessing that body, I was starting to become aroused when she gave her last instruction.

'Now don't come too fast, will you!'

That was it. That was the straw that broke the camel's back or in this case the rather uneasy erection. I rushed into the bathroom, dressed as quickly as I could and made my exit. Not a word was said and I have no idea what she was thinking, but she certainly wouldn't be late for the hairdresser.

As I entered the bar, Mike looked up in astonishment.

'Well, that didn't take long did it?' And then seeing my expression he asked me why I was looking so pale.

'Mike,' I said. 'We should have stayed on that boat.' I didn't go into details, but the look on Mike's face gave me the impression he wouldn't have left so soon if he'd had the chance. By now I was beginning to regret it myself. She had been very beautiful, and I mean – Hedy Lamarr!

We still couldn't get any firm news about the boat, so Mike suggested we go down to Cannes to wait for it, as he had a friend there who had invited him to stay. Mrs Winston – a full blooded Cherokee as she assured us – was the wife of a multi-millionaire construction builder who had rented the famous Château d l'Horizon for the season. We were in good company as Doris Duke, the tobacco heiress, was there, closely escorted by the notorious lover, Rubirosa. Doris was a tall, good-looking woman and to my amazement very nice. I thought she would be spoilt rotten and be an arrogant, rude bitch, but she was nothing of the kind. Spoilt yes, who wouldn't be with all those millions and all those potential husbands hovering round, flattering her. Poor Ruby was in there really pitching. She used to keep him waiting around at all hours to take her to lunch or dinner and both Mike and I were amazed that any man would stand for it.

Doris was obviously interested in these two English types who refused to be overawed by her wealth and, one day, for the hell of it, Mike and I asked her if we could take her to dinner? She graciously agreed and we made a date for eight o'clock the next evening. We waited until 8.15 and then, as not surprisingly she hadn't shown up, we took off. Next morning at breakfast, she asked us rather plaintively what had happened? We told her, very innocently, that we had waited until 8.15, and then as she hadn't shown up, thought she had changed her mind. We apologized and asked if she'd give us another chance that evening. She accepted and as we left for a swim we gave Rubirosa, who had been eyeing us balefully during the conversation, a cheery salute. Poor man. With us it was fun. With him it was business. At eight o'clock punctually Doris turned up and I think it was the first time in her adult life she arrived on time.

Instead of going to one of the expensive and, to our mind, boring restaurants that café society had decreed were 'in', we took her to a little bistro we knew and I think she enjoyed herself thoroughly, not having to tablehop and wave to friends as she would have been forced to do in the other places. Mike and I are complete opposites physically and mentally; he is very attractive in an aesthetic kind of way and very gentle; me, dark and dashing and seemingly very tough. In fact, mentally Mike was far tougher than I, but Doris wasn't to know that and, as we both flirted with her outrageously, we realized that she was rather naive and could be swept off her feet quite easily. She just couldn't make up her mind which of us she wanted. She had never been treated in this cavalier way before and it intrigued her.

Naturally many guests came to the Château and the only people who weren't obsessed with money were the actors and actresses. Michèle Morgan came with her boy friend, Merle Oberon was there and a very beautiful young French actress, Martine Carol, but the others, wealthy industrialist bankers, property tycoons, always seemed to talk about money. Every pronouncement made by one of these bores was treated with such deference by one and all – except us – that it made me sick to my stomach. The Cherokee would show off her jewellery at the drop of a hat – and what jewellery! Millions of dollars worth. Mike and I used to exchange glances and I know the same thing was going through his mind. Let's knock off the jewellery and blow – after all, she was asking for it and we were probably the most deserving cases there. A strange aura of degeneracy comes over you when you mix in such a set. Mike and I were both successful actors: we made good money, but we paid taxes and so didn't keep much, unlike these people whose other favourite subject was tax evasion. Tax havens, tax exiles, tax set-ups. Mike and I couldn't be bothered with it all – we just paid.

Merle Oberon was one of the most beautiful ladies I'd ever encountered, with the most attractive voice. She was a highly intelligent, sophisticated woman of the world, and I realized that conversation can be as important in a relationship as sex. Naturally I made a pass at her, as passes seemed to be the main sport in the Château. I was gently rebuffed. She explained that, although it would be fun, she was still married and, although the marriage wasn't particularly successful, she didn't want to make a fool of her husband. She went up even higher in my estimation. She told me, however, that if I wanted a flirt she had a very attractive friend who was free at the time, and she, Merle, would arrange a meeting. We agreed on a restaurant in Beaulieu and I waited in high anticipation. When Merle showed up, her 'friend' greeted me with a big kiss and we both shrieked with laughter while we explained to the bewildered Merle that we had met before and filled her in as to the strange circumstances of our meeting.

I had met Rosemary Riachi, my blind date, the previous year, when she had been in love with Prince Youka Trebetskoi. As I was then alone in Cannes, we would all go out together with Youka's brother Igor and Freddie McEvoy, an Australian adventurer. Youka and Rosemary each told me mournfully that, although they were in love, they couldn't afford each other as they both liked the good things of life. Neither had a penny and so they would have to make rich marriages. I found this rather sad as I had become fond of them both. It was all due to that degenerate atmosphere that had already hit me. There was so much money being flashed around, so much jewellery, so many yachts, so many sumptuous parties, so many beautiful women looking for rich husbands, so many unattractive rich men looking for beautiful wives and so many unattractive rich women looking for beautiful men. My two chums were certainly beautiful and would find no difficulty in finding rich mates, but it all seemed such a waste.

It so happened that Barbara Hutton, the Woolworth heiress, was there and a plan was worked out to catch this tempting morsel. First into the arena was Freddie McEvoy, but he struck out as, owing to a recent operation for a duodenal, caused no doubt by trying to please these demanding ladies, his performance was not up to scratch. Next went Youka. But he had an inexplicable predeliction for eating raw garlic sandwiches, which made him stink like a polecat and didn't endear him to the fastidious Miss Hutton.

Now they were desperate, as Igor, although beautiful, was not considered very bright. However, they dressed him up and, carrying a large bouquet of red roses, which took practically all of their remaining capital, he went into action. Success. She found him enchanting, as he neither smelt of garlic nor was recovering from an operation, so she became a princess and he became an heir.

I watched all this from the sidelines while Rosemary, rather tearfully, gave me a blow by blow description. Although her Youka had struck out here it was only a question of time before he met some rich lady who liked the smell of garlic and he'd be home and dry. Then what was to happen to her? Merle was enchanted by this story and we had a wonderful evening, swearing that all of us would make good marriages, good being rich, naturally, and to hell with love. I needn't have worried about either of them. Merle married a very rich Mexican and Rosemary one of the richest men in America. Years later I was to visit her at her fabulous château on Cap Ferrat. Strolling in the magnificent garden she pointed to a villa across the bay, perched on the side of a cliff.

'Do you know who lives there, Jimmy?' she asked me, rather sadly. 'Youka. He's married to an American heiress and is very happy.'

'Are you happy?' I asked.

She looked at me a moment.

'What is happiness, darling? I know one thing. I'm rich.'

With this in mind, after one drunken evening with the financially delectable Miss Duke, I remember rolling dice with Mike to see which of us was going to marry her.

'Now, understand, Mike. If you win I marry her and pay you half my settlement, and if I win, you marry her and pay me half yours.'

Solemn drunken nod from Mike. I threw and won. I remember thinking, thank God, Mike will handle it much better, as he's far more easy-going. Next morning, both with terrible hangovers, we met for breakfast on the terrace, the only other guest present being a very disconsolate Rubirosa. He was at the far end of the table and couldn't hear our whispered conversation.

'You weren't serious last night, were you, Jim?' pleaded Mike.

'Don't tell me you're trying to back out of it,' I replied indignantly.

The look of anguish on Mike's face made me break up and I couldn't keep a straight face any longer.

'Of course, I was joking, you clot. Do you really think I was seriously expecting you to marry Doris just for the settlement? It's this bloody place. It's not for us, Mike, let's get out.'

Mike gave a sigh of relief.

'Jesus, I thought you were serious. You're such a bossy bastard I wouldn't have put it past you.'

We looked down the table to Rubirosa and asked him to join us for coffee. He approached rather suspiciously. We apologized for our behaviour, swore we wouldn't interfere with his romance any more and told him that in fact we were leaving that day. We told him the whole thing had been done to tease him, as Doris had never stopped talking about him when she was with us. Not true, but it made him feel happier. However, as we were doing him a kind of favour we asked him to do one for us in return.

'Sure,' he said. 'Anything.'

'Ruby, what's the secret of your incredible performance with the ladies,' we asked, awestruck at the stories we'd heard.

'Simple,' he said. 'A lot of whisky. After a certain amount of whisky it becomes numb. It functions, I feel nothing, but the ladies do.'

Mike and I exchanged disappointed looks.

'Whisky?' we both asked – we'd expected some fantastic South American revelation, but whisky?

'Whisky,' he replied firmly.

After three or four whiskies I knew I couldn't even get it up, let alone perform.

Rubirosa and Doris were married. Gossip had it that his divorce settlement was around the two million dollar mark. So much for whisky.

We moved into the Carlton Hotel and a few days later heard that our boat had arrived in Marseilles. Private boat captains apparently are rarely a sober breed and ours turned out to be no exception. The tedium of the voyage had driven him to the bottle and he had managed to stove in the side of the boat which was now in dock for repairs. Not a very successful maiden voyage. At this point Mike had to report back for a new Anna Neagle film, so I had to oversee the repairs and the delivery of the boat to its final moorings in Cannes Harbour. I became sick of being alone and so returned to London to arrange the furnishing of my new home in a block of flats at Princes Gate overlooking Hyde Park.

The divorce had gone through successfully with no publicity, and Elspeth and I sighed with relief, as we had both dreaded the bombardment we'd have had from the press if they'd found out. She was still in her play and was busy arranging to move the furniture from Watchers and seeing to the decorations in her new home. Saying goodbye to Humphrey and all our other gardener friends was heartbreaking as only Louisa, Rushton and The Cog would be staying with me. Esther, still giving orders, had decided that she would stay with Elspeth and look after the children, but that I was to have Louisa, a splendid arrangement as this way I knew my kids would at least eat well. I don't think they knew what was happening, as they were only two and a half and four years old. It all seemed an exciting adventure to them. I took a last, sad look at the lovely flowers and shrubs, the fruit trees we'd planted and the wonderfully prolific kitchen garden, hoping the new owners would show them the same love that we had bestowed on the whole property. Divorce is a bastard in every way.

12

I had gone to Pinewood Studios to discuss a comedy they had in mind for me when I ran into a ravishing young beauty, Jean Simmons. After she had made an outstanding impression in a small part, singing in a film called *The Way to the Stars*, the Rank Organisation had pounced and so she was also under long-term contract. She was guarded and protected wherever she went as the Rank boys didn't want any outside influence to enter her young life. I used to see her at film premières, always accompanied by one of Rank's men, and give her an elaborate bow. Jean always responded to this joking gesture with a giggle and a furious blush. Here she was, definitely not a child any more and looking very delectable. I was in a low state after the divorce and she presented a challenge. Not only was she the most sought after young actress in England but also the most closely guarded. I would arrange meeting places to try and thwart the watch-dogs and Jean entered into the fun and excitement of it.

The whole thing began as a joke but very quickly developed into a romance. She was an adorable creature and, by doing everything possible to poison her mind against me, the Rank minions were only adding fuel to the fire. Her mother had been told that it was a disgrace for her young, innocent daughter to be seen with a married man, so I invited them both to dinner at my flat and, swearing them to secrecy, told them about my divorce. Her mother looked rather disappointed as I think she secretly enjoyed the idea of her famous daughter going out with an equally famous married man. I could imagine the conversation at her Cricklewood tea-parties as she dished out this scandal with the buttered scones.

Jean's reaction was quite the reverse. Turning to her mother she said calmly, 'You see, Mummy. I told you Jimmy wouldn't do anything wrong', and then gave me such a trusting look that I began to have misgivings. What was I doing explaining my marital status to this rather nervous mother? I wasn't about to ask for her daughter's hand in marriage. Jean was eighteen and I a very shop-worn thirty-four, but I had to admit to myself that I was becoming very fond of her and that it was more than just a passionate flirt.

I wondered if I should make my divorce public so as not to damage her reputation, though my original intention had been to wait until some time had gone by so that it was no longer newsworthy. However, Jean was preparing to go off to Fiji to make *The Blue Lagoon* so we would be separated for three or four months and anything could happen before she came back so I decided to wait.

About this time Johnny and Mary Mills invited me to a New Year's Eve party and I arranged to pick up Larry and Vivien, Rex Harrison and Lilli Palmer, in order to save petrol, which was still rationed. Johnny chose to offer the most peculiar mixture of drinks at this bash: rum cocktails followed by some rather sweet champagne. No one was partaking too freely but dear Vivien, thinking that Johnny would be hurt, downed large quantities of this bilious mixture with disastrous results. On the way home she started to get very sick and, as the Mills lived way out in the country, the Great West Road was dotted by Vivien's upchucking all the way home. We dropped off Rex and Lilli and eventually a very pale and shaken Vivien was helped out of the car by Larry.

'Oh, my God, where's my purse?' she moaned. 'I've lost my purse with all those lovely presents.'

Over the years Larry had given her a valuable jewel-encrusted compact, lipstick holder and cigarette case. We searched the car frantically, but no bag. Vivien must have dropped it during one of her excursions into the bushes – but which bush? She had been throwing up at frequent intervals along thirty miles of freeway. We dismissed all thoughts of searching for her missing property and Larry accompanied a now sobbing Vivien into their house. On the way back I suddenly had a vision of the handbag lying in a gutter. I saw it clearly. It was now about four in the morning and I asked Rushton if he would mind going back to take a look, and we set off, keeping our eyes glued to the other side of the road. We drove for miles and I was beginning to think my psychic flash had been wishful thinking when there was the bag, exactly as I'd pictured it. I leapt out, half expecting everything to have been stolen, but to my amazement it was all there.

We drove home triumphantly and at lunchtime next day I called Vivien to offer my sympathies. When she tearfully told me what a terrible hangover she had and how awful she felt about her loss I said I would be over soon as I had a small New Year's gift for her. I arrived with the bag wrapped in layers of tissue paper and hidden in a box covered in ribbons. Vivien took it rather half-heartedly and slowly started unwrapping it. I went into the next room where Larry was dejectedly sipping black coffee. As he was telling me how he'd warned Viv not to drink those bloody cocktails we heard a scream.

'My bag! My jewels! Jimmy! Jimmy, where did you find them? Larry, look, they're here – they're all here.' After profuse thanks and kisses I went home glowing with the success of my little miracle.

One day my agent called and told me that the master, Rank, would like me to have dinner with him in his private suite at the Dorchester Hotel. I'd never been invited to a private dinner with Rank before and I wondered what he had on his mind? I had a pretty shrewd idea, but maybe I was wrong, maybe he was going to offer me more money? John Davis was to be there also, so I knew the more money bit was out.

After a rather embarrassed and silent meal, and the departure of the waiters, Rank began.

'Now, it's about Jean Simmons,' he started in his flat Yorkshire accent. 'I like to believe we're all a big family and I regard Jean as my daughter.' (Well, you're a pretty damn mean father, I thought, knowing the ridiculous salary he was paying to Britain's top female star.)

'You're a married man with two children and what I hear is going on is wrong.'

'It's a disgrace,' added John Davis who had been eyeing me balefully all through dinner.

I looked at them in silence. They were both rich, powerful men who ran our lives, and neither was thinking of Jean's future happiness. They were only thinking that I might teach her my rebellious habits.

I decided to have a little fun with them.

'It's quite true, I do have two children, Mr Rank. But you don't have your facts quite right.'

'What d'you mean,' Rank spluttered. 'Do you deny that you're going round with Jean?'

'Not at all. I don't deny the going around, as you so quaintly put it, with Jean. I deny the other charge.'

Rank and Davis exchanged glances.

'What other charge do you deny?' snarled Davis.

I thought it was time to lower the boom on these two, so I told them I was no longer married and that I had been divorced for six months. Rank dropped his coffee cup and Davis choked into his napkin. There was a long silence. I could see them both mentally firing their entire publicity staff for not having informed them of this world-shattering event. I told them my divorce was a personal matter and any announcement to the press would be made when I was good and ready. Thanking them politely for their fatherly interest in Jean, I beat a hasty retreat. I realized at once that I'd have to make a release to the press and chose a good friend who promised that, in return for an exclusive, he wouldn't headline the story. I left for Paris, warning Elspeth not to answer the phone, and luckily it worked out as planned. Very little was said. It may sound strange today that anybody could attach any importance to our divorce, but in those days stars were big news.

In Paris I bumped into my friend Big John Mills, the restaurateur, who ran Les Ambassadeurs, the finest eating place in London. He gave a dinner party for me at which I met one of the most beautiful women I had ever seen in my life. John told me she was a famous French actress, actually more famous for her performances in bed than on the screen, who, at that moment, was at a loose end and looking around for another conquest. I have to admit I didn't put up much of a fight and was conquered very easily. John mentioned the names of a few of her former lovers, names like Baby Pignatelli, Rubirosa, Aly Khan, Errol Flynn, all notorious performers between the sheets. How was I going to be able to compete with these champions, I thought. However, we got on exceptionally well and she was the kind of woman who by just looking at you gave you the feeling you'd be a far superior lover to all those other famous names. Quite wrong in my case, but I was determined to put up a good show as this forceful lady, who liked her close friends to call her Minouche, had already arranged to spend an evening with me when she arrived in London a few days later. After all, Jean had been away for nearly two months and I was only human.

Naturally we dined at Les Ambassadeurs with John fussing over us and giving me a bad time with remarks to my lovely companion about not getting too excited as Englishmen were a cold-blooded lot and wouldn't she rather end the evening with a hot-blooded Pole, he, of course, being Polish. But I'd come prepared and, slipping out to the men's room, quickly swallowed three benzedrine, having heard from a fighter pilot friend that these kept you awake and up to the mark. Not having taken any form of drug before they had a most startling effect. Later, in my flat, even Minouche was staggered as I made my assault. Cold-blooded Englishman indeed. I'd bloody well show her. I pounded away all night, actually feeling nothing myself, apart from a buzzing in my ears and the sensation that my eyes were about to pop right out of my head. Minouche finally pleaded with me to stop as I'd worn her out and, murmuring that she must come to London more often, fell asleep. I immediately started cooking eggs and bacon as I was ravenous and, returning to the bedroom with a loaded tray, woke her up.

'Christ,' she complained. 'Don't you Englishmen ever sleep?'

'Not with a beautiful woman around,' I leered with popping eyes.

'Why are you looking at me like that?' she asked with her mouth full of eggs and bacon. 'Don't tell me you want more?'

'If you feel like it, yes,' I answered gallantly.

'God, no! Enough is enough,' she gasped.

During the evening I had admired a heavy gold identity bracelet she had been wearing and while we kissed goodbye she slipped it off her wrist and handed it to me, telling me to keep it in memory of a wonderful experience. I stammered my thanks at this very generous gift but was quickly corrected by the bleary-eyed but still attractive Minouche.

'Well, *chéri*, it's almost a gift because of the ridiculously low price I'm asking. Only four hundred pounds.'

Four hundred pounds. The bloody thing was only worth a hundred but how could you haggle over the price of a bracelet with a woman you'd been ravaging all night? I dutifully paid up and, telling me to keep myself free as she'd soon be back, she left. I thankfully closed the door behind her as the benzedrine was beginning to wear off and fell into bed. I slept for three days. Did she really imagine that was my normal performance?

About this time I received an invitation to dine with Alexander Korda at his lovely house in 'Millionaires' Row', as Kensington Palace Gardens is always called, for obvious reasons. I was expecting to see other guests, but to my surprise we were alone. I had admired this man for many years as he had been responsible for putting the British film industry on the map. He was a Hungarian but an entirely different character from my friend Gabby Pascal. He was charming and erudite, something rare in the film industry, loved beautiful women – he had been married to the lovely Merle Oberon – owned a collection of Impressionists, enjoyed good company and good food, so we had a great deal in common and devoured a fabulous meal, surrounded by some of his lovely paintings, one of which, a huge boating scene by Manet, I greatly coveted. But as yet I had no inkling of why I had been invited.

With the brandy, Alex got down to business. He told me that he would be interested in a deal after my Rank contract expired, knowing it had only one more year to run, and did I have any ideas or subjects I'd like to make? I thought if only I'd met this man when I came out of the army, perhaps I mightn't have had such a jaundiced view of the film business.

I told him how flattered I was, but that I had decided to give up film acting once I was free and change to the other side of the camera. I was already negotiating with Jon Godden's agents to buy her book, *The House by the Sea*, and I started telling him about my plans for the production, which I thought was a good subject to start with as it only had two characters and one set. He seemed amused that such a successful movie actor should want to give it all up for the responsibilities and problems of a producer. I tried to explain that I was getting very little satisfaction from being a star and, although I was quite aware of the problems, any mistakes that I was sure to make would at least be my own and not those of the producers I had been forced to work for.

I told him I was tired of trying to keep up my image as a swashbuckling lover, of the constant press interviews and personal appearances. Maybe as a producer-director I could have a little anonymity; in those days very little attention was paid to that side of the business.

As I thanked Alex for the wonderful evening he asked me to be sure to contact him when I started on my first production as he would like to be associated with it, but I was never to see that charming man again.

A month later Jean came back from Fiji and I was thrilled to see her. I had missed her more than I cared to admit and it was lovely to see her curled up on the couch after a party when the elderly were holding forth – I being one of the elderly. I still thought of her as a child, although physically she was anything but. I was determined to think of a subject we could act in together which would show her first as a child and then later as a young woman, because at that time nobody would accept her playing a love scene with an adult man. I was thinking of stealing an idea from an old silent movie, *Daddy Long-legs*.

However we still couldn't go out together openly as I didn't want the press to get hold of our affair and make it sordid with their snide remarks. She was their darling and I could imagine their reaction to her first love being old Swashbuckling Granger. She had got her own apartment by now and Rushton was kept busy alternately fetching her to my place and waiting round the corner for me to leave hers. In those days two people who loved each other didn't just shack up together, and we preferred it that way. We would shack up if and when we got married, which to be absolutely truthful I was still doubtful about.

I started work on my idea and, when I had the story outline completed, contacted a scriptwriter, Noel Langley, to collaborate with me on it. I told him I was sure if it turned out all right Rank would buy it and that he could have all of whatever they paid. But I asked him to keep his price low as I didn't want Rank to think I was holding him up. The main thing was to get a good vehicle for Jean and myself. I called the film *Adam and Evelyne*, and it turned out exceptionally well. It was a charming light comedy in which Jean started off as a teenager who goes away to finishing school in Switzerland and returns a sophisticated young woman. She played the teenage bit beautifully, which was to be expected, but her playing of the sexy, sophisticated young lady did exactly what I wanted for her and delighted the audiences.

It was quite extraordinary playing love scenes with someone you loved and who was in love with you. It was easy with someone you didn't give a damn about but with Jean I became self-conscious. She enjoyed it thoroughly and when, in the film, I was telling her how much I loved her but that I was afraid I was too old for her, she'd mutter under her breath, 'You're telling me, you dirty old man.' Later, when she had to tell me she loved me, she'd whisper 'and I mean it, too'. This threw me completely and I'd 'dry up' and the director would ask me to play the scene more sincerely, as I wasn't giving the impression I loved her at all. This, after the way we'd spent the previous night!

I've always been shy of telling a girl I really love that I love her. I become tongue-tied, but very early in my relationships with women I realized that they need to be told regularly how much you love them. I try to show I love them but find it almost impossible to say so. The words 'I love you' are so trite, so over used, that they just stick in my throat. But if you've told a woman you love her, you can screw her best friend and she may forgive you, but if you haven't said those three little words, look out!

Jean was very keen to try her hand in the theatre and Rank rather grudgingly gave her time off to do a play. But what play? It couldn't be a big part, as Jean, having had no stage experience, couldn't sustain it, and I knew she'd never experienced the terror of an opening night, so we looked for a suitable subject. Stephen Mitchell, a successful theatrical producer, who had presented most of Terence Rattigan's plays, approached us and promised to come up with something interesting.

In the meantime, Jean and I were at last to have a holiday together on the boat. Shortly before, Mike Wilding had completed a film for Hitchcock and had used the boat for a holiday with his leading lady, Marlene Dietrich. They had become very close and I had hopes that he might marry her, as she was such a super lady and adored him. She was the kind of wife Mike needed because in many ways he was helpless. His health had never been good and he needed someone to mother him and run his home. Marlene was not only a ravishing lady but was 'earth mother' to anyone she loved. Jean and I adored her. She was such a no nonsense lady, with a wonderful sense of humour and she treated Mike like a wayward child. She'd look at us with those enormous eyes and say with that throaty voice, 'You see, darlings, he doesn't eat enough. He doesn't get enough sleep. He needs me. Now, Jimmy, he listens to you. Tell him he needs me. He's rather stupid, you see. He doesn't know what's good for him.' All this in front of Mike as if he wasn't there.

One evening, after we'd all been to a Royal Command performance, we returned home for a nightcap and Marlene decided that Mike must have something to eat. Into the kitchen she went and, putting an apron round her priceless Balenciaga gown, proceeded to whip up Boeuf Stroganoff. Slightly indigestible at one o'clock in the morning, but Mike dutifully ate it with no apparent ill effects. What a shame they never married.

Anyway, Mike explained that he'd left the boat at Portofino under the care of our now slightly more sober skipper, so I went out ahead to pick her up and bring her back to Cannes, where Jean would join me. She had to stay in London for some personal appearances arranged by her masters, which would take her two or three weeks, so it worked out fine. I arrived in Cannes to make sure the ship's chandlers I was dealing with had prepared the moorings for my boat, and who should be staying at the Carlton Hotel but Tyrone Power with his fiancée, Linda Christian. I had met this extraordinarily good-looking man the year before on a flying trip he had been making to Europe and was hailed as an old friend. He introduced me to Linda, whom I'd met previously in London with Mike Wilding, but she didn't seem to remember. If she wanted to give the impression we'd never met before that was perfectly all right with me. I asked them if they'd like to accompany me to Portofino and spend a few days on the boat, and they accepted.

Portofino in the late forties was a dream place, as it had not yet been discovered by the tourists. All the houses surrounding the well-hidden little harbour were painted different colours with wooden shutters and masses of bougainvillea, plumbago and geraniums rioting over the walls like a travel agent's dream in glorious Technicolor: we sat at a table outside one of the quayside trattorias sipping Campari and were all entranced. My skipper had docked the boat right opposite one of these restaurants and, after our meal, we only had to walk two or three yards and we were aboard. That first night, lying in my cabin, I couldn't help envying Ty in the arms of the lovely Linda. Here I was in one of the most romantic places in the world, on a boat that Mike and I had spent a fortune to maintain, with my newfound friends noisily enjoying each other, and I was alone. This was not how I had planned it, I thought, as I eventually fell asleep.

We'd heard there was an extraordinary eating place a few kilometres along the coast tucked away in a cove, so next morning, after a leisurely breakfast and already sipping our midday cocktails, I casually gave orders to the skipper to get under way and, casting off the stern sheets, the electric winch started hauling up the anchor. As the boat gradually moved to the centre of the harbour, a strange thing happened. Instead of the anchor coming up, the bows of the boat started to go down. Our anchor had caught in something. The watching fishermen yelled instructions in Italian, none of which we understood. What we could understand was that we were trapped. Ty Power nonchalantly continued to sip his drink, waving to all the laughing fans crowding the shore enjoying the fun until three or four fishing boats came to our rescue and attaching lines to the cables and chains we'd hooked onto, eventually freed us. Naturally they all claimed salvage fees, which cost me several hundred thousand lira. I gave the skipper a dirty look and joined my guests as if this event was quite normal in yachting circles.

One thing this slight balls-up had taught me was that to be an international star you had to go to Hollywood. All the fans had been screaming out Ty's name but no one had noticed me and I had starred in about twenty British films.

We discovered the cove and this time I gave orders to drop the anchor. The clatter of the anchor chain seemed to go on for a long time and I jumped up in alarm only to see the end of the chain disappearing into the sea with a final plop. As the bloody skipper had forgotten to secure the end we had now not only lost I don't know how many fathoms of expensive chain but the anchor as well. There was quite a wind and we were gradually being blown on to the rocks. Shouting and waving to the watching fishermen we indicated our plight and a new team delightedly rowed out and towed us to a safe mooring. Of course they claimed salvage. Apparently the water there was so deep that there was a sunken Italian destroyer they couldn't salvage, so now my anchor was down there with her. That was the most expensive lunch I've ever given.

I found Big John Mills in Cannes and he accompanied me on the boat to pick up Jean from Nice airport. In those days the customs and immigration weren't so strict and Jean was able to go straight from the plane to the beach where our launch was waiting to take her out to the gaily decorated boat; with lights festooned all over her it made a very romantic sight. Generous John had insisted on bringing champagne and caviar, and our return to Cannes was hilarious, Jean getting hiccups from the champagne and me getting seasick from too much caviar.

But it was a marvellous trip and it was lovely having her with me again. I taught her to water-ski and we used to take the boat between the islands off Cannes and ski in that crystal clear bright blue water. After working up an appetite we'd go ashore on Ile Ste Marguerite where there was a restaurant famous for its langoustine: small crayfish cooked with onions, tomatoes and spices, served with a pilaff. Delicious. In a very short time we both put on about ten pounds each, but it was worth it.

You never realize you have so many friends until you own a boat. They would swarm aboard, always at mealtimes, wherever we were. How they reached us, I've no idea – I think they must have swum out. The meal over, having taken their siestas and their turn at the water-skiing they would somehow disappear, until the next meal.

One of our visitors was a wealthy Belgian girl who told me one day that she was planning to drive her Cadillac to San Sebastian to see a bullfight. I had always been a great aficionado, having read every book I could find on the subject since Hemingway's *Death in the Afternoon*, but I had never seen a 'corrida'. The chance was too good to miss and the lady in question agreed to take us if we paid our way – David was coming as chaperone because I didn't want to get involved with her. But how to explain to Jean? I knew that she'd loathe bullfighting and would be more interested in going to the Bal des Petits Lis Blancs which was to take place in the next few days. This I wanted to avoid like the plague as, although in a good cause, it was the kind of social function where all the ladies on the coast competed as to who would sparkle the most. Jean could compete because, in spite of not having much jewellery, she could outsparkle anyone.

I asked Big John if he would look after her while I went to Spain and he told me I was an idiot to go off and leave her with all those wolves on the prowl, but with my customary arrogance I pooh-poohed the idea that Jean could look at anyone else. Naturally she was upset when I told her of my plans, but calmed down when I explained it would only be for four or five days and I really didn't think she would like all the violence. I also told her it might be amusing to go to this gala without me and with a free hand to see what she could catch. She might come up with something much more exciting than old Granger. I didn't mean a word of this, of course, but should have taken more notice of a secretive smile that came to her lips.

It was a long drive to San Sebastian, not helped when all the electrical equipment on the Cadillac fused, we ran into a violent storm and couldn't get the top up. We arrived soaked to the skin, foul-tempered and I didn't need David's services as a chaperone as by this time the Belgian lady and I cordially hated each other.

The corrida was a very special one as it featured Luis Miguel Dominguin, Spain's Numero Uno and a newcomer called Aparicio. Luckily I ran into someone who knew me and the word went round that a visiting film star was present, so I received the VIP treatment. Being a star does have certain advantages. I was ushered into the presence of the handsome Luis Miguel and introduced to his sister and, as I thought, his girl friend, an exquisite Spanish lady named Vittoria. They were all very friendly and generous and arranged that I should sit with these two beauties. David, thank God, had taken the Belgian in hand and was sitting somewhere else.

This was my first experience of the madness that takes over a Spanish town during its principal Feria: thousands of people thronging through the streets on their way to the bullring: horse-drawn carriages with exotic, sultry señoritas in gaily coloured dresses and mantillas: their caballeros mounted in the Andaluz style on prancing horses, wearing attractive Cordovan hats; all converging on the different entrances to the ring, jostling and waving to each other, and all done in the best of spirits, carrying their goatskin botas and spurting streams of wine into their mouths. When I tried it, I nearly choked. At the hotel I had been honoured by being allowed to watch Luis Miguel dress in his 'suit of lights' and saw how he changed from a laughing, joking playboy into a serious, rather pale stranger. He left us suddenly and went into a little room adjoining to pray to Our Lady of the Macarena, the patron of all matadors, and it hit me suddenly that this wasn't just a spectacle, an entertainment for all those thousands of aficionados, it was an exhibition of bravery and skill between a man and a killer bull in which, if he put a foot wrong, the man would be rewarded by a bad goring or even death, but once back among the shouting, screaming mass of fans all this was forgotten as we waited for the entrance of the matadors.

The beautiful Vittoria excitedly waved to all her friends and whispered to me what man was having an affair with what wife and which girl was having an affair with which husband. Seeing my rather shocked expression she explained that in Spain, being very Catholic with no divorce allowed, this was the only practical solution. I watched this adorable young creature seriously explaining to me the possible attractions her life would hold for her should she get married. I began to feel jealous at the very thought of her preferring anyone else to me should I be that husband and then quickly looked away from those grey-green eyes. What the hell was I thinking of? She was Luis Miguel's girl and anyway I had Jean waiting for me in Cannes. But I was very aware of her all through the afternoon.

The matadors made their stately entrance and the trumpets sounded for the release of the first bull of the afternoon. In it rushed, a huge black creature with wide sweeping needle-tipped horns. It proceeded to charge the barrera behind which the matador was watching and I shuddered as I saw those horns tearing out great chunks of wood. Then Aparicio stepped out with the cape to face the monster. He did five or six fantastic Veronicas, passing the bull so closely that at one time he was almost knocked off his feet. Then followed the horrible but necessary business of the picadors, as they proceeded to stick lances into the bull's shoulder. Next the placing of the banderillas, done by one of Aparicio's cuadrilla, and finally the faena with the muleta. The bull was huge and brave and charged absolutely straight and I've never seen anything like it, this slim young man controlling that gigantic animal. He did it superbly, killing cleanly and to the cheers of thousands of fans and the waving of thousands of handkerchiefs the president awarded him both ears and the tail, a practically unheard of accolade.

Then came Luis Miguel. His sister spoke no English so Vittoria explained everything to me. Apparently he had signed very remunerative contracts with South America and wasn't going to take any risk of getting a cornada (wound) which would prevent him from fulfilling those obligations. He refused to work close to his bull in spite of the jeers and catcalls of the crowd. I became very embarrassed as he had dedicated this bull to me and we had his cape spread out in front of us. This puts the recipient of such an honour in a very invidious position because if the matador does well you share the applause and get slapped on the back but, if he does badly, as was the case that afternoon, you share the jeers and catcalls, as if you were partly to blame for spoiling their sport.

After a rather unexciting series of passes Luis Miguel fixed the bull and, turning his back on it, started towards the barrera in preparation for his next series of passes. But the bull wasn't fixed and charged, knocking our unsuspecting friend on his face. Although the horns hadn't penetrated, the bull had made a fool of him and, forgetting those lucrative contracts, he began the most breath-taking series of passes anyone had ever seen. He ended up kneeling between the bull's horns with his back to it and signalled with both arms his contempt of the crowd that had been jeering him a moment before. My two companions, unable to watch, had hidden their faces in their hands, they were so sure he'd be killed. But he wasn't, he was triumphant and, having also been awarded both ears and the tail, was carried round the ring on the shoulders of the aficionados. After my first introduction to bullfighting I realized that when the bulls were great and the matadors brave and skilled it could be the most thrilling experience, especially if you were lucky enough to have beautiful women on either side of you, but if, as was often the case, the bulls were treacherous and the matadors less brave and skilled, it could be a sickening spectacle.

That evening, exhausted by the emotion of this great corrida, not knowing I was never to see its equal again, I needed a siesta before the night's festivities, as I didn't have to join my friends until 11.30. Vittoria's mother was there too and turned out to be a very young looking, attractive lady who seemed to be paying more than the normal attention to her daughter's boy friend, Luis Miguel. They left together early, as he had to get his sleep in preparation for the next day's corrida. This didn't seem to surprise Vittoria and we all went on to a night club. Normally I avoid nightclubs like the plague as I can't stand the noise and crush, but this time it was fun as I had Vittoria to myself and, strangely enough, she didn't seem to miss Luis Miguel.

This programme was repeated over the next three days, and on the final evening Luis took me aside and asked me in halting English why I didn't find Vittoria attractive as she was rather hurt at my seeming lack of interest. In amazement I told him I wasn't in the habit of making passes at somebody else's girl friend, in this case his. He roared with laughter and said he thought I understood it wasn't

Vittoria he was interested in but her mother. I was flabbergasted and, that evening, having asked her out alone, I told her of my misunderstanding. Although the same age as Jean, Vittoria seemed so much more adult. I told her of my doubts about my future with Jean, how we were both in the same competitive profession, the inevitable separations that would pull us apart and my fears that it wouldn't work. I also asked if she could possibly understand how a man could love one girl and yet be terribly attracted to another. She replied with a smile that, although she hadn't had much experience, she thought she could. I remember trying to lighten the conversation by saying that anyway I was a divorced man and she was a Catholic. She shyly told me that she wasn't a professing Catholic and didn't necessarily have to be married in Spain. This kind of conversation after only knowing each other three days! Oh Christ, I thought to myself, here we go again! The next morning as we prepared to leave, I shoved some pesetas into Vittoria's hand and told her to hang on to them for me as a guarantee of my return.

I was very silent all the way back to Cannes, my thoughts were confused and I felt a sense of disloyalty. Big John was waiting for me at the hotel with an 'I warned you didn't I?' expression.

'Well, you've blown it, Jimmy. You were away just too long.'

'Why, what's happened?' I asked.

'Well, as you can imagine she's had everyone chasing her and I think there's a pretty special thing going with Orson Welles.'

'Orson Welles,' I said in outrage and stormed off to Jean's room.

A moment ago I had been searching for a way of telling Jean about Vittoria and trying to explain my seeming infidelity, now I was about to attack her over her interest in someone else. We had a tearful reunion and continued our relationship where it had left off. I didn't go back to Spain.

This little story has a very moving sequel. Two years later, when Jean and I were married and living in Hollywood, Luis Miguel came over with Ava Gardner to spend an evening. Taking me aside he told me that Vittoria had waited for two years and it was only the news of my marriage that made her realize I wasn't coming back. I felt a complete heel. Ten years later, when Jean and I were divorced, I was in Madrid having just finished a film in the south of Spain. The telephone rang and Vittoria's mother was telling me how excited she was to hear I was in Madrid and that we must get together. I told her it was impossible as unfortunately I was leaving that day.

'But what shall I do with the money, Jimmy?' she asked.

'What money?'

'The money you gave Vittoria to keep for you.'

It all came flooding back.

'How's Vittoria?'

'Oh, she's very happy, married and living in Chile. She has four lovely children,' said the proud grandmother. 'She'll be here in a week.'

I told her how sorry I was to have missed her and asked her to spend the money on flowers for Vittoria.

13

While searching for a play I heard of one done some years previously in Paris, called *Le Corsaire* by the French playwright, Marcel Achard, in which Louis Jouvet had starred. On my way to the boat I had called on Achard, and he had charmingly given me the English rights to the play. It needed adapting as well as translating, but seemed the perfect subject: it concerned two film stars making a picture about a pirate, and was wonderfully romantic. Although the girl's part was longer than I should have liked for Jean's first stage venture, I was sure she could handle it. In the flashback she had to play a young girl captured by the pirate, and in the modern sequence a young film star acting out the part. I took Jean to meet Marcel and he was completely captivated and very excited by the whole idea. I stayed on in Paris to complete the contractual details and Jean returned to London.

One day Marcel asked if I'd like to go to Brussels with him to see the fight between Marcel Cerdan and the Belgian Cyrelle Delannoit for the European middle-weight championship; the winner would go to Detroit to fight for the world title. As a great boxing fan I accepted enthusiastically. Jean had been horrified by the brutality when I took her to see my friend Freddie Mills fight Gus Lesnovitch for the light-heavyweight title, which he won, so I knew she wouldn't mind missing it. Marcel explained that we would be accompanied by Edith Piaf who was currently having a wild romance with Cerdan and because of this couldn't be at the ringside. If Cerdan lost, the fans would tear her apart, as she'd be blamed for 'draining' him, something this tiny man-eater was notorious for. Piaf would watch the fight on television with friends and we'd all join up later. The fight was one of the bloodiest I'd ever seen, but Cerdan, although receiving terrible punishment, won. Afterwards we all met for dinner with Edith's friends, and Cerdan eventually arrived with clips holding together the terrible cuts over his eyes and stitches in the skin below them; a terrifying sight. Cerdan was sitting next to me as Edith, on his other side, lovingly fed him morsels of food, caressing and crooning to him as she did so. Suddenly he picked up my hand and studied it for a moment.

'My friend, what I would give to have hands like yours.'

He put one hand alongside mine and showed me how his knuckles had been pushed back and smashed with the force of his punching over the years. Now he was forced to hit with the sides of his hands as he couldn't stand the pain of a straight punch. He was a sweet man and obviously adored Edith as much as she adored him. He went to America a short time later and became world middle-weight champion, beating Jake Lamotta but was to die tragically in a plane crash on the way home. Piaf never recovered from his death.

On my return to London Peter Bull, who spoke good French, undertook to translate the first two acts of Achard's play and I started to adapt the last act which I thought could be improved. I had the author's blessing on my ideas but I was worried about time. Jean only had nine months before her next commitment and Peter and I were working like mad trying to get the play in shape. At that moment a young man called Peter Glenville entered our lives.

Peter had already worked with our producer, Stephen Mitchell, and had a subject which seemed to solve all our problems, Tolstoy's *The Power of Darkness*; it had never been performed in Europe and would be a challenge. Everyone was expecting Jean and me to do some commercial play to cash in on our names, and our choice of a worthwhile controversial subject might confound the critics. Peter was a very persuasive young man and, although I had my doubts after reading this lugubrious, bloodthirsty drama, he triumphantly pointed out that Jean's part answered all our doubts about her stage acting abilities: she would have an important leading role but the character was a mentally retarded peasant girl. I thought this was carrying our doubts too far, but Jean was enthusiastic as it would mean that should she have trouble with the lines or projecting she would have the excuse that this was part of her character-ization and not her inexperience as a stage actress.

Peter arrived one evening with Tolstoy's grand-daughter who fascinated us with her story of how the play had come to be written. Apparently it was a true story and the character I was to portray had died in Siberia while serving a life sentence for murder. She didn't know what had happened to the girl. Peter also brought along with him a Russian set designer who had made brilliant sketches for the production; with all this excitement we were hooked. Stephen Mitchell was a little scared of the cost, the production having four sets and a huge cast, so I offered to co-produce with him and guaranteed half the money. As we lay in each other's arms that night I asked Jean if she was sure she wanted to do the play – we still had time to pull out. She told me she was really relieved not having to play a technically difficult speaking part, the thought of it had terrified her and this seemed to be the solution. Dear little Jean, she had so much faith in her Jimmy, who could do no wrong in her eyes, but her Jimmy was about to make the biggest mistake of his life.

We got together a wonderful supporting cast: Frederick Valk, Sonia Dresdel, Mary Clare, Herbert Lomas and other fine actors playing the lesser roles. It was a thrill to be back in the theatre after so many years and we opened triumphantly to a standing-room only audience in the Opera House, Manchester. We managed to fill this vast theatre for two weeks and, although the notices were very mixed, to say the least, all the actors received good write-ups, including our little peasant. We were already planning which London theatre would be the best and had decided that only one would be right, the Lyric, Shaftesbury Avenue. But there were problems: being one of the most popular theatres in the West End it was, of course, occupied. Stephen assured us that by the time our tour was completed he would come up with something.

During the tour, the London press was hounding us, interviewing Jean on her feelings about stage acting, asking me why I had cast her in such a thankless role, intimating that I was just using her for my own aggrandizement. I couldn't bring myself to explain that the whole idea had really been for Jean, to give her experience in the theatre without the risk of her making a fool of herself and had I only been thinking of myself I could have appeared in any number of different vehicles.

I began having grave doubts about the venture. One day in my hotel room in Glasgow, while Peter was lying on one bed and I on the other, with Jean curled up on the couch, I suddenly said:

'Peter, you know we shouldn't bring the play into the West End. They're all waiting for us. It'll be a disaster.' There was a pause after this bombshell.

'You're right, Jimmy,' Peter answered. 'You're absolutely right. We can pack the theatres on tour but London's a different proposition.'

We were just discussing the problems of arranging another six weeks tour so that at least we would all finish up making some money, when the phone rang. Peter answered, and after a moment turned to us with a triumphant yell, 'It's Stephen. He's got the Lyric.'

We all gathered round the phone shouting congratulations to Stephen, completely forgetting what we'd been saying a moment before. Everything is timing. If Stephen hadn't called at that precise moment, the play wouldn't have come into London and I wouldn't have had to face a problem which changed my whole life.

One of our last dates before coming to London was Liverpool, during Grand National week. Every evening on tour I used to make a curtain speech and bring forward Jean and the others. During this particular week I advised the audience to put their money on a 50-1 outsider called Russian Hero. I told them they'd just seen a Russian play in which I'd played the hero, so it was obviously a cinch. We left Liverpool to shouts of thanks from the crowd seeing us off at the station. Russian Hero had won the Grand National and we were the only ones who hadn't backed it.

Opening night at the Lyric was a nightmare. All our fears were justified. As the curtain went up, a wave of hostility came over the footlights, it was uncanny, we could feel it. The theatre was packed with professional first nighters come to see two film actors fail, with the critics ready to tear us apart and the gossip columnists watering at the mouth in anticipation of our humiliation. None of them was disappointed. The play was a disaster.

All those weeks on tour, playing to enthusiastic audiences, had lulled us into the belief that maybe our efforts to present something worthwhile might be appreciated, that two popular stars hadn't been content to appear in some commercial venture but had chosen instead a very difficult, challenging subject. Forget it. We'd failed. Next morning the cast was called together and Stephen told us that in his opinion the play should come off at the end of the week. I could see the despairing looks of all the small-part actors and the walk-ons who'd worked so hard during all those uncomfortable weeks on tour. It wasn't easy to get a job in the theatre in those days and they had made no other plans, thinking our play would have a long run. I felt I personally had failed them. I asked Stephen if he would wait a moment and went into a corner with Jean.

'Darling, would you be prepared to take minimum salary and see if we can't make a go of it? I hate to see all our friends out of work.'

Of course, being the darling she is, she agreed. I then asked the other leading actors the same question, and they all agreed. I told Stephen that I would take over the production as I didn't see why the hell he should suffer, but he sweetly said that he was prepared to put back any money he might have made on tour to see if we couldn't survive. So we sent out for drinks and all toasted our hopes of survival.

Peter Glenville, our director, who was initially responsible for the idea, on reading the notices, left town, and we didn't see him again during the run. The next few months were pretty hard going: we played to full houses but that was owing to the genius of the front of house manager in 'papering' the theatre. Hospital staff were offered free tickets, the services, students, universities, women's clubs, men's clubs, all accepted his offer and flocked to the theatre. This was a pretty depressing play and, in order to keep up the morale of the company, I used to make funny speeches at curtain time. I would lead forward a young actress all of seventeen playing a seventeen-year-old in the play and introduce her to the audience as the most brilliant character actress, telling them that in reality she was fifty. They would laugh and applaud and she would giggle and bow. I would ask all those who had paid for their seats to put up their hands, and on the appearance of a scattered few, we on the stage would applaud their courage. We knew we were fighting a losing battle but at least I thought we were entitled to a little fun.

There was one moment of hysteria every night which was not of my planning. The second act curtain was a very dramatic moment with me, slightly out of my head, imploring my mother to listen, as I thought I could hear the cries of my murdered baby. Of course there should have been complete silence in the theatre while this tragic character hallucinated, but the back walls of the Lyric stage were very thin, and outside in the street the buskers were entertaining the queues waiting to go into the adjoining Windmill Theatre, famous for its nude shows. A man with a piercing trumpet would choose this dramatic moment to burst into 'I dreamt I dwelt in Marble halls' so there was hysterical laughter on both sides of the curtain. It didn't really help the mood of the play but at least it kept our spirits up. Jean was a tower of strength throughout this ordeal and nothing seemed to faze her. She was with her man and that was all that mattered. Bless her.

One evening the front of-house manager came round to tell me that Irene Selznick was in front. She was the ex-wife of David O. Selznick and a daughter of Louis B. Mayer of MGM. A powerful lady. I'm afraid not even that news could inject much enthusiasm into the cast as we were all pretty depressed by this time. After the show Mrs Selznick didn't come round, so I thought, screw it, now they'll know how awful I am as an actor and co-producer in America as well as in England, but no, apparently not, because two days later an invitation came to meet her for a drink at Claridges after the show. I already had a soft spot for this charming lady as I'd heard her idea of a perfect weekend was to run about six films on her private projector with food and drink being brought in while you were watching. Lovely. Anyway, she amazed me by saying she had been very impressed by my performance and would like me to star opposite Vivien Leigh in the London production of *A Streetcar Named Desire*.

I looked at her in amazement and said: 'Mrs Selznick. I have just fallen on my arse playing a Russian peasant. Now you're asking me to play a Polish-Brooklyn peasant. And, incidentally, isn't the fellow in New York a bit of a sensation, young chap called Marlon Brando? He'd be pretty tough to follow, don't you think?'

She pooh-poohed this and said she thought I'd be great and wouldn't I consider it? Larry Olivier was going to produce and both he and Vivien were enthusiastic about the idea. I thanked her and said how flattered I was and I would certainly talk to Larry. Later Larry and I met and I told him I didn't think I could handle the Brooklyn accent and that wouldn't help his production at all. Larry put his hand on my shoulder.

'Jimmy boy,' he said, rather pontifically, 'just put yourself in my hands, and you'll have nothing to worry about.'

So we both started to giggle because it was pretty pompous and Larry didn't really mean it that way.

'Sorry, Larry,' I told him. 'I've had enough of the theatre for the moment. I'm going home to lick my wounds and try and raise some cash to pay my debts. That show has cleared me out.'

And I wasn't kidding. When we finally closed I was flat broke and owed the Inland Revenue about £15,000, a lot of money in those days. My accountant kept calling me to say he couldn't keep the tax authorities at bay very much longer and something had to be done. I knew Mike wouldn't mind selling the boat, there was the Rolls Bentley plus some furniture and paintings, but I also knew that if you try to sell things quickly you get about a quarter the price. What was to happen to my hopes of producing and possibly directing *House by the Sea*? Did I really have to go back to films just to pay the income tax – and hell, how dare any country demand up to ninety-eight per cent tax? What did it leave you? Nothing, and that's exactly what I had. After being one of the top earning film stars in Britain for six years I had ended up with a big zero and a pile of debts. Just then the phone rang and it was my ex-agent, Jack Dunfee.

'If I get you a film in America for MGM would you sign with me again?'

Naturally I said yes, and that was how I came to play in *King Solomon's Mines*. A call came from MGM in Hollywood and I talked to Benny Thau, the big wheel in star handling over there. He gave me the usual bullshit about how great the film was going to be, etc., etc., and said all the details would be handled by MGM in London. Of course my agent made the usual cock-up in the contract and I found I was being paid in pounds and not dollars. The day I set foot in Hollywood the pound was devalued from $4.10 to $2.80 and I lost a third of my salary.

When MGM wants something, they want it quick. I was rushed off to get immigration papers: explanation, it would make it easier for work permits, etc., with a blue card, whatever the hell that was. If I didn't want to stay in America I could just de-immigrate. Jean had finished her part in *Trio* and was preparing for a film with Dirk Bogarde, and I was apprehensive again about our relationship. Here I was off to Hollywood, followed by four or five months location all over East Africa and then back to Hollywood to complete the film. Was this going to be our life together – forever being pulled apart? Oh well, I thought, let's make hay while the sun shines.

So Jean and I made hay and it was great. But the day came when I had to leave my lovely flat and my lovely Jean and board my first Stratocruiser for New York. Quite a trip in those days, twelve or fourteen hours, I think; big party the night before; big send off and I'm poured on to the plane. If you'd booked a sleeping berth, the top (where now you put overcoats) was pulled down and converted into a bed. So I made friends with the steward and almost before the plane had levelled off I was into the bunk and it seemed no time before I was woken with breakfast. Wonderful trip. Any trip that I remember nothing about to me is a wonderful trip. I don't travel well. My ears pop, my sinuses swell, and I get airsick at the slightest bump.

This was my first sight of the US of A and that frightening city, New York. My God, it seemed immense. I'd heard about the skyscrapers, of course, and seen them in the movies, but in real life they seemed bigger and the city was certainly noisier. Apparently MGM had fixed things – in those days it was possible – so I was passed quickly through

Immigration and Customs, and the nice MGM representative, who looked and dressed like a very wealthy senator, had me ushered into an enormous Cadillac and sweeping along the freeways towards the MGM suite at the Waldorf-Astoria. They got a special rate, he explained, after making the film *Weekend at the Waldorf*. Fascinating, I thought, I wonder if I could get a free suite at the Dorchester for the rest of my life if I put together a film called *Weekend at the Dorchester*? Hell, no! They'd probably refuse to lend their name because it would be bad publicity. Difference between London and New York.

The Waldorf was very imposing, but my first impressions aren't too clear as I was still dopey from the travel pills I had taken. A swarm of bellhops dressed like drum majorettes took my bags, one each, and having deposited them in an enormous suite, looked at me expectantly. Oh God, I thought, I haven't a cent. At that time you were only allowed to take ten pounds out of Britain and that doesn't go far in New York. However, I was saved by the senator who arrived and handed out dollars all round. He then asked what I would like to do, as I had all day free; my plane to Hollywood was not taking off until the following afternoon. I looked at him rather nervously and explained my financial situation. He gave me a big grin and handed over a couple of hundred dollars, saying, 'That should take care of you until you reach the coast and then you'll be looked after by the Studio.'

'Thank God,' I thought. 'Somebody's going to look after me.'

I was already feeling nervous, shy and homesick. I remembered my first days at school, not knowing anybody, not knowing my way around, new faces, new challenges. I wasn't feeling at all like the big film star about to take Hollywood by storm. I just felt lonely.

'Would you like to have lunch at "21",' my new friend asked me.

'Sure,' I said. 'Lovely.'

'Okay. I'll call for you at one o'clock. Get some rest and freshen up,' and he left.

I went to the window and looked out. Immediately I got vertigo. Christ, what floor was I on? I'd never been so high in my life, but even so the noise was deafening – traffic, police whistles, sirens, aeroplanes, riveters on building sites, New York noise. Coming from sleepy old London it was overpowering.

The '21' is impressive, as everyone knows, but what impressed me most was my introduction to the New York cut steak, charred and medium rare. Don't forget I had come from England where we were still only allowed a few ounces of meat a week and here on my plate was two months' ration in one meal. I ate every bit of it. Wonderful. However, I couldn't tackle the salad. Very strange. Lettuce with a peach filled with cottage cheese, covered with Roquefort dressing. What a mixture! But the baked potato with chives and sour cream went down a treat. While I was stuffing, I looked around and saw at a table only three yards away a very familiar face I'd seen in so many Warner Brothers films: Joan Blondell, talking, or rather listening to a tiny, dynamic man. I asked my new friend who he was and he told me it was Mike Todd, the famous producer. I'd never heard of him. Little did I know then that he'd be responsible for breaking up Mike Wilding's marriage to Liz Taylor, that he'd eventually marry her and cause poor Mike so much misery.

I still couldn't work out why I was feeling strange and uneasy, and then I suddenly realized. I wasn't being looked at. For the first time in almost six years nobody was nudging and pointing. In one way it was great to be anonymous again but a little disconcerting when you've been used to it and taken it for granted. I learned at that moment, as I had learned with Ty Power in the South of France, that to be a truly international star you had to work in Hollywood.

The senator asked if I'd like to see a show that evening and of course I picked the hardest to get into – *South Pacific*, a smash hit and packed every night. But with MGM everything was possible, he would get me the tickets.

'Now what about a girl?' he asked.

I looked at him in astonishment.

'What girl?' I replied. 'I don't know any girls here.'

'Oh hell, that's easy. What kind would you like? Thin, fat, blonde, brunette. . .?'

I got slightly hysterical and told him to stop kidding. He told me very seriously that MGM had a sort of roster of ladies for the use of VIPs. I didn't think Jean would approve so I somewhat reluctantly refused; reluctantly because I was fascinated to see what he would have come up with.

The trip to the theatre that evening was a nightmare. I had never seen anything like New York traffic before: cars bumper to bumper, hooting, honking, the drivers yelling, pedestrians darting in and out among the cars, police blowing whistles. I'd never heard a police whistle blown with such ferocity. Before a British bobby blows his, somebody has to be after the crown jewels, but here they seemed to like blowing just for the sake of blowing. The crowds outside the theatres were thronging, milling, hustling, pushing, yelling and cursing, so unlike the sedate way the British go to the theatre, but it was exhilarating. I quickly got caught up in the mood and, pushing, shoving and yelling like the others, I eventually arrived at my seat.

The lights went down and the show started, and what a show! That had to be the greatest musical ever staged. Mary Martin was a dream and the other parts were beautifully acted; the chorus and choreography superb. My only criticism was that I got the impression Enzio Pinza didn't believe a word he said or sang. Later I learned that he understood very little English. What an experience! What a show! What energy! What talent! So much better than anything I had seen in London. It was later to take that city by storm as well.

I wanted to go round backstage and tell Mary Martin how divine I thought she was. In London I wouldn't have hesitated, but here nobody knew me, they'd probably throw me out on my ear, so I didn't risk it. As I left, I was astounded to see a whole crowd of autograph hunters waiting for me. How did they know I was there? How did they know me? Apparently this was my New York fan club. Yes, I had a fan club. Wasn't that great?

14

On the flight out to the coast I had one serious worry: the reaction of the leading lady who was to star with me in *King Solomon's Mines*. The last time I had seen her we had parted unhappily when we both agreed I should return to my wife. She had since married a man I had introduced her to during our European tour of *Gaslight*; a Battle of Britain pilot named Tony Bartlett. What would be her reaction to spending three or four months with me on location in Africa? I needn't have worried. As soon as the plane stopped, an MGM representative came aboard and arranged for me to leave first, and there on the tarmac were Deborah Kerr and her husband. I was very moved as we hugged each other and Tony slapped me on the back, welcoming me to Hollywood. Thank God. I already had some friends here. They told me they would meet me later at Mike Romanoff's where the producer of the film, Sam Zimbalist, would join us. Johnny Rothwell, a member of the vast MGM publicity department who had been chosen to look after me, took me to the Beverly Hills Hotel where a bungalow had already been booked.

The drive from the airport hadn't impressed me very much. Was this the famous Los Angeles? I'd never seen so many second-hand car lots, supermarkets, hotdog stands, hamburger joints, ugly clapboard houses, signs advertising everything from coke to Cadillacs and, worst of all, the tangle of telephone and electrical wires crisscrossing all over the place. But then we entered the residential part of Beverly Hills. Quite different. Streets lined with soaring palm trees, beautiful Mediterranean-style houses set back from lawns bordered with tropical flowers. This was more like it.

The Beverly Hills Hotel was everything I had imagined, with tall, bronzed, athletic, young men in beautifully cut uniforms to open the car doors and take your bags. I was never to get over how many beautiful girls served in restaurants and shops and the incredibly good-looking men working in gas stations and hotels. Of course this was the land of the beautiful people and they couldn't all be lucky enough to be famous. I was taken through the lobby, past the Polo Lounge and out through the gardens to my second-floor 'bungalow'. I noticed one or two beefy looking men lounging outside the door of the bungalow below mine and when I asked who they were, Johnny told me that Howard Hughes didn't like visitors. I asked who Howard Hughes might be and was told that not only was he one of the richest men in the world but the head of RKO Studios. My friend couldn't understand why I had never heard of this incredibly eccentric millionaire.

'Of course, he was the man who designed the special bra for Jane Russell,' I exclaimed. 'But if he's so bloody rich and important, why does he waste his time on nonsense like that?'

'You don't know Howard Hughes,' Johnny replied. No, I didn't. Not then. But I was to very soon, and how!

When I entered the famous Mike Romanoff's restaurant, I was greeted by the Prince himself and 'His Highness' led me to Deborah's table, telling me that not every customer received this royal treatment but that we European gentlemen must band together against the upstart peasant Americans, this with a twinkle and a courtly bow. I was still a bit groggy from the flight and, after a stiff drink, dazedly looked around. Yes, by heaven, they were there, the giants, Spencer Tracy with a beautiful girl, Humphrey Bogart with his wife Lauren Bacall, that lovely singer Dinah Shore, who had thrilled us during the war on the American Forces network, Jack Benny and George Burns with their wives, with Benny falling about laughing at something his friend

Burns had said – and then, my God, it really was, Gary Cooper. I was staring at this hero of mine so openly that he must have become aware and catching my amazed look he gave me a smile and nodded. I whispered to Deborah, 'He nodded at me, he actually nodded at me.'

'Stop acting like a tourist. You're a star yourself, behave like one,' she whispered back.

I couldn't eat with excitement but was able to drink so, when my producer arrived, I was slightly pissed.

Sam Zimbalist was an enormous man, very ugly until he smiled and then he became beautiful. He gave me rather an appraising stare. After all, he'd hired this actor without seeing him in person and I think he was rather taken aback by the sight of this tired, pale, rather groggy object smiling back at him. Then he asked me why I didn't have a decent agent as he'd had hell's own time contacting me. I replied that I thought Jack Dunfee had contacted him.

'Nonsense,' he replied. 'I saw you in *Saraband* and ran several of your other films and decided you were right for the part.'

He had then tried to contact me through my agent. The only agent on record was Dunfee, so Sam called him and Dunfee got his ten per cent for the next seven years for a phone call he hadn't even paid for. Deborah, who knew Jack Dunfee well, made one comment: 'Typical.'

Next morning an enormous Cadillac whisked me out to MGM. I was dropped off outside the immense Thalberg building, better known as The Iron Lung. Some say it got its name from the incredible air-conditioning system it contained, and some from the fact that no original thought ever came out of it. Sam Zimbalist met me and introduced me to the guards on the gates. I was given a sharp scrutiny by one of them who, to my amazement, was packing a forty-five revolver. The fans must be pretty rough out here, I thought. Apparently MGM had its own police force, headed by a Mr Whitey Ford who was a power to be reckoned with.

If you were a MGM personality and got into trouble with the law, a call to Whitey would certainly ease things.

I passed through those gates thinking I'd got it made. MGM! How many times had Mike and I queued at the Empire, Leicester Square, to see Norma Shearer, Greta Garbo, John Gilbert, Wallace Beery, Jean Harlow, John Barrymore, Joan Crawford, Clark Gable, or Spencer Tracy and here was I going to make a film for them. I didn't know till later that the roof was about to fall in: a power play between Nicholas Schenck in New York and the notorious Louis B. Mayer was to result in Doré Schary taking control and the days of the superstar would be over. It would be the day of the super producer, then the super writer, Doré having originally been a script writer, and the super director, and the star would come a bad fourth. Louis B., with all his faults, had had one credo, a star could do no wrong as long as he was box office.

Anyway, I wasn't to know this as I went into the wardrobe department. I was met by a charming old man, a Mr Winter, who was head cutter and who assured me that I would get the best service possible as his son, Ralph Winter, was the editor on our film. I went through some hysterical moments as I studied the sketches of what they thought a white hunter should look like. No one connected with the film had ever been to Africa. Strange, I thought in Hollywood they were perfectionists. Their answer was, well, the audience hasn't been there either, so what's the difference?

One day in the MGM commissary I was introduced to Cary Grant who invited me to his home for a meal, as he wanted to hear all the news from England. He warned me that his wife, Betsy Drake, had been given a French cook book and was determined to go through the whole list of entrées and try them out on her guests. He had a charming home up in the hills and Betsy was in one of those wonderful American kitchens toiling over a stove with all sorts of pots and pans bubbling away. I knew by the way she was measuring everything out that she wasn't an instinctive cook. However, the flush-faced Betsy proudly served up her latest concoction, which couldn't have been all that good because I don't remember what it was. Betsy made me laugh when she triumphantly declared she only had 108 more recipes to get through but, judging by the look Cary gave me, I don't think he was going to allow her to continue much longer.

Cary asked me if I'd like to visit the Farmers' Market with him, an experience I shouldn't miss. It was an incredible place with stalls from all over the world, even their recent enemy Japan. But my eye went immediately to the British stall and the sight of the different teas, cheeses and hams made my mouth water. I excitedly asked Cary how much of each item I was allowed to buy? He told me I could buy as much as I liked. I just couldn't believe it – any amount I liked! It had been ten long years since I'd entered a shop and been able to buy more than a few ounces of each article. I started with ten pounds of sugar, then ten of tea, ten of butter, five pounds of bacon and forty-eight eggs, remembering my one egg and one rasher a week, ten pounds of Black Angus steaks, two legs of Canterbury lamb and finished off with a whole Stilton cheese. The man serving me exchanged looks with Cary as much as to say who is this lunatic? While we were piling it all into the car, Cary reminded me that I was living in a hotel and what the hell was I going to do with all this food?

'Cary,' I told him solemnly. 'I'm just going to look at it.' He obviously had no idea what it meant to be rationed.

We got back to my hotel and I lovingly stacked my purchases round the sitting-room and put the perishables away in the fridge. I had such indigestion that night I couldn't sleep. I had eaten an omelette of eight eggs with six rashers of bacon and a fried steak on the side, followed by chunks of Stilton cheese, washed down with cup after cup of heavenly, strong, well-sugared tea. I wasn't able to cook again during the rest of my stay as I was expected to eat out, and eventually I was asked by the management to please get rid of the lamb and the steak as they had begun to smell.

James and Pam Mason called me up inviting me over; they were giving a party for me. Dear James and Pam, of course I had forgotten, they were already well-established in Hollywood. They told me I couldn't miss their house as it was just behind the Beverly Hills Hotel and to look out for Pamela Drive. Well, well. Only there three years and they'd already named a drive after her! I was very impressed.

George Sanders was there with an incredible non-stop chattering, voluptuous lady named Zsa Zsa Gabor; a good-looking man with flashing teeth that after the first flash you realized were capped, called Greg Bautzer, who turned out to be one of the principal Howard Hughes lawyers, and Ava Gardner, being held in earnest conversation by an obviously doting admirer. When the lovely lady was alone a moment I sat down beside her and introduced myself. When I told her that I had come out to work for MGM, she warned me whatever happened not to sign a long-term contract. She had, and it had been a disaster.

'Look what happened to Judy Garland,' she said: This was when Judy had been taken out of *Annie Get Your Gun* and was supposedly on drugs. Hell, if they could ruin a talent like that, what would happen to us lesser mortals? She then asked me if I'd like to squire her the following night to the opening of a restaurant owned by Esther Williams. MGM were arranging the publicity for this bash and would naturally like two of its stars to appear together. I asked Ava if that was the only reason, just the publicity, and got a very enigmatic look in reply.

It was strange meeting the lovely Esther Williams dressed in an evening gown – I expected her any moment to rip it off and expose a bathing suit underneath. The place was over-crowded and swarming with photographers and MGM publicists, so after a suitable interval Ava and I slipped away.

This sophisticated beauty was not at all what she seemed. As we sipped a drink together she confessed that she too was insecure and hated all the ballyhoo that went with being a film star, the interviews and photographic sessions, the feeling of being a commodity, pushed from one film to the next. She had come off a farm in the south and just couldn't adjust. She'd also had two pretty traumatic marriages, one to Mickey Rooney, the other to band leader Artie Shaw. Much as I liked her I didn't see any more of her on this trip; I think she was otherwise occupied with a famous singer but I'm glad to say we were to work together in the future and she was to become one of my greatest friends.

While I was at Metro I got the impression I was being summed up by everyone because I was an Englishman, and the English had a reputation for being stuffy and condescending. They found out eventually that I wasn't either and I received the highest accolade, being told that, apart from my accent, I could be an American. I remember being asked quite early on whether I wasn't going to become an American citizen. I would ask, if the positions were reversed and they were working in England, would they become British? I always received the same reply, 'Shit no, I'm an American.' That's what endeared them to me, they were so proud of America, of being Americans. They never envied you your position because they believed with the right breaks they could become equally successful. Everything was possible in America. The first time I drove my imported Bristol into a gas station, the young attendant admired it and told me one day he'd get one like it. He was studying in night school to be a lawyer. Knowing what lawyers make in America, he's probably got three Cadillacs by now. I found it very refreshing.

Of course I met all the famous names in The Iron Lung: Benny Thau, handler of stars, Eddie Mannix, troubleshooter now but originally a bouncer back in New York for one of the nickelodeons, L.K. Sidney, public relations, Doré Schary, new head of production, and eventually the great man himself, Louis B. Mayer. He greeted me as a kinsman, telling me that he was also British, being of Canadian extraction and so we ought to get on fine. I gathered from that he expected me to work well, hard, cheaply and give no trouble.

While fittings were going on, Benny Thau asked me if I would mind testing for the leading part in *Quo Vadis*. I replied rather haughtily that surely they could run some of my films, as I hadn't done a test for seven years. He told me that the director, John Huston, simply wanted to see if the chemistry would work with the lady they had in mind to play opposite me, Elizabeth Taylor. I think she was seventeen at the time. I grudgingly agreed and, after being dressed in a skimpy tunic and having had my hair curled, Roman style (I'm glad to say they didn't suggest pinning back my ears), I reported on the set. The director was waiting for me. John Huston. One of the most prestigious names in the business. Remember his *Maltese Falcon*, with Bogart, Lorre, Astor and the unforgettable Sidney Greenstreet? I had never worked with a director of his calibre before and hoped I could please him. I was introduced to the incredibly beautiful and curvacious Liz Taylor, who disappointed me by having a rather squeaky voice, but you can't have everything, can you, and she had practically everything else in abundance.

I had most of the dialogue in the scene, as she was playing a demure slave and I the lecherous Roman conqueror. Before the take, Huston came up and told me in that phlegmy, ginny voice of his, 'Now, Stewart, I want you to play this like a drunken buck nigger. Know what I mean?' I thought I did, but at nine o'clock in the morning? However, I did my best and broke the crew up with my ogling of Miss Taylor's assets. Huston seemed to be satisfied and next day my new friend and producer Sam told me that everybody was impressed and I was a hot favourite to get the part. The film would be shot after I had completed *Solomon's Mines*.

Sam then asked me what I thought of his choice of director for our film: Compton Bennett, who had directed the popular British picture *The Seventh Veil*, with Mason and Ann Todd. I cautiously asked where he was and, when Sam said he was already in Africa preparing our film, I kept my mouth shut. How could I tell him what I knew, that James Mason and the producer Sidney Box had directed *The Seventh Veil* and all Bennett had done was to say 'action' and 'cut', after being given his instructions by those two. Unfortunately for everyone involved, I said nothing.

Before I left for England, Deborah rang and asked me to dinner, saying my date would be Toni Mannix, my boss the bouncer's wife. I asked if he would object and Deborah assured me that everything was fine, the lady just wanted to meet me to pass judgement on this new MGM acquisition. We met at a fabulous Hollywood restaurant called Don the Beachcomber, which specialized in Polynesian food and drink. Toni Mannix turned out to be a very luscious lady of a certain age and sat next to me while we were presented with the most exotic rum punches, served up in all kinds of different containers – mine, I remember, was in a scooped-out frozen pineapple. We all sucked away at each other's drinks and after about three rounds were feeling no pain. The food was exotic, too, sweet and sour pork, spare ribs, egg rolls, fried shrimps, squab legs, all garnished with incredible sauces and eaten with chopsticks.

While I was tucking into these delicacies, I suddenly became aware of a hand groping at my flies. I glanced in amazement at my companion who was expertly handling her chopsticks and nonchalantly chatting to Deborah while her other hand was very expertly handling my flies. As she grabbed me I choked on a piece of fried shrimp. This at least made her remove her hand in order to help me mop up the mess but, when it was cleared away and I was starting on a spare rib, back came the hand, which seemed oddly unconnected to my table companion who didn't even glance at me. I mean, there's a time and place for everything, but during a Polynesian meal eaten with chopsticks was in my opinion not the time. As she got a firmer grasp on me again I looked in amazement at Deborah. She gave me a questioning look and, realizing what was going on, got a fit of the giggles and choked on her egg roll. I strongly suspect she had known this sort of thing would happen when she invited me. Toni apparently had quite a reputation. Eventually this bizarre meal came to an end and as we left I begged Deb to drop me off first. I politely wished the groper goodnight and with, 'I'll call you tomorrow' to Deborah, let myself in to my bungalow and locked the door as I had a suspicion the night's games had not come to an end – I'd noticed the way Toni looked at me when she said goodnight. I was right as there was a bang at the door.

'Let me in, Jimmy, let me in.'

I thought she was going to wake the whole hotel, including the powerful Howard Hughes below who would probably have me bumped off for disturbing him, so I opened the door. In she staggered and, having shut the door behind her, proceeded to start undressing with a muttered, 'All right, let's take up where we left off.'

'Left off what?' I asked as coldly as possible, grabbing her arms to stop her undressing any further.

'What's the matter, kid, can't you get it up?' she snarled.

'No, madam, not with you,' I countered.

'Fucking pansy,' she shouted and left.

I went to bed wondering what the bouncer Eddie Mannix would have to say to me because I was sure she would tell him I had tried to rape her. Luckily I heard no more, but Deborah went into hysterics when I told her. She had suspected what would happen and, knowing what a square I was, wanted to see my reaction.

The time came for me to return to England and get the

necessary shots for our venture into Darkest Africa. Sam wished me good luck and my agent, Jack Dunfee's associate, a very strange man called Fefe Ferri, who insisted on kissing and calling me darling at every opportunity, assured me that my rather staggering hotel bill would be taken care of by Metro. I pointed out that I'd put a lot of personal items on the bill, not having any money apart from what Metro had advanced me, and was assured 'not to worry' as it would be Metro's pleasure. Later I was to find out what that 'pleasure' would cost me.

15

I was met at London Airport by a battery of reporters and photographers, asking me what I thought of Hollywood. When I told them that my brief visit had been a very pleasurable experience and that I had found everyone very generous and friendly, that the studio had been immensely efficient and the climate wonderful, their faces fell. In those days it was the fashion for every returning celebrity to run down Hollywood and say how much better everything was in London. Not true. I found poor old London, not surprisingly, rather drab and battered looking, the food non-existent and the climate horrible. Being summer, it was naturally pissing with rain and, as to the film industry, no one seemed to show any interest in my experiences in Hollywood.

Jean had just finished her film with Dirk Bogarde and we were able to spend some time together but I wasn't the best of company as I had to receive interminable shots in preparation for my safari to Africa: typhoid, para-typhoid, tetanus, cholera, smallpox and, worst of all, yellow fever. The first lot had been given almost painlessly by my own doctor, but the last had to be given by a government nurse at the Hospital for Tropical Diseases. She was obviously a sadist since she seemed to delight in pushing the large needle in very slowly. The reaction to all these jabs was horrific and both my arms were swollen and inflamed. Poor Jean. Our attempts at love-making were continuously interrupted by my yells of pain if she touched one of my arms. One day, while sitting rather miserably with a fever of 102° from the typhoid shot, the director, Compton Bennett, arrived. His first words cheered me up immensely.

'I have to tell you right now that I wanted Errol Flynn in the part.'

How's that for openers? We looked at each other in silence, I mean, a remark like that is a bit of a conversation stopper. I decided to pretend I hadn't heard and offered him a drink. We made desultory conversation about the weather and, thankfully, a short time later he departed. I was left with the exhilarating thought of spending three or four months in the African bush with this twerp. I didn't blame him for preferring Errol, but why tell me?

On this trip I hoped to try my hand at big game hunting and so went along to Westley Richards to choose some guns. I was advised by the owner, a charming fellow called Malcolm Lyell, to take along light, medium and heavy rifles. I chose a beautiful Holland and Holland .240 magnum, a Holland and Holland .375 magnum and a .577 Westley Richards single trigger, double-barrelled rifle. This rifle had originally been ordered by the Polish Count Potocki. He had been incredibly rich before the war but had now lost everything. Malcolm told me a sad story about the Prince shyly asking if he could borrow a pair of shotguns, as he had been invited to the Duke of somebody or other's shoot. Not only did Malcolm lend him the guns but he went to the trouble and expense of having the Prince's initials embossed on the stocks and his crest engraved on the guncases so that it wouldn't appear that the guns were borrowed. Apparently the Prince had wept at this thoughtful gesture. Now I was ready for anything and, as I left with my purchases, it occurred to me that I might reserve the light rifle for the director.

I received the news that we were travelling to Africa by flying boat and Jean and I drove down to Southampton where we were met by Deborah and Tony. The huge machine lay out in the Solent and, sipping coffee together in a little quayside bar, we wondered if it would ever get into the air. Customs and Immigration had already checked us through and the time came for us to embark. Jean was in floods of tears as we kissed goodbye. We'd only been together a week or two and now here I was off to Africa for three or four months. How I wished she could come with me, but of course that was impossible. Again I had a sinking feeling in the pit of my stomach as I saw Rushton, with his arms round her, help her gently into the car and drive away. How could two people who loved each other, yes, by now I knew I loved her, lead a life of constant separation? Deborah saw my misery and gave my arm a squeeze of comfort. The boat was alongside and we got in and started out to the enormous machine in which we were to travel to Lake Naivasha in Kenya. It was the first time any of us had been in a vessel like this and the take-off was very scary as the waves it threw up on either side mounted above our look-out portholes. It felt as if we were submerging and then suddenly the waves fell away and we were airborne.

It was a slow and tiring flight with many stops, but I wouldn't have travelled any other way. The trip took three days as we stopped at Naples for refuelling and at Khartoum, where we spent the night, but eventually we were flying low over the bush country of Kenya and approaching our destination, fifty miles outside Nairobi. In those days Africa was the mysterious and little known Dark Continent and we gazed out of the windows like excited tourists. Below us we could see the movement of wild game and at one point our low-flying machine terrified a herd of elephants as we passed over them. We skimmed over the lake, disturbing a family of hippos and came to rest a few hundred yards from a pier on which we could see the welcoming group, with the inevitable photographers. As we were rowed in we could see monkeys jumping around in the trees surrounding the lake and I longed to tell the cameramen to stop flashing their bulbs and give us a chance to take in all this wonder. But we were here to do a job. This was not a sightseeing tour, so we dutifully posed and shook hands with some of the local officials, district commissioners, game wardens, governor's aides, etc., who were to help us make the film.

Our drive into Nairobi took a long time as we often stopped the car to watch a herd of 'Tommies' or Grant's gazelle staring at us in disdain before trotting off, not having liked the look of us. We saw impala doing their incredible circus leaps, and the trees lining the roads were full of baboon, scratching and picking their toes as they contemptuously observed us. At one spot we all got out and gazed in amazement up the Rift Valley, the whole of East Africa seemed spread out beneath us, the road at that point being about 6,000 feet above sea level. The driver pointed to a tiny church tucked into the side of the hill which had been built by the Italian prisoners of war, who had made the road, to show their love of this spot. Many came back to live in Kenya after their release. A large herd of hump-backed cattle, grazing on the plains which swept away into the distance, were being guarded by creatures straight out of the Middle Ages, and we were immediately taken back a thousand years. They wore cloaks draped over their shoulders, gathered at the waist by a belt holding a short stabbing sword. They carried long, broad-bladed tapering spears, but it was their faces that made us gasp, daubed with ochre, fringed with hair twisted into ringlets also covered in ochre, they gazed into the distance, proud and arrogant, as if we weren't there. Nearby their women, with babies tucked into slings on their backs, were mixing some concoction in earthen bowls. Their arms were covered in bangles with coil after coil of copper wire edged with gaily coloured beads wound round their necks. Some were bare breasted, wearing only a short apron, and to our amazement their heads were completely shaven. They showed incredibly white teeth as they smiled at us for, unlike their warrior husbands, they deigned to acknowledge our existence.

We were told that these were the nomadic cattle-loving

tribe of the Masai, the most feared warriors in East Africa. Their usual diet was milk mixed with blood and, although seemingly skinny and lightly muscled, could throw those heavy spears accurately with a flick of their wrists, and outrun practically any European trained athlete. One of the settlers had tried out an experiment when he first arrived in the district. He had measured out the equivalent of the Olympic Marathon course through the bush and, knowing the Masai would do anything to own a cow, he offered one as a prize for the first to reach the finishing line. On the morning of the race about twenty *moran* (young warriors) arrived, carrying their heavy buffalo hide shields and their long tapering spears. He asked them to leave these behind as they would hamper them on their twenty-five-mile run, but the *moran* refused to part with their treasured implements. He sent them off with a couple of blasts on his whistle and this group of lithe, ochre-smeared athletes happily took off, laughing and joking, and disappeared into the bush. After a suitable interval the settler drove down to the finishing post. He could hear the cries and laughter of the approaching runners surging up the hill together in a bunch. At the last moment they spread out in line abreast in a perfect photo finish. Not one of them had discarded either spear or shield and they had obviously planned this trick in order to get a cow each, but the settler was pleased to pay up when he discovered that their time was within minutes of the then Olympic record.

As we entered the European parts of Nairobi, we were amazed at the blazing colours of the flowers in their gardens, hibiscus, frangipani, bougainvillea and, of course, having mostly British owners, geraniums, while the streets were lined with Flame of the Forest, jacaranda and flowering eucalyptus trees.

We arrived at the Norfolk Hotel, made famous by Lord Delamere, one of the original settlers. He used to give parties there for his other settler friends which went on for days during which incredible amounts of liquor were consumed. We were met by the owner, Tubby Block who, with his brother Jack, owned and ran most of the best hotels in Kenya. We were led through the foyer into a courtyard, ablaze with flowers and cages of brightly-coloured birds, and with an old covered wagon in the centre. This was the very wagon their grandfather had used when he came out seventy years before and traded with the settlers. Surrounding the courtyard were bungalows with little verandahs, comfortably equipped and spotlessly clean.

Our first location was within driving distance of Nairobi, a small town named Machakos. This was the scene where Deborah and I took off on our safari into the great unknown. The district commissioners who were helping us had got together hundreds of natives to do tribal dances, accompanied by their weird orchestras consisting mostly of drums and, to our amazement, police whistles. Stalking disdainfully among these Kikuyu, were a group of arrogant Masai warriors carrying their spears and shields. The assistant DCs were worriedly watching them as they explained to us that they, the Masai, were sworn enemies of the contemptible Kikuyu. In the old days they would raid them, killing all the men and taking the women as concubines, and that had been in the not too distant past. The DCs hoped there would be no trouble between them, but this turned out to be a very vain hope indeed. All the local settlers had assembled to watch these strange people playing around with cameras and shouting orders to the natives who, of course, didn't understand a word and were having a high old time. It was as if the whole scene had been organized for their amusement.

I felt very self-conscious in my Hollywood's idea of a white hunter outfit. One of the spectators was a Colonel Dean Drummond, DSO and three bars, who turned out to be an avid film fan and was fascinated by what was going on. He told me that Philip Percival, the dean of white hunters, lived nearby and might give me some tips on what I should wear. Phil Percival! How often I'd read of this character who had taken Ernest Hemingway on safari, and whose partner, Baron Von Blixen, had accompanied Teddy Roosevelt and most of the crowned heads of Europe on their hunting trips. Although Deborah and I had been called to be ready for the first shot, the director, now dressed in what he thought was a dashing outfit (any man with his kind of legs and knees should never wear shorts), had suddenly changed what little mind he had and decided to concentrate on the natives before they got out of hand and started killing each other. It had been his brilliant idea to mix the Masai with the Kikuyu.

Phil Percival took one look at me in my outfit and started to laugh. Having managed to quiet him down, I asked him what I should do to improve it. The first thing, he told me, was the hat.

'We've got to do something about that bloody hat. Now wait a minute. I knew a man once who wore a snakeskin round his hat, let's try that.'

We tried it, but it looked like one of those coloured hatbands worn in Florida and California.

'I've got it,' he said. 'Another friend of mine wore a leopard tail round his hat. Very dashing.'

We tried that with one of the leopard skins flung over the sofa. It was too thick, so we cut a strip off the skin itself and wound it round the brim. Perfect. And that's how the bush hat with the leopardskin band came into being. Now they're sold all over Africa, not with real skin of course, but I wish Phil and I had patented the idea. We'd have made a fortune. Next he suggested sewing cartridge loops on to my shirt and advised me to try and get a revolver from somewhere to wear on my hip. Apparently hunters in the 1880s always carried sidearms, not for the game, but as protection against the savage tribes. I eventually borrowed one, strangely enough an American frontier Colt .45, from Alan Tarleton, the man who was supplying the snakes used in the film. Now I felt better and more able to face the onlooking settlers without being sent up.

Phil Percival had a wonderful farm at Machakos and I envied him his life. Off into the bush on safaris with some rich American or titled European to earn money, and in between relaxing in his comfortable house, waited on hand and foot by his native servants, who obviously adored him. His wife was a sweet woman who was addressed by one and all on the farm as 'Mama'. She too was adored and was doctor, nurse and midwife to the hundreds who worked there. I saw only smiling faces when I visited the little huts with their allotted *shambas* where they grew corn to make *pombe* (strong African beer). I get so tired of hearing from the media, who usually know nothing about Africa, how the African has been exploited and enslaved by the British. I'm not referring to the Dutch, German, Belgian and French colonists – I'm not an authority on their methods – I can only talk from my own experiences. The farmers and planters of Kenya, Tanganyika and Uganda that I met looked after their workers, saw to their health and comfort and the education of their children. Are they faring any better now?

Phil and his wife invited me to stay with them while I worked nearby and I gladly accepted. Many evenings, sitting by a blazing fire, looking out over the plains where Phil had once hunted lion from horseback, we would discuss the 'atrocities' of the hated white man. Phil had very definite ideas about the slave trade. He admitted that, without the white slavers, there'd have been no transportation of negroes to the Americas and the Caribbean. But who captured and delivered those slaves to the coasts? The whites? Hell, no. No white ever went into the interior to capture the black man, he insisted. They were captured by warring tribes of their own race and, shackled together, were bought by the Arab slave traders, whose only interest was to use them as beasts of burden to convey ivory to the coast, for sale to India

174

and China. Phil in no way denied the culpability of the whites in taking advantage of this lucrative business, but he was tired of hearing that it was solely the whites who were involved. He pointed out that there were slaves in Africa, Arabia and India long before the white slavers arrived. The blacks sold their own people into slavery. The Arabs, the most brutal of all slave traders, delivered them, so if we're going to pass judgment let the black and the Arab take their share of the blame.

When I showed up next day in my modified and, in everyone else's opinion, vastly improved outfit, the director, of course, had to find fault. Head office hadn't approved a leopardskin hatband and therefore I couldn't wear one. Naturally I wore it. We finished our work in this area and after I had thanked the Percivals for their help and hospitality we moved off into the Rift Valley for the next sequence.

After I moved back into the Norfolk Hotel, Tubby Block asked if I would like to do a bit of hunting on his farm as the buffalo there were ruining his crops and they needed teaching a lesson. I don't know why he thought I'd be able to teach these ferocious animals anything but I was willing to have a go. So on Saturday evening I was driven to the ranch manager's home where I was welcomed by a charming English family and spent the first evening regaling them with stories of the film business. Personally I wanted to hear about Africa and the farming life out here but they naturally preferred to hear about England and the films, never having met a movie actor before, so I did my best. Next morning we drove all over their beautiful farm and, although seeing every other kind of game, couldn't find the marauding buffalo. Disappointedly we returned home but over a large Scotch and soda planned to give it another try at dawn the following morning. I told my host I had to be on the location at 8.30, but he assured me that if we got going by 5.30 we might get some sport and he would deliver me back on time.

We drove out in darkness, with his Masai gun-bearer in the back of the Land-Rover and reached some meadows where we could hear the buffalo feeding. We could scarcely make out their dark forms and crept into position, waiting for the dawn to break. I had often read of this terrifying animal, whose reputation was amply justified in the Nairobi cemetery with the headstones bearing the ominous words, 'Killed by a Buffalo'. I silently shook in my shoes. At first light we realized that our position was right in the centre of this huge grazing herd and we were only protected from discovery by a clump of bushes. My host pointed out a large bull and told me to thump him. Being assured that once I fired the herd would take off, I squeezed the trigger and down the bull went. But the others didn't take off. They started milling around trying to find out where the shot had come from. The Masai gun-bearer was already up a tree – I'd never seen anyone move so fast – and my host suggested that that might not be a bad idea for us as well, so we made a dash for the nearest large thorn tree and scrambled up. Bloody painful. The buffalo had now seen us and menacingly watched us with their noses pointed out in that frightening way they have. There were a lot of females in the herd with calves which probably accounted for their belligerent attitude.

I think the farmer was as scared as I was, as he had never seen them behave like that before and nervously suggested that I fired a shot to scare them off. I tried it, but it had no effect, they just stood their ground and continued glaring at us. This stalemate went on for what seemed like hours and I realized that I was going to be late for work. I didn't fancy spending the morning up a tree with thorns sticking into my behind and, after all, I was working for Metro. Didn't these bloody buffalo realize that they were holding up a motion picture? Unheard of. Until now we had been conversing in nervous whispers, so I thought I'd try the effect of a well-

The 'little darling' with Mummy and Iris. *(National Film Archive)*

My poor suffering father.

'Uncle'.

'Nanny'. The trouble-making old
battleaxe. *(National Film Archive)*

On the beach in my beloved Cornwa

'Upper class playboy type'. Film extra.

Waving that handkerchief around: 22-year-old 'Charles Surface'.

'Subtle acting' with Robert Donat and Constance Cummings. 1939 Old Vic Season. *(BBC Hulton Picture library)*

Slightly chubby-faced husband. Elspeth looking lovely of course.

Provisional Lance-Corporal Unpaid, Gordon Highlanders. *(National Film Archive)*

Dyed hair, plucked eyebrows, painted out upper lip and ears stuck back. My first starring part in THE MAN IN GREY.

Lowest form of animal life in the British Army. 2nd Lieut. in the Black Watch.

That stricken look would come into her eyes and I just couldn't slug her again. Poor Maggie Lockwood in THE MAN IN GREY. *(Kobal Collection)*

LOVE STORY. I'm going blind, she's dying of some illness, why the hell don't we get together and exchange ideas?

FANNY BY GASLIGHT. James had just done his scene-stealing trick with the rose.

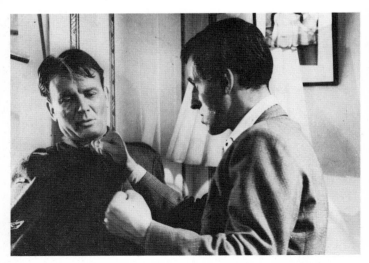

WATERLOO ROAD. Waiting to be beaten by Johnny Mills, which I hated.
(Kobal Collection)

CARAVAN. One of the kind of characters I always seemed to be playing.

At last, a father. Jamie, our firstborn. *(Keystone)*

With Deborah Kerr somewhere in Europe, 1944, performing for the troops. *(Kobal Collection)*

THE MAGIC BOW. David McCallum with his precious 'Strad'. *(BBC Hulton Picture library)*

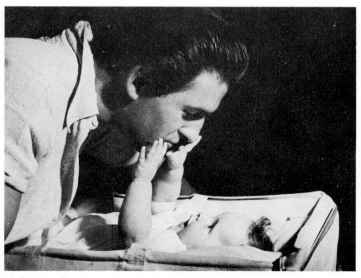

Lindsay, my first daughter. She was an angel. She still is.

'Family man'. *(Mirrorpic)*

Exhibition with old friend, Freddy Mills, world cruiser – weight champ. *(Keystone)*

ADAM AND EVELYNE. Embarrassed to play love scenes with someone I really loved.

KING SOLOMON's MINES with Deborah and the famous leopard skin hatband. *(Cinema Bookshop)*

SARABAND FOR DEAD LOVERS. One of the few films I really liked.
(National Film Archive)

WOMAN HATER. My introduction into comedy with the bewildered Edwige Feuillière. *(National Film Archive)*

Last holiday on the boat before taking off for Hollywood.

The incredibly bizarre
marriage organized by
Howard Hughes. *(Kobal
Collection)*

The unfriendly 'buff' who didn't realize I was making a film for MGM and
knocked me on my arse.

trained theatrical voice. I let go with an enormous yell that even Olivier would have been proud of. To my relief and astonishment this proved too much for them and they left. Shakily we scrambled down and, after pulling thorns out of each other's backsides, we jumped into the car and took off for the location. My friend assured me that he would skin out the buffalo and hand the meat to his farm help, keeping the horns for me.

We arrived in a cloud of dust and I tried to sidle up to Deborah as if I'd been there all the time, but the po-faced director was waiting for me and even my assurance of what a wonderful publicity story it would make: 'Star treed by ferocious buffalo. Risks life to be on the set in time, etc.' didn't impress him.

'But you weren't on time,' he said in his schoolmasterish voice. 'Don't let it happen again.'

'No, sir,' I said, choking back my fury. But of course he'd been right. I was late, the first time in my career, and that's inexcusable. The boys made up for my public humiliation as they demanded all the gory details. Of course I built up the story, making myself out to be the intrepid hunter, not a scared amateur, hiding up a tree with thorns in his bum, to get away from buffalo that were probably only curious.

The day came when we all left the comforts of the Norfolk Hotel and moved up to the Northern Frontier District where we would be living under canvas. Safariland, the famous hunting outfitters, had organized the camp, and I remember with what pride they showed Deborah her double tent (she had her husband with her, the lucky bastard) and its bath with hot and cold running water. This miracle was explained when they showed us two large oil drums at the back of the tent, one containing cold water and the other propped up over a wood fire, delivering the hot. There was a young black in attendance whose sole duty was to see that the drums were topped up with water and that there was always a fire going. I was allocated a bucket hauled up into a tree which released tepid water.

The country here was glorious and on our way to location we passed herds of elephants. I longed to jump out and photograph them but there was no time and elephants didn't feature in our film. It was amazing, lying in our tents at night, being lulled to sleep by the distant grunting sighs of lion and the giggling of hyena. Our camp always had these companions as they could smell the food and on many occasions the kitchen boys, camped a little distance away, would be woken up by marauding hyena snuffling among the pots and pans.

Our next stop was at Rumaruti where Kerr Hartley, the famous animal trapper, had his headquarters. He had every kind of game imaginable in his corrals waiting for shipment, and we were to use some of these animals in the film. One of his captives was a tame rhino, very young, with not very impressive horns, which was supposed to terrify us on our safari. I told Kerr I didn't think those tiny horns were all that frightening and he asked if I'd like to see a real giant? Apparently he'd been keeping this trophy up his sleeve for an important client and promised to show him to me on my day off.

We took off the following Sunday and he pointed out this massive beast sheltering under a thorn tree right out in the centre of the Rift Valley. He explained how rare this was, as normally rhino will seek cover in daylight among the thick thorn scrub which bordered the Valley. But there he was, with his massive horns, snoozing under the tree in the middle of the day. Kerr told me how he had learned to 'call up' rhino on his trapping expeditions. He used an empty cartridge case and blowing into it, produced a noise very like the rhino's whistling snort. Rhino have very poor eyesight and as long as the wind was right, so that they couldn't use their keen sense of smell, Kerr could call them right up to him. If he wanted them to charge, he would just start

178

swaying, which seemed to infuriate them and on they would come.

An idea came to me which, if it worked, might be a high spot in the film. I asked Kerr if he could call up this rhino, and if he could make him charge, I would try 'the matador shot'. Just before the end of its charge, a rhino puts its head down offering a chance to shoot it between the shoulders which would kill it instantly and often results in the animal doing a complete somersault. It was dangerous, but I knew that if I had Kerr on one side of me and a man called Hunter, one of the most famous big game hunters in Africa who happened to be staying with Kerr at that moment, on the other, the chances of being knocked down were small. I would ask the unit manager to let me have a cameraman holding an aeroflex to film this and I would walk into shot as the rhino charged and fire when it was almost on me, confident that Kerr and Hunter were backing me up. After I had brought the rhino down I would turn to face the camera, so that the audience would know it was me and not a double. This could be joined up by a reverse shot of Deborah with the safari boys behind her and make a wonderfully exciting sequence.

Kerr was enthusiastic at the idea of his trophy-bearing rhino being immortalized on film, so we returned to the ranch and excitedly discussed the idea with Hunter, who agreed wholeheartedly to take part.

That evening, having received the okay from Bob Surtees, MGMs famous cameraman who was filming this epic, we approached the director. On hearing of the plan he turned a sickly shade of green. Seeing this change of complexion, I quickly pointed out that he and Deborah could stay a mile or so back and not come anywhere near until everything was over. The director's colour returned when he learned he didn't have to participate but the disapproving sour look remained. He told us he'd think it over.

Next morning I was greeted by the director who thrust a

telegram into my hands. Apparently the SOB had wired off to Hollywood, telling them that I was endangering the whole unit with my crazy ideas and of course received a reply vetoing the whole plan. I argued that he'd had the assurances of two experienced big game hunters that there was no risk, and anyway did he think I was idiot enough to risk my own life just for a film, but he was adamant. He'd received orders from The Iron Lung and that was the same as a direct-message from the Almighty. So we used the tame rhino with the tiny horns and the scene went for nothing. The next free day Kerr and I took off and, calling the rhino up, this magnificent animal charged and I shot it cleanly, everything happening as we'd planned. We came back that evening with the trophy and Hunter, who had been on rhino control and had shot over 2,000 in his life, admitted it was the finest trophy he'd ever seen.

Our stay with the Hartleys came to an end and, thanking Kerr again for his incredible generosity in giving me the chance to shoot his 'private rhino', we made our way to the prepared camp near Mt Meru. Here the warriors of the Meru tribe were supposed to chase us into the forest, brandishing their spears. Again the DCs warned us to take care. There had been a tragic sequel to our visit to Machakos. Apparently the Masai had gone on the rampage, as the DC had feared, and killed two Kikuyu, raped some Kikuyu women and in turn had been beaten up by the more numerous Kiuks, resulting in two more deaths. This had caused a furore at government level and we had damned nearly been kicked out of Kenya.

'What do these bloody film wallahs think they're doing, coming here and upsetting everything we've been trying to control for fifty years?'

Of course they were absolutely right, and I believe the Metro powers paid heavy compensation to the families involved.

We asked the DC what his problem was with the Meru

and he told us that they were very like the Masai in that they suffered from hysteria and, if they got over-excited, weren't to be trusted with their spears. The scene called for Deborah, Richard Carlson, who played her brother, and myself, to run into the forest and be chased by the Meru, brandishing their spears and screaming their war cries. They had all daubed themselves in war paint, which had been outlawed except for special ceremonial purposes, and the DC thought they had been knocking back some *pombe*. He advised us once we started to keep going, as his men might not be able to control the hysterical Meru. That's all we needed, a spear up the behind, so we arranged to have a truck standing by.

Nervously we waited for the word 'action', with all the screaming natives milling round us, blowing horns and beating their shields with their spears. We hoped they didn't understand the word 'action', as we were supposed to start a little before them. They would receive their own signal from the DC. Because I brought up the rear I warned Richard and Deborah to go like hell or they'd be trampled to death by a very scared Granger so, when the word came, Deborah was off like a bloody hare. I couldn't even keep up with her, and thankfully we passed the camera and leapt into the truck, slamming the doors. Just as well, as some of the Meru got carried away and started hurling spears, but eventually they quietened down and rushed back to their compound where they continued to drink beer, tanking up for the next take, in which I suppose they hoped they'd catch us. We told the director, who was standing safely on a platform, that we hoped the shot had been all right, as we had no intention of giving those drunken savages another go at us. The cameraman gave the okay signal, and we all hastily packed up and pulled out, thanking the DC for his good advice.

I congratulated our leading lady on her Olympic performance and she told me she hadn't even reached top gear. What a super woman. Never any complaints, no playing around with her make-up, always cheerful and co-operative. Without her courage, as we shall see, the film would never have been finished.

The next sequence entailed us running around in the forest trying to evade our pursuers and eventually taking shelter by climbing up an enormous tree. During this sequence, my trusty gun-bearer, a marvellous 'Nandi' who used to carry needles and a spool of thread tucked into his elongated ear lobes, was supposed to be shot by the villains. I was to pick him up and carry him through the forest until at last I had to rest and, on laying him down, realize he's dead. I was then to pick him up again to hide his body from the cannibals chasing us. Now this man was no light-weight and his body had been greased, so as I lifted him he slipped and I felt a sharp pain in my chest and back. I thought nothing of it and continued the scene. Afterwards I felt a slight spasm between the shoulder blades which gradually wore off, so I didn't report the accident to the doctor. But this 'accident' was to have a very strange sequel.

Our last location in Kenya was to be a hotel just outside Isiolo, in the foothills of Mount Kenya. This beautiful house had originally been owned by a rich French lady who had built it for her lover many years before. She had named it Mawingo, meaning Clouds, and now after her death it had been turned into a hotel.

Later, when we told Bill Holden about its beauty, he bought it and turned it into the fabulous Mount Kenya Safari Club.

After a hard day's work we would all sit out on the bougainvillea-covered terrace sipping drinks and looking up at Mount Kenya, with its incredible varieties of trees and vegetation. I wished Jean could have been with me as it was one of the most idyllic spots for lovers. Deborah's husband, Tony, was getting a few dirty looks from the rest of us as we'd been on safari about two months now and were beginning to get a bit oversexed. The only other female in the group was Deborah's hairdresser, who actually was very plain, but in our female-starved eyes was getting more and more attractive every day. However, our noble director had snaffled this one, which none of us thought was a very good example of leadership.

While I was staying with him, Phil Percival had introduced me to another famous white hunter, Eric Rungren, who was lying in hospital, having been chewed up by a leopard. The only thing that had saved his life was his enormous strength. He had wrapped his legs around the animal to stop it ripping his stomach out with its hind claws, a favourite trick of the leopard, and throttled it to death while the animal chewed on his arms and shoulders. He had been in a terrible state when brought to the hospital and nearly lost an arm through blood poisoning, but had now recovered and was back in our area.

He had a job on buffalo control and asked me if I would like to join in the hunt for a *kali* (killer) buff that had been terrifying the villagers nearby. I swore him to secrecy and arranged to meet him the following Sunday at dawn. His safari car had a pack of hounds in the back and he explained that hunting with dogs was allowed, as this animal was a killer. We stopped the truck and, while Eric was handling the dogs, Miles Turner, his assistant, assembled the .470 magnum for me – unfortunately I didn't have my lovely .577 with me. My gun had a single trigger but this one had the normal two triggers and the change nearly led to my death. At that moment another car joined us and Dean Drummond and Tubby Block got out. They were also friends of Eric and had come to see the fun. I suspect they had really come to see an actor make an ass of himself and they weren't to be disappointed.

While we were whispering together, Miles suddenly pointed, indicating that the buff was lying nearby. I couldn't see a thing as I didn't have the sharp, trained eyes of my companions. Then it stood up and I saw it. It was only about seventy yards away and, shaking with excitement, I tried to line up on its shoulder as it took off. There was a shattering roar in the stillness and the buff flinched as I heard the thunk of the striking bullet. Then, before I could get in another shot, it disappeared into the thick thorn brush with the dogs baying at its heels. We took off after it and came to a kind of tunnel the buff had made in this impenetrable stuff and Eric warned me, as I prepared to enter, to make sure the buff wasn't coming back as there wouldn't be room for us both. I crawled in with Eric behind me and a little way ahead could hear the dogs baying and the grunts of the buff.

After about fifty yards I stopped and peered through the roots at the buff ahead. I could just make him out in the half light, hooking at the dogs who were snapping all round him. Suddenly it looked up and for a moment we stared at each other, then it turned and disappeared. Whispering to Eric to follow I scrambled down the tunnel but at that moment the light was blocked out and I realized that the buff had come round in a circle and was now heading straight for me. Eric yelled to me to shoot and as the gun came up to my shoulder I remember thinking, 'This can't be happening. I'm making a picture for Metro. What's this bloody buff think it's doing trying to kill me?' After another yell from Eric I fired and the bullet hit the buff high up in the head, dazing it a bit. It was now about two yards off and coming on again. Frantically I squeezed the trigger but in my excitement I'd squeezed the same one and of course nothing happened. I think the buff was as confused as I was, as it hit me in the ribs with the side of its horn, throwing me into a thorn bush and I could feel the blast of Eric's gun as he let off with both barrels. But that didn't stop the buff either. He trampled over Eric and started to turn. I finally squeezed off my second shot and reloading, put two more into its shoulder, but it still wouldn't go down. It stood glaring at us from about three yards away.

'I've got no more bullets, Eric,' I murmured despairingly. Eric's answer was a final shot which dropped the buff.

All this had taken place in a few seconds and within a very

confined space as we were still in the 'tunnel'. Miles came down out of a tree and congratulated us for giving him such a splendid view. We thanked him for his help.

'Christ, you don't think I wanted to tackle a wounded buff with my bare hands, do you?' And then we realized he hadn't brought his gun. Eric, mopping a cut on his forehead, asked me if I was hurt and I told him I was okay as it was only a smack in the ribs, but reaction had set in and I started to shake.

'God, I thought it would never go down,' I said.

'It's amazing what punishment those animals can take. Your first shot took it too far back, Jim, and your second too high up in the head. It just dazed it. Your next ones killed it, but it takes some time for the buff to realize it's dead, and in the meantime it can do a lot of damage.'

Tubby and D.D. joined us and asked what the fusillade of shots had been about. Had we encountered two other buffalo? When seeing only one corpse they eyed me rather sceptically, but on hearing the story congratulated us on our narrow escape. We took photographs to record this triumph for posterity and all had a drink to celebrate, but as I sipped mine I wondered whether I would ever shoot a buff without getting either treed or trampled on. By this time a crowd of villagers had arrived and started to divide up the carcass of their former adversary. I reckoned they'd all have indigestion that night as it was a tough old brute.

The next morning my ribs had stiffened up and I was in misery. I confided my exploit to Deborah and asked her to back me up when I explained to the director that I'd had a fall.

'Of course,' she said. 'You fell horsing around with Tony. I was there, wasn't I?' Bless her. So I escaped being ticked off once more.

In our next sequence Alan Tarleton, the snake man, came into his own. The scene called for the safari, led by me, to be held up by a cobra. This frightening reptile was supposed to rear up and threaten me as I approached a bank. I nervously asked Alan if he was going to milk the snake of its venom to make it harmless in case it chose to bite me.

'Can't do that, Jim, it wouldn't throw its hood. A snake isn't stupid. If I milk its venom it'll know it's harmless and just try and get away. It won't attack you.'

That's perfectly all right with me, I thought.

'Well, what are you going to do, Alan?' I asked nervously. Nervously? I was shitting myself. Like most people I have a horror of snakes, but I couldn't show this fear in front of all the boys.

'Don't worry, Jim. I'll scotchtape its mouth. It'll attack you but won't be able to bite. Now, when you grab it, grab it just behind the head and hold on until I can take it away from you. Okay?'

'Okay,' I replied. I hoped the snake understood all this. Alan knelt down on my side of the bank so the camera wouldn't see him and held on to the snake's tail until the magic word 'action' came. I saw the snake trying to get away and Alan pulling it back through the brush but, before he could signal to me, the director called 'action'. I approached the bank and the snake reared up, throwing its hood in a very threatening way. I swiped at the swaying head with my hat, as in rehearsal, and grabbed it behind the head. As I held it, the snake curled right up my arm. The feel of that cold, dry scaly horror gripping my forearm made me feel sick with fright, and I was thankful to hear the word 'cut'. Then I heard Alan's voice, chillingly quiet.

'Don't move, Jim. Hold on tight, whatever you do, don't let go.'

I held on like grim death and Alan cautiously put his hand over mine and, gripping the snake behind the head, pulled it off my arm and shoved it back in its box.

'What was the problem?' I asked.

'Christ, man, didn't you see? When I pulled it back

through the brush the tape came off its mouth. It could have bitten you.'

I nearly fainted.

'Why the hell didn't you warn me,' I yelled.

'Hell, I was going to, man, but the director said "action".'

Of course. Nothing must waste MGM film even if it meant the leading man getting bitten by a cobra. I told Alan severely that in future I would take full responsibility for the waste of film: if he saw any risk of any of us being bitten by his bloody snakes he was to yell 'stop' as loudly as he could.

'Try it, Alan. Yell as loud as you can.'

Alan yelled.

'That's right, Alan, only louder if possible. Understand?'

Alan assured me he understood. I caught the director's eye. I thought he was looking rather disappointed.

Alan also had a python which would feature later in a scene with Deborah who was already shaking at the thought of it, poor darling. She had been behind me in the cobra scene and could have been bitten too. That evening I had a drink with Alan in my tent. I was still shaking and needed the alcohol.

'You're either stupid, or a brave lad, what you did today.'

'Neither, Alan,' I answered. 'Just a show off.'

'There's something else I didn't tell you, man. That's a spitting cobra. He could have blinded you.'

'Oh, thanks,' I said, wondering if I'd ever finish this film.

Alan had another experience with that bloody cobra. He couldn't get rid of it until we got the okay on the 'rushes' and, being high up in the mountains, the nights were very cold, so Alan had to sleep with the snake to keep it warm. It lived in a slatted box and one morning, after shaving, he had stubbed his toe on the box and without thinking, picked the box up to put it out of the way. The cobra spat through the slats and the venom hit his neck where he had just nicked himself shaving. He came to my tent, shaking, shouting for brandy.

'Brandy, Alan! At eight o'clock in the morning?'

'Give it to me quick, man, quick.'

I poured a tumblerful and he drank it down in a gulp. After a moment he told me what had happened and I downed a brandy too. Alan's neck had already turned a bright red where the venom had hit, but the brandy must have worked for he experienced no other effects. After Deborah did her scene with the python, where it had to slither over her legs, and having received the news that the 'rushes' were okay, Alan blew the cobra's head off with his pistol, but lovingly drove the python a hundred miles into the country to release it where he had caught it.

'Don't like cobras, but pythons are nice people,' he explained.

16

Now the hard part of the trip was at hand as we were off to take a boat up the Victoria Nile to Murchison Falls, where we would camp for two or three weeks in the heart of a game reserve. We were told that, as a precaution, we should all have anti sleeping-sickness shots, because the area we were going into was infested with tsetse fly and some might carry that dreaded disease. Typical, I thought. MGM didn't want me to take a tiny risk in getting a memorable shot for the film but was quite willing to let us all go into a sleeping-sickness area which could have permanent effects on the health of anyone who contracted it. The shots had startling and different effects on us all. I went to bed for three days with a fever of about 103°: Deborah, who was proving to be tougher than any of us men, showed no ill effects at all. One of the crew walked out of the doctor's office after the shot with no apparent symptoms and fell flat on his face in the street and split his head open. He was out for about two hours. Most of the crew had some reaction but I was too miserable to hear about them. Later the doctor told us that they had used us as guinea pigs as this serum hadn't been tested publicly before. Great!

We flew off to Butiaba on the shores of Lake Albert in Uganda, to await the arrival of the paddle steamer which would take us up-river. I thought the crew needed cheering up so I threw a party for them all. We were a mixed group: the actors consisted of two British and one American, there were twelve Americans and twenty-four Kenyans on the crew with an English director, a Hungarian second unit director, who had a South African female assistant, an American production manager, an English husband, Tony,

189

and a few German and Italian interpreters, assistant directors, etc. With all these men around, lusting after her, Deborah found herself in a difficult situation and handled it beautifully. Never did she try any coquettish gestures or sexy innuendoes, she just made herself out to be one of the boys and showed her remaining fondness for me in always backing me when I was in trouble, which was often. Of course we were all jealous of Tony and no one thought he was good enough for her, but we had to admit he did a wonderful job keeping her happy.

The party was a great success: everybody got pissed and let down their hair. After four or five Scotches, even the director (wearing shorts, of course) looked human and gave us an exhibition of ballroom dancing which gave us all hysterics.

The paddle steamer arrived and we all embarked on our two day trip up the Victoria Nile. We would all sit out on deck watching the natives in their dug-outs fishing, the crocodiles lining the banks slithering into the water as we passed, ploughing through herds of hippos who would disappear as we seemed just about to hit them, surfacing a little way off with just their two ears and nostrils showing above water. Elephants on the banks guarding their *mtotos* (babies) as they played in the river, spraying each other with their trunks. The big tusker in attendance would raise his head and let out a piercing scream of defiance as we passed. It was a paradise and I would have loved to have bought a piece of land there, built myself a shack and spent the rest of my life just watching the animals.

The next morning we gradually became aware of a faint roaring sound in the distance and the current of the river seemed to become much stronger. We were approaching the Falls where the broad Victoria Nile narrows to a few yards as it rushes through the rocky gorge and tumbles two or three hundred feet to the river below. This was to be our home for the next three weeks. The din was fearful and we had to shout to make ourselves heard, but gradually we became accustomed to it. The tented camp was laid out along the river bank in rows, reaching back to the surrounding forest, and looked very picturesque. We all went ashore and were allocated our different tents where we unpacked and then started to investigate our new home.

The Ugandan Game Wardens warned us not to stray too far as we were in the middle of a highly populated game reserve containing many elephants and rhinos, apart from the crocs and hippos infesting the river and its banks. Sadly we watched our paddle steamer disappearing round the bend of the river, giving us a forlorn farewell hoot on its siren. Whatever happened to us it wouldn't be coming back for three weeks and there was no other transport around.

Sitting outside my tent that evening, watching the crocs snapping up the stunned fish as they came hurtling over the falls and listening to the strange honking of the hippos, I drank quite a lot of whisky and fell into my camp bed wondering what the hell I was doing here. I knew the answer, of course. Making money for the MGM shareholders, and paying off my own income tax.

Next day we were shown where most of the scenes would be shot. Right on top of the falls. That meant a very steep climb of about 300 feet through tangled scrub and slippery rocks. The men had to carry their equipment up there each morning and bring it down each evening as they daren't leave it up there for fear of it being trampled on by elephants. Poor buggers, I thought, I'm glad I don't have your job, little knowing that both Deborah and I would be helping them very soon. Once up there the views were breathtaking. We lived in a kind of mist from the spray of the water as it rushed through the canyon and up above the roar was even more deafening. Wearily we descended that first evening and I envied Deborah her bath. I didn't have the nerve to ask if I could share it as I didn't think Tony would approve.

After a few days the drawbacks of this Garden of Eden started to emerge. First, there was a mad hippo, who lay in wait for us as we started our trip up to the top and charged us, scattering the men, who would drop anything they were carrying and run for their lives, me with them. We asked the game warden, who always accompanied us, why he didn't shoot the bloody thing? We received a shocked look as he told us this was a game reserve and no shooting was allowed unless it was to protect life. I asked him if it was necessary for the hippo to be actually chewing one of us up before he fired, and after that he let off a few token shots over her head (she was a female with a baby hidden somewhere) which scared her off for a bit, but she was always lurking about somewhere.

The other drawback was dysentery. Malaria hadn't felled anyone yet, as we were all full of attabrin and looking rather yellow, but dysentery was something else. We all drank boiled water, of course, which lessened the chance of typhoid but there was no way of protecting the food, cooked by our black help and laid out on tables in the messing tent. All the blacks apparently suffered from dysentery, and some of them from amoebic dysentery, a really dangerous disease. One after the other, the crew became infected to different degrees of seriousness. Some were so sick they couldn't get out of bed and by the end of the second week our white manpower was down from thirty able-bodied men to eight. This meant Deborah and I had to lug some of the equipment up the cliff. Once again Deborah showed her courage and, although I knew she was suffering discomfort like all of us, never missed a day's work.

This was the location where the famous hair-cutting scene took place. Deborah was supposed to get fed up with her long hair and hack it off, afterwards washing her head in a pool and roughly drying it. The hair stuck out all over her head in little spikes. Deborah has the kind of classic beauty that doesn't need elaborate hair styles to set it off, and I begged her to play the scene just like that. She looked adorable but, even more important, it looked real. She agreed but the director insisted that his hairdresser lady friend be called in to tong and curl it. When we got back to Hollywood the powers that be thought it hadn't been tonged enough and reshot the scene. She looked as if she'd just come out of the hairdresser's which, of course, she had. It got a big laugh which was a pity as the rest of the film was so realistic.

At last the twenty-first day dawned and we were all packed and standing on the wharf by seven in the morning, waiting anxiously for the steamer to appear. One of the unit was strong enough to make it up to the top to get a better view and suddenly we heard him yelling that he could actually see it. And then we saw her coming round the bend giving welcoming toots on the siren. There was a mad rush up the gangplank as if there might be a chance of her leaving without us and we all sighed with relief as the roar of the falls faded into the distance.

The entire unit was flown to Kampala where there was a good hospital and the really sick men were put to bed. The crew had just about had this trip by now and none of us could see why we should go on risking our health. I mean, it was only a film and not a test of endurance. When we complained to the unit manager he told us it would be impossible to cancel our schedule and go back to Hollywood since it would cost a fortune to build the Watussi Village, our next sequence, on the back lot. Of course our health didn't matter but money, that's something else. The crew, he explained, could easily be replaced but if either of the stars should contract amoebic dysentery, that would mean packing up and going home. Deborah, being strong as a horse, was not a good bet, so all the men looked hopefully at me.

'Come on, Jim, have a test. You never know, you may have it.'

I didn't really want to test as I knew it would be rather

painful, but I agreed and off we went to the hospital. I was ushered into the doctor's lab and the boys stood outside, peeping round the door in hopeful anticipation.

'Take your trousers and pants off, hop on the table and kneel down in a praying position with your buttocks in the air.'

I did as I was told. Out of the corner of my eye I saw him pick up a glass tube about two feet long and about two inches wide. He started greasing the end. What the hell was he planning to do with this instrument of torture, I wondered? I soon found out. Here was I, kneeling on a table with a foot of tube up my behind, with all the boys watching and offering remarks like, 'Don't do that too often, Jim, or you might get to like it.' I really felt like a star at that moment. After several Aha's and Mmm's the doctor withdrew the instrument and told me to get dressed. There was a hushed silence. Then he turned and with a smile told me I had a pretty healthy colon with no signs of amoeba. There was a roar of disappointment from my watching friends and I felt very ashamed. I had let them down. I didn't have amoebic dysentery.

The unit then left for our last location in the Belgian Congo, a town called Kigali in Ruanda Urundi. Deborah and I were to be flown in by private plane a little later. We said a last goodbye to the poor blokes who were left behind in hospital and boarded our charter plane, a tiny Cessna. We asked the bush pilot whether it was safe to fly over the mountainous areas ahead in such a small aircraft?

'Christ, man. This is a peachy machine, get us anywhere.'

We took off with our garrulous pilot diving and turning to show off the different beauty spots below. I was already airsick and clutching Deborah's hand for comfort. At one turn we passed over an extinct volcano and our mad pilot friend asked whether we'd like to take a closer look? Before either of us could answer we were flying around inside the bloody volcano at a steep angle with the centrifugal force of

194

the vertical turns draining all the blood from my brain and I blacked out. After we emerged from the crater our pilot asked if we hadn't thought it a beautiful sight? I believe Deborah muttered something but I was still unconscious. Eventually we landed and thankfully alighted from that tiny deathtrap. As we went forward to meet the welcoming group there was a loud vroomp and our plane burst into flames. Our intrepid bush pilot exclaimed, 'Must have been an electrical short. I told the bloody mechanics to check it,' and then with a sweet smile 'Lucky it didn't happen while we were inside that crater!'

Shaking, Deborah and I got into the car and were driven to the Belgian hotel where we were to stay. We were met by a grim-faced doctor who warned us not to touch a drop of water or any food that didn't come out of a can. Apparently ninety per cent of the inhabitants of this garden spot had malaria and ninety-five per cent dysentery, to say nothing of possible typhus, cholera, yellow fever and the clap. We looked at him in horror.

'What do we eat and drink?' we asked.

'Oh, we've commandeered all the tinned food in town and there's plenty of beer and wine. I've sent a charter plane into Stanleyville, 300 miles away, to bring us out a distillation plant. It should be here in a week.'

We asked if boiled water wouldn't solve the problem, but were told that only distilled water would guarantee total protection. During the next week we had to have beer or wine with all our meals and even had to brush our teeth in the stuff. Neither beer nor wine go with bacon and eggs at breakfast time and, strangely enough, the crew, who were a hard-drinking bunch, were all dying for a drink of water.

We were taken out to the location and had our first meeting with the Watussi whom we were to work with. Incredible people. The men were all giants, seven to eight feet tall, with their hair done in that strange style you see in Egyptian wall-paintings. Their features were neither negroid nor Arabic, but had an air of great gentleness and nobility. The women, also tall and slender, were carried around in litters by the Bantu, a tribe that they had conquered centuries before when they came down from the north.

Unlike all the other African tribes we had worked with, who had always been friendly and curious, these people were strangely aloof. They liked acting and were very good in the film, but never tried to mix with us. They had built the palace, which had featured in the film, entirely out of bamboo, plaited by hand, without a single nail, all lashed together by thongs. There was an intricate maze at the back, leading to the different huts of the king's wives. In the old days, the only person who knew the plan of the maze was the king himself. This secrecy was necessary as there was much jealousy and many attempted assassinations, so the king didn't want his staff to know which wife he would be visiting on which night. This maze must have taken weeks to prepare and was only shown for a few brief seconds in the film. It had been necessary to build all this as there were no original examples in existence. When the different kings died, all their personal belongings and living quarters were burned to the ground, so when the Belgians conquered the country and controlled the rulers, no more palaces were built.

The distillation plant eventually arrived from Stanleyville and we were able to have a glass of water. Lovely. We were to spend Christmas of 1949 there and MGM had the kindness to fly in turkeys and plum puddings. So at least we had one meal that didn't come out of a tin. It was a wonderful dinner and at last the men could see the end of the road. With luck and good weather there were only a few more weeks to go.

At long last the final day arrived and we all behaved like school children packing up to go home on holiday. We sadly said goodbye to our friends who had to be left behind in hospital and took off in different directions. It was wonderful to hold Jean in my arms again and to gorge myself three times a day with the glorious creations of my faithful Louisa.

During my few days in London I had a visit from Carol Reed who was enjoying world-wide acclaim for his latest film, *The Third Man*, with its incredibly successful musical background played on the zither by Anton Karas. Reed was planning to do Conrad's *Outcast of the Islands* and offered me the leading part. I accepted immediately, as the thought of working with a director of his calibre, after my recent experience, was an exciting challenge. The film would start after the completion of *Solomon's Mines*, so things seemed to be looking up. Jean and I had taken delivery of the first two Bristol cars off the line and not wanting to be separated from my new toy I arranged to have it flown over to Hollywood. I thought it might impress the rather patronizing Hollywood contingent – it did, especially the accounts department, as I had had the freight costs charged to MGM.

The day I reported to Sam's office, I passed our director, Compton Bennett, in his car, leaving the lot. I thought he looked rather strange as he acknowledged my wave with a sickly smile. On entering Sam's office I remarked on Bennett's appearance and Sam explained that Bennett had been sending letter after letter alibi-ing as to his failure to deliver what was asked of him and putting all the blame on Tony and me. According to him we had disrupted the whole unit and it was only his, Bennett's, efforts and devotion to duty that had saved the situation. Louis B. Mayer had smelt a rat and called in our cameraman, Bob Surtees, to tell him the true story. Apparently Bob had said that far from being a trouble-maker I had had to work out every shot with him as the director really didn't have a clue, so Mayer had fired Bennett off the picture. Tony was delighted since he'd always hated him, but I was rather sorry for the poor SOB. I never enjoyed kicking someone when they were down however much I'd disliked them before.

Bundy Marton, the second unit director, who had been

responsible for all the fantastic shots of animals and scenery, took over the film and we started shooting the interior scenes. It was so strange to be wearing the same clothes and apparently working in the same African sets, but having all the comforts that we'd been without for four months; to have good food, not to be attacked by swarms of flying insects, to work in air-conditioned studios and to be able to visit a real lavatory instead of squatting in the bush during the day when we'd been away from camp. But once again we had to go on location, this time to Death Valley, where the desert sequences would be shot. This part of California well deserves its name as it is the most desolate, hot, uncomfortable place imaginable. But at least we would come back to civilized living conditions in our hotel. The air there was so dry that if you picked up any metal object you'd get an electrical shock, which took some getting used to.

One evening I started to get terrible chest pains and had difficulty in breathing. I was so scared I sent for the assistant director as I was rolling about on the bed in agony. He tried to call the doctor and kept dropping the phone because every time he touched it he got an electric shock. In spite of the pain I started to laugh. Here was I in the process of dying and he was in terror of being electrocuted trying to use the phone. Eventually he got through and the doctor arrived. When I described my symptoms, he looked rather grave and gave me a shot of morphia.

Before passing out I overheard him telling the assistant to get an ambulance as quickly as possible as he thought it was a heart attack. Things became a bit hazy after that but eventually I remember coming to in the largest Cadillac ambulance I'd ever seen. I was in a euphoric state with the effects of the morphia and, when the driver asked if he might stop and get a hamburger, I happily agreed and asked him to get one for me too. I had a nurse in the back with me and she spent the rest of the trip feeding me bits of delicious hamburger. She even asked if I'd like the onion ring and I told her that as I didn't think I had long to live I'd better not miss the chance. Normally I hate raw onions but the effect of the drug made me love everything and everybody.

When I eventually arrived at the Cedars of Lebanon Hospital I was rushed to a cardiograph machine and, having had different electrodes stuck all over my body, I was put to bed. The next morning a very puzzled doctor entered my room and told me that there was nothing wrong with my heart and he couldn't understand why I had suffered all the symptoms of a cardiac attack. The pain in my chest had now eased but I still had a sharp pain in my back and left shoulder. He asked if I'd had any accidents in Africa and I suddenly remembered the pain in my chest and back when that heavy black body had slipped when I was lifting it. I told the doctor this and he immediately ordered X-rays of my back. These disclosed that I had damaged some vertebrae and I must have done something during work in Death Valley to cause the muscles of my back to go into spasm and give the symptoms of a heart attack. Very frightening. I suffer from that back problem to this day. I was put in traction, manipulated, given deep heat treatment and gradually the pain went.

While I was going through all this, Sam Zimbalist visited me and told me that he had inherited the job of producer on *Quo Vadis* and that he very much wanted me to play the lead. I told him of my obligation to Carol Reed and he assured me that that was no problem as *Quo Vadis* wouldn't start for quite a time. The problem was that Mayer, much as he wanted me to play the part, would not give a chance like this to anyone not under long-term contract. I told Sam that I had no intention of signing for another seven years hard labour. I was adamant and Sam left to report my decision to Mayer. Anyway it wasn't the time to discuss a long-term contract while I was lying in a hospital bed. I wanted to get fit first – that attack had scared the hell out of me.

When I was let out of hospital, Metro thought I ought to have a few days in the sun before starting the rather energetic ending of the film. They sent me to the Racquet Club in Palm Springs where I was welcomed by Charlie Farrell, the owner, whom I remembered so well in *Seventh Heaven* with Janet Gaynor. He didn't seem to have changed much, so this Palm Springs climate must have something. I spent a week lying in the sun and it was very relaxing.

My next-door neighbour was Gene Tierney who was resting there with her husband, Igor Cassini. Having drinks in the bar one day he told me how he had 'thumped' the notorious Howard Hughes for making a pass at his wife. That man's name seemed to be cropping up wherever I went. I asked him how he had dared 'thump' anyone so powerful? He told me calmly that 'Hughes bled like anyone else.' Tough character. Cassini, I mean.

Gene just sat there looking very pretty but rather sad. There was always a haunted look in her eyes, even after a few drinks. William Powell was there, too, with a very young, sportive wife who was always playing tennis with bronzed good-looking young men. He just watched. So did I. I reported back to work and everyone asked very solicitously whether I had completely recovered from my 'heart attack'. I didn't disillusion them as I thought I would get better treatment, but they soon found out I was faking and it was back to the grind again.

In a way it was sad when the picture came to an end. After all the experiences we'd gone through together we'd become very close, almost like a club. The others went their separate ways but I had still to be on call in case there were any retakes or dubbing necessary.

One day my agent rang me to tell me that Cecil B. de Mille would like to meet me as he thought I might be right for a lead in his forthcoming production of *The Greatest Show on Earth*, a film about the circus. De Mille had taken over the Ringling Brothers Circus the following day and wanted me to come out there to meet him. Fefe said he would call for me and mentioned that he would have another star with him that de Mille was also interested in.

'Who's that?' I asked.

'Hedy Lamarr,' he replied.

'Hedy Lamarr!' I almost shrieked.

'Yes, Why? Have you met her?'

'Well, kind of,' I stammered.

'Well, that's great. She's sweet, isn't she?' and he rang off. Sweet! Well, that wasn't exactly my idea of her but, more important, what was her reaction going to be when she laid eyes on that sorry excuse of a lover who had crept out of her bedroom only two years before. Oh dear!

The next day I nervously waited in my bungalow, thinking what a small world it was and dreading the outburst from Miss Lamarr when she realized whom she'd be travelling with. At last my agent was at the door and I sidled out, trying to hide behind him. As we approached the car, he stepped aside and there I was face to face with the lovely Lamarr.

'Jimmy, how wonderful to see you again, and how do you like Hollywood?' She held her face up to be kissed. Gratefully I kissed her and, breathing a sigh of relief, squeezed into the seat beside her. She looked ravishing, of course, and once more I had regrets that I'd failed so dismally on our last meeting. If only she'd kept her mouth shut. But that wasn't the way with Hedy. On the journey she was even giving instructions on how to drive the car and which route to take.

We arrived at the enormous Ringling Brothers Circus and were ushered by waiting attendants into the presence.

Cecil B. de Mille was a very overpowering character. He wore riding boots and breeches and carried a riding crop which he used to point out his different camera angles and to sweep out of his way any curious onlookers. The place was packed and the acts were in progress, but de Mille and his party moved around as if no one was there. It must have infuriated the paying public and I became very self-conscious at the remarks hurled at us to 'get the hell out of the way'. A man with a chair followed the autocratic figure of de Mille wherever he went and had the chair in position whenever the maestro sat. De Mille never looked round. He just sat, knowing that the chair would be there. I knew I would never be able to work with this man even if he should want me. I respected what he had done in the cinema. He was indeed a giant and had worked with all the great names of the movie world; those dazzling personalities I had queued up to see as a boy. But I knew I wouldn't be able to contribute to the kind of slavish adoration shown by all the people around him and which he obviously demanded from anyone working with him. To hell with it, I thought. Life's too short and, anyway, now that my debts had been paid I didn't really want to do any more acting. I just wanted to get back to England and prepare my first production. So having nothing to lose, and being fascinated with this chair business, I quietly asked the carrier how much he would take not to have it in place at a certain moment. He looked at me in horror.

'Christ, Mr Granger. I'd never work in Hollywood again.'

'I don't mean on purpose,' I whispered. 'Make it look like an accident.'

'Shit. Accident or no accident, if his arse hit the ground I'd be out,' and he quickly shoved the chair in place as de Mille sat. Oh well, it was just an idea.

Hedy had decided to stay until the end so, making our excuses, Fefe and I drove back alone. On the way he casually asked me if I would like to meet another of his clients, Miss Betty Hutton. I admired this raucous beauty, particularly her smashing pair of legs, so I said I was available. He told me he would arrange a dinner date and left.

At about this time I was getting severe headaches and my

sinuses were giving me hell. I suppose this was from all the dust I had inhaled in Africa but, whatever it was, I realized I would have to see a doctor. Unfortunately the only appointment I could get was on the morning of my date with Miss Hutton. The doctor told me that my sinuses were badly blocked and infected and that he would be forced to open them up and drain them. Not really knowing what this entailed, I told him to go ahead. He stuck some cotton wool dipped in anaesthetic up both nostrils and then took a wicked looking metal tube and pushed it up my nostril, puncturing the membrane. I thought the bloody thing had gone into my brain, but he told me not to worry as he was only going to wash me out. You can say that again, I thought, what about my date? He repeated the exercise on the other sinus and triumphantly pointed to all the 'guck' that had washed out.

'You'll be a different man now,' he told me. 'Just take these antibiotics for the next few days and everything will clear up.'

Clear up hell. I still suffer. I had seen a lot of blood in the basin and asked him if the bleeding would continue for long as I had an important date that evening. He told me he'd packed the two punctures with cotton wool and there'd be no problem.

Feeling slightly dizzy from the antibiotics and with a very 'stuffed up' feeling in my nose, I duly reported at Miss Hutton's house. She was beautifully turned out and was obviously ready for a long night on the town as she told me what she had planned. We would dine at Chasens and then go on to Ciro's to dance. I hoped my cotton wool plugs would hold out. I had a different evening planned but thought I'd better go along with her ideas on the first date. After showing me round her lovely home (everyone in Hollywood seemed to want to show you round their home immediately you set foot in the door), she asked me if I'd like to see her baby. Christ, I didn't even know she had a baby, I didn't even know she'd been married, and I certainly didn't want to be part of this cosy domestic scene.

As I reluctantly followed her to the nursery I couldn't help wondering if she'd had the sort of trouble my poor Elspeth had had. My ardour was quickly cooling as I looked at the little bundle lying in the cot. What can one say about a baby? It's a baby. They all look the same unless, of course, they're yours and then they take on very special attributes, unlike any other baby in the world. I made the usual compliment-ary remarks and then leant over the cot to have a closer look at the red wrinkled face staring up at me. At that moment one of the plugs popped out and my nose started to bleed all over the baby who naturally resented it and started to scream its lungs out. With my head held back and a handkerchief pressed to my nose I spluttered some apologies and got out of the house as quickly as possible. So much for my efforts to be a ladies' man.

The next morning Fefe rang me to ask what the hell had happened as his client had been yelling down the telephone telling him not to lumber her with any more bleeding English actors. I didn't bother to explain as in my efforts to stop laughing the other plug was threatening to pop out.

Having been informed by the studios that my services would no longer be required, I started getting ready to leave, but when I phoned Fefe to say goodbye he told me I couldn't leave until the next film had been decided.

'What film?' I asked.

'Haven't you read your contract, Jimmy? Metro has an option on another film.'

'But what other film?'

'I'm not sure, darling, but I think it's a costume picture called Ivanscott.'

'Ivanscott? What the hell's that?' And then I realized he meant *Ivanhoe*.

'Anyway, darling, Benny Thau wants to see you as he's got something interesting to tell you.'

Benny Thau was a strange, tiny man, who always spoke in

a whisper. I think this was studied as you could never sprawl back comfortably when he was speaking but were always forced to perch on the edge of your chair, leaning half over his desk to try and understand what he was saying. I gathered that he was offering me a long-term contract as the big boys had seen a rough cut of *Solomon's Mines* and were very enthusiastic. I thanked him for the honour and refused. A glint came into the steely eyes.

'You do realize, Jimmy, that we have an option for another film,' he whispered. '*Ivanhoe* will be a very important film and we had you in mind for the lead but, if we don't have you under long-term contract, we shall be forced to put you in a lesser role.'

He pushed the contract across the table and it nearly hit me in the eye as I was leaning so far forward to try and hear this last piece of good news. He pointed to a complicated legal rigmarole which, translated, meant Metro had the right to put me into any picture in any role. My bloody agent hadn't stipulated that it had to be a starring part. My fault, of course. I should have read the small print but I had stupidly left all the details to my agent. I trusted him to look after my best interests which, incidentally, would be his. I resented this 'generous' offer of a seven-year contract with a lethal body blow attached in the event I should refuse it. Politely I told him what he could do with his contract. His manner changed from benign royalty about to confer an earldom on a deserving vassal to a hard-faced bank manager refusing a loan. Apparently he had pressed an unseen button because at that moment a man appeared with a sheaf of papers.

'What about these, Mr Granger?' (I had been Jimmy until then), Benny asked.

The sheaf was prefaced by a list of everything I had purchased and put down on my hotel bill. Cash advanced for expenses, bills from various shops for clothes, booze, meals, tips, all the necessary extras we'd had on location in Africa, the cost of transporting my car to Hollywood, every single item, even down to the newspapers I'd ordered with breakfast. It came to the staggering sum of something like ten thousand dollars. I didn't have a penny as my salary was being paid in England and had gone straight to the Inland Revenue. Fefe Ferri had urged me to charge everything and assured me that MGM would be delighted to pick up the tab with those famous words, 'Not to worry', so naturally I'd thought he'd made some contractual agreement with Metro. I couldn't believe my agents had left an important item like my living expenses to the whim of Benny Thau. He then pointed out that even if Metro agreed to pay these bills, the American tax authorities would treat the result as salary and expect a hefty piece as their cut. Foreigners working in the States could not get their exit visas until all taxes had been paid. He gave me a sweet smile as he dropped this last bombshell.

My mouth went dry. Christ, unless I came to some arrangement, or managed to borrow the money, I couldn't even leave the country. I was trapped. Seeing the stricken look on my face, Benny whispered that I had nothing to worry about: everything would be taken care of. All I had to do was to sign a contract. I was leaning so far over his desk I was practically in his lap. It would have been more bearable if the SOB had shouted at me, but that bloody whisper seemed even more threatening. I told him I would think it over and left.

Entering Fefe Ferri's office I was greeted with a big kiss and congratulations. I asked Fefe if he'd please stop kissing me and lend me ten thousand dollars. I got that bank manager's look again and wearily sank into a chair.

'Why didn't you warn me? Why were you always encouraging me to charge everything? Why did you tell me Metro would be happy to pick up the tab. "Not to worry". Why?'

'Darling, I thought you understood. You didn't really think they'd pay everything, did you? Do they in England?'

He had me there. And then, of course, I realized that he'd been as anxious as Metro for me to get into debt and force me to sign up. That way he'd be guaranteed his ten per cent for seven years without having to do any more work on my behalf.

'You bastard,' I said, and left.

I walked about Beverly Hills for hours. After all we'd been through in Africa to make a good film, the discomforts, the illnesses, the dangers. I had been in large part responsible that the film had been completed at all, and here I was with infected sinuses from the dust, a permanently damaged back, and an irritated ulcer from the food. Couldn't Metro show a little appreciation and not repay me with a kick in the teeth? Then suddenly I realized how unfair I was being. Metro was showing their appreciation. They were offering me the greatest reward they could think of, a seven-year exclusive contract, and they couldn't understand why I hadn't jumped at the chance to sign. They, quite rightly from their point of view, thought I was being difficult and ungrateful. How often that word 'difficult' would be applied to me for wanting to lead my own life, for wanting some kind of individuality. But they didn't think as I did and couldn't understand my misery at the thought of having to cut my roots and leave everything I loved, my mother, my children, my friends, which included my ex-wife, my home, my country, and most of all, my Jean. She was still under contract to Rank and wouldn't be able to come with me. Oh well, I was apparently never to be a producer. Once more *House by the Sea* would have to be shelved.

We all met in Benny's office and the interminable wrangles started about the details of a seven-year contract. In order to repay my 'debts' they agreed to buy my London apartment and assured me that they would keep it for visiting MGM VIPs, myself included, so that maybe one day I could buy it back. By an 'oversight' it was sold six months later.

Before the final signature I made one stipulation. I had heard that *Scaramouche* was being prepared as a musical for Gene Kelly and I insisted that that film should be written into my contract as a vehicle for myself, and not as a musical. I remembered the little boy with the upset stomach being so thrilled at this romantic adventure story, and I wanted the chance to thrill other little boys – and girls too, for that matter. I was given time for the Carol Reed film and wouldn't have to report back to Metro for six months. Naturally there were the usual publicity blurbs about this momentous event and I was to encounter for the first time those two horrors of Hollywood, the gossip columnists Louella Parsons and Hedda Hopper. Puffed up, egotistical, vain, conceited monsters. I wondered why my publicity man, Johnny, was shaking even before he ushered me into their presence.

'You don't understand, Jim. They have the power of life and death out here. They could get me fired tomorrow if I upset them.'

Like hell they can, I thought to myself. Parsons was a bloated, over made-up, simpering, inebriated, pathetic creature, who was not basically unkind, just overwhelmed by her power; Hopper was a different matter, tall, horse-faced, arrogant, funny, dangerous, with a penchant for outrageous hats. If she disliked you she was vicious and unforgiving, and wouldn't miss a chance to inject some bitchy remark about you, your family and your films into her column. Needless to say, there would be fireworks between us in the not too distant future.

17

Pandro S. Berman, one of the producers at Metro, approached me one day in the commissary just before my departure for England. He had made a very exciting film some years before called *Gunga Din*, with Cary Grant, Victor McLaglen and Douglas Fairbanks, Jr. He told me he wanted to do a remake and would like me for the lead; the script wasn't completed but all would be ready by the time I returned. I wasn't used to being approached about a film while having lunch, but told him I remembered the film well, it sounded an exciting idea and I would be happy to talk with him when I came back. He had a very good name, having been responsible for producing the Fred Astaire-Ginger Rogers epics, when quite a young man, so I was flattered that he should approach me soon after my new commitment. I wasn't to feel so flattered when I read the script.

I asked my agents if they would be kind enough to look out for a small house for me to rent on my return, since I would have to move out of the Beverly Hills Hotel. As I have said, I hate flying and yet in the last nine months I had flown thirty-five thousand miles and was off on another fourteen thousand mile round trip within a few months: almost fifty thousand miles in one year. That doesn't seem much today with fast jet planes, but in those days it meant a lot of hours in the air, far too many for my liking.

As I passed through English Customs I was acutely aware of all the lovely Cockney accents, mixed with others from all over England and thought sadly that in a few months I wouldn't be hearing them again for years. I seemed to see the countryside with different eyes. I'd never realized it was so green, so gentle, so cosy. I was becoming homesick already at the thought of living in Los Angeles, not at all gentle or cosy. As we approached London I was immediately at home. This was where I had been born and spent thirty-five years of my life. I was much more aware of all the beautiful old buildings, old churches and museums, Buckingham Palace, St Paul's Cathedral, the parks and gardens, Piccadilly Circus and the theatres. There was nothing old in Los Angeles, no traditions, so sprawled out, so aptly called fifty towns in search of a city. I had loved it when I first arrived, as I knew I was there only on a visit. I realized that it was exciting and new but God, it was so different.

I was practically in tears at what I had done when I entered my lovely apartment and gave Louisa and the 'Cog' a hug. Neither would be coming with me. Wendy had her own life to lead and a boy friend in the offing. Louisa was Hungarian and there was no chance of her emigrating with me so that she could work out there. How I would miss her lovely cooking and thoughtfulness. I remembered her outraged look when I returned from Africa. I had lent the apartment to a good friend of mine, Commander Kehoe who, with his chum Errol Flynn, had apparently held Bacchanalian parties that had deeply shocked her and she had only stayed on in loyalty to me and, in her words, to protect the Mr Sir's silver. I couldn't see Errol pinching my silver but apparently anything had been possible in her eyes.

Elspeth came round with the children and I felt a complete deserter when I told her I would be leaving for seven years. Of course I would be coming over to see everyone from time to time and they could all visit me, but it wouldn't be the same. My children needed a father, someone who would lovingly kick their behinds from time to time. I didn't want them to think I was leaving them because I didn't love them, but how could children of that age understand contracts, careers and income tax? They only understood one thing. I was going away. I just hoped it would all work out. It was the same with Jeannie. I tried to explain how I had been trapped;

what an ass I'd made of myself. She only had three more films to make for Rank, but they might be spread over the next two years. There was one bright spot. Paramount would be distributing one of her films and she would be visiting America for a publicity tour in about six months' time, so at least that was something to look forward to.

Unfortunately there was a problem about Carol Reed's film. Locations were to be in the Pacific or somewhere, and, owing to the climate, it had had to be postponed for three months. This meant I was to lose the chance of working with one of the finest directors in the business, but it gave me an opportunity to carry out another cherished plan.

Big John had bought the Lindsay II, our boat in the South of France, so Mike and I had a little cash to play with. I knew I couldn't take this money out of the sterling area and, as cash always burns a hole in my pocket and, having four months to kill before reporting back to Metro, I thought to myself that here was the perfect chance to go on a safari in Africa. Extravagant maybe, but I couldn't resist it as I longed to see Kenya again, free of the control of a film company. I'd be able to visit all the friends I'd made out there and be in a position to invite them to my camp and return some of their hospitality. I explained my longing to Jean and told her I knew I should stay in London to be near her but that I would only be able to see her in the evenings when she returned from work and that anyway she always fell asleep the moment she got home. She understood and I felt like a naughty schoolboy playing hookey as she watched me excitedly packing my things.

A phone call to Eric Rungren in Nairobi had fixed the safari and within a few days I once more found myself on a plane going back to the country I had so thankfully left only three months before. But this time it was going to be different. I would be my own boss and wouldn't have a po-faced director telling me what to do and where to go.

There has been enough about Africa in this book and so

the story of that amazing experience where I managed to get myself charged by a furious lioness with cubs, by a rogue elephant and a very bad-tempered rhinoceros, apart from being operated on by the famous 'flying doctors' who unfortunately had forgotten to bring the anaesthetic, will have to be told elsewhere.

On my return home I kept poor, tired Jean up till all hours of the morning recounting my experiences and narrow escapes. I was talking to myself most of the time as Jean would be quietly asleep in my arms, but then the day came when once again Jean and I had to be parted and, having packed up the few things I was going to take with me, some paintings, china, silver, books and a few odds and ends, not much to show for being a top star in Britain for seven years, I sadly kissed her goodbye and flew off to my new life in California.

I arrived back to the Beverly Hills Hotel because of course my agent had failed or forgotten to find a house for me, and the first person I ran into when I reported to the studio was my friend Sam. I hadn't been able to see him when I left as he'd been in Italy preparing for *Quo Vadis*. He told me how he'd tried to get me into the film, but Robert Taylor had been cast and Mayer had refused to replace him.

'You told me you weren't going to sign, Jim. If you had, it would have been easy as you were the first choice. What made you change your mind and why the hell didn't you tell me?'

'Sam, you weren't here so I couldn't tell you, and if you've got three or four hours I'll explain why I signed, though even then you wouldn't believe me.'

Pandro C. Berman's office was right opposite Sam's in The Iron Lung so, wishing him fun in Rome and telling him to be sure to sample Alfredo's fettucini, I went to see Pandro.

He told me he had got together a wonderful cast for *Soldiers Three*, as the epic was to be called, including Walter Pidgeon,

Robert Newton, Cyril Cusack, David Niven and Greta Gynt. I knew that dear old Bob Newton was one of the biggest drunks in the business, so life wasn't going to be dull. Tay Garnett, a real old timer, was to direct, with Yakima Canutt as the second unit director. This man's name was a byword in Hollywood for his stunts, having done the most dangerous one doubling for John Wayne in Ford's *Stagecoach*. He had been champion cowboy at all the rodeos for years and was built like the proverbial brick shithouse. It was a pleasure to work with this big gentle Indian, and we became good friends. But the script. Oh dear! If Metro had planned to ruin my career they couldn't have chosen a better subject. I went to Benny Thau with my problem and asked if my first film under the new contract couldn't be something more suitable. His answer absolutely rocked me.

'Don't worry, Jimmy, if it's as bad as you say, nobody will see it so it won't do you any harm, will it?'

My jaw dropped as I looked at him in amazement. He couldn't be serious, could he? This was one of the heads of this vast empire, someone responsible for the personal handling of the stars. As I continued to look at him in silence he pressed that unseen button again and Eddie Mannix, L.K. Sidney and Doré Schary entered. They started to congratulate me on the success of *Solomon's Mines* and told me that with what they had planned for me I would be the new Number 1 on the lot, as Gable's last two pictures had bombed.

This was supposed to be a compliment, but it just disgusted me. To their amazement I told them that I was shocked they could speak so contemptuously about a man of Gable's stature, a man who had made millions for them. They had pushed him into two unsuitable, second-rate pictures, which of course had failed, but the fault had been theirs not his, and added that the film they were pushing me into would also fail. They looked at me as if I was out of my head. As I left in the deafening silence I realized I'd made another mistake. I really must study the book, 'How to make friends and influence people.'

I consulted Cary Grant to see if he could give me any tips but, having read the script, he advised me to do the best I could and get it over with. Tay Garnett, the director, was enthusiastic and told me it was one of the funniest slapstick comedies he'd ever read. That was just the point. After my disastrous experience with that lovely French actress, Edwige Feuillère, in *Woman Hater*, I knew comedy wasn't exactly my line. You don't build up a reputation as a romantic actor with slapstick comedies. Walter Pidgeon was a veteran and, being under contract, had no say in the matter, but what the hell David Niven, who was playing a supporting part, was doing, I can't imagine. He must have been very hard up.

Work on the film was pleasant enough with Tay laughing hysterically at every scene we shot. If everybody in the audience had laughed half as much when the film was shown we would have had a winner, but of course they didn't. Bob Newton was absolutely impossible, bless him, and arrived practically every morning incoherent with booze. Tay was very understanding and would shoot around him until we could pour enough coffee down his throat to get him at least half way sober. It's difficult to work with an actor who when not incoherently drunk is suffering from a frightful hangover. Yakima Canutt was a joy to work with but was surprised when I insisted on doing my own fight scene. He had thought an English actor would need a double. I don't know why the Americans should think we English are so effete. Maybe we had exported too many horizontal heavyweight boxers, but I was going to prove that at least one of them wasn't and in all my future films I insisted on doing as much of my own stunt work as possible.

While this masterpiece was being made, preparations went ahead for an epic production of *Scaramouche*. The producer was to be a man called Carey Wilson who had the reputation that if you asked him the time he'd tell you how a Swiss watch was made. I soon realized what that meant when I met him. He didn't stop talking for one second, but the appalling thing was not the verbal diarrhoea but what he was saying.

'Now, Stoo' (I had told him that my friends called me Jimmy but he took no notice), 'I know this is a costume picture but I want you to give the impression you're wearing grey flannel trousers. I don't want any of this waving hands around and taking snuff.' (Bang goes my training as Charles Surface, I thought to myself.) 'And another thing. This film is about the French Revolution but we're not going to have any of that storming the Bastille shit. That's been done. Forget the revolution. We're going to make a rip-roaring comedy.'

Holy Mackerel. I'd been looking forward to making this romantic costume film about the French Revolution and here was the producer telling me to forget about the costume and the Revolution. Also, I had been hearing the words Andy Hardy every now and then thrown in to convince me on some point. Then in a flash I got it. Of course. This was the producer of the Andy Hardy series and damn good they were, but not exactly the same type of film as *Scaramouche*. Now I began to understand his attitude but I hoped he wasn't expecting me to play the part like Mickey Rooney. I tottered out of the room with my head buzzing from the torrent of nonsensical rubbish and made my way to Sam's office. I poured out my troubles to him but he was too excited about the reception of *Solomon's Mines* to give me much sympathy. He was clutching a bunch of notices and read one of them out to me.

'This is from a very tough lady called Dorothy Kilgallen of the *New York Journal* who says: "I lived through the Clark Gable vogue, the Robert Taylor excitement, the Van Johnson hysteria and I did some fluttering over Gregory Peck. But so help me I have never seen anything like the way ladies with high boiling points and high intelligence are falling to pieces over Mr Granger.'' Then she quotes: ''He's divine...makes me sick to my stomach.'' ''I've dreamed of him every night for six weeks.'' ''The greatest thing since sliced bread.'' ''He made me feel as if I were drowning.'' How does that grab you, Jim?'

It didn't really 'grab' me, it embarrassed me. Then Sam gave me the rest of the notices to read and they were all extraordinarily good. Being a new face I received very flattering praise: the script had been good, the locations staggering and that strip of leopard skin round my hat had done the trick. According to the press I was now accepted as one of the top stars in America. I wondered dismally how long it would last after films like *Soldiers Three* and the proposed Carey Wilson idea of *Scaramouche*. Anyway, I was happy for Sam and the crew that all our efforts had paid off and we had a box office smash. From Sam's office I dropped in on Benny Thau and told him that in view of the producer's ideas I would like to be released from *Scaramouche*, but at the look of astounded outrage on his face I quickly got the hell out before he could hit me with a suspension.

Johnny Rothwell, my publicity man, phoned me at home that evening, home being a little house I had rented way out in Santa Monica, to tell me that his opposite number at Paramount had called him from New York with the news that Jean had arrived. Jean, I must point out, was not the greatest letter writer. In fact, in the twelve years we were together, I think I had ten letters from her, less than one a year wasn't really overdoing it, especially as during those twelve years we spent about three of them apart. There had been no way for her to phone or wire me as I hadn't yet told her my new address, and messages to the studio would go to the fan department and be lost among the sacks of mail which apparently I was now receiving. Johnny and the Paramount boys who were, of course, already captivated by this little English beauty, wanted to work out a surprise for her. An airport would be too public so they had the idea that I should take the train to Chicago and they would have Jean there on some pretext or other and we would travel together on the famous Twentieth Century to New York. I jumped at the idea. The thought of seeing my little Jean again pushed all my studio problems into the background.

Johnny and I booked two staterooms on the 'Super Chief' and started the almost three-day trip to Chicago. I remember in later years Spencer Tracy telling me that he would like to spend the rest of his life living at Claridges where the service and comfort were so outstanding. Well, I wouldn't have minded spending at least three months every year travelling backwards and forwards on the 'Super Chief'. It was a fantastic experience. The stateroom was large, the bed comfortable, with a choice of piped-in music day and night, and the service memorable. I had a lovely old black gentleman with grizzled white hair looking after me; he seemed to adopt me the moment I stepped aboard. He was always popping in to see to my comforts and to have a chat if he thought I was lonely. I remember him coming in on the first morning to tell me that we were approaching Gallup, New Mexico, and would I like him to get me some fresh baked bread as we would be stopping there for a few minutes. As the train started up again I found myself tucking into an amazing American breakfast of fried eggs, bacon and sausages, flapjacks smothered in butter and syrup, pushed down with hunks of steaming fresh baked bread. I think I put on five pounds on that three day trip and had excruciating indigestion practically all the way. He must have thought I needed fattening up as the size of the steaks he brought me for dinner were challenging even to a man of my voracious appetite, but I never disappointed him and with a satisfied smile he would clear away the empty plates.

The third day came and we were rattling into Chicago. Johnny ordered me to stay put and not to show my face at the window as it would spoil Jean's surprise. I waited excitedly and suddenly Jean was standing there at the door of the stateroom with two Paramount chaps proudly showing off this surprise present, me. Jean's reaction was to break into floods of tears and I saw the look of amazed disappointment on the faces of the escorts as I grabbed her in my arms.

'Jesus, kid, I thought this would make you happy. What are you crying about?' one of them asked.

'I always cry when I'm really happy,' Jean snuffled. 'Ask Jimmy.'

I assured them that this was so and thanked them for their thoughtfulness. It was indeed a wonderful surprise.

'Nothing's too good for that little lady,' they assured me. 'She's the greatest.'

I introduced her to my hovering black friend and of course she captivated him too.

'You have mighty fine taste, sir, if you'll allow me,' and then with a sweet smile to Jean, 'And may I compliment you, Miss Jean? He's a mighty fine gentleman.'

This may have been because of the twenty dollar tip, but I was certain of one thing. He was a mighty fine gentleman, too.

Our love-making on that trip to New York was one of the most difficult I'd every experienced as I kept falling out of the narrow bunk every time the train bumped and swayed over the points, and I arrived in New York covered in bruises.

New York wasn't nearly so frightening with Jean at my side as we window-shopped all the way down 5th Avenue, gaping at the skyscrapers, and I showed her off proudly at '21'. Johnny asked me if I'd like to see the fight between Joe Louis and a newcomer called Rocky Marciano. Would I not! Joe Louis had been another of my heroes and I had seen practically all his fights on film and had met him during the war on his trip to London. I had even been in the ring with him for a publicity shot, but thankfully not with the gloves on. I remembered going into the ring with the gloves on once with another world champion. I had been persuaded to give an exhibition bout with Freddie Mills in front of the thousands of employees at the Ford Motorworks at Dagenham. I had begged Freddie to allow me to spar with eight-ounce gloves in order to look more professional but eventually had to wear the sixteen ounce which were like pillows and made me look clumsy. Freddie told me later that he had no intention of risking me 'laying one on him' with an eight ounce.

'You're a heavyweight, Jim, and I'm only cruiser-weight and you can hit. I could tell that when we sparred.'

I looked at my friend Freddie and his jaw like a granite block and assured him that I would never have 'laid one on him' even if I'd had the chance, which was doubtful.

Anyway, the thought of seeing Joe Louis in person at Madison Square Garden was a chance I couldn't miss and I persuaded Jean to accompany me, as I assured her Joe would make short work of this clumsy brawler, Marciano. It was a sad evening and we were both miserable when Joe was being counted out. He had come into the ring overweight and a mere shadow of that tigerish figure he had been a few years before. At the beginning he had made Rocky look stupid as he easily picked off his clumsy swings, but gradually his arms tired and inevitably Rocky finally connected and that was the end of poor Joe. Like many other boxing fans I had misjudged this street brawler Rocky, as he went on to become the only unbeaten world heavyweight champion in the history of the ring and the last white champion we were to see (I don't count Johansson). Jean and I sadly went back to our separate suites at the Waldorf.

The next day I received a message from the coast to report back, as Doré Schary wished to see me about something. Trouble, I thought to myself. That night holding Jean in my arms, both sad at the thought of another separation, I told her my thoughts.

'Jeannie, I'm fifteen and a half years older than you, I'm grouchy and difficult to live with but I love you. Do you think you'd like to risk it and get married?'

Her answer was floods of tears, so I knew she was happy about the idea. We sat up half the night planning our next move. She'd come back with me to Hollywood where we would announce our engagement and then she'd fly back to London to work something out with Rank. She had no intention of trying to get out of her commitments and we both agreed that we would just have to face up to the inevitable separations. I explained to Jean that she'd have to wait a bit for her engagement ring as I would have to work something out with my business manager who kept me very short, thus preventing me spending the money I would have to pay out in taxes. This strict control of the stars out here was another new experience for me. I never saw the huge sums of money I earned. The studios paid my salary direct to my agents who, after deducting their ten per cent, passed the remainder on to my business manager who would bank it in two different accounts: ninety per cent into the tax account and ten per cent into my current account. The business manager would turn up weekly with my allowance and cheques for me to countersign for rent, shop accounts, servants' salaries, car, television, refrigerator etc., it being impossible for me to pay cash for anything, and for this dreary service he received five per cent of everything I earned. How could I persuade him to let loose enough to pay for a diamond ring? Screw him. It was my money and I'd just have to dip into the tax account, a fatal mistake as I was to find out to my cost. I never seemed able to catch up again.

I took Jean along to meet Cary and Betsy Grant and told him my problems.

'Wait a minute, Jim,' he said. 'I'm sure I've got a diamond ring here somewhere.'

To my amazement he went to a safe and started ladling out all sorts of jewellery, pearls, gold cigarette cases, gold compacts, brooches, pendants, earrings, and then with a triumphant, 'Here it is', showed me a beautiful little diamond ring. He told me I could have it at a very reasonable price and generously suggested I could pay him back when I could. It was a beautiful stone, but it was 'little', being only about four carats and I, broke as I was, wanted Jean to have something in the neighbourhood of eight carats. Cary told me I was quite right, Jean deserved nothing but the best, and he introduced me to a dealer who came up with a very nice looking stone of the required size and, having persuaded my business manager to part with some of my money, I was able to present Jean with her first diamond. She was thrilled. But both my connoisseur friend Cary and I had been taken in. When later I had the ring valued for insurance I discovered that it had a flaw. Well, it wasn't exactly a flaw, it was a chasm.

My meeting with my boss Doré Schary wasn't all sweetness and light as in spite of his undeniable charm there was always the 'big stick' hovering in the background. He told me how upset he was at my decision not to do *Scaramouche* but that the studio had decided not to suspend me if I would agree to do a film called *The Light Touch*, written and to be directed by a chap named Richard Brooks. He had just made his first film, *Crisis*, starring Cary Grant, and I wasn't particularly enamoured of the thought of working with him as I had heard he had reduced a small part actor to tears. That actor was Ramon Novarro. The thought of anyone reducing one of my childhood heroes to tears filled me with anger, but that's Hollywood. When a star is down he's fair game for anyone. I had to agree in order to avoid suspension and went along to meet Brooks. His opening words reminded me of the illustrious Compton Bennett.

'I have to tell you that I wanted Cary Grant.'

He puffed away at his pipe as I took this in. I answered that, having read his script, I could understand why the much-in-demand Cary Grant had refused to do it, but as we were both under contract we'd better make the best of a bad deal. Oh dear, I thought. Here I go again. Why couldn't I keep my bloody mouth shut? Anyway Brooks seemed impervious to my sarcasm and told me proudly what wonderful locations he had picked out in Sicily and Tunis and then showed me photographs of a very attractive young lady.

'That's Anna Maria Pierangeli who'll play opposite you. Doesn't speak very good English but we'll get round that.'

I spoke very good English but wondered how the hell I would get round his dialogue.

18

Howard Strickland, head of MGM publicity, had made the announcement of our engagement and the calls started to come in from Louella, Hedda, Sheilah Graham, Harrison Carroll, all demanding exclusive stories of the marriage. Strickland warned us not to give any details or any promises to anyone, as that would only antagonize the rest and, what was more important, the British Press would be very upset to read of our marriage in an American column, so we spent our last days together dodging these leeches and not answering the phone. Jean had to return to England for a week or two and boarded the plane, proudly flashing her slightly flawed diamond.

The Press was out in force to meet her at London airport and were horrified to see a weeping Jean in her mother's arms as she came through Customs. The bastards had taken her ring away. This was bureaucracy gone mad. Jean was Britain's most popular female star. Everyone, including the Customs officials, must have seen the headlines announcing her engagement to me. Did they really think she was smuggling her engagement ring into England to sell at a profit? She explained that she was only staying for a couple of weeks and would guarantee to take the ring with her when she returned to America. No, replied the hard-faced unrelenting officials of HM Customs. She must either pay a huge amount of duty or leave the ring with them. I heard all this from a still weeping Jean when I called her from Hollywood. After I had got over my natural fury I told her how sorry I was that her engagement finger was still bare.

'No, it's not, darling,' Jean told me. 'I'm using a piece of string that you tied up a parcel with. That's my engagement ring, a piece of your string.' I was practically in tears now, too. Poor Jeannie, she'd been so proud of her ring. How could anyone be so cruel? But there's always someone with a little power ready to throw his weight around.

I had to dip into more of the tax money as the transatlantic phone calls weren't cheap and we'd talk together practically every evening. Naturally the English Press were onto her all the time to give details of the date and place of the wedding. She said she didn't know and she'd be as pleased as them when she did. That shut them up.

While she was away I approached Benny Thau about a loan to buy a house. Surely Metro wouldn't want one of its top stars to move into a rented house after his marriage because he couldn't afford to buy his own home? Not good publicity. I tried to sound as plausible as possible and wished I had a good agent to handle it. But if Fefe joined in, it would probably end up with me buying a house for him. Benny eyed me coldly and then muttered something about *Scaramouche*. I pretended not to hear, which wasn't difficult in his case, but he went on whispering about how upset everybody was that I had turned it down.

'Now, Benny,' I said, 'about the house?'

'Now, Jimmy,' he answered, 'about *Scaramouche*?'

I got the message.

'All right, Benny, but please, for God's sake change the producer.'

He promised he would see what he could do about both the house and the producer.

As I was leaving The Iron Lung I saw a very tall, good-looking man approaching me. He introduced himself as Bert Allenberg, head of the William Morris Agency, and asked if I had a minute as he would like to discuss something with me. Over a drink, he asked whether Jean had a good agent? I told him her situation with Rank but that didn't deter him.

'She'll be free soon and then she'll need the best agent in the business.'

'And you think you're the best?' I asked.

'No, I don't think I'm the best. I know I'm the best.'

We looked at each other a moment and then burst into laughter. I liked this charmer. I liked his quiet arrogance. In fact I liked everything about him. I promised him I would arrange a meeting with Jean directly she returned. When they met she liked Bert as much as I did. For the rest of his life he managed her career, looked after her interests and behaved like a father to her. He became one of my best friends and did a lot to restore my faith in human nature, especially agents.

Strickland was again on our backs about not informing the Press of the place and date of our marriage. Jean asked why we couldn't just go to the nearest church and have a normal wedding? Strickland assured us that that was not the way things were done in Hollywood. He had arranged all the details of Clark Gable's secret marriage to Carole Lombard most successfully. The Press received due notification after the event, when the newly-weds were safely away and so they were able to have their honeymoon in peace and quiet. I pointed out that we were nowhere near as newsworthy, but Strickland replied that we were newsworthy enough. Again we took our problems to Cary and Betsy. I think they both liked the undercover intrigue of this romance and we sat up until all hours discussing different plans.

Suddenly Cary said, 'I know who'll arrange it. Why didn't I think of it before? Howard Hughes!'

That name again. The man who had occupied the bungalow below mine when I first arrived in Hollywood, who had been 'thumped' by Igor Cassini for making a pass at Gene Tierney, the man whose chief lawyer had so many capped teeth.

'Why would he want to help us?' I asked.

'Don't worry, Jim. He's a very good friend of mine and he'd get a hell of a kick out of this sort of intrigue as he hates the columnists too. Just leave it to me. All your troubles are over.'

Famous last words. Our troubles had just begun.

A few days later Strickland was on the phone.

'Well, you two, you seem to have powerful friends. Get ready to leave at a moment's notice. I'll give you the details later. But it seems you're going to be married in Tucson, Arizona.'

I told this to Jean.

'Where's that? In America?'

Strickland assured us it was.

'What about Mike Wilding?' I asked. 'We want him to be best man and he's in New York.'

'Tell him to stand by,' said Strickland and rang off.

We called Mike who sounded a bit confused, but promised he'd 'stand by'. Jean and I looked at each other a moment. I knew she was thinking the same thing. Marriage was a pretty personal affair and ours seemed to be entirely under the control of an invisible multi-millionaire and the head of MGM publicity. What a crazy situation. I think we both started to have second thoughts at that moment, but Jean broke the rather gloomy silence by saying that we'd better pack. So we packed – among other things. If you're hiding in a hotel suite with a beautiful girl packing isn't the only thing on your mind.

The call came.

'I'll pick you up in about half an hour and take you to a private airfield. Tell you all the details when I see you.'

Strickland sounded very mysterious. We got our things together, not really knowing quite what to take with us. It was December 1950 and it was cold in Los Angeles but what was the temperature in Tucson? To hell with it, we'd find out when we got there. There came a long blast on a horn and we went out with our bags. An enormous Cadillac was waiting with a driver wearing dark glasses holding the door for us. I wondered what he was doing at nine o'clock on a winter's morning wearing dark glasses? Anyway it added to the intrigue. We found Strickland tucked away in the back and he filled us in.

'You're going to fly to Tucson. A car will meet you and take you to the Arizona Inn. You'll check in there under the names of Smith and Jones.'

'Which is which?' I asked.

'Take your pick,' he replied, laughing rather hysterically. 'Someone will call you and tell you what the next move is. Apparently you're going to be married in the home of a lawyer friend of Howard Hughes.'

'In a lawyer's home?' we both exclaimed.

'Yes. Hughes has arranged everything.'

Jesus! Couldn't we have any say in our own marriage? I could see the disappointment on Jean's face, as I know she had pictured a little church somewhere and the thought of a lawyer's home wasn't too inviting. I was about to tell Strickland to forget the whole thing and we'd just live in sin when the car pulled into a field and there was a Convair waiting for us. Apparently Hughes manufactured them as a side-line. Before we could tell Strickland anything we were being buckled into our seats by a very charming stewardess and the plane was revving up. We waved to our poor press agent and, if I'd been in his shoes, I'd have been praying for the day of retirement so that I could wash my hands of all this bullshit with movie actors. During the flight the stewardess fussed over us and told us we'd just love Tucson as it was a real keen town, whatever that meant. During this weird flight Jean and I sat, nervously holding hands, wondering if there was anybody at the controls. Maybe Hughes was manipulating them from some remote centre in Los Angeles? We never did see the pilots behind the closed doors to the cockpit because after landing and we'd got off, the plane was already taxiing away and we had no chance to go round to the front to thank them.

Another enormous Cadillac met us and again the driver was wearing dark glasses but, this time at least, there was some sun. We seemed to have landed in the middle of a desert with a small town in the distance. On the horizon strangely-coloured mountains surrounded us in a complete silent circle. We saw small wild cactus wherever we looked and huge saguaros standing up like policemen directing traffic. We drove along a dusty desert track and came to a highway sweeping away to the south in a seemingly endless straight line. Our driver told us it led to the border town of Nogales and beyond that was Mexico, but we turned north and eventually reached the small cow town of Tucson. To us it looked just like a film set with high-heeled Stetson-hatted cowboys sauntering down the streets. The shops offered saddles and hand-tooled gunbelts in their windows and there were bars with colourful names like 'Dead Man's Hand', 'The Quick Draw', and 'The Last Chance'. Quite a change from the Old Brompton Road, London.

We swept through the town and out into the desert again and pulled up outside a Mexican-style building. This was the Arizona Inn. The foyer had Indian rugs on the floors and hunting trophies, Indian and Mexican artefacts on the walls, while the bar leading off the foyer had swing doors like the saloons we'd seen in so many Westerns. We were welcomed by the manager, dressed Western style, with a turquoise studded belt and a strange leather thong held by a turquoise buckle round his tight-fitting shirt-collar in place of a tie. Very picturesque. We registered with the fictitious names and were led out through a patio to our bungalow. The manager told us that the adjoining one was reserved for our friend Mr Brown. So we were to be Smith, Jones and Brown. Not very original.

We'd barely started to unpack when we heard the door of the bungalow next to ours slam and knew that 'Mr Brown' had arrived. We rushed in to welcome him and were met by a very dazed, white-faced Mike.

'What in God's name is going on?' he asked.

We tried to explain that this was the Hollywood way of

228

arranging a secret marriage and how was his trip? He told us that at three o'clock in the morning he'd received a call to be ready to leave in half an hour. A black Cadillac had arrived at the door and taken him to a private airfield. We asked if the driver wore dark glasses.

'Yes, now I come to think of it, he did. How did you know?'

We told him we were psychic.

'Then I found I was the only passenger in an enormous plane. A stewardess came up and thrust a note into my hand which told me to register at the Arizona Inn under the name of Brown. I spent the next nine hours watching the stewardess snoring in a seat up front. I couldn't sleep at all as I was so confused. Anyway here I am and congratulations. I hope you'll both be very happy.'

Poor Mike. But what organization. Our trip from L.A. had taken three hours, Mike's nine hours and yet we'd both arrived within ten minutes of each other. This Hughes was really something. Mike asked plaintively if he might be allowed a drink and, leaving Jean to finish her unpacking, we took off to the 'saloon'. We were greeted by a mustachioed, long-haired barman who looked just like Wild Bill Hickok. As we thirstily downed our drinks I felt a hand on my shoulder and a voice said, 'Howdy folks. Welcome to Tucson.'

We turned in astonishment and saw a tall figure wearing a Stetson, tinted glasses and carrying a forty-five on his hip supported by a bullet-studded belt. He wore smartly pressed khakis and high-heeled cowboy boots.

'This is Sergeant Thompson of the Highway Patrol,' the barman introduced us. Highway Patrol? Did he need all that artillery to control speeding cars? We'd better pay our bills here or we'd never leave the State alive. We hastily finished our drinks and left.

That afternoon the Reception called us and told us a car was waiting for us. It wasn't a Cadillac but the driver was wearing dark glasses. He drove us to a very pretty house on the outskirts of town and a matronly figure welcomed us at the door.

'Come in, come in. How nice to meet you. Mr Hughes has explained everything and it's all been taken care of.'

I'll bet, I thought to myself. We were shown into the drawing-room and our hostess explained that this was where the marriage would take place.

'I'm terribly sorry my husband can't be here to welcome you but he's just had a riding accident and broken his leg. So untimely. Do come up and meet him.'

We trooped upstairs and were introduced to the bedridden lawyer who had his plastered leg in traction suspended from the ceiling. He peered round the plaster and introduced himself, apologizing for his condition and asking us not to mention his accident to Mr Hughes as he might not take it kindly. I gathered from this remark that Hughes's employees were not allowed to break their legs when they were on the job. The whole scene was getting weirder by the minute. Promising him we wouldn't say a word we went downstairs again. Our hostess then offered Mike and Jean tea as she told me I had an appointment with the clergyman who would officiate at the wedding the following day. The car took me to a very modern-looking building with a small cross stuck up on the roof. Apparently this was the church. A small, mild-looking man, dressed in Western-style khakis, but with no gun visible, took me into a book-lined room and, sitting me down, told me that he'd have to ask me certain questions.

'Mr Granger' (well at least he knew my name), 'I gather you are a divorced man. Now I must satisfy myself that you are not an adulterer, otherwise I could not in all conscience join you in holy matrimony to some unsuspecting girl.' What was this sanctimonious twerp talking about? Jean an unsuspecting girl? Again I was about to jump up and tell everyone what they could do about this bloody marriage and then I had second thoughts. We'd come so far it would be a shame to blow it now. I explained as calmly as I could that, although technically I had committed adultery in order to obtain a divorce, in the eyes of God I hadn't. This seemed to satisfy him and his manner became more affable. As I left, he called after me, 'See you in church.' I turned in surprise and said I thought we were to be married in a house?

'Just my little joke, son.'

With jokes like that, I thought, you'll never get your own comedy programme on TV.

I picked up Jean and Mike and, promising our hostess that we'd be on time the next morning for the main event, we returned thankfully to the Inn. By now we were all feeling the effects of the journey and the dashing about. Arizona has the most wonderful climate and the combination of the altitude of 2500 feet after coming from sea level and the dry, crystal clear desert air sent even Jean and me to bed early. Mike, poor devil, having started his day at three o'clock that morning, was already tucked up. We decided that at least we should be celibate that night, as marriage was only a few hours away, but next morning, while Jean was prancing around half-naked preparing herself for the great moment, she looked so adorable that I couldn't resist it. I was slightly weak at the knees from this effort as we all got into the car and drove to our wedding.

Our hostess took us into the drawing-room and introduced us to two charming middle-aged ladies, beautifully dressed alike, and holding identical bouquets, telling Jean that these were her bridesmaids. She'd thought of everything. In all the confusion I hadn't even thought of getting a bouquet for Jean, so one of the bridesmaids handed over hers. The room had been filled with flowers and, although it was a sweet thought, it looked more like a funeral parlour. We took our places in front of the parson who was now suitably dressed and the ceremony began. I could see the two bridesmaids and a couple of friends who were acting as witnesses eyeing us both all through the proceedings. They'd obviously been told that these were two famous film stars who were eloping, but couldn't place us and were wondering what all the fuss was about. Presumably *Solomon's Mines* hadn't reached Tucson as yet.

Mike, of course, lost the ring and, when he eventually found it in the first pocket he'd searched, I couldn't get it on Jean's finger. She started giggling, which I thought very inappropriate on this solemn occasion, and I started to feel sick. All in all a not very orthodox wedding. It was well organized with a lot of thought going into it on our hostess's part, but I just didn't feel married. It was like a scene from a film without the cameras.

At last it was over and in a thick Western accent the parson pronounced us man and wife. Of course champagne had been laid on and Jean, whose giggling now was almost hysteria, swallowed hers the wrong way and started to choke. After that she got the hiccups and I went to the lavatory and threw up. What a wedding. I returned and gave the parson a handsome contribution for his church fund and kissed the bridesmaids who by this time were giggling as helplessly as Jean. We visited our crippled host where more champagne was produced and he assured us that he was at our disposal any time. I told him we weren't planning another marriage in the near future and, thanking them all, 'Smith, Brown and Jones' were driven back to the Inn. We had to return almost immediately as we'd forgotten to sign the register, so of course more bottles were opened and by the time we left we were all thoroughly pissed, especially our hostess who, with her flowered hat falling over one eye, tearfully told us she'd never witnessed anything so beautiful. Later that evening we all remarked on the kindness of those sweet people who had let their private home be invaded by total strangers. We should all have gone back the next day to thank them and give them a memento but for some reason, mostly thoughtlessness, we didn't, for which I feel ashamed.

If Mr and Mrs Schoenhair should read this book I hope they'll realize I've never forgotten their kindness.

After a special dinner the Inn had laid on with more champagne, I watched Jean getting ready for bed. After three years of being more or less together, three years of doubts and uncertainties, we were finally married. I loved her dearly, nobody could help loving Jean, and I just hoped I could make her happy, but I had grave doubts that Hollywood and our careers might tear us apart. This travesty of a wedding wasn't the greatest way to start off a marriage, which is a difficult institution at the best of times. I felt emotionally exhausted and hungover as I crawled into bed beside her. I told her that after the day's events I felt slightly confused and would she mind if I read a little?

'Of course not, darling,' she replied. 'but not too long, please.'

As she snuggled up to me I opened a book. Before leaving Hollywood Sam Zimbalist had told me he very much wanted to do another film in Africa and he thought that this story might be suitable for myself and Deborah. It was a fascinating book and I got completely engrossed in it. I was conscious of Jean turning over out of my arms and going to sleep, but the book held me. After about an hour I thought I should really stop and pay some attention to my bride. I studied the sleeping figure for a moment. She had one of those faces that is even more beautiful without make-up and at that moment she looked about fourteen. I knew I should wake her and show her how much I loved her but I was really too tired and so the rather shopworn bridegroom turned out the light and went to sleep. That was a big mistake and I would live to regret it. Incidentally Susan Hayward and Robert Mitchum played in the film of that book, so all that reading was for nothing.

The next morning Jean didn't remark on my inattention and, thinking that maybe I'd got away with it, we joined Mike at the swimming pool for breakfast. We noticed him eyeing a rather striking-looking blonde sitting alone a little distance away. Her face looked familiar and I suddenly realized it was Barbara Hutton, one of Cary Grant's ex-wives. Cary Grant and Howard Hughes. Their influence seemed to be popping up all over the place. I told Mike who she was and he quickly stopped his ogling.

'Christ, she's way out of my league. Isn't she one of the richest women in the world?'

'Yes, but that shouldn't stop you. Look at the success you had with Doris Duke.'

He gave me a dirty look.

'Anyway, Mike, you've only got a couple more days so make hay, man, make hay.'

We soon discovered why one of America's richest heiresses was alone in a little cow town in Arizona. Her son, Lance Reventlow, suffered badly from asthma and was there in school because the dry air of Arizona helped him. That evening Miss Hutton was very aware of the attractive Mike's interest and, after receiving an encouraging smile, he went over and introduced himself. He was invited to sit with her, so Jean and I left him to his haymaking.

The next evening Mike told us he had invited her to have dinner with us. She turned up, beautifully dressed, coiffeured, manicured and made-up, but all this elegance next to Jean's fresh-faced beauty made her look slightly raddled. Apart from an eye-blinding diamond ring, her only jewellery was a necklace of black beads, which surprised me a little as I knew she owned a fabulous collection of jewellery. After dinner, during which the delicate Miss Hutton had only toyed with her food, she remarked what a pretty engagement ring Jean was wearing and asked to see it more closely. I expected her to get out a jeweller's glass and screw it into her eye, and while she was examining our slightly flawed stone, she made sure Jean was suitably blinded by the blue-white gemstone she was wearing herself. Then she noticed the rather unpretentious pearl necklace I had given

Jean as a wedding present and, after saying how sweet it was, asked Jean if she liked the one she was wearing. I tried to kick Jean under the table as I had a suspicion of what was coming, but Miss Hutton got there first. She held out her black beads and thrust them across the table into Jean's face. They weren't beads at all, they were black pearls, a unique and absolutely priceless string which had been given to her by one of her husbands. (After she'd given him the money to buy it, I thought to myself.) I wanted to kick her skinny arse all round the pool as I couldn't stand the way she was trying to humiliate Jean. She failed dismally as darling Jean said, 'They're very lovely but I prefer mine because Jimmy bought them for me.'

I leant over and gave Jean a big kiss which was my way of telling her that she didn't need any jewellery anyway, it would only be gilding the lily.

We saw Mike off at the airport and he told us he was returning to England straightaway as there was somebody there he was interested in. That somebody turned out to be Elizabeth Taylor, who had just obtained her divorce from young Hilton.

'Don't think you're the only one who can pull a beautiful bird, mate,' he told me with a wink. We both wished him luck and, after thanking him for coming, watched his plane disappear into the distance.

One day a young lady introduced herself to us. She was Sharman Douglas and her father, who had been Ambassador to England, lived in a town quite near, named after his family. I had seen pictures of Sharman in the English Press, accompanying Princess Margaret on many occasions, and had even met her father in London. Sharman was good company and knew the area well. She suggested we hired a car and saw something of the countryside. After visiting her parents' home, our next trip was down that straight ribbon of road, fifty miles to the border town of Nogales. Customs and Emigration officers waved us through and we found ourselves in Mexico.

Nogales Sonora was one of the dirtiest and most depressing tourist traps I'd ever seen. The over-spiced Mexican food was lethal, but in spite of my delicate stomach the tequila, with the accompanying suck of lemon and lick of salt, went down a treat. Jean hated it but Sharman and I managed to knock back quite a few and I realized why the road from Nogales to Tucson had been named El Paseo de Muerto – The Road of Death. The sides of the road were peppered with white crosses to mark the accidents, mostly caused by Mexican drivers going across the line to work in the States after a boozy weekend and the tourists who poured into Mexico and weren't used to the lethal effects of tequila. I made sure I had several cups of black coffee before we started back.

Eventually our two weeks 'honeymoon' came to an end and we happily made our way to the airport. We quickly discovered the contrast to our pampered arrival as we queued up at the reservation counter, and finally took our places in an overcrowded plane. We both had to admit that there were some advantages in Howard Hughes's way of travel.

19

There was good news when we got back to L.A. Metro had agreed to loan me the money for a house. I think they had their eye on Jean for a film and wished to ingratiate themselves. We bought a large Mediterranean-style mansion in Bel Air, a very prestigious neighbourhood, and moved in. Jean was very enamoured of the nursery suite and eyed it speculatively.

'Oh no, you don't,' I told her.

'Of course not, darling. Only when you want a baby, too,' she answered sweetly. But the way she looked at me warned me that I'd better be wanting one soon. I hung my few paintings and African trophies on the walls and thanked God that it had come fully furnished as Jean and I had practically no household possessions.

As expected we were sternly reprimanded by the outraged Louella and Hedda for having 'sneaked off' and denied them this scoop. To make up for it they demanded we gave each of them an exclusive on what it was like being newly-married stars in Hollywood. I told them both we'd 'post a bulletin' in due course and hung up.

Cary called and asked if we'd like to meet our benefactor, the mysterious H.H. The usual bespectacled chauffeur called for us and we were whisked off to an airfield. Cary was already there talking to a tall, thin man with a droopy moustache who was tinkering with something on the plane. Cary introduced us and, having thanked him for his kindness, we both studied this legendary figure. He didn't seem so special or so frightening, for that matter, and he sure as hell wasn't smart. He had on a five dollar open-necked cream shirt stuffed into creased baggy khaki trousers and wore scuffed sneakers. Being a watch freak I immediately noticed that he was wearing a cheap chrome one on his wrist. Well, you could have fooled me. This was a multi-millionaire? But, when we got to know him better, we realized that this was his way of showing his contempt for everything and everyone. He really had it, he didn't have to impress people and he liked to see the reactions. But his face was extraordinary. The skin seemed stretched like parchment and we learnt later that this was the result of many plastic surgery operations after a bad plane crash. The eyes were pale and lacklustre but you got the impression they didn't miss much. He spoke with a slight Texas accent in a strange high-pitched toneless voice, apparently caused by the head injuries he had suffered in that same plane crash which had left him deaf. Very unnerving.

We got in the plane and took off. Hughes was alone at the controls and immediately we realized that this was a superb pilot from the ease and assurance with which he swung the plane round and headed down the runway. Cary was sitting with Jean so I asked Hughes if I might sit in the co-pilot's seat. He welcomed me and asked if I could fly a plane? I told him I'd had lessons years before when my sister had been married to a pilot instructor. 'Okay,' he said. 'Take over', and he took his hands off the controls. Shit, I thought, as I grabbed the half-wheel, I'll probably go into a spin. I had been taught in an old-fashioned Avro with a joy-stick and so was pretty clumsy with the wheel, but Hughes was patient and completely relaxed, knowing he could get the plane out of any scary position I might put it into. He was much friendlier here in the cockpit and I quickly realized that this was something he really loved. Strangely he seemed to hear better than I did in the noisy cockpit and I've often wondered since whether he was really deaf, as he always seemed to hear whatever he wanted to and just 'tuned out' when he was bored. Jean and Cary started to complain about the bumpy ride so I handed the controls back to the master.

We were flying to the Grand Canyon as Hughes thought we might like to see it. Of course a large black car met us at the small airfield where we landed and we were whisked off to a lodge perched on top of the cliff looking out over that vast gorge. It was very impressive but somehow rather sad, it was so barren, so stark, with nothing moving, but the air was crystal clear and you could see for miles. Hughes told us the canyon was so vast that if all the people in the world were compacted into cubes they couldn't fill it. I tried to imagine this and wondered what Benny Thau and Louis B. Mayer would look like in cube form. I was sure that Rank, Davis, Compton Bennett and even Hedda and Louella would look much better. We wandered about and had a meal in the impressive dining-room with bay windows overlooking the canyon and, while the others were busy, I quietly sneaked off to the lavatory as I was still suffering from the Murchison Falls runs. I was attending to my business when I heard footsteps outside and realized that Cary and Hughes were taking a leak.

'Well, what do you think of her,' asked Cary.

'I'd sure like to get my teeth into that,' I heard in that high-pitched voice. 'He's a goddamned lucky son of a bitch, that Granger.' Then there was silence. 'Oh shit. I've got my cock caught in my zipper.'

I wondered what I would have heard if he hadn't, and I kept very still until they left. I didn't realize until much later what effect that innocent question of Cary's would have on our lives.

I had only just got used to sharing a home with Jean when I was kissing her goodbye. I don't know why Jean didn't come with me, money I think, as Metro refused to pay her expenses. Making *The Light Touch* was fairly uneventful and I knew as I made it that it would add nothing careerwise to anybody connected with it. Pier Angeli was adorable with an anxious mother in attendance at all times and Brooks was his apparently usual, unpleasant self. It's sad to think that Pier Angeli was to take her own life a few years later, but that's what Hollywood can do to you if you let it.

When I got back I began taking fencing lessons from Jean Heremans, the European champion, in preparation for *Scaramouche*. We had a new producer and the son of L.K. Sidney, George, was going to direct. He had just made the musical of *Annie Get Your Gun* with Betty Hutton and I'm sure was disappointed that there would be no singing or dancing in our picture. Thank God we got on very well and were both determined to make it an outstanding film. While I was going through the different fencing routines worked out by Heremans, Walter Plunkett, the top Metro costume designer, was working on my many different outfits, the most important being the one in which I would do the now famous ten-minute sword fight all over the theatre with Mel Ferrer. Walter eventually designed an eye-riveting costume which helped me outshine everyone else and was exactly right for the character. Mel was and is a charming person and, although a very good actor, I think he'd agree with me that he isn't the greatest swordsman in the world, so Heremans doubled for him, as they both had the same slim figure. But I presented a very different problem as I am heavily built and fencers aren't usually made that way. The studio hired Paul Stater to double for me, a champion swimmer and acrobat, who had doubled in the past for Johnny Weissmuller in the Tarzan pictures, but a swordsman he wasn't, anyway not an elegant one, so I did all the stunts myself. I avoided fencing with Mel as much as possible as he never could concentrate if there was a pretty girl around, which was often, and I would find his sword coming straight for my face instead of my body as rehearsed. But you couldn't tell the difference when Heremans took over for the shots favouring me and I felt more secure.

The accidents and near accidents on this film were incredible. The first happened to poor Heremans and I was

THE LIGHT TOUCH with a very young, innocent Anna Maria Pierangeli who had such a tragic ending.

SOLDIERS THREE. Not the way to build a romantic image. Bob Newton looks fairly sober for once. *(IPC Magazines)*

SCARAMOUCHE, just before I slipped and smashed myself up for the second time. *(National Film Archive)*

X marks the spot where Jean was to take Hughes and the lower X marks the spot where I hoped he'd land, preferably on his head.

Our house guests, Mike and Liz. No wonder H.H. got over-excited. *(Associated Press)*

Looks easy but moments later I nearly broke my neck.

The chandelier that 'missed'. *(National Film Archive)*

YOUNG BESS. Jean played the 'virgin' Queen! *(Kobal Collection)*

THE WILD NORTH. Wild dogs as tame as rabbits. Anyway I've got more teeth than he has.

THE PRISONER OF ZENDA. Two for the price of one. Shot in 28 days and great fun in spite of a sabre in the mouth! *(National Film Archive)*

On the set of ZENDA with One-take Thorpe, Louis Calhern and Bob Coote. Jean, of course, has captivated them all. *(IPC Magazines)*

Beloved Spence with the overbearing Cukor and Bessie. *(National Film Archive)*

BHOWANI JUNCTION.
Ava in a sari was pretty
goddamn irresistible.
(National Film Archive)

BEAU BRUMMELL. Both
separated from our 'mates'
and hating every moment of
it. *(National Film Archive)*

Royal Command of BEAU BRUMMELL. A tasteless choice.

My two darling 'monsters' on the MGM lion which had been presented to me.

GREEN FIRE. Final 'wet' embrace. It doesn't seem to stick out here! *(National Film Archive)*

My cockney stand-in, Bob Porter, who didn't much like Pakistani hospitals.

GUN GLORY. The not-so-quick draw. At least here I got the bloody thing out of the holster! *(IPC Magazines)*

Jean happy and pregnant when we became US citizens. *(Associated Press)*

HARRY BLACK AND THE TIGER. In India with star I. S. Johar. *(© Daily Mail Syndication)*

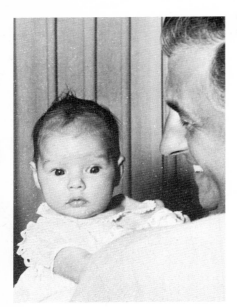

Tracy. You must admit she was a pretty baby.

Cheyenne, Elvic, Sundown and Harry Boy with their proud owners. Our new ranch in background.

Jean was as impressed as I was with $50,000 worth of 'bull'.

Tracy riding over the ranch with her doting Dad. *(Globe Photos)*

My last Christmas with Tracy.

Just before the break-up *(Globe Photos)*

Idyllic scene on our own lake with Tracy's Island in the background.

NORTH TO ALASKA. My last film in America. I always thought I was big until I played opposite Wayne. *(National Film Archive)*

Saying goodbye. *(Globe Photos)*

responsible. At the beginning of the film my character can't fence and, when his best friend is killed by the villain, Mel, he picks up a sword and goes at him (now doubled by Heremans) as if the sword were an axe. Heremans parried one of my smashing blows and the sword broke halfway down the blade and the tip slashed his eye open. Like everyone else I was horrified as Heremans clapped his hands to his face and we saw the blood running through his fingers. He was rushed to hospital and, as I waited in the corridor, I was thankful to learn that the blade had only sliced along the eyelid and not touched the eye. He had to be bandaged for several days but no real damage was done. On another occasion I didn't parry his blade sufficiently and the point sliced a little piece out of my face only an inch from my own eye, so I thought it was about time we all had some insurance. My request to Eddie Mannix was met by a howl of outrage almost as loud as the one from his wife Toni when she learnt I wasn't going to screw her.

'Insurance,' he yelled. 'Gable never had insurance. Barrymore, Tracy, Novarro never had insurance. Why the hell should you have insurance?'

'Eddie, they only paid ten per cent in tax and kept ninety per cent. I pay ninety per cent and keep ten per cent. If I'm hurt who's going to look after my family – my children, my ex-wife, my present wife, my future children, and what about my poor old mother?'

By the time I'd finished Eddie who, in spite of his roaring, was a soft-hearted Irishman, was practically in tears. He promised he'd arrange everything and told me for Christ's sake to take care as Metro had a lot invested in me. He summoned the MGM insurance man who started discussing how much compensation I should get for the loss of one eye, both eyes, one leg, both legs, paralysis from spinal injuries, total disablement and finally death. By the time he'd finished this grisly list, Eddie was almost as green in the face as I was. I hadn't realized how many vulnerable parts I had and began to wish to hell I hadn't raised the subject.

The next duelling scene was with Mel when I wasn't supposed to be very professional and he was to make a fool of me, slicing my clothes with his sword and finally, having positioned me under an enormous iron chandelier, cutting the rope holding it up. The chandelier would come crashing down and narrowly miss me. We did the master shot with Heremans doubling for Mel but each time we came to the chandelier bit, they stopped the cameras and told us they would do it later in a trick shot. Eventually the scene was finished and I was asked to wait in my dressing-room while they rigged up the scene with the falling chandelier. I was tired after all the takes and snoozed for about an hour. Eventually there was a knock on the door and I was told that everything was ready. George the director explained the peculiar position of the camera. They had taken up the floorboard of the sound stage and the camera was in a hole. I was supposed to lie down so that the camera would see my profile and the chandelier high above. The falling chandelier would stop a foot from my face and they would get me rolling out of the way in another shot. 'A very effective scene, Jim, as the audience will see you helpless and the chandelier crashing down on you before it stops.'

There was a slight pause as he waited for my reaction.

'Suppose it doesn't stop, George?'

'What do you mean, doesn't stop? Of course it'll stop.'

'But supposing it doesn't, George? That bloody thing weighs a ton. I'll be mincemeat if it hits me.'

'Jim, we've had our special effects man rig the whole thing. He's the best man in the business. You don't think he'd risk anything, do you?'

'No, George, I don't. But it's me lying there, not him. Let's see one without me in place, just to make sure.'

'Oh Christ, it's taken an hour to rig, if he lets it go it'll take ages to haul it up again and arrange all the special safety gadgets.'

That 'difficult' look came into my eyes.

'Let's see one, George,' I said quietly.

He reluctantly agreed with a 'these fucking difficult actors' look on his face.

'All right, Cedric,' he said to the waiting special effects chief. 'Let's try one. Clear the stage. All right. Let it go.' And Cedric let it go. Down came that chandelier, the chain holding it snapped and the gigantic monster crashed and sank its serrated iron edges two inches into the solid wooden floor. They'd left the mattress I'd been lying on for rehearsal in place and it disintegrated. In the deathly silence I could hear the director being sick and the sobs of the now blubbering Cedric.

'It's never done that before,' he choked. 'In all my years in the business I've never had anything happen like that,' and he buried his face in his hands. As he left the stage I noticed he had a slight limp and two fingers were missing. I didn't like to ask him how that particular accident had happened. There was still a stunned silence as by now George had stopped being sick. I felt I'd better say something to ease the tension.

'Interesting. Very interesting. George, I think I'll direct the film for a change. You do the acting', and there was a nervous laugh.

When I got back to my dressing-room I found I was shaking as I'd very nearly told George I'd do the scene without a rehearsal, since I didn't want to hold him up. What made me insist on seeing one? Maybe it was the thought of that insurance policy, one eye, one leg, etc. That chandelier would have guaranteed the jackpot.

There was a tap on the door, 'Jim, everyone's going home as they're a bit shaken up, so you're free. Have a nice evening.'

They're 'shaken up' I thought. I don't think I was able to change for about an hour.

I didn't tell Jean anything about the day's events when I

243

got home as I didn't want to frighten her. She was bubbling over with the news that Bert had confirmed to her that Paramount wanted her for the lead in *Roman Holiday*, to be directed by William Wyler. She had read the script and was absolutely thrilled with it. Bert assured her that he would work something out with Rank as it would be to their advantage for Jean to be in a successful American picture. Her leading man was to be Gregory Peck whom we both admired. I felt so happy for her as I also knew that Metro wanted her for another film, *Young Bess*, the story of Queen Elizabeth I as a young girl. Metro were planning to go to town on this film and give it an all-star cast and a large budget production, so things were looking rosy for my little wife.

The next day on the set Bert came to visit me in my dressing-room. He had heard of the near disaster the day before and told me that he'd stormed into Eddie Mannix's office and demanded that some insurance should be worked out for his client's husband. Eddie had explained that I'd already been to see him and we'd agreed all the details. Bert asked when the policy had come into effect and was told by a shamefaced Eddie that it hadn't actually been signed.

'So you see, Jimmy, if anything had happened yesterday you weren't covered at all. You'd really better have someone to look after you.'

'I know, Bert. I wish to hell I had you, but I've got Jack Dunfee in England who does nothing and Fefe Ferri over here who just keeps kissing me and telling me not to worry.'

'Would you like me to handle you,' Bert asked.

'Of course. But how? I'm signed up with them.'

'I hope you don't mind. I've bought them out.' Bert held out his hand. 'Welcome to the Morris office, Jim.'

'But Bert, you'll make nothing out of me,' I said in bewilderment as I shook his hand.

'Money isn't everything, Jim. I'm kind of fond of that little wife of yours and you're sort of growing on me. So let

244

me take care of you from now on.'

Dear Bert, he didn't know what he was letting himself in for.

A fews days later, the director having recovered his nerve, we started the complicated acrobatic fencing sequence in the theatre. The first scene took place on the edge of the theatre boxes about twenty feet off the ground. The edge was only about six inches wide and, as I was supposed to be being driven backwards, the special effects had rigged a corset for me, with a steel wire going up to the gantry to hold me in case I fell off. This damn wire got in the way and, after several rehearsals, I took off the corset as I felt confident I could manage without it. Of course I fell off the balcony. Twenty feet may not be very high but it's high enough. I landed on my hands and feet but crashed over on to my right shoulder which took much of the shock. Painful, and I'm still troubled by it today, but after massage and heat treatment I was able to continue. I'd been lucky since, if I'd landed on my head, I'd have broken my neck.

The next near fatality came a few days later. The theatre set had been constructed in the eighteenth-century style but the seats were modern. I think they'd come from a demolished cinema. They were covered in red plush so didn't look too out of place but naturally had tip-up seats. When the seats were in the upright position there was a small gap between them and the backs and I was warned not to slip and get my legs caught. The scene called for me to fight Mel between the seats with me straddling the backs and, as he retreated into the aisle, I was to run along the narrow backs of the seats and leap down to continue the fight. Everything went well in rehearsal but of course in the take I tried to be that much more acrobatic and slipped. My foot and leg went down between the seat and the back and the impetus of my rush carried me headfirst into the aisle. I managed to twist as I fell or I'd have snapped my leg off at the knee which, as everyone knows, only bends one way. The noise the twisted knee made as it snapped the chair seat from its hinge, together with the crunching sound of my fall, convinced everyone that the worst had happened. My knee was giving me hell and I was lying on my back semi-conscious when I heard the assistant director say as he rushed up, 'Oh, Jesus Christ, he's killed himself.'

I thought I'd have a bit of fun with him so I lay absolutely still with my eyes closed and tried not to breathe.

'It's bad, George, he's not breathing. I think the poor bastard's dead.'

I heard George come up while the extras and crew swarmed around to have a closer look at the lifeless body. I was giving the performance of my life trying to take a breath without the assistant noticing so I was beginning to choke. Then I heard my friend and director George utter the true Hollywood sentiment.

'What the hell are we going to do? The film's only half finished.'

'Call a doctor, you mercenary prick,' the corpse suddenly said. Everybody gasped in shock as I sat up and they all crowded round to congratulate me on my escape. Actually I was really badly hurt as my knee had been wrenched and the sides of my leg were scraped raw, to say nothing of the effects on that already damaged shoulder and back smashing into the ground. They carried me to my dressing-room and the doctor strapped me up.

A very sore husband came home to his little wife that night and Jean was appalled as I got into a hot bath holding the bandaged leg over the side, but I assured her it was nothing and that the fight sequence would soon be over. With youth on my side I quickly recovered and returned to work. Youth! What am I saying? I was almost forty then, but anyway the film was finished without any other major incident. Years later I had to have the knee operated on as it never completely recovered. Unfortunately the insurance had expired so I wasn't able to make a claim.

On the whole it was a happy film, but very tiring, and darling old Lewis Stone, the man who had starred in the original *Scaramouche* with Ramon Novarro, the man I had queued up to see so many times when I was a boy, played a small part. The crew were always surprised at my concern that he should be looked after, brought coffee when he wanted it, have a chair ready when he was tired. I fussed over him like a hen because I remembered him as a star and to me he would always be someone special. Screw the fact that he was now only playing a small part, he'd been a star and I made damn sure he was treated like one.

My insistence on doing all the stunts and swordplay went for nothing as, after the première, one fan remarked on what a wonderful 'double' I had. When I replied that I had done it all myself he scoffed at me. 'Oh, come on, Mr Granger, we know you actors never take risks. We know it's always somebody else.' Fuck him.

20

Jean was surprised that she hadn't heard from Rank asking her to report for her next film but I was delighted as it gave us time to be together with neither of us working, but one day the reason for this unexpected situation was made clear. Bert arrived, looking very serious, and told us that he had some disturbing news. His London office had been in touch with the Rank Organisation to work out a deal to clear Jean for *Roman Holiday*, and had been informed that Rank no longer had any call on her as they had sold her contract. We both looked at Bert in amazement. We couldn't believe it. We just couldn't believe that Rank, with all his avowed affection for and obligation to his faithful young star, who'd served him so loyally over the years, would sell her like a piece of merchandise without even consulting her. Then Bert produced the real bombshell. Jean's contract had been bought by Howard Hughes, the man who had a pretty unsavoury reputation where women were concerned. We asked Bert if he couldn't be mistaken, but he assured us solemnly that not only was he not mistaken but Hughes had already been on to him to discuss a new deal for his latest acquisition.

'What deal?' we both asked together.

'Can't you guess,' Bert replied. 'He wants a long-term contract. He says he can do nothing with only three films, but, if Jean would sign for a seven-year contract he would make her the biggest star in the world.'

Oh God, here we go again.

'And if she doesn't sign?' I asked. Bert looked embarrassed.

'I don't suppose he meant it, but he threatened to put her

into three lousy productions which would ruin her career.'

There was a miserable silence.

'Do you really think he meant it, Bert?' I asked hopefully.

Bert looked at us for a moment.

'Yes, he meant it, Jim. He's a real bastard when he wants to be.'

We were talking about the mysterious man who had so kindly arranged our secret marriage, taken us on a trip to the Grand Canyon, who had been so quiet and self-effacing. And then I remembered his reply to Cary's question as to what he thought of Jean. 'I'd sure like to get my teeth into that.' Well, he'd started with a hell of a big bite.

I don't think Jean realized the implications, as she told me that at least now we wouldn't be separated.

'But darling, you don't understand. You can't be under long-term contract to a man like that, can she, Bert?'

'God, no. It's bad enough for you, Jim, but at least I can talk to Metro. You can't talk to Hughes. If he felt like it he could keep her off the screen for years. Money means nothing to him, women do and you know what that implies.'

'All right. What are we going to do?'

'Play him along. See him. Make a fuss of him, but don't discuss business. Leave that to me and we'll try and work something out.'

Bert left two very miserable and confused newly-weds to discuss the situation. Jean wasn't really thinking much about the Hughes problem, she couldn't get over the way Rank had behaved. Not a word from anybody in that vast organization. She'd been sold off and they were no longer interested.

We didn't have long to wait for the first probe from Hughes. A rather nervous flabby character called Walter Kane got in touch and asked if he might visit us. He was Hughes's right-hand man, he explained, and spent about two hours telling us what a great, kindly and philanthropic character his master was, that his only desire was to give

Jean full scope for her talents and see she got the kind of treatment she deserved. Bullshit, I thought to myself. I asked Kane why he didn't get in touch with Jean's agent and was told that Hughes mistrusted all agents and preferred to deal with his artists direct. Well, we had something in common, I thought, with the exception of Bert. Kane knocked back quite a few gins during this meeting and started to relax.

'Get to know him, Jean. You'll find he's an easy man to deal with. He's lonely and I'm sure he'd appreciate it if you invited him up here.'

He gave us a number that would always reach Hughes, with strict instructions not to divulge it to anyone. This was like the presidential hot line, only maybe more secret and certainly more important. We both tried to show the reverence due to this confidence, and Walter staggered off.

While all this skullduggery was going on we received news that our best man Mike would be arriving with his new fiancée, Liz Taylor. Naturally we told him that, until he found a house, they should both stay with us, so when Hughes turned up for the first time to dine with us, he was met by two of the most beautiful girls in the world. His pale eyes bugged out of his head, and he literally drooled as he stood looking down at them sitting demurely side by side on a couch. He practically overbalanced trying to look down their cleavages, both of them being well endowed in that department. I'd heard the rumour before but now I was certain. Hughes was a tit man.

Michael and I watched this performance with amusement.

'Which do you prefer, Howard?' we asked teasingly.

'Goddamn, I can't make up my mind,' he replied, practically watering at the mouth.

'Well, hard cheese old boy. You're not going to get either of them, so up yours.'

Howard turned and looked at us with those pale eyes. We thought we were teasing a nut. We were teasing a cobra.

Howard loved the Beachcomber food and all the Hawaiian

drinks they served there. He never went to the restaurant, he'd order everything and it would be served up at one of the many houses he had dotted all over Beverly Hills, all with projectors and, after seeing some movie or other, he'd tuck into the food and drink. His favourite was the same as mine, the Pi-eye, served in a frozen scooped out pineapple so, being the good host and hoping to keep the cobra happy, I went to the Beachcomber and bribed one of the barmen to give me the recipe. Very involved. Three different kinds of rum, fresh pineapple, lime juice, honey and angostura bitters all beaten up in a Waring Mixer and poured into the scooped out frozen pineapple. The next time Howard came to dinner I handed him the surprise. He took a sip and said in amazement, 'Shee-it, it is a Pi-eye. How did you get the recipe?'

I told him I'd bribed the barman.

'How much did you pay?'

'About a hundred dollars.'

'One hundred dollars', he yelled. 'Just for a drink. Are you rich or something?'

He wasn't at all impressed that I'd gone to all that trouble to please him; he just thought I was an idiot. I probably was. He didn't even ask for the recipe.

The question of letting Jean do *Roman Holiday* came up with Hughes and his factotum Kane.

'If she'll sign, no problem, Jim. Hughes will buy the whole project from Paramount and do it at RKO.'

'But Walter, Jean doesn't want to sign. Can't we come to some arrangement of a multiple picture deal, but not an exclusive?'

'Sorry, Jim. You know Howard' (I was beginning to), 'he doesn't like to share his property with anyone.'

After a lot of pleading with Walter to get in touch with Howard, as even his hot line wasn't answering, we got the news second-hand that he had refused. That was Howard's trick, when anything came up that was vital to anyone connected with him, he'd just disappear. Jean lost the film and was heartbroken. Willie Wyler was so disappointed that he threatened to shelve the picture as he had been set on Jean and felt there was no one else, but he was persuaded to see a newcomer in a play called *Gigi*, tested the young lady, was thrilled with the result, and Audrey Hepburn played the part. She was brilliant and won an Oscar. Although Jean had sworn never to see the film she confessed one evening that she'd sneaked into a cinema where it was showing. She went to the phone and I overheard the following conversation.

'Miss Hepburn, my name is Jean Simmons.' Pause. 'Thank you, Miss Hepburn. I've just seen *Roman Holiday* and, although I wanted to hate you, I have to tell you I wouldn't have been half as good. You were just wonderful.' She hung up, and realizing I had been listening, sat down beside me. 'I meant it, darling. She was better than I could have been and I wanted to tell her so. D'you know she told me she'd been a fan of mine for years. Wasn't that sweet?' I hugged her and told her how much I admired her for her generosity, but if it hadn't been for the machinations of Hughes maybe Jean would have won that Oscar instead.

To make up for Jean's disappointment, Hughes, the dirty, double-crossing Machiavellian son of a bitch, asked us all to go with him to Lake Tahoe. I had been planning to take Jean to Acapulco for a holiday, and Mike and Liz wanted to come too. Walter Kane heard and came hurrying along to say that Hughes was very worried that we should risk our health in that 'Mexican hellhole' as he called it. He still considered Jean as his potential property as, although we had refused all his offers, he couldn't believe we'd go on saying no. He thought money could buy anything. Kane told us that, if we still insisted on going to Acapulco, Hughes would arrange a yacht for us to stay on and a seaplane to take us down and stand by in case we wanted to leave at a moment's notice.

We just wanted to get away for a little and be tourists like everyone else and didn't need all this pretentious bullshit, but Walter pleaded with us not to disappoint Hughes and so, in order to 'play him along' as instructed by Bert, we found ourselves on our way to inspect the seaplane. The usual car and plane were laid on and Hughes met us at the airfield. He took us to a jetty on Lake Tahoe and there in the centre of the lake lay a PBY. It had been luxuriously converted and the two 'blisters' which had held the machine guns were now a bar. It was an eerie feeling sitting in those glass bulges as there was nothing beneath us – it was as if we were sitting outside the plane.

Hughes was in his element as he had never flown one of these machines before and took off and landed about ten times. I had arrived suffering from a bad cold with my nose completely blocked up and these changes of altitude weren't doing my eardrums any good. On the last circuit Hughes took her up high and said he wanted to try out her diving capabilities. As he swooped down towards the lake far below, I felt an agonizing pain in one ear.

'Howard, for the love of God, bring her down slowly and keep her down. I think I've burst an eardrum.'

Everyone was very solicitous, including Howard, but later I strongly suspected he had done it on purpose. He knew I was 'blocked up' and what might be the result of the constant changing of pressure.

We made our way to Las Vegas and checked into a large bungalow attached to one of the big Casinos, *The Silver Nugget*, I think it was, and a doctor was called. I had indeed perforated an eardrum and needed a lot of attention. Howard told me that his own aeroplane was suffering from pressurization problems and he didn't want to risk taking me back to L.A. in my condition. He suggested we all stay where we were for a few days until the plane could be repaired. While I lay miserably in bed, holding different kinds of compresses to my aching ear, the others went out on the town. Hughes was a good host and they visited all the best casinos and saw all the marvellous floor shows with Sinatra, Dean Martin, Sammy Davis Jr, Joey Bishop, etc. They would get back at about two in the morning and tell me all about it, then go off to bed, Hughes in one room, Mike and Liz in another and I with Jean. We would be woken for breakfast at about ten o'clock and Hughes would join us. This went on for four days. Eventually Hughes announced that the plane was ready and with the doctor's instructions to continue the treatment, we returned to L.A. We thanked Howard for everything and told him what a lovely idea it was to fly down to Acapulco in the PBY and go aboard the yacht. He beamed with seeming pleasure and left.

We looked at each other in tired confusion and wondered how the hell we were going to get out of it. At that moment the phone rang and Bert was yelling at us for disappearing without letting him know where we were. We explained what had happened and how I couldn't fly because of the plane's pressurization troubles.

'What are you talking about,' Bert said. 'I've been meeting with Hughes at about three o'clock in the morning for the last four mornings. I'm exhausted.'

This was a favourite way Hughes had of doing business. He would arrange to meet whoever it was on the corner of Sunset and Vine at two, three or four in the morning.

'Bert, how could it be possible? We've seen Howard go to bed at two o'clock every morning and met him for breakfast again at ten. When the hell did he sleep?'

'That SOB doesn't need sleep like the rest of us. That's why he's so successful in his dealings, he just breaks the opposition down through sheer exhaustion.'

Uncanny. He'd got up every night while we were sleeping, crept out, flown his plane to L.A., driven to his meeting, flown back, crept into bed again and risen bright and shiny a few hours later to join us and spend the rest of the day sightseeing with Mike and the girls, and not a word to any of us, not a hint. Holy cow, what kind of monster were we dealing with? We were soon to find out.

One day Mike and Liz got the royal command from Hedda Hopper to pay her a visit for tea. She considered Liz a special protégée of hers, having known her and written about her since she was a child. They came back that evening with Mike white in the face with shock and fury. Liz was in tears as Mike kept on asking her how she could have listened to all that bullshit, why hadn't she just walked out? As I poured Mike a stiff whisky he told me what had happened.

'Directly I had been handed a cup of tea, I was completely ignored. Hedda started to have a long and impassioned argument with Liz. "How can you think of marrying a homosexual?" Hedda demanded. "What do you mean?", bleated poor Liz. "What I say," thundered Hedda. "He's a known homosexual. What are you thinking of, throwing your life away on someone like that?" Liz started to cry. I was just looking at Hedda like a mouse with a snake. I was paralysed. Jim, how do you deny you're a queer? And she was so goddamned persuasive she even had me believing it. And you, you silly cow,' Mike turned to the sniffling Liz, 'Why did you listen to all that crap? Why didn't you walk out?'

Liz let out a howl and Jean led her out of the room. 'Give me another Scotch, for Christ's sake. I'm still shaking. You wouldn't believe it, Jim, the fucking bitch talked about me as if I wasn't there. Who in God's name does she think she is?'

'I'll find out,' I said, seething with fury and dialled Hedda's number.

'Yes, who is it?'

'May I have the pleasure of talking to Miss Hedda Hopper? This is Stewart Granger.' I spoke in well-modulated mellifluous tones.

'Oh, one moment, Mr Granger. I'll put you right through.'

'Yes, Stewart, how are you?' came the voice of the one and only.

'I'm fine, Miss Hopper. I'm just calling to say that I think you're a monumental bitch. How bloody dare you accuse a friend of mine of being a queer, you raddled, dried up, frustrated old cunt.'

I heard a shocked intake of breath and before she could reply I hung up.

'Not very gentlemanly I'm afraid, but I feel better now. I'll join you in a Scotch.'

We both drank in silence. I looked at my old friend who, to my certain knowledge, was one of the biggest cocksmen in the business and thought he had to come all the way across the Atlantic to be accused of being a faggot. Hollywood! With the beautiful homes, the lovely climate, the efficient mighty successful studios, it seemed to us the perfect place to work. But we'd only been there a few months and look what was happening. Of course Mike and Liz made it up with Hedda, but she never forgave me and never missed a chance to sink her barbs into me in her columns, but eventually I got my own back. But that comes later. Much later.

One of the three films that Howard had bought from Rank had to be *Androcles and the Lion*, produced by Gabriel Pascal. Gabby told us of his plans to make this one of the most expensive films ever made in Hollywood – it would make *Caesar and Cleopatra* seem like a quickie. (A quickie, I thought. It practically put Rank out of business.) Rank had only been a millionaire but Hughes was a multi-multi-millionaire and Gabby's eyes gleamed in anticipation of the budget. We tried to warn him that it might not be as easy as he thought, but he had met the seemingly innocuous Hughes and considered him a pushover.

The film started and Gabby got up to his old tricks of wanting to change sets, costumes, casting, etc., while the film was in progress. The inevitable happened. Gabby came to see us one night, practically in tears. He had been thrown off the picture and was barred the lot. He wasn't even allowed to collect his personal papers from his office; they had just been dumped in a box and left outside the gates. Hughes had struck. Gabby tried to get a ruling through the courts but for every lawyer he could employ, Hughes had ten and every legal move attempted by Gabby's lawyers was blocked. He never set foot on the lot or handled another foot of his film. He never worked again either and a couple of years later we heard he was dead. We think he died of a broken heart. The cobra had struck again. Poor Gabby.

In spite of Hedda's warnings and Hughes's behind-the-scenes machinations (he was unsuccessfully trying to buy Liz's contract from Metro), Liz and Mike were married and moved into their own home. We missed them and felt rather lonely in our enormous Hollywood house. We realized we'd made a mistake in this purchase and had our eye on a much smaller, cosier place that we'd seen up in the hills overlooking the San Fernando Valley. Of course Kane promised us that Hughes would buy the property for us, but again that was dependent on Jean signing up. Tempting, but no way. *Scaramouche* had been released and was a great success, thank God, so Metro was looking around for another swashbuckling vehicle for me.

One day we were invited to dine with Ronald Colman and his darling wife, Benita Hume. It was to be an all-English evening with David Niven and his wife, Deborah and Tony and ourselves. After dinner Ronnie asked if we'd like to see one of his old pictures? He showed *The Prisoner of Zenda*, as David had played a small part in it and Ronnie thought it might amuse him. We sat enthralled all through that marvellous romantic drama and, as we were leaving, I told Niven that I was going to try and persuade Metro to buy the rights and do a remake. Niven thought it was 'a jolly good idea' and next day I went to see Doré Schary. When I told him what I had in mind he almost had a fit.

'Do you know how much Selznick would ask for the rights?' he yelled.

I told him it didn't matter what he asked as we could reproduce it shot for shot and thereby save the money invested in the purchase price. It had never been done in colour and I thought, with careful planning, we could shoot it in thirty days, unlike Selznick who had taken something like six months. Doré agreed that it was a good idea and a surefire follow up for me after *Scaramouche* and promised to look into it.

My next film was to be an outdoor epic about a Canadian mounted policeman and a trapper. I was rather startled when I entered the producer's office and found him in front of a tickertape. He quickly dropped the handful of tape he had been studying and made like a producer, but I soon discovered he didn't know what he was talking about and I doubt if he'd even read the script. He was a charming man and later I discovered he was really a stockbroker who advised the Metro brass on what to buy. They couldn't have a stockbroker on the payroll so they made him a producer. Well, that figured. The director was to be my old friend Andrew Morton, who had taken over and completed *Solomon's Mines*.

The Wild North, as the film was called, was going to cover a lot of territory including Jackson Hole Wyoming, Sun Valley Idaho, and the Rogue River. Wendel Cory, the other actor, and I had to cross vast distances on snow shoes, be attacked by wolves, fall into snow drifts and pull each other out of freezing rivers. Lovely. As I was to play a French Canadian trapper, I asked if I couldn't attempt a French Canadian accent, which would give the part some credibility. I was immediately whipped into Eddie Mannix's office again, as apparently accents were his forte as well as insurance.

'Jesus, Jim, what you want to try an accent for? They're fatal. Look what happened to Gable when he tried an Irish accent in *Parnell*. Practically ruined his fucking career.'

'Maybe, Eddie, but look what happened to Spencer Tracy when he used a Portuguese accent in *Captains Courageous*. It won him an Oscar.'

'You think you're gonna win an Oscar by trying a frog accent?' Eddie asked.

'Hell, no, Eddie, of course not. I'm not Spencer Tracy and this film ain't *Captains Courageous*, but at least it'll make a change. Let me try it and if you don't like it, I'll dub it in my own voice.'

'Okay, Jim, it's your career.' And that's why I put on that bloody frog accent. I wish I'd listened to Eddie.

Cyd Charisse played opposite me and used to cheer me up on the cold mornings in make-up by 'pointing' for me. She had the most perfect legs I'd ever seen and was a marvellous ballet dancer. She would stretch out one of those fantastic legs and 'point' as only ballet dancers can and I'd feel better. She was beautiful and should have had a much more brilliant career but unfortunately she was tall and Gene Kelly, who made all those wonderful musicals at Metro, is only about five feet eight, so that short, rather plain lady, Vera-Ellen, got all those juicy parts.

Jean was able to join me in Jackson Hole and it was wonderful coming back in the evenings to a warm cuddly wife after freezing my butt off in the snow.

Running in snow shoes isn't the easiest thing in the world and on one occasion I tripped and took a dive into a snow bank. I had my hands manacled in this scene and couldn't get up. After they had pulled me out, the men told me how funny I'd looked with just my feet showing and they had all fallen about laughing. They were rather surprised when eventually my blue face emerged, choking up the snow I'd inhaled. They hadn't realized the snow was slushy and I'd nearly drowned. Another time we had to be attacked by wolves and the animal trainer appeared on the scene.

Now if there's one thing more lethal to the poor long-suffering actor than the special effects man whose effects never go wrong, it's the animal trainer with his dogs that never bite, cats that never scratch, lions like kittens, elephants that won't crush an egg, crocodiles that won't snap, horses like rocking chairs, etc., etc. This one had ferocious looking Alsatians that at a command would snarl but of course were really as harmless as rabbits.

In one scene a wolf was supposed to leap on my back as I was fighting off a pack, which in reality were stuffed heads thrust at me by the prop men. Very realistic when the wolf noises were added to the sound track, but the one behind me had to be the real thing. I was assured that the snarling demon was as gentle as a rabbit and would merely jump on me and proceed to lick my face. Action came and the 'rabbit' sank his fangs into my shoulder. As I was yelling in pain and everyone was trying to pull off the 'rabbit' who seemed reluctant to release his clamped jaws I could hear the trainer muttering, 'Can't understand it. He's never done that before.' While I was being dabbed with iodine and shot with anti-tetanus, I understood that there always has to be a first time, but why did it always have to be me?

Wendel and I were nearly drowned in another sequence when the boat was overturned and we were thrown into an icy river. In the scene Wendel was supposed to save me as I was acting unconscious having been struck on the head by something but I quickly realized that it was Wendel who was in trouble. He was quite a drinker and I think the shock of the icy water on his ravaged liver had sent him into a coma. We were both tied off with rope concealed underwater and, as the men tried to pull us in, the force of the rushing river dragged us under and made things worse. Yelling to the men to release us, I managed to float the unconscious Wendel down and get him to shore. Thanks to Uncle I've always been a fish in the water, but with all the heavy clothing we'd been forced to wear, this fish had nearly drowned and taken Wendel with him. But it was all in a good cause, dear old Metro.

Walter Kane was coming up to the house more frequently now with a variety of proposals, but all containing the same seven-year clause. He would always drink a lot of gin during these meetings and then beg us for a mouthwash before he left. Amongst other things apparently Hughes didn't like his employees to drink on the job. Bert told us on the phone that H.H. was pressuring him now and had drawn up a contract for him to study.

'It's a very attractive offer, Jim and, if it were any other studio, I would advise Jean to sign and get it over with, but apart from Hughes being psychotic, he's in the process of running RKO into the ground and she might find herself without a film for years.'

'Don't worry, Bert. Jean has no intention of signing.' Jean was shaking her head furiously in the background.

'I suggest Jean accepts any bad film Hughes throws at her and gets the commitments out of the way. They can't hurt her career, she's got too much talent.'

'Okay, Bert, I'll tell her.'

Hughes was furious when Bert told him to do his worst, that he could only use Jean for two more films anyway and she didn't care what they were. One day the phone rang and it was Hughes himself, something that rarely happened, and he asked to speak to Jean. I passed the phone to her and she listened nervously. I saw an amazed look come over her face and she gestured to me to listen in. The SOB was propositioning her.

'When are you going to get away from that goddamned husband of yours? I always have to see you either with him or Bert Allenberg. I want to talk to you alone, honey. We can go away somewhere and thrash the whole thing out. You won't be sorry; I promise you.'

I snatched the phone.

'And I'll promise you something, Mr Howard Bloody Hughes. You'll be sorry if you don't leave my wife alone,' and I hung up.

'He doesn't care about the contract, Jean. It's you, he

wants to screw you. I don't blame him but he'd better not try anything or I'll kill the bastard.'

Jean had a huge smile on her face.

'Darling, I believe you care.'

'You're goddamn right I care,' I yelled.

Jean loved it as she'd never seen me show jealousy before.

Everything was quiet for a bit. Walter Kane still paid us brief visits but I think he knew it was hopeless and just came for the gin, but he couldn't get over the fact that Jean had turned down an offer from the mighty H.H. He was a god in Walter's eyes and he didn't understand why we refused to worship at the same shrine.

Bert rang to tell us Jean's next film was to be a 'pot boiler' called *Angel Face*.

'But there's one good thing about it. Bob Mitchum is co-starring and he'll look after her.'

Bob was serving a long-term contract with RKO and was one of Bert's clients. Bob really took Jean under his wing and, in spite of the bullying Otto Preminger who was directing it, Jean enjoyed the film. She adored Mitchum and used to tell me what a good actor he was, how funny and amusing and how easy-going, he just wouldn't let things get him down. I wished I could have been more like him.

In one scene Bob was supposed to smack Jean, and she told the very gentle Mitchum to really let go. Otto insisted on take after take and poor Jean's cheek was getting redder and redder. As Otto insisted on yet another take, Mitchum turned to him and let him have one right across the face.

'Would you like another, Otto?' he said.

Otto quickly agreed to print the last take.

Although not especially successful at the box office *Angel Face* wasn't a bad film and did no harm to Jean at all. I expect H.H. was furious. It's difficult to plan a bad film to hurt somebody's career. The result is sometimes quite successful whereas it's the carefully planned blockbuster that can really kill you.

21

The Prisoner of Zenda started and I worked my arse off. Doré Schary had had to pay Selznick half a million dollars for the rights, an unheard-of price in those days. It had been my idea and I'd guaranteed Doré it would be a financial success so I'd better look out. He'd given us a super cast including my old friends James Mason and Deborah Kerr; then there was Louis Calhern, a wonderful actor and a dear sweet man, Robert Coote playing Niven's part, Robert Douglas, and Jane Greer, a very funny dishy lady. 'One take' Richard Thorpe was directing it.

I'll never forget my first scene which was very complicated with me having to get slightly drunk as the king and play around with a monocle. The scene lasted about five minutes during which I never stopped talking but I managed to get through it on the first take. I heard the director say, 'Cut. Print.'

'Christ, Richard, aren't you going to let me have another try?'

'Sure, Jim, if you want to. Do you think you can do it better?'

I hesitated.

'I don't really know, Richard. Did you like it?'

'I liked it fine, but if you want another one, let's go.'

'No, Richard, if you liked it that's fine with me.'

And that's how the film went. If you remembered the lines and got through the scene, Richard would print it. He didn't believe in ten or fifteen takes in order to catch some subtle difference only appreciated by the director. I loved working like this and that's the reason the film was made in such an incredibly short time. With all the fights, the coronation and

263

ballroom scenes as well as having to shoot many scenes twice over because of the split screen, when I'd appear as both characters at the same time, the film was finished in twenty-eight days. Bloody hard work but great fun. We even had time for some practical jokes as Louis Calhern was a great giggler and I adored working out tricks to make him break up. The fight sequence was effective, I think, and although I could never compete with Ronnie Colman as an actor, at least I could fight better.

No remake was ever made so exactly like the original. We had a moviola on the set and ran the Selznick version and then went on the floor and copied it shot by shot. I even tried to imitate Ronnie Colman which was fatal. Coote didn't try to copy Niven and that's why he came out so well. In spite of some bruising, James Mason and I escaped any real damage in the sabre fight, though there was one moment when I nearly got 'spitted' on Heremans's sword. He arranged all the fight sequences again after his success with *Scaramouche*, and doubled for James. One scene was a close-up on my face against a large oak armoire, and Heremans, standing by the camera, had to thrust his sabre at my face while I parried, first to one side and then to the other. On the second thrust the sword was supposed to go past my face and stick in the oak door behind me. I realized that Heremans was nervous and aiming not for my face but slightly to one side. I stopped the scene and asked him to thrust straight at me and it would be up to me to parry. Much more effective. He thrust straight at my face and I parried to the right; he thrust again and I was so pleased with the success of the first parry that I forgot to parry to the left. The blade caught me in the mouth and there was a horrified silence as the blood started to pour out. Heremans was paralysed and didn't dare pull out the sword, the crunching sound it made as it went into my mouth having convinced everyone that it had come out the back of my neck.

'Take that fucking sword out of my mouth,' I spluttered

and Heremans nervously obliged.

Again a miracle had saved me. Owing to my habit of flashing my 'pearly whites' whenever I swashbuckled, the blade had hit my teeth and skidded, making that horrible crunching sound and only sliced my gums open. Painful but not too disabling. With three or four stitches closing the wound I was able to continue the next day, though I have to admit that if I hadn't guaranteed the film's success I would have taken a few days off.

Richard was sick when the accident happened as he told me it looked absolutely horrible. I seem to have the knack of making all my directors throw up.

During the filming a team from *Life* magazine came down to interview me. They were unpleasantly patronizing and I longed to tell them all to piss off and let me get on with my work, but the publicity department persuaded me that this visitation was an honour and begged me to co-operate. Apparently this co-operation paid off as I got the cover of the June edition, 1952, with the caption 'Stewart Granger. Swashbuckler'.

Jean had finished *Angel Face* and was more relaxed, as she only had one more picture to make for Hughes. Bert told her that he had several very interesting offers so not to worry about her career and, as I had completed *Zenda,* we both had some free time and once more started planning our trip to Acapulco. One day Bert asked Jean if she would mind meeting Hughes face to face and telling him that she didn't want anything to do with him or his offer. Bert assured her that he would be there to back her up and, unpleasant as it was, it was necessary, as Hughes just wouldn't believe that Jean was serious and thought that Bert was lying. They took off together and I waited anxiously for their return since I'd seen how nervous Jean was when she left. Hughes had become a sort of threatening monster in her eyes and she couldn't get over the power this man wielded in that vast empire known as Hollywood. I was nervously sipping my third Scotch when they came bursting in. Jean hugged me and said at last it was over, she'd told him and that was that.

'You'd have been proud of her, Jim. This little figure stood there and told Hughes that she wanted no part of him or his contract and couldn't wait for the day when she'd be free. She thanked him politely for his offer of yachts and planes and asked if she could go now?'

Hughes had apparently been speechless with fury and just stood there when they left. We all had a drink and toasted Jean's approaching freedom. Our happiness was shortlived. Bert arrived one day white in the face.

'You won't believe it. You just won't believe what he's done, the bastard.'

'Oh God, what now,' we exclaimed.

'He's served papers on all the studios saying that he has a seven-year ''moral'' contract with Jean and, if they should employ her for any picture, they'd find themselves in litigation with him. You know what the studios are, Jim, they hate the thought of any trouble with the powerful Hughes, so that's where it's at.'

Jean and I looked at each other in horror. Oh Christ, were we never going to be out of this man's hands?

'But Bert, we were only negotiating. Jean didn't sign anything. How can he stop her working?'

'Legally he can't, but he's powerful enough to scare the studios who never want any trouble and certainly don't want Hughes for an enemy. That's the problem.'

'All right, Bert. What are we going to do? Just sit down under this and have Jean out of work for years?'

'We'll have to take him to court. Get a legal ruling that he has no rights over her.'

'Take Hughes to court! The government tried and lost. A senator tried and lost. What chance do we have?'

'It's the only way, kids. Tough as it's going to be, it's the only way.'

We sat there, looking at each other miserably. Oh God,

why had Davis and Rank sold Jean's contract to a man like this? Why had we allowed him to arrange our marriage? Why had Cary made that fatal remark asking Hughes what he thought of Jean? I was back in that lavatory hearing that high-pitched voice saying how he would like to get his teeth into 'that'. And I'd thought it was funny. Funny, Jesus!

Bert brought along a top lawyer, and we went through interminable interrogations. Bert was asked to hand over the different unsigned proposed contracts and we had to give approximate dates and times of all our meetings with Kane and Hughes, with what was said and done in each case. Tiring, boring, frustrating, aggravating and so bloody unfair. Our lawyer had served notice on Greg Bautzer that we were taking legal action.

Messages came back through the grapevine telling us how foolish we were, pointing out that we had no chance of winning against a man of Hughes's power, and asking what was all the fuss about. Was a seven-year contract so awful? To many people maybe not, but to Jean, who had just finished one stretch and longed to be free to pick and choose her parts, longed to be able to have a baby without asking a studio boss's permission, to have holidays when she felt like it, it was unthinkable. But the main feeling was that we didn't have a chance – don't rock the Hollywood boat, don't make waves, don't challenge a studio head's authority. Wherever we went people would come up to warn us, out of friendship of course, not to take on the powerful Hughes. Louis B. Mayer called me into his office and advised me to settle. A court case would be bad for the industry, for my career, for Metro. Joe Schenck, the brother of Nicholas Schenck, head of Loewes Inc., saw us at a restaurant and urged us to drop the case. Bert, who had promised to testify on our behalf against Hughes was threatened that, if he went into court with us, RKO would never employ any of the Morris office clients again. This was a very heavy stick indeed, as that meant their writers, producers and directors, as well as actors and actresses, would be barred from one of the major studios. Bert had a meeting with the Morris office head, Abe Lastvogel, who asked him if it was really necessary to get involved, as it would mean the loss of hundreds of thousands of dollars in commission to the company. Bert was adamant.

'They're in the right, Abe. Jean is our client and she has the right to ask me to testify as to the truth in this matter and by God I'm going to.'

Why weren't there more people like Bert Allenberg in the world?

We had to give endless depositions in front of Hughes's lawyers who seemed to be asking questions that were nothing to do with the case: questions about my youth, my schooldays, my army career, my divorce, where I had bank accounts, what businesses, if any, I was connected with. I was completely confused and didn't know where all these questions were leading, which I suppose was the object of the exercise. The lawyer was lighter on Jean and only discussed the actual offered contracts. Then we heard, through our relations and friends in England, that a mysterious American was asking questions about our past, trying to dig up any scandal, without any success, I'm glad to say.

We were both getting absolutely paranoid about the whole thing. One night, when Liz and Mike were commiserating with us and trying to plan our constantly interrupted holiday to Acapulco, the doorbell rang and a dark-glassed chauffeur handed over an envelope with the words 'from Mr H. Hughes'. I asked him to wait and we all gathered round as I opened it. It contained two pieces of paper. One was a cashier's cheque for $187,000 (about a million dollars at today's values) and the other a receipt for Jean and me to sign, showing we'd accepted the cheque. This was the amount promised us if Jean would sign the contract, representing the purchase price of our house and the rights to the book, *The House by the Sea*. There was a hysterical moment as we all laughed and said to each other, 'Let's just take off for Acapulco and blow the lot in one glorious long binge and to hell with the consequences.' And then sanity prevailed. I called Bert who advised us not to do or say anything but just to wait for him. He wasn't long and arrived with the Morris office lawyer, who took possession of the two pieces of paper and, having notified the chauffeur that he, the lawyer, would personally deliver them back to Hughes, left with him. As we all slumped down, Bert explained this last little trick.

'He just couldn't imagine you refusing all that money, but if you'd cashed that cheque, even if you hadn't spent any of it, he'd have had you over a barrel. It would have been the same as Jean signing the contract.'

We became even more paranoiac. One evening Pam Mason asked us to dinner. It was a fun party as hers always were and Greg Bautzer was among the guests. He was a great friend of Pam's and, being a very attractive man and a bachelor, was always in demand. I avoided him as, although I found him a nice enough guy, he was Hughes's Number 1 lawyer and I certainly didn't want to discuss the case. At dinner he was sitting across from me and, when there was a lull in the conversation, he said, 'Well, Jim, you're a hell of a brave guy.' I immediately took offence, thinking he was having a crack at me and, in spite of Pam pulling at my arm and assuring me that Greg meant nothing, I jumped up and challenged Greg to come outside and continue the conversation in the garden as I was sick to death of all these insidious innuendoes. Eventually I was quietened down by Pam and a rather pale Greg assured me he meant nothing more than what he'd said.

'I really meant it, Jim. I admire your guts. I represent Hughes but it doesn't stop me respecting you.'

I apologized and left. On the way home we miserably wondered if we'd ever be able to spend time together without that bloody man's name cropping up. I 'moodied' round the house for days. Neither of us wanted to go out and the only telephone calls we would take were from Bert or our lawyer. We were beginning to distrust our friends now, too, and I think this was partly due to 'Big John'.

We hadn't seen Big John Mills for almost two years, the last time being when he'd given a party at Les Ambassadeurs for Jean and me before I took off for Hollywood. Apparently Big John had signed a very lucrative contract with TWA, then owned by Hughes, to supply all the food for their transatlantic flights. He was over in Hollywood to discuss business with the Master and had dropped in to see us. He was very welcome as both of us were very fond of him, but he happened to ask why we didn't make it up with Hughes and I hit the ceiling. The poor bastard hadn't realized what had been going on and Hughes had tried to use our friendship with John to get to us again. Being paranoid I thought he was in on the plot and it was some years before we became friends again. The accumulation of all this well-meant interference in my private life finally sent me round the bend.

One evening, alone in the large house with Jean, and having knocked back a little more Scotch than usual, I suddenly heard myself saying: 'That monster is going to ruin our marriage, ruin your career, ruin our lives. I'll have to kill him.'

Jean looked at her rather white-faced husband and murmured quietly, 'Of course, darling. How?'

'Oh, I've got it all worked out,' I told her with a rather mad satanic look on my face, and I had too. 'Now Howard is always trying to get you alone, right? Okay, I'm going to pack up tomorrow and go to the airport as if I were leaving on a trip. I know somebody is watching this house, so they'll see me go. But I'll make damn sure they won't see me come back.' I didn't know how I was going to do this but in my rather drunken state everything seemed feasible. 'Now some time after I've gone, you'll get on the hot line to Hughes and tell him that you're alone and want to see him. Tell him that you're upset about the whole thing as the thought of a court case terrifies you. Cry a little. You're a good actress. Sound a bit hysterical, right?'

'Yes, darling, of course,' said the rather mesmerized Jean.

'Now when he gets here, take him out onto the terrace. I'll be hiding upstairs. After a few minutes of tearful conversation, scream. Get it? Scream loud in case any of the neighbours have got their binoculars on us' (a completely paranoiac thought, of course). 'I'll rush out and knock the sonofabitch over the railings and with any luck he'll break his bloody neck on the rock garden below. Right? You got that?'

'Yes, darling. I get him outside and I scream. You come out and knock him over the railings. He breaks his bloody neck. What then?'

'What then? What do you mean, what then?' I was pouring myself another large slug and congratulating myself on this brilliant plan which would solve all our troubles. 'What then? I call the police, of course, and tell them that I found Hughes attacking you, lost my temper and hit him. The poor chap fell over the railings and Bob's your uncle. With his reputation and the witnesses we'll have to prove that he's been hounding you, I'll get away with it. Well, what do you think?'

'It seems a very good idea,' Jean said soothingly.

I was beginning to feel sick by now with all that Scotch and, with a muttered apology, rushed to the bathroom and threw up. I don't know whether it was just the Scotch or planning a murder, but I felt like hell, collapsed into bed and passed out. The next morning I woke with a ghastly hangover and gradually what I had been planning the night before seeped through into my addled brain. I looked down at the peacefully sleeping Jean. She looked so innocent, so unlike an accomplice in a murder plot that I just couldn't understand how she could have agreed to it. I woke her up.

271

She came out of her sleep as she always did, fresh-faced and clear-eyed although not entirely awake.

'Darling, do you remember what I said last night?'

'Of course,' she answered.

'You really remember – all of it?'

'Yes. I'm to call Hughes, get him out on the terrace, scream, then . . .' I cut her off.

'Okay, okay. You remember. But don't you realize what I was saying? I was planning to murder someone. Murder. Don't you understand? It's impossible. It's ghastly. I must have been mad.'

'I know, darling, it's awful.'

'Well, why the hell did you agree?'

'Because I knew you were pissed and you'd change your mind in the morning.' She gave me a kiss. 'I'm awfully tired, darling. We were so late last night,' and with that my accomplice turned over and went back to an untroubled sleep.

Of course it was madness, of course it had been mostly play-acting but that's the state Howard had got me into.

I had been loaned out to Columbia to make *Salome*, a film co-starring Rita Hayworth, so I had everyone at Columbia warning me that I was fighting a losing battle. There was a girl I ran into in the hairdressing department, a very beautiful young actress called Terry Moore, who at the mention of the name Howard Hughes practically went into hysterics. He had somehow screwed up her life, too. My co-star gave me a pitying look and said she hoped I knew what I was doing. Rita apparently had had some dealings with the monster some time before. It wasn't the best atmosphere in which to give a good performance. Charles Laughton was in the picture and it needed all the concentration possible to deal with that scene stealer. He didn't like leading men and did everything to screw me up. Much as I admired his acting I was in no mood to put up with his tricks and told him if he didn't stop them I would kick him in the balls. He stopped.

The day of the trial came nearer and the schedule of the picture had been arranged to allow me time off to attend. Any court of law gives me the shivers. I had been in the witness box once in my life and that was only for a friend up on a drunk driving charge, but I remember even then being paralysed with nervousness by all the panoply of Justice, so as I walked to the stand and took the oath I was literally shaking. I faced the battery of lawyers representing the mighty Hughes and hoped to God I could stay calm and not lose my temper. Jean's future depended on me and Bert Allenberg being good witnesses, and I hoped I wouldn't blow it. The first impression I got was that Hughes had bought the judge. He overruled every one of my lawyer's objections and sustained every objection the opposing lawyers made. I remember thinking to myself that, if this was American justice, and we lost the case because of a man's wealth, Jean and I would never do a film again but go back to England and just work in the theatre.

I was six days on the stand being questioned about things that seemed irrelevant to the case. Eventually I lost my temper and, when asked why I had been so averse to Jean's signing a contract with a reputable studio, I burst out that it had nothing to do with the studio, I objected to the studio's boss wanting to screw my wife. Of course the Press loved this and the judge gave me a ticking off for using that kind of language. I apologized and felt like telling him that if he thought that was bad language he'd be in for a shock if I really let go.

Every evening Jean and I, Bert and our lawyer held a post-mortem. We were all very depressed as our lawyer also thought that Hughes had influenced the judge. The consensus of opinion was that, although I hadn't been too brilliant, I hadn't been too bad and finally my cross-examination came to an end and I went back to *Salome*.

After a day spent trying to save John the Baptist's head, I would come home to hear how the others had made out in court. Jean was only kept on the stand one day and the lawyer treated her with kid gloves. In no way could he show this innocent creature as a scheming, greedy actress, so he wanted to get her off the stand as quickly as possible. Bert, apparently, had been brilliant and let Hughes have it with his denunciations of this ghastly blackmailing behaviour coming from a studio head.

While the trial was going on, another of Hughes's lawyers had been approaching us behind the scenes urging us to withdraw. According to him we hadn't a hope in hell of winning our case and the damages Hughes could claim would take every penny I could earn for the rest of my life. I assured him that not only were we not going to withdraw but that we were eagerly looking forward to Hughes's appearance on the stand. I told him that I would be sitting beside my lawyer advising him as to which questions to ask that would really embarrass Hughes. I knew where quite a few bodies were buried.

The time came for our side to open our defence. The first witness naturally was to be Hughes himself and, because of his deafness, the court was being wired for sound. Jean and I didn't sleep that night and at 8.30 were dazedly getting dressed in preparation for the new ordeal, when the phone rang. It was Bert.

'Jimmy, Jean's won her case. Hughes's lawyers are here and want to settle.'

I couldn't believe it. Jean broke into tears of relief and I started laughing rather hysterically.

'Jimmy, are you there?' Bert's voice came anxiously.

'Sure, Bert, We're here. Still can't believe it after all this time but go on. What happens next?'

'Well, they want to know what damages you want.'

I turned to Jean.

'Darling, do you want damages?'

'No,' Jean answered firmly. 'I want nothing. Do you?'

'Not if you say so,' I replied.

'I just want to be free. God, I want to be free.'

'Okay, darling, leave it to me. Bert, we want nothing from that sonofabitch, nothing at all.'

'Jim, I must point out that you could get a hell of a lot in damages. Libel against you' (Hughes had intimated that I had a deal with Metro to evade tax), 'insinuations about your background, damage to Jean's career, mental stress, attempted blackmail, I could go on forever. He obviously has no intention of showing his face in court, you could take him for a couple of million at least. You have a right to it and you both deserve it.'

'I know, Bert, but Jean is just glad it's over and wants nothing. Let him pay our legal expenses and that's it. Come round and have breakfast and let's celebrate.'

We still couldn't believe it. Although we cooked up eggs and bacon they remained uneaten on our plates as we went over and over the last ghastly months. Our lawyer phoned and asked us to get down to the court as quickly as possible as he had a pleasant surprise for us.

We had been playing to full houses for two weeks as the public loves cases involving famous names, but that morning as we were led into court, the promise of Hughes's appearance had them hanging from the rafters. Our lawyer explained that the judge could simply announce that the case had been dismissed but on this occasion he had expressed a wish that we should be present. The judge took his seat and read out a statement completely exonerating us and expressing his disgust that a man like Hughes could think that by using batteries of lawyers he could win a case so obviously unjust. Later the court stenographers sent us a signed copy of this statement with their congratulations and best wishes. We met the judge in the corridor and thanked him for his kindness.

'Not at all,' he said. 'After studying the depositions it was quite clear to me that Hughes had no case. You noticed I overruled all your lawyer's objections and sustained all theirs? I did this so there could be no chance of their appealing my verdict. These appeals are tiresome and can continue for months, years even. I didn't want to give them any chance of that.'

Then he asked us to sign autographs for his daughter. And we'd thought this kind man had been on Hughes's side! Wealth and power didn't count in his court, only facts. Thank God.

The press were amazed that we hadn't asked for damages as Hughes's public relations department had put out that we were greedy actors trying to get what we could out of a rich man. They congratulated us on our victory, but we hadn't really won, nobody admired us for fighting for a principle. We had made waves and challenged the Establishment. Unheard of. It had made us both nervous wrecks and almost ruined our marriage. I'm sure Jean had been thinking that, if she hadn't married me, none of this would have happened. She would have been happily working in England and coming to Hollywood one day on her own terms. I couldn't help thinking that it was hard enough to try and protect my own career and look after all my other responsibilities without these added complications. It took us both months to get over it but eventually we realized that in spite of the traumas of the last year and a half we still loved each other and that was all that mattered. But we never did get to Acapulco for that second honeymoon.

Looking back on it now, the most incredible thing is that I almost liked Howard Hughes. I certainly respected his undoubted genius and I admired his bravery and guts. He insisted on testing every new plane his company built himself and had some pretty horrific crashes. Somehow he always survived and seemed to be back at the controls of some other plane as soon as he was out of hospital. One story that had really endeared him to me was when he was romancing Katharine Hepburn. She was on tour in a play and he had flown down to spend the weekend with her. On leaving his plane and crossing the tarmac he had spotted a rather sporty looking motorbike leaning up against a fence. He studied it in fascination for a moment and then putting his leg over the saddle, kicked it into life and took off. He didn't return the bike until the following evening. The owner found it in the same place with an envelope attached. In it were a couple of hundred dollars and a detailed plan of some suggested improvements. Anyone who could stand up a beautiful woman for a motorbike must be endearing. I would have liked to have been his friend, as he was a very special person, but Hughes didn't understand friendship, he had no friends.

One person at least made money out of the case and that was our lawyer. He presented his bill and when Hughes saw the amount, he exploded and accused him of being a crook. There were two other lawyers present, so our man sued him for libel and won. Hughes had to pay out a sum equal to five times the original amount. Poor Howard. RIP.

22

During the making of *Salome,* I ran into the much maligned Harry Cohn, the boss of Columbia. I heard a raspy voice call out 'Granger' and turning I saw a squat pugnacious figure approaching. 'Yes, Cohn,' I said. His cigar nearly fell out of his mouth. Everyone, but everyone, addressed him obsequiously as Mr Cohn. There was a moment's pause as we eyed each other.

'Mr Granger, Mr Cohn, Jimmy, Harry, which do you prefer?'

He gave me a grin. 'Okay, Jimmy, I heard you were a difficult SOB. Glad to meet you.'

We shook hands and became friends. I liked him. Everybody had told me he was a bastard and it was fashionable in Hollywood to run him down and call him the meanest man in town. But he was always straight with me and that's what counted. He came on the set one day and threw me a script.

'There you are, you Limey bastard, there's a part for you.'

I looked at the title. *From Here to Eternity.*

'Which part?'

'Which do you think. The lead. The Marine sergeant.'

I looked at Harry in amazement.

'I can't play an American Marine sergeant. I'm English.'

'You're a fucking actor, ain't you? Of course you can play it.'

To Harry's surprise I turned it down. What an idiot I was. If I'd played it, nobody would have known how marvellous Burt Lancaster was going to be and it was such a great part I'd probably have got away with it. After the star-studded première I ran into Harry.

'You see, I did you a favour, Harry, turning it down.'

'Bullshit, Jim, you'd have been great.' Maybe the fact that I was probably cheaper than Lancaster coloured Harry's opinion.

The star-studded première of *Salome* was memorable in a different way, to say the least. At the climax of the film Rita Hayworth appeared, carrying the head of John the Baptist on a silver salver and one enthusiastic member of the audience yelled out, 'Hey, man, dig that crazy dessert.' It didn't seem to worry Harry. 'It'll make a fucking fortune, Jim,' was his reaction, and he was probably right.

Jean's first film after her freedom was *Young Bess* for MGM. They had given her a fine supporting cast (including me), Charles Laughton repeating his brilliant performance as Henry VIII, and Deborah Kerr played Catherine Parr. George Sidney was directing and as there were no sword fights I hoped I wouldn't make him sick on this film.

Being married to my leading lady was a new experience for me. Actors by nature are egotists and love to tell their partner how brilliant they've been that day and all the problems they've had to contend with. You can't get away with that if your partner happens to be playing a larger role than you, but with Jean it was easy as she was one of the most undemanding, professional actresses I've ever worked with but I could imagine what it must have been like to be married to tigresses like Crawford and Davis. With them you'd have to bottle up your own problems and just listen to theirs, or else.

We'd had a normal social life the first year we were married but the second year, owing to the Hughes case, we'd practically gone to ground. Now that it was all over we began to accept invitations again. The great hostess of that time was Edie Goetz, wife of the former head of Twentieth Century-Fox, Bill Goetz. They had a magnificent home with the most incredible collection of Impressionist paintings I'd ever seen. We were greeted in the entrance hall by the famous bronze figure of the little ballet dancer by Degas, drinks were served in a small study where the 'Japanese' self-portrait by Van Gogh glared down at us, after dinner we were led into the drawing-room which was literally plastered with paintings by Manet, Monet, Cézanne, Sisley, Vuillard; name it, it was there. I remember my horror when, on my first visit, after dinner the usual film was shown. On the wall above the couches hung some of the most valuable paintings in the house. As the lights dimmed I saw this wall tilt up and recede, revealing the film projectors. If something had gone wrong with the mechanism, several million dollars worth of pictures would have been ruined. I suppose they could always have bought some more.

Everyone who was anyone was at these parties. In fact you could judge the success of your last film by the number of invitations you received. If you'd had a flop that phone didn't ring, but happily *Scaramouche, Zenda* and *Bess* were successes. It was there that we met all the 'greats' of the industry and it was incredible to see so many of them in the same room at the same time. We always forgot we were stars ourselves and just gaped. On one occasion, after the gracious hostess had greeted us, I was hailed by Alan Ladd. We had met a few years before in London at a Royal Command Performance and Alan had never forgotten a little gesture I had made on his behalf. Alan was short and I had been asked by the thronging photographers to pose with him. Being used to having pictures taken with my old friend Johnny Mills, who is also short, I went into my crouch which brought Alan's head and mine to the same level. Alan couldn't get over it. He told me all tall actors delighted in going up on their toes to make him look even shorter and added, as he thanked me, that any time I visited Hollywood I would find a friend there and to be sure to look him up. And here he was. That man had stature even if he was short.

Gary Cooper, of course, stood out from everyone, not only because of his height, but because he was the most beautiful man I'd ever seen. There's no other adjective to describe him, he was just beautiful. He was fascinated by big game hunting and we agreed that, when we got the chance, we'd go on safari to Africa together. Whenever we met we would ask each other 'Are you packed?' Unfortunately we never did make that trip.

We met Bogart often, but I shall never forget the first time. It was at some party or other and 'Bogey' had taken a few too many which was his wont and started to needle me, which was also a habit of his. I didn't know that he was only kidding and started to take his gibes about the bloody British seriously. I remember telling him rather pompously that he had to be a much bigger man than he was to be making remarks like that or he'd get his head knocked off and I, for one, would be delighted to oblige. Bogey was amazed at my reaction and asked rather plaintively why I was getting so upset, that he was only kidding. I realized I'd made a fool of myself, apologized and after that used to laugh good-naturedly when he tried to take the mickey out of me. I'm glad to say we became good friends and on some occasions I even protected him from getting his head knocked off by other large opponents lacking a sense of humour.

Gable was another star attraction at these parties whenever he appeared, but although charming enough, he seemed uneasy in the obligatory tuxedo and wasn't a pastmaster at small-talk. I think he was bored by the social whirl and I don't blame him. The queens of Hollywood were there, showing off their latest fashions and jewellery and also their latest men. But the real catch at all these parties was a newcomer called Marilyn Monroe. Amazing the effect this zany beauty made on her entrance, which was invariably late. I was always amused by the silence that came over the room and the looks of envy on the faces of the other famous beauties. Only a few years previously, on a visit to MGM with Bert Allenberg, I had seen a forlorn figure coming towards me. I couldn't take my eyes off her, or to be more exact, off the swaying behind as it passed. No behind ever swayed like Marilyn's. I went up to her and introduced myself. I was dying to ask her for a date but I felt a tug on my arm from Bert. I excused myself and sadly watched that behind disappearing through the MGM gates.

'Why did you stop me, Bert? It was an innocent invitation. You don't think I was trying to date her for myself with Jean waiting for me at home, do you? I think Jean would like to meet her too.'

Bert grinned at me. 'Well, I wasn't sure, but you see my partner, Johnny Hyde, is madly in love with her and he's in hospital, poor devil. He's very sick, in fact I don't think he's going to make it.'

He told me Johnny wanted to marry her but Marilyn refused because she wasn't in love with him. If she had become his wife he would certainly have left her a great deal of money as he was a very rich guy indeed. I think this says a lot for the integrity of the much maligned Monroe.

We found out later that she was looking so forlorn because she had just been fired by MGM. She had played a small part in *Asphalt Jungle,* directed by John Huston but, before the film was released one of the drama coaches at MGM advised them to let her go as she didn't think Monroe had any talent. The real reason was she had too much sex appeal for that envious, unattractive female. Stupid cow. And here Marilyn was, the star of the evening, outshining all the other stars. Incredible young lady.

The other amusing thing about these parties was the 'help'. Even the very rich would augment their permanent staff with agency personnel, so you'd see the same butlers and maids at all the parties and, after a time, they would become friends and tip you off on what to eat.

'Don't touch the chicken à la king, Mr Granger, it's been heated over. Go for the beef.'

Most of the food had been sent in as permanent staff in Hollywood didn't like to be overworked, so everything always looked delicious but tasted more like warm soggy flannel. When Jean and I returned the hospitality I used to do the cooking myself so my guests were guaranteed a real home-cooked dinner. Because of this our parties were very successful but we didn't give them very often as they were too bloody exhausting. Cooking for thirty people isn't exactly relaxing. Our close group, apart from Mike and Liz, were Bert and Mildred Allenberg, Sam and Mary Zimbalist and Spencer Tracy.

We had met Spence at Metro one day and were completely captivated by this Irish charmer. Apart from being the best actor in the whole movie industry he was also the most attractive. Apparently he'd been a great lush in his day and he fascinated us with the story of how he finally decided to stop drinking.

'I would get drunk and disappear in the middle of a film, get into fights, become a complete bum. At the beginning the studio heads and my friends would rally round and cover up for me, but eventually the only one left who seemed to care at all was Victor Fleming, who had directed several of my pictures. The last booze-up I had was one of my worst. I'd been picked up by the police and thrown into the drunk tank; I was filthy, unshaven and ill. Vic found out where I was, squared the Press, the police and the studio and took me home. He had a Filipino servant and, giving him instructions to bath, shave and put me to bed, went to get his doctor.

'After being given a thorough examination, I was lying there feeling like death when Vic came in with a case of Scotch. He put it down beside my bed and went to the door, turning back he said, ''Spence, I've just talked to the doctor. He tells me one more bash like that and you'll be dead. I want you to do me a favour. Drink that whole case of Scotch. It's the last time you'll see me, Spence. I'm through,'' and he went out and left me alone.'

Spence looked at Jean and me for a moment. 'It was a hell of a decision, kids. I was dying for a drink but I knew it wouldn't be just one. I knew that I'd lost my last friend and there would be nobody left to give a damn about me. Either I took Vic's advice and drank the whole case or I shouldn't take another drink, ever. I decided to give it up and I haven't had one for twelve years. But the terrible thing is I know even today that if I was to take one drink I'd start off all over again. We're never cured, you know.'

The group would come up to the house twice a week regularly and naturally we all had drinks before dinner. I had warned Jean, when asking known alcoholics or lushes what they would like to drink, never to say 'what would you like, Coca-Cola or tonic or ginger ale', just to ask them what they would like. Spence would always think for a moment and then decide on one or other of the soft drinks. One evening when Jean asked 'What's yours tonight, Spence?', he paused before answering 'You know Jeannie, I think I'll have a Scotch.'

Jean never turned a hair, she just came over and asked me to pour Spence a Scotch. I could see she was white in the face but without a word she handed the drink to Spence, sat down and started an animated conversation with Bert. We were all watching Spence out of the corner of our eyes as he looked at the drink in his hand. Suddenly he called Jean over. 'Jeannie, would you mind very much if I changed this for a coke?' and he gave her a wicked grin. Jean took the glass out of his hand and hurled it into the fireplace. 'Spence, don't you ever do that again,' and she ran from the room crying.

Spence looked around innocently. 'What's she going on about? I was only kidding.' But he knew that he'd upset her badly. He could be a devil sometimes and loved to tease the people he knew were fond of him.

About this time I struck out in a film I was very keen to do.

Bert assured me that he could arrange a loan-out from Metro as it would be a very prestigious film and help my career. The film was *A Star Is Born*. It had been one of my favourites when played by Janet Gaynor and Fredric March and I was thrilled to learn that I'd been thought of to try and repeat his magnificent performance. At last I was to be given the chance to play in a modern film with a real character part I could get my teeth into and also to appear opposite the legendary Judy Garland. Sid Luft, Judy's husband and the producer of the film brought her to dinner and of course Jean and Judy became a mutual admiration society. Jean, like practically everyone in the world, adored the talented Judy and apparently Judy returned the compliment. Jean had made a film the previous year with Spencer Tracy called *The Actress*, directed by George Cukor, who was to direct *A Star Is Born*. Spence warned me that, although brilliant, George had a habit of telling you how to say your lines.

'Don't let him, Jim, it's fatal. Whenever he tries it with me I just tell him to play the part and I'll direct the film.' But that was Tracy who had made several films with George and was one of his best friends. Cukor was a fascinating man. He had worked with all the greats like Garbo, Barrymore, Hepburn, Dressler, Harlow, Grant, and I felt pretty small fry in comparison and wondered how I was ever going to tell him anything. However, he called me one day and told me he thought it would be a good idea if I could come over and rehearse with Judy at his home. I arrived and to my consternation found that we were going to rehearse in the garden. George had several yapping dogs who didn't help one's concentration much, but as they didn't seem to upset Judy I felt I couldn't complain.

'Let's start with the scene in the bar where Judy is singing and she comes over to your table. All right, Jimmy, go ahead.'

I nervously spoke my first line.

'Do you always sing like that?'

'No, no,' said George. ' "Do you *always* sing like that?" Try again.'

I tried again.

'No, no. "Do you always *sing* like that?" '

The dogs started to bark, Judy started to laugh and I got paralysed. I remembered Spencer's advice not to let George tell me how to say the lines. Lines. I hadn't even got one out. The afternoon wore on with George giving me every bloody inflection and I began playing the part like a New York Jew, which George was. He also had a habit of jabbing his forefinger to emphasize his words. That night in bed beside Jean she saw me jabbing my finger as I repeated over and over: 'Do you always sing like that?'

'What are you doing with your finger, darling, and why are you using that funny voice?' Jean looked at me as if I'd gone mad, which I very nearly had.

'George wants me to play it like that,' I replied.

'He couldn't, it's awful,' said Jean.

The next day was just the same. I couldn't get a word out without George correcting me and pointing that bloody stubby finger. It didn't seem to affect Judy at all as she would listen to his corrections with a faraway look in her eyes and then say the line exactly as she'd said it before. But he was absolutely demoralizing me. One night, after having had a few drinks to bolster my courage, I phoned George and told him I was coming down to see him. After taking another big slug I arrived at his home and he nervously welcomed me into his drawing-room. He had every right to be nervous as I was furious and rather drunk.

'Now sit down, George Cukor, and don't open your mouth or wag that fucking finger in my face.'

'Yes, Jim, of course.'

'This is how that scene should be played,' and I started off. I had the script with me and went through to the end. George applauded when I'd finished and asked why I hadn't done it like that in rehearsal.

'Because you won't give me the chance, George. If you think I'm going through this kindergarten lesson in acting from you every day, you're mad. Take the script and shove it.' And I walked out. What a shame. I could have played that part on my head.

Jean and I had managed to get rid of the vast Bel Air mansion and had bought a lovely little house perched on top of a hill overlooking the whole of Hollywood on one side and the entire San Fernando Valley on the other. It was a paradise and we were really happy there. Our first guests from the 'old country' arrived one day, Richard Burton and his wife Sybil. I remember spotting the young Burton playing a small part in a West End play so, when I read he was appearing at a small theatre in Hammersmith, I went to see him. He was startlingly good and I went round backstage to pay my respects, though I hesitated a bit because I didn't want him to think I was being patronizing. The door of the dressing-room opened and there was young Burton in a jockstrap, clutching a glass of beer.

'Oh, my God, a bloody film star,' he said with that slight Welsh accent.

'Excuse me, but I just wanted to tell you that I think you're the most brilliant young actor I've ever seen. I just wanted to tell you, that's all.'

As I turned away, Burton grabbed me by the arm and invited me into the dressing-room.

'Damn, I've only got beer, I'm afraid, but if you'd like one . . .'

'No, thanks, I've got someone waiting, but when you come to Hollywood, look me up. I'm off there in a few weeks.'

'Hollywood?' Burton said. 'I'm not going to Hollywood.'

'Oh yes, you are. That's for sure. Promise to look me up, eh?'

We shook hands and Burton promised that if that unlikely

event took place he'd be sure to give me a ring. And here he was. In his first film he starred opposite Olivia de Havilland in *My Cousin Rachel*; his second was to be with Jean in *The Robe*. Small world. And later he was to marry my best friend's ex-wife, Liz Taylor. Small unhappy world!

Just before leaving the big house we had other visitors from England, my two children Jamie and Lindsay. They'd come over with their nanny for the holidays. I hadn't seen them for three years and, my God, how they'd changed. Jean coped wonderfully, considering the situation. Young children have a cruel way of putting their father's new wife in her place.

'What do we call you? I mean, you're not our mother, are you. Daddy's our daddy but you're not our mummy.' This said in such accusing tones. Poor Jean, she looked really scared.

'It might be a good idea if you called her Jean, don't you think? After all, that's her name.'

I tried to match their belligerence but the way they said 'Jean' had us in fits of laughter after they had haughtily stalked off. She won them over in about two days and eventually they adored her, but they were so undisciplined. I realized how difficult it must have been for Elspeth to control them because they needed a man to kick their behinds when it was necessary which, like all children of that age, was often. After a few weeks of Daddy being the heavy, boring but essential, they were almost human. My daughter Lindsay, although the younger, was the ringleader. She's an Aquarius, with all that that implies, plus her Daddy's temper. A difficult combination.

Jamie, a Cancer, meekly, but joyously, followed her bad example. I loved them both but, God, where did they get all the energy? Jean and I were absolutely exhausted after a day trying to entertain them. We were almost praying for the holidays to be over so that we could have some peace and quiet, but of course when they did go back we both missed them desperately.

I remember the last night. Jamie was about to go to his first boarding school and proudly showed me a pair of boxing gloves. Freddie Mills had given them to me when he'd won his world championship and apparently Elspeth had given them to Jamie to encourage him to be a good boxer like his father. As Jamie held out the gloves I asked him if he liked boxing? His young face broke up and he tearfully told me that he didn't really like the idea of hitting other boys or of being hit. I took the gloves away from him and tossed them out of the window.

'Now listen to me, Jamie. Never try to be a hero. If you have an argument with a boy smaller than yourself, let him run. If you get into a row with a boy bigger than yourself, you run. If you want to have a go with a boy your own size, have a go, but it's not necessary. It doesn't really prove anything. But whatever you do, don't try and be a hero, it just doesn't pay. Right?'

My son was already looking happier. He grew to be six foot three and a half inches and is very powerfully built. He was rarely in a fight. He didn't have to prove himself, like his father. That was the best advice I could have given him and I'm proud that he took it.

It was not long after I had recovered from the exhaustion of my children's visit that I was woken by the phone at about two in the morning. It was David Niven.

'Jim, I've got a problem. Viv [Vivien Leigh] is very sick and there's a fellow here who's upsetting her. Can you help?'

'Who's upsetting her?'

'Fellow called John Buckmaster.'

I'd heard of this unfortunate chap, Gladys Cooper's son, who had already been confined to a mental hospital on a couple of occasions.

'Well, he shouldn't be a problem, David. I'll be right down.'

Jean sleepily asked where I was going and when I told her said, 'Poor darling Viv. Give her my love', and went back to sleep. David met me outside the house and explained that Viv appeared to be having a nervous breakdown and the last person who should be with her was the unstable Buckmaster.

'I've been trying to get rid of him for hours but he won't go and won't let me near Vivien.'

'Leave it to me,' I said and marched in. I don't know what I was expecting but I was certainly taken aback at the sight of Buckmaster, clad only in a towel, standing on the landing at the head of the stairs leading to Viv's bedroom and proclaiming that he had been sent by a higher power to protect her. Sod this for a joke, I thought, he's got to go.

'Mr Buckmaster,' I said, advancing in my most belligerent manner, 'you don't know me but I know you and I've been sent by an even higher power to see that you get the hell out of here. Now I'll give you one minute to get dressed or I'm coming up after you. If you're a good boy I'll drive you back to your hotel, otherwise you'll go in an ambulance.'

There was a moment's silence while he thought it over. David was nervously fingering his moustache and giggling in the background. To my relief Buckmaster turned and, with a muttered 'I'll only be a minute', disappeared.

'You see, David, you're not the only one who's got charm.'

'Well done. Look, Jim, here's the phone number of the studio doctor. When you've dropped off our friend, give him a call. I'll look after Vivien in the meantime.'

Buckmaster appeared, fully dressed, and I drove him to the Garden of Allah (very appropriate) where he was staying. I apologized for my belligerent behaviour and explained that it was Vivien I was worried about and not his feelings. He said he quite understood and went into the hotel. I phoned the doctor who said a prescription would be waiting for me at Schwab's all-night drugstore.

'They'll give you four pills, Mr Granger. They're very strong and one will be sufficient to sedate her. When you've managed to get one down, call me and I'll come over with two nurses who are used to handling this sort of thing. But I don't want Miss Leigh to be fully conscious when we arrive or the shock might do her great harm.'

Oh God, I thought, what have I let myself in for? But Vivien was an old friend and that's what friends are for – to help each other. I returned to the house and whispered my instructions to David.

'How the hell are we going to get anything down her, Jim? She's behaving very strangely.'

And she was. She had copied Buckmaster and only had a towel draped round her. She was sitting in front of the TV, watching it as if hypnotized. Of course, at that hour of the morning there was nothing to see, just lines, with a high-pitched buzzing sound, but it seemed to fascinate Viv. Suddenly, with that over-hearty voice one uses when thoroughly scared and embarrassed I suggested we all had breakfast and winking conspiratorially at David, went into the kitchen. My brain couldn't have been working too well at that hour as, like a fool, I only prepared breakfast for Viv. I put the contents of one capsule into the scrambled eggs and another into the coffee. Of course, when I brought in the tray Viv became suspicious and asked why we weren't eating too. I stammered that I was on a diet and David muttered that he'd just eaten, the idiot, which wouldn't have convinced anyone.

Suddenly Viv thrust a forkful of egg at David and told him to try some. I had signalled to him that the coffee and eggs were loaded so he desperately tried to avoid the fork. But Vivien was a very overpowering lady and in her present manic state got very suspicious. David for once was giving a bad performance and Viv immediately caught on that he didn't want any part of that breakfast. She didn't try it on me, just David. It ended with him drinking half the coffee and swallowing half the eggs, forcefed by Vivien. I was trying to hide my hysteria, as at any moment I expected David to pass out. I didn't have long to wait. With a stifled yawn he said he must catch a few moments sleep and happily zizzed off on the couch.

I was left alone with the frightening Miss Leigh. We had been friends for years and yet the strained, white-faced, oddly-behaved woman facing me was nothing to do with the Vivien I knew. Suddenly she dropped the towel and walked out into the garden. It was dawn now and she said she was going to take a swim. She sat down by the edge of the pool and I joined her. Here I was at six in the morning sitting by a pool opposite a totally nude and utterly deranged stranger. I thought a direct approach might work.

'Vivien, you know I love you and wouldn't want to hurt you. You're tired, darling, and you must rest. Please take one of these pills.'

I had brought a glass of water with me and handed it to her. She smiled sweetly, studied the pill for a moment and then tossed it into the pool. With her green eyes studying me intently she looked exactly like a cat that was ready to pounce. Oh Lord. I was down to the last one now and didn't know what the hell to do. I went inside to see if I could get some help from David but he was snoring away peacefully with a contented smile on his face. Although I shook the hell out of him, I couldn't wake him up. Vivien was still sitting by the pool gazing out into space. Okay, I thought, charm hasn't worked, I'd better be brutal. I seized her by the shoulders.

'Now, Viv, cut out the crap. I'm tired and if you don't behave, I'm going to shove this bloody pill down your throat. Now open your mouth.'

Viv obediently 'opened' and as I started pushing the pill in, grabbed it out of my hand and threw it into the pool. She looked at me with a triumphant smile and started to laugh. I couldn't help laughing too. The whole scene was so uncanny. Me trying to force a naked forty-year-old film star to take a pill. I put the towel round her and led her back into the house. I phoned the doctor and explained my failure. He didn't seem surprised and told me they could be very tricky in that state. He told me to hang on and he would be up very soon with the nurses. That wait seemed like hours. Vivien was watching the empty TV screen again, as if her whole life depended on her concentration. Finally there was a ring at the door and Vivien darted up the stairs and stood at the top glaring. I let the doctor in, followed by two enormous nurses, who told me to leave it to them as they were used to this kind of situation. I noticed one of them was concealing a hypodermic syringe, as they advanced to the foot of the stairs. They may have been used to this kind of situation but they certainly weren't used to a person like Vivien.

'How dare you burst into my house! Get out! Get out!'

Vivien could be very imperious when she wanted to be and very frightening. The nurses were completely shattered and started to back away. Then one of them cooed at Vivien, 'I know who you are. You're Scarlett O'Hara, aren't you.'

'I'm not Scarlett O'Hara, I'm Blanche Dubois,' Vivien screamed and they retreated even further.

Vivien had been working on *A Streetcar Named Desire* for nearly two years, both in the theatre and in the film studios and many people thought this demanding role had caused her nervous breakdown. Muttering to them to get their hypodermic ready, I went up the stairs and took Vivien in my arms. I whispered to her that everything was going to be all right and, lifting her up, carried her into the bedroom. I fell across the bed, pinning Vivien underneath me and yelled at the terrified nurse to stick the needle in. As Vivien felt the point, she looked at me as if I had betrayed her.

'Oh, Jimmy, how could you? I thought you were my friend.'

After hospitalization Vivien recovered and when next we met she was her old self again, but I never forgot that look on her face. I *was* your friend, Vivien, believe me.

23

I expected my next picture would take me back to Africa as Sam Zimbalist had been looking for a follow up to *Solomon's Mines*. He had wanted to make a sequel but I'd talked him out of it. We'd got away with it once but a sequel would only be an anti-climax. It was Marlene Dietrich who gave me the idea of remaking *Red Dust* and setting it in Africa. Brilliant. Gable and Harlow had made a romantic outdoor smash of the story twenty years earlier, and I thought Deborah would be great as the haughty English lady with Ava Gardner perfect for the Harlow whore. I went to see Doré Schary who, after the success of *Zenda,* listened to me more sympathetically and we got the go-ahead. Sam Zimbalist hired the top script writer of the time, Johnny Lee Mahin, to prepare the first draft and it was coming along great. We were all excited about Johnny's idea of making the main theme of the film capturing gorillas. Ava, Deborah, me and gorillas. Unbeatable. One day I was summoned to Doré's office.

'Jim, congratulations. *Solomon's* was a smash, *Scaramouche* was a smash and now *Zenda* is doing fine. Congratulations.'

I noticed he didn't mention *Soldiers Three, The Light Touch* or *The Wild North.*

'Now we've got a problem, Jim,' Doré continued in his avuncular, confidential man-to-man approach. 'We've got a real problem, Jim. Your career is going great guns, but Gable's – Gable needs a good picture. He's just made two bombs' (and whose fault is that, I felt like saying), 'and we've got to keep the King happy, no?'

I was wondering when the knife was going in. I didn't have long to wait.

'He wants to do your African picture.' (It had been called *Mogambo*.) 'Now, Jim, you've been to Africa, you don't want to go there again, do you? You don't want to be separated from that lovely little wife of yours, do you?' (No I didn't, but I wanted to make that African picture.) 'So we've decided to take you out and put Gable in. Okay?'

There was a deathly pause.

'But Doré, that picture was my idea. Nobody would have thought of doing a remake of *Red Dust*. Shit, it's not fair, Doré.' Why the hell I was using the word 'fair' in Hollywood I don't know. I was bitterly disappointed and outraged at being double-crossed but I wasn't really surprised. I should have walked out of the studio and told them to shove their contract, but I had to pay for that house. I was a little disgusted with my friend Sam Zimbalist too for not taking a stand on this and, as producer, insisting I played the part, but he was a company man and had to take orders like everyone else.

Instead of *Mogambo* they handed me a script called *All the Brothers Were Valiant*, a crappy melodrama about whaling, pearl-diving in the South Seas, mutiny and lust. Some of my scenes were to be made on location in Jamaica but Jean couldn't come with me because she was preparing for the blockbuster Cinemascope production of *The Robe* with our new friend Burton. Another separation, though this time it was not to be for long as 'One Take' Thorpe was at the helm again. We stayed at the Tower Island Hotel on the north coast and with all the tourists thronging about it was very hard to concentrate and remember we were making a film. The different rum punches were impossible to resist, especially with the accompanying calypso bands which serenaded us every evening and far into the night. Try sleeping with a calypso band playing just outside your bungalow when you have to get up at six in the morning.

We worked in a palm grove bordering a white sandy beach with a coral reef lying fifty yards offshore forming a lagoon of dazzlingly clear water. God, what a beautiful spot, idyllic except for one thing. Where there are coconut palms there are jiggers. These animals burrow under the skin and form festering sores so, before long, most of us had our ankles and legs covered in scabs especially those, like me, who had to run around barefoot. This disenchanted me somewhat with the place and when I was offered a hundred acres by the owner for around $50,000, I turned him down. The fact that I didn't have $50,000 was neither here nor there. I hadn't appreciated that palm groves can be cleared, jiggers got rid of, and hotels and villas built overlooking that perfect beach. The land was near Ocho Rios which became the most fashionable tourist spot on the island and the hundred acres I was offered was eventually sold for real estate development for about five million. Actors just aren't businessmen.

Bob Taylor was the easiest person to work with but he had been entirely emasculated by the MGM brass who insisted that he was only a pretty face. He was convinced he wasn't really a good actor and his calm acceptance of this stigma infuriated me.

'Your problem is that you're too bloody good-looking and it's fashionable to say that good-looking guys can't act,' I used to tell him, but nothing would convince him.

'Do you know what they did, Jim, when they put me into *Quo Vadis*? They showed me your test and told me to play the part just like you.'

I roared with laughter. 'But that's typical, Bob. If I was so great why didn't they use me? They chose you because you're a bloody fine actor. Just look at those arseholes in The Iron Lung, stunted, pot-bellied and bald, most of them. They're jealous, that's all.' He was such a nice guy, Bob, but he had even more hang-ups than I had.

In this film I was allowed to play the bad brother, a nice change which I thoroughly enjoyed, and at the end there was to be a very effective death scene with me giving my dying blessing to Bob and his wife in which I would move my audience to tears, or so I thought. The climax of this rip-roaring melodrama was a mutiny for which I was responsible but, finding at the last moment that blood is thicker than water, etc., I change my mind and side with Bob. During the resulting free for all, the principal villain comes at me with a harpoon; I crush his skull with a club and he runs me through. Now the place the special effects man had chosen for this thrust was the centre of my chest and I suggested to the director that my stomach might be a better target as it would give me rather more time for my death scene. Thinking it would take too long to change, Thorpe said it looked fine the way it was. But, when the film was previewed, there was a howl of laughter from the audience at the miraculous durability of the hero who could still speak after having had a harpoon through his heart. Naturally I asked for a retake but was told it would be too expensive as the set had been demolished, so the scene was cut. What a waste of that tear-jerking performance.

Jean had completed *The Robe* and been signed up for another costume epic, *The Egyptian,* so this had her tied to Hollywood for the next six months. Sam Zimbalist had come up with another idea for me, *Beau Brummell*. I was enthusiastic about it as I remembered the silent version with John Barrymore and set to work excitely on the script (I wasn't doing any of the writing, naturally, but Sam would show me each scene as it was completed).

We were discussing the all-important costumes with Walter Plunkett when I heard a rumour that it wasn't to be shot in Hollywood but at the MGM studios in England. This was to be a major film with a four-month schedule and would mean another long separation from Jean.

Bert and I pleaded with Benny Thau to have it made in Hollywood but were told that MGM had 'blocked pounds' which could only be used in England and where money came into it I knew we were fighting a losing battle. I tried to explain that my marriage came before any film, but naturally I was accused of being 'difficult' and a bad friend to Sam who had reactivated the film especially for me. Bert and I asked to see the mighty Nicholas Schenck, head of Loew's Inc., the owners of Metro, in order to plead my case. The meeting was arranged and Bert suggested that Jean should come too as he was sure Schenck wouldn't be able to resist her.

Schenck was known to all his studio underlings as 'The General' but when we met him we thought 'The Lizard' would have been a more appropriate title. He was small and ugly and gazed at us with cold, heavy-lidded eyes that didn't blink once during the entire meeting. I told him my problems, with Jean snivelling dutifully beside me, adding that I felt sure he, as a good family man, would understand my reluctance to be continually separated from my wife. It was useless. I even offered to do a film a year for nothing, as long as it was made in Hollywood, if they would release me from my contract but those unblinking, hooded eyes looked at me expressionlessly as he told me I was far too valuable to the studio and eventually I gave up. As we left the presence, Jean burst into floods of tears and when Benny Thau worriedly asked her why she was crying, she replied through her sobs: 'Because Jimmy has to work for that awful man.' Benny went white. Obviously that wasn't the way to refer to 'The General'.

So, having succumbed to the threats of suspension and the pleas of my friend Sam, I once more found myself packing and getting on a plane that would take me away from Jean for months although it was wonderful to be back in London and to see my family and all my old friends again. My mother came and stayed with me at the Dorchester and my two children would come bursting in with Elspeth, just like old times, and I thoroughly enjoyed myself, until it was time to start the film.

I can't remember a thing about my performance except that I seemed to be constantly changing from one tight-fitting costume to another and having to compete with the extrovert and unpredictable Peter Ustinov and Robert Morley, a formidable combination. We had a very pompous German director (naturalized American, of course) called Curtis Bernhardt, and Elizabeth Taylor endeared herself to me by yawning in his face when he was giving her minute instructions as to how to play a certain scene. She was bored with the whole thing as she too had been forced into the part against her will and hated being separated from Mike.

At the beginning of the film this German director had ordered the prop man to get him a stick.

'A stick, sir? What kind of a stick? What for?'

'Never mind vot for. I vant a schtick.'

'Yessir,' and he got his 'schtick'.

The director started slapping it on the furniture when giving orders and poking people with it until I took him aside one day.

'I know you're an American, Curtis, and you know you're an American but the crew don't know you're an American, they think you're a German, and don't forget they were rationed until two years ago because of the war. You know, the war between Germany and England. So be a good chap and don't use the stick.'

'Vy not?' he asked.

'Because if you do, they'll drop a lamp on your head. Know what I mean?' and I took the 'schtick' out of his hands and broke it. He got the message but I don't think I endeared myself to him.

My stand-in was a lovely cockney character called Bob Porter, an old mate of mine who had stood in for me on many of my English films. A stand-in is a very important person in a film star's life. He has to be a real friend and in many cases is the liaison between the star and the outside world during filming. If you want to get to the star you'd better be in with his stand-in. It was winter in England, so of course I caught intestinal 'flu which gave me colitis. This is not a comfortable complaint if you're wearing skintight costumes. After a few hours' work my stomach used to swell up and the tight clothes became torture. I had to have colonic irrigations to relieve the inflammation and one day I overheard my friend Bob describing this treatment. In London a real cockney uses rhyming slang. Up the apple and pears (stairs), put the loaf of bread (head) on the weeping willow (pillow). So you go up the apple and put the loaf on the weeping, meaning you go upstairs and put your head on the pillow, go to bed. So Bob's explanation came out like this.

'Poor old Jim, every night he has to have a splosh up the H.' Slightly confused I asked, 'Splosh up the H? What d'you mean, Bob?'

'You know, Jim, Aristotle – bottle – bottle and glass – arse splosh up the arse. See?'

'But why H? Aristotle begins with an A.'

'Oh, not Aristotle – it's Harry Stocle. See?'

One evening after work a friend of mine brought a very beautiful blonde round for a drink. She found me completely enthralled by an ant colony. I had bought this fascinating present for my children but hated to part with it and used to watch it for hours. It was a real ant colony encased in glass constructed in such a way that they could exist in it for years. Fascinating. At that time in America there was a dirt rag rather like the English *Private Eye,* called *Confidential.* Stars, of course, were their favourite target and we were all getting fed up with the scurrilous lies reported in this filth magazine. So far I had escaped but on returning to Hollywood I was told that I had featured in one edition: 'Granger gets his kicks from ants' was the headline and there was a photo of me absorbed in my ant colony. That bitch had been working for *Confidential* and must have had a concealed camera. The article stated that, after watching the ants, I would get turned on and attack the nearest female, meaning her, I suppose, but I certainly hadn't attacked her as I found the ants far more attractive. Eventually I had to hand the colony over to my children as it was time for me to go back to America.

Jean was still on *The Egyptian* and found making epics as boring as I did. I had to die with a harpoon in my chest and she had to die with an arrow in hers. She agreed it was difficult to act with those dirty great things sticking out of you. In *Beau Brummell* I died of pneumonia in a garret and in *The Robe* she was eaten by lions in the Colosseum. Our careers were running neck and neck.

We had talked of a family but Jean was put off by Liz Taylor's pregnancy. Mike and Liz would often visit us during this period and Jean was horrified by the suffering Liz seemed to go through. She had hurt her back at some time and the pregnancy caused her considerable discomfort. She was always complaining of pains in her stomach, her back, her legs. Poor darling, I'm sure she was really suffering but Jean thought this was the normal result of pregnancy and didn't want any part of it. However, the thing that really postponed any addition to our family was Mike's talent with a paint-brush. As the months passed, Liz's stomach became enormous. She would wear a skirt cut out round the bulge with a smock-like blouse over it. One day she raised the blouse and Jean was horrified to see that Mike had painted a face on that distended stomach. That did it. It took Jean two years to get over the shock.

In 1948 Jean had been nominated for an Oscar for her performance as Ophelia in Olivier's *Hamlet* and, when she came to Hollywood to attend the ceremony, she had been entertained by Walter Wanger, a famous producer married to the beautiful Joan Bennett. He had been very kind to Jean and had given a lavish party in her honour. We had seen him several times and often dined at his home. Walter had been shattered by the discovery that his wife was having an affair with her agent. He had followed them one day and, finding them together in a car, had shot the agent in a very delicate part of his anatomy. Poor Walter got five months in jail for this righteous act of aggression, the Beverly Hills police apparently disapproving of its residents shooting people's balls off, though Walter's aim had been poor and he'd only managed to hit one.

Jean and I came into the MGM commissary one day and saw Walter lunching by himself, stuck away in a corner, with everyone in the crowded restaurant studiously avoiding him. Naturally we went over and joined him. He was our friend and we resented the way he was being ostracized. When I went back to the set a publicity woman came over to us.

'I've never seen such a brave thing,' she gushed. 'In front of everyone you went over to that man and sat with him. Such courage.'

'Balls,' I said, not realizing the epithet was so appropriate in the circumstances. 'He's our friend. What do you expect us to do, cut him?' Hypocritical bitch. But that was typically Hollywood. When a man was down, avoid him like the plague. I think the real reason Walter was being avoided was not because of the jail sentence but because his last film had been a flop! If you're a success you can get away with murder, as was proved about the same time.

Khrushchev was visiting Hollywood and being fêted as if he were God Almighty himself and a party was given for him at Twentieth Century to which all the big names were invited. Spyros Skouras, President of Twentieth Century, was on the dais with Khrushchev and made a rather bumbling speech about in what other country in the world but America could a poor Greek boy get the opportunity of becoming head of a great organization controlling 5,000 workers? The wily Khrushchev replied in what other country but Russia could a poor peasant rise to be head of an organization controlling 200 million workers. I was about to jump up and shout that Skouras had succeeded without murdering millions of his countrymen but I was stopped by the applause and cheering from every other person in the room. To my shame I kept quiet. But that's the point. Khrushchev was a success and Hollywood reveres success no matter how it's attained.

24.

The fabulous Grace Kelly was to be my next leading lady. Many people, the press especially, have asked me what it was like to play love scenes with all those incredibly beautiful women.

'My God, Jim, it must be great to hold all those smashers in your arms and kiss them. Come on, confess, you get a kick out of it, don't you?' A kick out of it, hell. I think any leading film actor will agree with me that there's nothing romantic or sexy about kissing all those fabulous mouths. Personally I don't like kissing in public and on a film set there are always about sixty bored faces looking on. Then there's the positioning. When you're kissing someone you really fancy you're not concerned with where the noses go and what's the best angle of the half face exposed to the cameras. You're not concerned with mucking up her make-up which you are warned will take half an hour to repair. Then I've always found it difficult to make love at nine o'clock in the morning. After a few belts, in the evening, because the day's work is almost over, it's easier to get in the mood, but having to pick up the same scene next morning and show the same enthusiasm takes more acting ability than I possess.

Many of my films were in costume and naturally you didn't have many duplicates because of the expense. It's hot working under the lights and you sweat. After a few weeks the costumes become high and, although dried and disinfected by the wardrobe department each night, it only took a few hours under the lights for them to start ponging again.

Then there's halitosis. Not everyone has a breath like

new-mown hay. When you're nervous in a scene it often affects your stomach which in turn affects your breath. I must have acted with many nervous actresses. One, I remember, was the most beautiful enchanting creature it was possible to imagine but she had the breath of a lion. Playing love scenes with her was torture, especially the ones when you breathe your passion for each other with your mouths inches apart so that you can both be in the lens at the same time. I used to take a deep breath and try to play the whole scene without inhaling. I made three films with that lady and it was very good for my breath control. I'm sure actresses had the same experience with some of their leading men. I would gargle and try to make sure I offended as little as possible, but I've been told that not all actors were so thoughtful.

Grace Kelly had been an immediate success after her first film *High Noon* in which she co-starred with Gary Cooper. After that she was lucky enough to co-star with Bing Crosby, Ray Milland, James Stewart and Clark Gable. Now she had me. Hitchcock wanted her for *To Catch a Thief* and, if the dates fitted, she would go straight from our film, *Green Fire,* as the epic had been named, to her next leading man, Cary Grant. Poor Grace was worried all through our film that she wouldn't finish in time because Hitchcock waits for no man or woman.

Our locations were in Colombia. I had never visited South America before and was shocked by the poverty. We only worked near the coastal towns of Cartagena and Barranquilla but if the rest of the country was anything like them the outlook was depressing. Grace arrived with her sister as her chaperone and Paul Douglas with several bottles of Scotch as his. Everywhere was dusty, dirty and swarming with flies and God knows why we went there as I didn't see any emerald mines, which was the theme of our story. When we came back to Hollywood for the interiors we matched up some missing exterior shots in the hills off Mulholland Drive and you couldn't tell the difference. A wasted trip.

We were running behind schedule and Grace was getting more and more worried. If the scenes continued in sequence she was going to be too late but if they concentrated on hers she would just make it. The director, my old friend Bundy Marton, was quite willing to rearrange the schedule but the production manager hated to have his plans altered and refused.

'What happens if I get sick,' I asked him one day.

'Well, I'd be forced to alter the schedule and it would cost a lot of money. Why?'

'Because I'm not feeling too well. But if you concentrate on Grace I'm sure my health will improve. Know what I mean?' I looked at him innocently but he knew what I meant. He changed the schedule and Grace got away in time but, of course, once again I was being 'difficult'.

Grace had one phobia, her behind. For me it was the most delicious behind imaginable, but it did stick out a bit and she was very self-conscious about it. Our last scene was played in a torrential downpour and when the final kiss came we were both soaking wet, which accentuated that fabulous behind. To save her embarrassment I covered it with both hands. She was so delighted at finishing the film that she didn't even object but if you look closely at that kiss you'll see Grace give a start as those two eager hands take hold.

Jean was preparing for another film at Twentieth Century, this time with Marlon Brando. It was to be called *Desirée* and she played one of Napoleon's mistresses. Marlon made it obvious that he was bored with the whole thing and was merely getting rid of one of his commitments. He muttered and mumbled his way through the part and I didn't see how Jean could have heard him, let alone acted with him, but Marlon can never be bad all the way through a picture and some of his scenes were brilliant. Jean liked him a lot but I found him fairly insufferable.

306

About this time I received a letter from my mother telling me that she was very worried about Elspeth's health and suggesting that the children should come and live with us as their mother just couldn't cope. I discussed this problem with Jean and she told me that if Elspeth was willing she was quite agreeable and, although terrified at the prospect of having them on a permanent basis, said she would do her best.

Elspeth was in a nursing home and agreed that I should have custody of the children. As soon as she was better she planned to come over to America to be near them. The travel details were fixed up and we waited anxiously for the arrival of my two beloved terrors. Of course a lot of arranging had to take place. The only servant's room was turned over to my daughter, Lindsay, while Jamie had the spare room. I've said the house was cosy. It was, it was also tiny. It was L-shaped with nearly all the rooms opening on to a patio with a swimming pool. At first we used to jump out of bed and straight into the pool but soon the novelty wore off and we used it less and less. But with the arrival of the kids we once again started to use it. We had no option. We would be woken early every morning by their shrieks as they splashed about in that infernal pool and of course one of us always had to be there in case of accidents. I hadn't realized Jean and I lived such a peaceful life until my two monsters turned up.

I had made enquiries about schools, pretty difficult in Beverly Hills which wasn't noted for its large selection. Naturally they were co-educational which thrilled my two who had always been to segregated schools in England and, when the headmistress gave them a test to find in which grade they belonged, I discovered how backward they were. She advised me to arrange special coaching for them before the next term and recommended a tutor. He turned out to be a small, nervous man and I wondered how he would get on with the monsters. He arrived for the first morning's tuition and all seemed to be going peacefully as Jean and I eavesdropped outside Jamie's bedroom which had been turned into a temporary classroom, complete with blackboard and desks.

Thinking that they deserved a break after their hard studies I sent in some fruit in the middle of the morning. Suddenly all hell broke loose. There were shouts and screams of laughter and loud squishy noises. I rushed in and was appalled at what I saw. Unfortunately I had chosen ripe plums and grapes on this occasion and my children had thought it fun to throw them at the blackboard. The poor little tutor, in trying to protect it, had come into their line of fire and the children soon found he made a more amusing target. Letting out a roar of fury that could have been heard in the next county, I ordered them to clean up the mess and led the terrified tutor into the bathroom and started picking squashed fruit from different parts of his anatomy. I begged him to give them another chance and guaranteed that nothing like that would ever happen again. He said he would only return if I would always be there during the classes, so at the age of forty-one I went back to school.

Jean, of course, had locked herself in her bedroom as she didn't want the children to see her laughing and it was left to me to mete out punishment. Nobody could look more innocent and angelic than my two and I couldn't understand why they behaved so fiendishly. I should have thrashed them both, I suppose, but I just couldn't bring myself to do it. I told them sternly that they wouldn't get their favourite food, couldn't watch TV or swim for a week. That really hurt. But it hurt us too as we couldn't swim or watch TV either. It was really hot that summer and all next day we were both dying to take a dip but couldn't, so we waited until they'd gone to bed. One night we were relaxing in the cool water when I had the feeling we were being watched and looking up, saw two little faces peering out of their bedroom windows. I've never felt so guilty in my life.

Bringing up children is hell. If you discipline them you must discipline yourself. But they were a joy in so many other ways and Jean was absolutely marvellous with them, though it can't have been easy for her to have two unruly children thrust into her life. She was only about twenty-five herself at the time and I often got the impression I was bringing up three children instead of two. She loved having midnight feasts with them romping about on our bed. I think she enjoyed herself more than they did and her protests were as loud as theirs when I ordered everyone off to sleep. They adored her and there was no more resentment about her not being their real mother. She never tried to usurp Elspeth's place. She was Jeanniebags, their pet name for her, and Elspeth was Mummy. Of course I had to be the heavy as Jean refused, quite rightly, to discipline them.

'It's not my job, darling. I love them and I want them to love me, but as a friend.' She wasn't only their friend. As often as not she was their accomplice and I wish I'd had a friend like that when I was a child.

Although she loved the new house and the easy-going informal life of Hollywood, I could tell that Jean was getting very homesick for London and her family, as it was three years since she'd been back. I was determined to try and find a film for us both and asked Benny Thau if there wasn't something that MGM wanted to do over in England to use up more of those frozen pounds. He promised me he'd look into it. We had an absolute treasure working for us, Vivienne Walker, who had been head of the hairdressing department at Pinewood Studios where she had looked after Jean on many of her films. Now she had come over to America and was working for us as secretary, companion and beloved friend, so there would be no problem with the children.

I was working on another dreary costume epic called *Moonfleet,* directed by the once brilliant Fritz Lang, but as it was a story about English smugglers in Cornwall, Lang was a little out of his depth. I remember one day, the production manager telling us that we were to be visited by the elusive Louis B. Mayer. He arrived with Doré Schary and to our amazement ushered in a young actor called James Dean, who had just made his second successful film, *Rebel without a Cause*. Dean epitomized rebellious youth in both films and was certainly carrying that characterization on in real life, being dressed in a cracked leather jacket, open-necked shirt, unpressed trousers and sneakers. Mayer called me over and introduced me to Dean as if he were visiting royalty, but he was obviously unimpressed by this historic meeting, and his conversation left much to be desired, being simply 'Hi there'. I told him how much I had enjoyed his last film, but he didn't return the compliment.

Mayer and Schary were obviously trying to get him to sign a long-term contract and their fawning over him was laughable. Apparently they didn't impress the twenty-five-year-old Dean either, as he never signed with Metro, or any other studio for that matter. I learnt later that he'd met Gable and Tracy with the same indifference and I was astounded that a boy that age could be so self-satisfied and unimpressionable. Hadn't Gable's performance in *Gone with the Wind* moved him at all? Or, more important, even if it hadn't, couldn't he have had the good manners to pretend that it had? I'm afraid I was as unimpressed by him as he seemed to be by all of us.

Jean had better luck. She was introduced to Elvis Presley and told me that apart from being one of the best-looking men she'd ever seen, he was charming with a great sense of humour. He seemed to know that I was her husband and explained he was a great fan of mine, having seen *Solomon's Mines* sixty times.

'Sixty times! You're not serious!'

'Oh, I sure am, Miss Simmons. I was an usher in the cinema.'

310

While we were pressuring Benny Thau to find that English-based film, we were visited one day by Mike Frankovich, a producer at Columbia. He had a script he wanted us to read as it had parts for both of us and was to be made in England. It seemed the perfect answer. We sat up in bed that night anxiously reading the treatment, which was pretty awful, but I thought with rewriting we could make something out of it. At least it gave Jean an off-beat dramatic part with a nasty two-faced villain for myself. We met Frankovich the next day and told him that in principle we were agreeable, provided the script was rewritten. It was then that Frankovich let go his bombshell. He was contractually obliged to have Arthur Lubin as the director.

'Arthur Lubin,' we both chorused. 'But he makes those awful Francis the Mule pictures.'

'Well, he's made others,' Frankovich said defensively.

'I know. *Ali Baba and the Forty Thieves,* and that was worse.'

'Never mind. With you and Jean he can't go wrong and I'll keep my eye on him.' That'll be a great help, I thought, how many pictures have you directed? But we were so keen to get to England together we'd have said yes to practically anything and we were offered very generous expenses indeed. Metro kindly lent me out and Jean and I were on our way to London.

We had taken a large suite at the Dorchester and there was a constant stream of family staying with us – Jean's mother, brother and sisters, my mother and sister, friends dropping in, late night tuck-ins, we hardly had time to study our lines and used to arrive at the studio madly going over our scenes together in the car. What we both missed in the States were the fish and chip shops, so on our way back from a long day's work, we'd tell the chauffeur to nip out and buy us four portions of fish and six of chips, liberally sprinkled with vinegar. By the time we reached the Dorchester the whole interior of the car stank and the very supercilious porter who opened the door would try to hide his shock as he was almost knocked down by the blast. We would rush through the foyer hugging our packages and hoping we could get a lift to ourselves. I'm afraid a good many residents were equally shocked by the two famous film stars stinking of fried fish.

While we were in London *Beau Brummell* was chosen for the Royal Command Performance, a most tasteless choice as it showed one of Her Majesty's ancestors, George III, as a raving lunatic, realistically portrayed by Robert Morley, built like a whale, who had endeared himself to me by treading on my toes in his mad scenes.

Before the performance we were presented to Her Majesty who, after she had said her usual tactful and complimentary few words to Jean and me, passed on to the next group and I was faced by Prince Philip. He leant over and whispered, 'Do you think this film is all right for Her Majesty?'

I hesitated. What could I say? Of course it wasn't 'all right'. 'If you could manage to distract her attention when Robert Morley appears, it might be better, sir.'

He laughed and said he'd do his best. I needn't have worried. On their way out the Prince gave me a smile. 'Everything was fine. That was her favourite scene.'

Lubin 'mulishly' directed the film called *Footsteps in the Fog* which had been rewritten by Lenore Coffee and myself, and our hard work in the car paid off when it won an international award. Thanks to Jean's performance and the success of the film, Mike Frankovich was promoted to be head of Columbia in Hollywood and I never saw him again, but long before the picture was finished Jean and I were beginning to miss our little home, the children and Bessie.

Bessie was a toy poodle and the bane of my existence. A year or so before Mike Wilding and I had been out shopping and I'd spotted this tiny object in a shop window. I knew Jean was longing for a pet and very selfishly I hadn't bought her one, knowing what pets can entail, but I decided this would be perfect for her. We entered the shop and I told the elderly couple in attendance that I wanted to buy the puppy, but it wasn't that simple. Apparently this was a very special puppy, with a pedigree that went back to the Ark and the owners had to be convinced that she was going to a good home. I don't think my pedigree impressed them at all, but when I told them that we had a large house in Bel Air they relaxed a bit and eventually graciously agreed to accept 500 dollars for the tiny object. In those days you could buy a second-hand car for less. Then they insisted that she had to be shampooed while we were lectured on the care of this ball of fluff, what kind of food to give her, where she should sleep, what vet to call and of course she had to have a special drinking bowl, food bowl, sleeping basket, collar and lead, dog coat and toys, all of which were very expensive. The purchase had taken about two hours instead of the five minutes I'd expected and I was now very late and I knew Jean would be worried. She wasn't worried, she was furious but as she was ticking us off, the puppy poked her head out of my pocket and Jean caught sight of her.

'That's why we were late, darling, getting a present for you, but of course if you don't want it, I'll take it back.' I knew Jean was happy because she was in floods of tears as she fondled her new baby. I named her Bessie after Jean's performance in *Young Bess* and from that moment on I was definitely second in importance in that household. Of course the sleeping basket was never used as Jean insisted on having the puppy on our bed and I never had another night's uninterrupted sleep. Nothing ever woke Jean but I'm a very light sleeper. During the night Bessie would decide to jump off the bed and then couldn't get back. Her whimperings and scratchings meant that poor old Dad had to lean over and help her back up. After a few weeks she became very possessive and I would have to ask her permission before I made love to Jean, otherwise she'd take a piece out of my behind.

When we got back to Hollywood we realized that our beloved little house would have to go and a larger one found to accommodate the children, so after a lot of paper signing with banks and mortgage companies we were able to buy a beautiful house which was perfect for the kids, again in Bel Air. We enrolled them in the local school, so our lives became a little calmer and better organized.

Strangely, Mike and Liz had decided to change their home too and had bought a lovely 'Bird' house up one of the canyons, Bird being the name of the architect who had built our own little house. We were invited one evening for dinner and who should be there but James Dean. He and Liz had just completed *Giant*, directed by George Stevens, and Liz and James had become very close friends. He was the proud owner of a new high-powered Porsche and I had just bought a Mercedes Benz 300 SL so there followed a heated discussion on the speed and merits of the two sports cars. I warned him not to hit anything as the Porsche had the engine in the back and very little protection up front, unlike the strongly constructed Mercedes. James was unimpressed and the conversation was forgotten over dinner.

I had begun to change my opinion of this young man who had not allowed the offers of money from studio heads to alter his determination to be independent, and secretly envied and admired his contempt for the Hollywood scene. As we said goodnight I had no premonition that we'd never see him again. The next day he wrapped his Porsche round a tree and was killed instantly. Liz was inconsolable. With only three films to his credit young James Dean had practically all of Hollywood in mourning.

How sad for Liz that only a short time afterwards another of her closest friends nearly died after a party at this same house. Montgomery Clift crashed his car on the winding road leading down the canyon and Liz dazedly cradled Monty's bleeding head in her arms until the ambulance arrived. Poor Elizabeth was rarely lucky with those she truly loved.

25

Pandro S. Berman called me into his office one day and told
me that at last he'd got something worthwhile for me.

'I owe you a good one, Jim, after *Soldiers Three* and *All the
Brothers*. You know that book about India you were keen on?
Well, we've bought it for you and Ava Gardner.' He was
talking about *Bhowani Junction,* a marvellous novel by John
Masters. I'd told Pan how much I'd like to do it and here he
was offering it to me. 'Now, Jim, there's a catch. It'll mean
at least four months' location in Pakistan and a month in the
British Studios, and I know how you hate to be separated
from Jean, so what about it?'

'Don't worry, Pan, this time she'll come with me.'

Excitedly I told Jean about the project and everything
seemed to be working out fine as we prepared for the trip
until Bert called up and told us that he had wonderful news
for Jean. Apparently Sam Goldwyn wanted her to co-star in
Guys and Dolls with Frank Sinatra and Marlon Brando,
directed by the brilliant Joe Mankiewicz. I saw the look on
Jean's face.

'Well, darling, we'll just have to postpone that trip to
India. You've got to do that film.' Of course she had to. It
would give her a chance to sing and dance and act with top
stars, working with a top director. It would mean another
separation but as Jean pointed out, even if I could get out of
Bhowani Junction I wouldn't see much of her as she'd be
working all day and probably be exhausted at night.
Anyway, that ghastly fight with Hughes had been about this
very thing, that she could choose her films and I certainly
wasn't going to stand in her way.

It seemed odd that she would be working with Sinatra and

I with Ava. The last time we'd seen them they'd been having an awful row. We had gone to join them before going to the Ambassadors where Frank was singing. As we entered the house we knew something was wrong as they practically weren't speaking to each other. It was decided that Frank would go on ahead and we would bring Ava and all the way she was carrying on about how impossible he was to live with, but when we were seated at our table and Frank came on, everything changed. He sang love songs as only Frank can sing them and he sang them straight at her. Ava started to cry. 'Look at the goddamned SOB. How can you resist him?' He joined us later and everything seemed to be all right.

I had decided to have a crew cut for the part of an Indian Army colonel and was showing the effect to an approving Pandro when the door burst open and in walked George Cukor. Pan beamed at me as he delightedly told me how lucky we were to have George as director. When he saw the look on my face he asked what was the matter.

'Oh, Jimmy and I had a bad experience on *Star Is Born* but that's in the past. We'll have a ball on this one, won't we?'

George looked at me rather pleadingly. Apart from that traumatic experience of being directed by him, I liked George enormously. He was witty and amusing and gave the most interesting parties in Hollywood. His house was beautifully furnished and had personally signed photos from all the greats of stage and screen in every room. Jean had adored working with him and anybody who had directed a masterpiece like *The Philadelphia Story*, one of my favourite films of all time, couldn't be all bad, so how could I refuse?

Having put the kids in school and worrying more than a little about leaving Jean in close contact with the triple menace of Brando, Sinatra and Mankiewicz, I prepared to take off. It wasn't that I didn't trust my lovely wife, I was just nervous that she would find out that I wasn't as fascinating as maybe she thought I was. Never give a woman the chance to make comparisons or you'll come up with the short end of the stick.

SAS had a new flight over the North Pole to Copenhagen where Ava was to join me and then we would fly on together to Karachi. My parting from Jean was very tearful as this was to be the longest separation since we'd been married. What a bloody prospect. How could I stay celibate for six months and, what was more important, how could she?

I arrived in Copenhagen completely exhausted and checked into the hotel. Ava was already there and, although we were both tired, we decided to go out on the town. This was the first time in five years that I'd been alone with this irresistible lady and in celebrating this event we got completely sloshed on the local Aquavit, chased with beer, and staggered back to the hotel. The Danes seemed to be able to knock the stuff back as if it was water and we had been 'Skolled' by everybody who had recognized us. When someone holds up a glass and says 'Skol' it's impolite not to lift your glass in return and drink it down. We hardly managed to make it to our rooms.

I woke with the most ghastly hangover I'd ever had in my life. What with the time change and the Aquavit I wasn't thinking about being lonely any more, I was thinking about how I was going to go on living. I went down to the bar and asked the barman if he had anything that would help. He looked at me pityingly and asked if I'd been drinking Aquavit. I couldn't nod as my head would have fallen off, but he guessed from my expression that I had the usual tourist's reaction to his national drink. To my horror I saw him pour out a stiff shot of the same poison to which he added Fernet Branca and I think some gunpowder and told me to hold my nose and knock it back. I followed his instructions and the effect was miraculous. Immediately my head stopped spinning, the nausea went and my arms and legs once more seemed to belong to me. I asked him to mix another and took it to Ava. She didn't answer my knock so I just went in. Later she told me that she'd heard the knock but was quite incapable of response. In spite of her pleadings to be allowed to die in peace, I held her nose and poured the nauseating liquid down. It had the same miraculous effect and in a very short time she was suggesting we go out and give the Aquavit another try.

Ava was a good flyer and during the flight was tucking into a meal of pork chops as the plane was thrown all over the sky and her leading man was trying his best not to disgrace himself. After what seemed like years we touched down in Karachi, I staggered off the plane held up by the Junoesque Ava and faced the battery of cameras. That's the terrible thing about being a movie star. I remembered once flying the Atlantic with Greer Garson. It had been a terrible flight and poor Greer had been sick all the way, but the Press and photographers were waiting at Heathrow Airport and I watched as she frantically repaired her make-up and arranged her hair. No one suspected that the radiant redhead who smiled gaily at all the cameras had only a few moments before been heaving her heart up. We're not actors for nothing.

We had to give a Press interview that evening and were in hysterics as the Pakistani Press tried to emulate Hedda and Louella, but with Pakistani accents. We had to wait in Karachi before making the trip to Lahore where George Cukor and the unit were waiting and to our amazement we received a royal command from the young King Hussein of Jordan to pay our respects that evening. What the hell King Hussein was doing in Pakistan at that time was beyond me, but the two swarthy guards who delivered the invitations made it clear that he wouldn't like to be disappointed.

'Who in God's name is King Hussein?' demanded Ava.

'Darling, he's one of the few last kings in existence and we can't very well refuse.'

'Speak for yourself, baby, I sure can. Anyway, what's he king of?'

'Jordan. He's king of Jordan.'

'Where the hell's that?'

'Christ, you ignorant American. Haven't you heard Paul Robeson sing about crossing over Jordan? Well, that's where it is.' To tell the truth I wasn't sure where it was myself.

We arrived at the palace which was guarded by fierce-looking Arab tribesmen and were shown into His Majesty's presence. The whole family was lined up, sisters, aunts, mother, wife, uncles and several generals. I heard Ava mutter 'Oh shit' to herself as the majordomo made the introductions. I'd told her to be a good girl and curtsy to the king and queen.

'I'm an American. I don't curtsy to anyone. If I didn't curtsy to Frank Sinatra I'm sure not going to curtsy to some lousy Arab. You curtsy.'

I was still inwardly giggling at this remark as I approached the tiny young king. Alan Ladd would have been quite happy having his photo taken with him, in fact Alan would have had to stoop, but before I could bow the king whipped out his autograph book and asked us to sign. It was a 'dry' palace and Ava was getting even more gritty at having to sip Coca-Cola when we were asked to take our seats and, guess what! They showed a movie. Apparently that's all they did in Jordan, watch films. From morning till night they watched films, in between making rude gestures at the Israelis.

We were flown to Lahore by charter plane and met at the airfield by a mob of Pakistanis who put 'leis' round our necks and made a big fuss of us, but I realized it was a publicity job when George Cukor appeared and put the final 'lei' round Ava's neck to the snapping of many cameras, after which we were driven in a cavalcade of cars to the largest hotel and led up to our suites. They were on the first floor at either end of a long verandah and the head of the stairs was guarded night and day by ferocious-looking Sikhs.

George had had Ava's suite sumptuously decorated at MGM's expense and he'd had mine cleaned.

Next morning, taking coffee in the hotel gardens, we were immediately surrounded by performing monkeys, a dancing bear, a fakir lying on a bed of nails and last, but by no means least, a hooded, pockmarked one-eyed flute player with a basket of performing cobras. That saw me off and I took the rest of my coffee indoors. I'd had enough of cobras, thank you. But as I looked out at the beggars and performing animals, I could imagine a young subaltern, seventy years before, just arrived from England, seeing all this for the first time just as I was. My father had served with the Indian Army for thirty years and had been stationed in the Punjab and very likely taken his first 'chota peg' at this very hotel. But I think he would have been appalled at what partition had done to his beloved India.

In *Bhowani Junction* I played a Lt-Colonel Savage, DSO, MC and bar, and of course while filming wore uniform with the medal ribbons attached. Cukor had arranged that a battalion of Pathans would be at my disposal so that I could get the feel of the part. The stupid sod had forgotten that I'd been an officer in the Black Watch and knew how to drill, salute and behave in a manner befitting an officer, but Cukor insisted that on my days off I should spend time with 'my' regiment. The Pakistani colonel was a charming man and a great admirer of the British army that had trained him and was fascinated to hear about my father. He insisted I review the men in costume and I self-consciously reported to the barracks where I was treated with great respect by all the NCOs who recognized the ribbons I was wearing. I begged the colonel to explain that I was just an actor who in reality only rose to the rank of 2nd Lieutenant, but he refused and said it was good for morale, so I took the march past. I felt a complete phony but secretly rather enjoyed it and gave a great performance. No colonel has ever stood more stiffly to attention or flashed such a snappy salute.

In spite of the heat, dirt, smells and the millions of flies, Lahore was the most colourful place I'd ever seen. This was because of the wonderfully attractive women daintily picking their way amongst the beggars and rubbish. They wore saris, for me the most sexy woman's attire imaginable, of every different colour and combination of colours, with one end thrown casually over their pitch black hair. They were made up with caste marks on their foreheads and wore brilliants in their pierced nostrils. Their eyes were rimmed by kohl and they wore bracelets on their arms which jangled as they moved. They even wore rings on their toes with little bells attached and I found it hard to keep my eyes off them and used to have erotic dreams in which Jean appeared dressed in a transparent sari. And this was only the first month.

What made it worse was that Ava dressed like this in the film and became even more desirable, so I established a strict routine. After work we would have a drink together but at seven o'clock I would determinedly say goodnight and go back to my bachelor quarters. She couldn't understand why I behaved like this and used to tease me that I had someone hidden away in my rooms. It became a kind of challenge to get me to go out with her. Her usual companions were Bill Travers, who had been in *Footsteps* with me and was playing a lead in this film, the publicity man and some of the other actors, so she was never hard up for men, but she was determined to make me one of them. It wasn't necessarily that she found me so attractive, she just couldn't understand my attitude. She used to put on a sari in the evening, because she knew they turned me on, and it was getting harder and harder to say goodnight. That room of mine was pretty lonely and if it hadn't been for my stand-in, Bob Porter, I think I would have succumbed, but he'd keep my spirits up with his wonderful Cockney sense of humour and we'd go out together with some of the other chaps and eat that godawful curry. But all that hot food makes you randier than ever and I was constantly running the cold shower to quieten things down.

I always sleep in the nude and one night Ava burst in about two o'clock and demanded why the hell I wouldn't take her out.

'I have to go with Bill and that boring publicity man. Why won't you take me? Don't you find me attractive?'

I looked at this vision in one of her saris.

'Ava, you're probably the most attractive woman in the world but I'm married. Remember? I'm married to Jean.'

'Oh fuck Jean,' said the rather pissed Ava.

'I'd love to, darling, but she's not here,' and then we started to laugh. Here I was with the sheets pulled up to my chin like a frightened virgin and here was Ava looking ravishing, we were alone in my bedroom and just laughing.

'All right, you faithful husband. I'll see you tomorrow,' and as she left I was literally sweating. Apart from being so damned attractive I liked and admired her. She was just like Jean and Deborah. There was no movie star thing with Ava. She never kept you waiting while she played with her make-up, like so many others. She was always on time and entirely professional, never complained of the heat and the flies. In fact, she was a hell of a woman which made matters even more difficult. I started wondering if Jean was having the same problem. I'd been told that it was different for women, that they didn't have the same urges as men, but miserably thought that that was probably wishful thinking.

Cukor was in his element, controlling his mass of extras and all his trembling actors. Of course he was telling me how to say all my lines, to expect otherwise would be like putting an alcoholic in a wine cellar and hoping he wouldn't take a drink, but he was amusing and enthusiastic and worked like a black (pardon the expression). One of the big scenes in the film takes place on the railway station with Colonel Savage trying to move the train against the wishes of the Congress party members in their little Gandhi hats. The mob breaks into the station and starts stoning the soldiers, myself included. Bits of cork and balsa wood had been handed out in place of stones and the scene was ready to shoot. 'Action' called out the excited director and the extras advanced on me, throwing their prop rocks. Suddenly a train window exploded behind my head and I realized that somebody was using real stones.

'Shit George, they're throwing bricks,' I shouted.

'Doesn't matter, dear, it looks great. Carry on, carry on.' A stone hit me on the shoulder.

'It's all right for you, George, you don't have to stand here.'

'Go on, Jim, go on, don't stop, it's great.'

All this dialogue took place while the scene was being shot and I was walking up and down pretending to be a stiff-upper-lip British Colonel. Then a rock hit me on the head and at the sight of the blood streaming down my face even George thought it was time to stop. 'Cut,' he shouted, 'Cut. Great, Jim, great. Looked really realistic.'

'It should have done. The scene's about a mob throwing rocks. They threw rocks, so that's realistic isn't it? Do you mind if I have my head attended to?' But George was already arranging close-ups of the different rock throwers while I had iodine poured into the cut. Later I dubbed in different dialogue to match my lip movements, but I wasn't talking to the crowd at all, I was complaining to the director. I saw the film for the first time on television about twenty years later and practically the whole scene had been cut, so my heroic performance had been all for nothing.

The time came for George to concentrate on Ava in her scenes with her Sikh lover and I wouldn't be needed for about ten days. I had already planned what I was going to do but said nothing to the production manager, I just took off. I went to New Delhi and on my first night was lucky enough to run into the owners of the hotel. Tiki and Biki Oberoi were

323

rich Parsees and owned practically all the important hotels in India. They were a fun-loving and generous pair and, when they heard what my ambition was, promised to help. James Corbett had been a hero of mine, I had read all his exciting books about hunting man-eating tigers and leopards and was dying to visit the jungles of Nani Tal where it all took place. Biki or Tiki knew the chief forest officer of that district and arranged for me to pay him a visit. They even provided a chauffeur-driven car.

I was accompanied by a friend of theirs, who knew the exact position of the forest lodge and who was a keen hunter himself. We stopped off at his home on the way and picked up a couple of rifles in case there was a chance of a shoot and he told me that there were still several tigers around harassing the villagers, and eating their water buffalo. If I could knock off one of these killers the villagers would be eternally grateful. I wondered what Metro would think if they knew their precious leading man was off chasing marauding tigers.

Eventually, after two days travelling, we entered the forest area which in turn became jungle. There was nothing like this in East Africa and I wondered what it would be like going after ferocious animals in impenetrable matted stuff like this. The jungle gave way to an open clearing and there was the lodge. It was a white stucco building with a verandah running the full length of the front, covered in hibiscus and bougainvillea. Our host was a fat jovial Pakistani and we were quickly ensconced in our bedrooms where I fell into a mosquito-net covered bed, or rather onto something resembling a mattress laid on top of wooden boards.

The next morning we breakfasted on the verandah and my host asked me if I'd like to accompany him on his rounds through the jungle, visiting the local villages. He told me that we would be using elephants and, handing me a bunch of sugar cane, told me to feed them. I had my back to the garden so I didn't know what the hell he was talking about.

324

'Behind you,' he said. I looked round and nearly fell off my chair. Two enormous elephants were standing about three feet away and I hadn't heard a sound. The mahouts riding them had large grins on their faces at the success of their trick which apparently always took place on the arrival of a guest.

'How do I feed them?' I asked nervously.

'Just show them the cane and you'll see.'

I held up the cane, the elephants raised their trunks into a question mark revealing pink mouths and I shoved in the cane. They were so gentle, they made sure I had withdrawn my hand before closing their mouths and lowering their trunks as they contentedly munched their treat.

I've never experienced anything like the thrill of travelling through the jungle on the back of an elephant. The sambur and spotted deer seemed to accept the huge beasts and didn't notice the humans perched on their backs. My host and I were sitting either side of a hunting pack strapped to the elephant's back with the mahout riding on its head with his feet behind its ears. The other elephant carried my friend and a local shikari to guide us. The 'pack' consisted of a kind of mattress with loops of rope to fit our feet into, not too secure. Suddenly there were screams and a flight of peacocks flashed in front of us. I stupidly asked who was raising peacocks, not understanding that of course they were native to this jungle.

I had always hunted in a Land-Rover with the accompanying whine of the gears and protesting squeaks of the springs as we bounced over the ground, so the silence of the great monsters as they picked their way delicately through the forest and bush was uncanny.

We visited two villages that day and discussed their problems with the local headman. Everyone chewed betel nut as they spoke in gutteral Pushtu and I was offered this disgusting delicacy but couldn't stand the acrid taste and the numbing effect it had on my gums. I gathered from my friend that the villagers had suffered loss among their precious cattle from both tiger and leopard so, telling the chief to send a runner to the lodge when the next kill took place, we went on to the other village where a similar conversation took place.

As we returned to the lodge I was assured that I'd definitely see some sport before long. The next day we had no news and my hosts suggested we go hunting that night. When I asked how one hunted in the dark, it was explained that you shone a torch into the jungle on either side from the safety of a hunting car and when eyes were lit up you just aimed between them and fired. As this wasn't my idea of a sporting way of getting a trophy I refused the generous offer. Two more days passed without any news from either village and I started to worry about the time. I only had a few more days and would then have to start back.

That evening, sitting out on the verandah sipping my drink and listening to the noises of the jungle as the sun set, I thought of my father again. He seemed very close to me here in India and I wished I had listened more attentively when he'd spoken of his time out here. There was one story I remembered vividly and it came back to me that evening as, like him, I was daydreaming. He'd told me rather shyly how he'd been sitting outside his bungalow up in the hill station of Peshawar, gazing into the sunset just as I was, taking his turn for a spot of leave away from the heat of the Punjab. He had given his *syce* (groom) the usual instructions about the care of his polo ponies and, as he was his senior servant, had made him responsible for his house.

'I was having my second "sundowner" when I suddenly saw my *syce* walking across the lawn towards me. I asked him what he was doing up here and who had given him permission to leave his post? He just stood in front of me and placing his hands together in the prayer position, bowed deeply and left without a word. I thought maybe he had family up there and had come to see them and decided to give him a good talking to when I got back. When I did return I sent for him and was told he'd died two weeks before at exactly the time he had appeared to me. He had come to say goodbye.' There were tears in my father's eyes when he told the story, and I believed him totally. He wasn't an imaginative man and would never have thought of making such a story up.

Having seen some of the vastness of India in the last few months, its wildness and mysticism, I could imagine the excitement and challenge it must have offered in my father's time. I could understand his unhappiness at having to leave it all and it wasn't only my mother's behaviour and the awfulness of us children that had saddened him. He must have missed his life out here desperately. Silently I toasted his memory and went to bed.

A runner arrived breathlessly at the lodge next day while we were having lunch and told us that a tiger had killed a fully grown buffalo and dragged it into the jungle. A *machan* (chair), ropes and axes were piled on to the elephants, a flask of tea and a package of sandwiches were thrust into my hands together with rifle, ammunition and a torch. It was explained that if a suitable tree was near the kill they would fix the *machan* about ten feet off the ground and I would spend the night there. I hoped they wouldn't find a tree for miles as I was beginning to shake. They had been told that I'd hunted a lot in Kenya and naturally thought this would be child's play for me. After James Corbett every Englishman was supposed to be a crack shot with nerves of steel.

We made our way to the village and were led to the place where the buffalo had been killed. I noticed that the elephant shuddered a bit as the mahout drove him along the path where the dead animal had been dragged and my companion explained that the smell of tiger always made elephants nervous. I was about to tell him that that made three of us, when a 'cooee' came from the other mahout as he pointed excitedly ahead. There it was, the already bloated body of the buffalo with flies swarming all over it, conveniently placed at the foot of an enormous tree.

'We're in luck,' whispered my companion. Speak for yourself, I felt like saying, but tried to look pleased. The elephants, trembling even more, gingerly stepped round the body to make sure the tiger wasn't anywhere around, though I knew there was no danger of that as in the heat of the day he would be lying up near water and would return to his kill as soon as it was dark. The men chopped away some branches to make a place for the *machan* and then strapped it in position. I took my place and the branches were cleverly arranged to hide me. The rifle and torch were handed up, together with the tea and sandwiches and I tried to look as if I knew what I was doing. I was assured that at the sound of the shot my companions would come back for me and, wishing me good hunting, silently disappeared into the jungle. It was dusk now and I never realized anyone could feel so alone as the light gradually disappeared.

When it was almost dark a sudden scream came as a peacock went to its roost and I nearly fell out of the tree. Now it was quite black; the moon hadn't risen and I was aware of the horrible smell coming from the corpse. What the hell was I doing here, I thought. I was beginning to long for my hotel room in Lahore with only Ava knocking on the door and thought of letting off a shot so that my friends would come and fetch me. They had told me that a tiger could jump twelve feet in the air and when I asked why I was only ten feet up they explained that if I was too high the angle of fire would make the shot more difficult.

I could hear the langurs calling to each other and some animal was snuffling around among the dead leaves at the base of the tree. With a snort it took off and I got a glimpse of a wild boar. What had frightened it, I wondered. There was an uncanny stillness for what seemed like hours and then far away a solitary monkey let out a warning call. Another called, much nearer and then another almost from the next tree. Then utter silence. I strained my eyes in the darkness as I heard heavy padding sounds coming towards me. Whatever was moving uttered grumbling moans and I realized the tiger was approaching. I was frozen with terror as the sweat poured off me and I even forgot the mosquitoes that had been whining around me for the last hour. There was absolute silence again while I strained my ears to try and make out where the animal was. Cats can see in the dark and I could imagine him gazing up at me and preparing for his twelve foot leap. Then I heard a crunching noise and realized the tiger was beginning to feed. I had always imagined them eating stealthily and quietly but this one was making a hell of a noise. Then I realized that he had no need to be quiet as he feared nothing – I was the one who had to be quiet.

Inch by inch I raised the rifle with the torch clutched under the barrel in my left hand. Dare I switch it on? What was I going to see? There might be more than one. The beam would give away my position and if I didn't kill cleanly the tiger would be in my lap. Then I thought, to hell with this. I was a good shot. Let's go. I pressed the button and the light flooded out illuminating a bloody great tiger gazing up at me in outraged surprise. For a moment I stared paralysed into those gaping jaws and then I fired. There was a roar from the gun and the tiger at the same time and the recoil sent the torch flying out of my hands. Black darkness. Not a sound. Had I hit it? Surely I couldn't have missed at that range. But I'd been so scared I had pulled the trigger and not squeezed it and maybe I had missed. Perhaps it was waiting a few yards away, furious at having its meal interrupted, gathering to spring. I sat there in the darkness absolutely frozen with terror and then to my relief I heard a distant 'cooee', and realized my friends had come.

'Did you get it?' a nervous voice called from far away. I didn't utter a sound. Another 'cooee' came, nearer this time. 'Did you get it man, are you all right?' I thought I couldn't let my friends walk into a wounded tiger so I summoned up courage and answered, 'I'm not sure. Take care. I've dropped the torch.' A light suddenly cut through the darkness, shining straight onto me. 'Not on me, you silly sod. On the ground.' The beam shifted and I could just make out the tiger lying across the buffalo. It didn't move. 'It's all right, come on, it's dead,' I called out in relief. I hoped they hadn't noticed the quaver in my voice. By the time the elephants came up I had pulled myself together and told my friends to give me a hand down, as if shooting tigers in the dark was an everyday occurrence in my life. The askaris had lit flares by now and we could see that my shot had taken the tiger straight in the mouth, killing it instantly.

While I was being congratulated by my friends I looked at the still form of the enormous beast that had been so terrifying only a moment before and regretted that anything so beautiful had to be destroyed. But I was assured that the villagers would be overjoyed as this one had taken quite a few of their precious livestock. What a shame I couldn't take photos as the tiger was loaded onto one of the trembling elephants, but I knew it had to be skinned immediately we got back to the lodge or the fur would slip. Now that the experience was over I was glad I had done it, but never again, thank you.

I thanked the forest officer for his hospitality and gave him a camera in remembrance of that thrilling night's work and wearily drove back to Delhi where I took a plane to Lahore. I told everyone I'd had a wonderful holiday seeing the sights and I think Ava was sure I'd been shacked up with some dolly bird. I didn't tell her what I'd almost been shacked up with.

Next day on the set I noticed Bob Porter wasn't around. When I asked where he was I was told that he had been complaining of bad headaches and had been taken to hospital. 'Which hospital?' I asked. 'Oh, the local, I think,' one of his mates replied. The local Pakistani hospital! Christ, poor Bob. That evening Ava and I drove over and started searching for him. We found him in a ward tucked away in a corner, desperately ill. The overworked Pakistani doctor seemed very uninterested as he told us Bob had a form of meningitis and couldn't be moved, we'd just have to wait and see what happened. I had seen Bob look at us imploringly through his puffed-up eyelids and decided I was going to get him out. The chauffeur and I picked him up between us, together with the blankets and, in spite of the protests from the doctor and nurses, put him in the car and took off. Ava cradled Bob's head in her lap and whispered to me that he was burning with fever. We carried him up to my room and put him to bed while Ava went for ice to make compresses for his head and I sent the chauffeur for the best doctor in town. He looked very grave as he examined Bob and after giving him a variety of shots told us that he would send a nurse over.

'We don't need one,' said Ava. 'I'll nurse him.' And that's what she did. For two days and nights she nursed Bob, sending me off for towels and ice, sponging him down and cooling his head. Bob was completely delirious and the doctor explained he had an infection of the membrane covering the brain and only hoped that the antibiotics would work and the infection would drain away, relieving the pressure. Poor Bob's face was swollen up to twice its normal size, but it didn't stop Ava's devoted care. I won't go into details but on the third morning something like an abscess seemed to burst and the crisis was over. Thank God we'd got him out of that hospital as they hadn't realized what the problem was and weren't giving him the right treatment. In a few days he was able to go back to his own bed and I could get a good night's sleep. But that darling Ava. What a woman! George Cukor had been sweet and arranged that we wouldn't be needed for those few days but I don't think either of us would have left Bob anyway.

26

We were now in our third month and I was getting desperate. I just had to see Jean. During our waits on the set Ava would tease me with remarks like 'What are you thinking of, baby, Jean? Jean with Frank, with Marlon or even with Joe? Don't worry, baby, I'm sure nothing's happening,' but the wicked look she gave me would make me worry even more. I had another break coming and George guaranteed that I wouldn't be wanted for at least six days, giving me time for the two days flight back to L.A., two days with Jean and then two days back.

I took off with Ava's mischievous 'Have fun, baby. I'm sure everything will be all right', following me and started on the tiring flight to Karachi, then on to Copenhagen and over the pole to L.A. I arrived at the house in the afternoon and had to wait for hours until Jean got back from work, but eventually she was once more in my arms. I dressed her up in the saris I'd brought with me and was able to experience in reality all the erotic dreams I'd been having for months.

Apparently she was having great fun on the picture and the way she talked openly about Marlon and Frank relaxed me a little but Joe Mankiewicz was something else. When I visited them on the set next day I could see the way he was eyeing her and the respect and obvious fascination she felt for him. I thought I'd try a little bribery. I discovered that 'Barling' was his favourite pipe and promised I would bring back a set from London when we'd finished our film. He couldn't really make a pass at the wife of someone who was bringing him his favourite pipes, could he? I hoped not. I talked lovingly of Ava, how I admired her, what a professional she was, but Jean just agreed and told me she knew I'd like working with her. Didn't seem jealous at all. I asked her about it. She looked at me in amazement.

'Why should I be jealous? Of course Ava's beautiful, but so are a lot of other women you've acted with. I know you love me and I trust you. You're not jealous about me, are you?' I told her the thought had crossed my mind. She looked at me with those amazing eyes. 'Well, you don't have to be. I love you.' And that was that. But I still brought back the pipes, just in case.

I felt I had only been home five minutes when I was leaving again. Another month in Pakistan and a month in England before the film would be over. Miserably I started the flight back. Coming over, with the thought of seeing Jean, the trip had passed quite quickly, but the return seemed interminable. Ava gave me an odd look when I reported on the set. 'Well, was it worth it, baby?' I looked back at her with a self-satisfied smile. 'What do you think, Ava. You're goddamned right it was worth it. Every minute of it.' Ava gave me a pitying smile. 'You poor idiot,' and then she kissed me on the cheek.

Things hadn't changed. It was still smelly, noisy and hot and somehow, having seen Jean in a sari, the pretty little girls in the street didn't turn me on any more.

The day came when our work in Pakistan was over and I was having my last breakfast alone in my room. The waiter brought me some rather soggy warm toast and I was reminded of another of my father's reminiscences.

'You know I like my toast crisp and hot? In India my cook would have the toast hot but it was always soggy. I thought I would get up early one morning and show him how to do it, but on entering the kitchen quarters I found him lying on his back reading a magazine. He had the bread between his toes, toasting it at the fire, and he was keeping it hot by putting it under his armpits. I had bread for breakfast after that.' I wondered if the same thing had happened to my toast. Like my father I asked the waiter to bring me some bread.

While I was back in England I was visited by the director Richard Brooks. He had a script that he'd adapted from a book called *The Last Hunt*. Apparently Doré Schary was going to produce this film personally and wanted me to play the lead opposite Bob Taylor, who this time was to be the villain. I'd had my hair cut short for *Bhowani* and it would mean wearing a wig which I hated and what was worse the film would start immediately I had completed this one. But a request from Doré was a royal command and I had to admit that the part of a buffalo hunter intrigued me. I'd always wanted to appear in a Western so I told Brooks that I'd be delighted.

By the time I got home Jean had finished *Guys and Dolls* and had loved every minute of it. She told me proudly that the fight sequence had been a great success and that I wasn't the only one in the family who could throw a punch. In trying to get fit for *Scaramouche* I'd had a punching bag rigged up in the garden and Jean would sometimes put on the gloves and have a go. I taught her how to 'put her shoulder' into a punch and after a few lessons she became the only woman I've ever seen who could throw a punch convincingly.

One day Walter Kane, of the Hughes era, knowing how interested I was in boxing, brought the great Jack Dempsey along to meet us. Of course Jack hit the bag a couple of times and we jokingly sparred together. He congratulated me on my footwork and the power of my punch against the bag. I told him that the real slugger in the family was Jean. I'll never forget the surprised look on Dempsey's face when, having told her to let one go, the tiny Jean knocked him back about two yards with the force of her punch to the point of his shoulder. He signed the glove 'For Jean, from one slugger to another. Dempsey.' I lost that glove somehow, dammit. Anyway, Jean had astounded the crew with the professional way she'd 'coldcocked' another female in a comedy sequence and it got one of the biggest laughs in the film.

Our first locations on *Last Hunt* were in the Custer National Park, South Dakota. There was a very comfortable tourist hotel there and Jean was able to join me for most of the time.

I met a man on this film who would be responsible for changing our whole way of life in America. His name was Elmer Black, a cowpuncher, rodeo rider and general tough Western cowboy. The studio had hired a lot of Hollywood 'wranglers', held in contempt by the real cowboys, to help drive the horde of buffalo for the camera. One or two of the herders were the real thing, and Elmer was one of them. I needed someone to teach me the Western drawl and I picked out Elmer. We'd spend hours together going over the lines and talking about the West. He had me completely fascinated with the idea of one day owning a ranch. The life he described of raising cattle, the yearly round-ups, the nights on the range in sleeping bags, with the attendant 'chuck wagon', the cowboy cook serving up fried eggs, bacon, coffee and hot biscuits out in the open on a cold morning, the building up of a fine herd of whiteface, dependable cowponies, sing-songs over the campfire in the evening – all completely romanticized by the wily Elmer, but by God he had me hooked. I used to tell Jean about it in bed at night.

'That's where we should bring up our children, darling. Not in Hollywood. On a ranch.' She looked at me in amazement.

'Darling, you come from the Old Brompton Road, I come from Cricklewood, what do we know about ranching?'

'I'll learn, don't worry. I'll learn all about it,' I declared confidently in my ignorance. She could see how serious I was and, treating me like a little boy with a new toy, promised me she'd think about it.

My next discussions with Elmer were all about how we could find the right ranch and it was agreed that after the film was finished he would take off and find one for me.

'New Mexico's the place, Jim. I used to cowboy there years ago, up in the Hila Wilderness Area, north of Silver City. Great country and cheap. California's too dang expensive, Nevada's too barren, Arizona's expensive too, but New Mexico, that's the place.' My God, I was already thrilled by the names, Hila Wilderness Area, Silver City, New Mexico. Quite a change from Cricklewood, Fulham and Chelsea. 'Right, Elmer, I'll bankroll you and directly the film's over you take off. Don't worry. I'll persuade Jean.' I could already see myself gazing at my thousands of contentedly grazing cattle from the saddle of my trusty cowpony. Elmer Black was indeed going to change my whole life and not entirely for the better.

In a way I think I can take some of the credit for the fantastic career of that brilliant actress Anne Bancroft. She was under long-term contract to MGM and was cast as the Indian girl in this film, a fairly dreary part which would give Miss Bancroft no chance to show off her acting talents. As usual the last scene in the picture was shot fairly near the beginning and this entailed me sweeping Anne up onto the saddle and galloping off into the sunset. Not an easy thing to do, to pick up a girl from the ground one-handed while trying to control a fractious horse. I pointed out the danger of this shot and suggested a double should be used but Brooks, although he must have known that nobody in the audience would tell the difference, insisted that Anne did the shot. Telling her to spread her legs as I lifted her up so as to avoid the pommel, I got ready.

The horse was one of the Hollywood types who, on the words 'get ready' starts to play up and when 'action' comes, takes off like a bullet. Trying to control him with one hand, I lifted Anne with the other, but the horse put in a buck at that moment and she landed hard, hitting her coccyx painfully on the pommel. I did my best to hold her off and stop the galloping horse but I'm afraid the damage was done and by the time I finally pulled up she was in agony. Quite rightly

336

her lawyers sued MGM and as part of the settlement they agreed to cancel her long-term contract. She went on to have a brilliant career in the theatre and movies and, if it hadn't been indirectly for me, she might still be playing Indian girls for MGM. I know it was painful, Anne, but you really have me to thank. If I'd been stronger it would never have happened.

There was a lot of buffalo killing in this film and the crew like the rest of us were pretty sickened by the whole thing. Brooks seemed to revel in taking close shots of maggots crawling out of the corpses littering the plains or of the skinning and butchering of the stinking animals that had been shot days before.

Although Bob Taylor and I, as the hunters, gave the impression we were shooting, the actual killing was done by the Park game wardens. These protected buffalo were increasing rapidly and every year had to be culled to keep their numbers in line with the grazing available. Fifty or so animals had to be slaughtered each year and in those days they were offered to hunters who could come and shoot their trophy, chosen by the game wardens. The hunters paid a large price for the pleasure of assassinating these harmless beasts, not really my idea of sport. Presumably MGM had bought up all the licences so we were allowed to have a prescribed number shot by the wardens. But the corpses had to be there for many days for the sequences necessary in the film and naturally in that heat decomposed pretty rapidly. To prevent this, refrigerated trucks would winch the bodies aboard each evening and the frozen corpses would be dumped back in their original positions the following morning, a ghastly business that turned our stomachs and we were glad when it was all over and our last memories could be of the remaining herd grazing contentedly in the distance. What horrors are sometimes necessary to entertain the cinema audiences of the world who demand realism!

The last sequence in the film was supposed to take place

during a freezing winter. Naturally the film couldn't be suspended for five months and had to be shot at the height of summer. The location chosen was the nearby Bad Lands, aptly named, an area that is freezing in winter but a cauldron in summer. The surrounding hills had been sprayed with a white powder to give the impression of a snowfall and the propellers of two high-powered plane engines created the gales that were supposed to be blowing. By throwing gypsum into the slipstream we had a very realistic snowstorm. It was about 120 degrees at the time and Bob and I had to dress up in thick clothes with scarves round our necks and ride into this stinging blast. The sweat was pouring off us as we pretended to be fighting for our lives in this 'freezing' blizzard. Twice I passed out and the clothes had to be ripped off me to give my dehydrated body a chance to breathe.

Bob and I must have drunk about fifty gallons of water between us as it seemed to stream out of us quicker than we could pour it down. I was worse off than Bob as I had to wear that bloody wig but in spite of being dehydrated, thrown off a horse, nearly killed in a buffalo stampede and almost crushed by an overturning waggon, 'things' must have been working as a few weeks after we returned to the studio, Jean triumphantly told me that she was pregnant.

I'd never seen her so deliriously happy and quickly took the opportunity to persuade her to allow me to look for a ranch. She was in such a euphoric state she would have said yes to anything. Telling Elmer Black I had the go-ahead, I gave him his expenses and he took off on his search.

While I was anxiously waiting for news from Elmer, Jean, of course, was full of plans for the expected baby. Once again we'd have to move as Jean wanted space for a playroom as well as a nursery. Her baby was going to be brought up in style. While all these plans were being excitedly discussed, a sudden thought came to me.

'Do you realize our baby will be an American citizen and we're British?'

'What do you mean? We're both British so she'll be British.'

'Not if she's born in this country. We're both residents here, we emigrated, but we're not American citizens. Any child born in the States of immigrant parents is automatically an American citizen. Do you realize the baby will have an American passport and ours are British.'

'What shall we do? Go back to England to have the baby?'

Jean was hesitant about this as she had great confidence in her gynaecologist, Red Crone.

'The simplest thing would be for us to become American citizens.' We looked at each other a moment. This was a big decision. All our roots were in England. My two children and both our families were British. What would they think. What would our friends, the press and our fans think. I already knew what they'd think, but there seemed no other way out.

We discussed it all with the legal department at Metro who enthusiastically advised us to take the step. They couldn't understand why we hadn't done it sooner, but becoming citizens wasn't as simple as we'd thought. We had to go back to school again and learn all the amendments by heart, the names of all the presidents, the forms of government and the complicated paraphernalia of elections. We used to sit up late into the night hearing each other repeat the lessons we'd been studying that day. We both passed with flying colours and, in the spring of 1956, swore our allegiance to the American flag. Now our expected baby would be safe. We'd all have the same passports.

27

The call came from Elmer Black that he was waiting for me in El Paso, Texas. I asked what the hell he was doing in Texas and learnt that that was the nearest airport for Silver City and also that the owner of the ranch he'd picked out for me in New Mexico lived there, so kissing my slightly pregnant wife goodbye, I set off for El Paso.

Elmer met me with his Buick station wagon and we started on the long drive to Silver City, passing through the cow towns of Lordsburg and Deming. The country was beautiful and at last I was looking at the much-filmed rangelands of the West. Cattle were everywhere, predominantly 'white face', but sometimes the small black blocky figures of Aberdeen Angus dotted the countryside. When we did get to Silver City there wasn't much to see; one hotel, with what passed for a restaurant, offered fairly comfortable rooms and we decided to spend the night there before exploring the country. I felt very self-conscious in my 'Hollywood' outfit and already questions were being asked about the 'dude', so I went to a local store and bought myself Western shirts, pants and boots. If you weren't dressed in this fashion you stuck out like a sore thumb, but in spite of my change of apparel they soon discovered that the dude was a 'fella from the fillums'.

The drive to the ranch took us over the Great Divide and, after climbing up to about 8,000 feet, we topped out over the Rockies and entered rangeland with juniper, cedar and Ponderosa pine on every side. Thrilling country, vast country but, to someone from London, frightening country. Miles and miles with hardly a building in sight. Elmer explained that most of this was Federal forest with deeded land spotted around: a rancher owning deeded land had the right to graze his cattle on a specified number of Federal acres. This was called his forest permit. He could run so many cattle and paid so much a head per year to the government. The ranch we were going to see consisted of 66,000 acres, of which only 3,000 acres was deeded land, but there was a permit to run 1,500 head of cattle on the rest. Elmer explained that we'd have to work closely with the 'Forest service rangers' who made sure these permits were not abused. My mind couldn't take these figures in: 66,000 acres. That was more than 100 square miles, more than forty acres to a cow. In England forty acres was considered a farm. I was dozing off in the car when I was suddenly woken by a handful of snow in my face. Elmer was making sure that I appreciated my surroundings.

Although we had left a beautiful warm spring day in Silver City, up here the winter snow still lined the road, and he had driven me to the highest part of the ranch to see the magnificence of the country. It was breathtaking and I was completely sold. We drove another ten miles along the eastern border of this colossal property to the headquarters, with Elmer pointing out the different grasses beginning to pop up through the scattered snow, then turned west along the Hila River, more a stream than a river, and arrived at a collection of corrals with a ranch house tucked away among trees. There were about twenty horses grazing in the meadows along the river bottom and I asked Elmer what they were doing here? He told me they went with the ranch. My God. Twenty horses! We were greeted by the English-speaking Mexican manager and shown the maps of the property with the different fenced-in pastures and watering places. It was all too big for me to take in but after Elmer explained how one valued a property like this I realized we were on to a good thing.

In those days a Forest Permit was valued at $250 per cow unit. If the permit was for 1,500 cows that gave a value of $375,000. On top of that was the value of the house and corrals, the horses and the 200 odd steers that were on the property. Another $50,000, making $425,000. The asking price was $250,000. It seemed like a steal.

'Come on, Elmer, let's get back to El Paso before he changes his mind.'

Elmer was beaming in anticipation as we started the six-hour drive back. Naturally he would be the foreman of this 'spread' and I would be totally in his hands until I learnt the ropes and that would be some years off.

'Bull' Adams was a fiery old gentleman who owned the best motel in El Paso as well as the ranch we were interested in and many other properties. He was obviously liked by the attractive waitresses who served us in the coffee shop and had won the nickname of 'Bull' from being the most famous bull trader in the area. If you wanted good herd sires you came to 'Bull' Adams. I think he was amused that a 'dude' from Hollywood was prepared to take on a venture of this size and asked me kindly if I realized what I was getting into. I assured him that I did, or rather I was willing to learn, and the haggling started.

I offered $200,000, and he patiently explained that I must appreciate the property was underpriced already and he had no intention of coming down. Eventually we settled for $225,000. I felt I was a hell of a trader with this small victory but the hard part was to come. I looked at the tough, weatherbeaten, wise old face across the table, took a deep breath and started.

'There's one problem, Mr Adams. I have big income but very little capital. I can only come up with ten per cent down and the rest over five years at six and a half per cent interest.' The normal bank rates were around five per cent in those far-off days. His jaw dropped and then he let out a roar of laughter.

'Goddamn, you've got a nerve, young fella. You trade me down $25,000 and then have the gall to offer that $25,000 as down payment. I ought to throw you out on your ear.'

He looked at me a moment and then called over to one of

the girls to bring some Bourbon. There was a silence while he poured out stiff drinks for Elmer and me and an enormous one for himself.

'I admire your guts, young fella, drink up. You've just bought yourself a ranch,' and then, rather anxiously, 'you do have the $25,000 I trust.' When I brought out my cheque-book and started to write, he added, 'I wouldn't put it past you to try and borrow it from me.'

Contracts were drawn up that same evening and it was all over. Jean and I were the proud owners of an area in New Mexico roughly five times the size of the Isle of Wight. I phoned her rather nervously and told her what I'd done but to my amazement she didn't turn a hair.

Next morning Bull asked me what cattle I had in mind to put on the ranch. 'Stick to whiteface, young fella.' (I was forty-two at the time.) 'Get a good bunch of young cows and I'll help you with the bulls. I know a fellow in Deming who's got some heifers for sale and I'll give you an introduction, but look out, he's a rough trader.' That turned out to be the understatement of all time.

The problem with stocking the ranch was money. For a good start we'd need at least 500 head. Cows cost around $200 each so with only $40,000 left I could only afford 200. I worked out with Elmer that if we sold those 200 steers on the property at around $125 each, that would bring us $25,000, and if we bought 500 weaner heifers at around $100 each, I could just swing it without having to dip into our tax money. I talked as if the steers could be collected in a few days. I'd forgotten that they were spread over 100 square miles. Three months later, having paid ten hired hands $200 a month each, plus their food, we only came up with 150. Of course, when I sold them the price was down and with the expenses incurred we broke about even, so bang went that $25,000.

We met Bull Adams's rancher friend at Deming and over interminable cups of coffee started negotiations. He was an immensely fat man of about sixty and I wondered what kind of horse he had to carry him over his land. I learnt that he hadn't had a foot in a stirrup for twenty years, but did all his 'cowboying' from a pick-up truck. He 'avowed' that he did have 500 heifers weighing about 325 pounds each that he'd held over through the winter and that they were the prettiest bunch of young ladies in those there parts. The market price was about 25 to 27 cents a pound. He was asking 30. I offered 25.

His face went purple and he started to gasp as he clutched his chest. 'Give me a little water, young fella,' he croaked. I passed him a glass and he swallowed it down. The colour in his face slowly became normal and he breathed more easily as he pleaded with me not to give him shocks like that as he had a 'bum ticker'. He looked at me reproachfully.

'What shock did I give you, sir?' I asked, completely shattered by this apparent heart attack.

'You did say 25 cents, didn't you? I offered you these beauties for a ridiculously low price of 30 cents and you insult me. Please, young fella, don't do things like that, you'll finish me off.'

I stammered out that I had no intention of insulting him and of course I would pay his generous price. I looked across at the poker-faced Elmer who was giving me no help at all and made a quick calculation that at 30 cents a pound I was still just below my $100 a head. Elmer had told me that it was usual to get a three per cent 'shrinkage' reduction on cattle being delivered any distance away and, as these would have to be trucked over 150 miles, I thought I would just mention this detail.

'Now, sir, about the three per cent shrinkage?' I started. There was a gasp, the face started to go purple, the hand went to the heart. 'No, no, forget it, I didn't mean it, forget it.' The normal colour came back into his face and the panting stopped more rapidly this time. I'd just lost another $1,500 but that was only money, this poor man's health was far more important.

Papers were signed, trucks ordered, and two days later at

about eight in the morning I was looking at 500 bawling fat heifers milling around in his corrals. In groups of ten they were run onto the scales and the weights were called out. To my horror they were averaging 425 pounds each, not the 325 I'd been promised. The fat-gutted, weak-hearted owner explained that they'd done better on the range than he'd thought but anyway I was getting fat heifers in prime condition that would be ready to breed the following spring. Christ, that was another $15,000 more than I'd bargained for. Oh well, we did have that tax money. The final heifer was loaded and we followed the trucks all the way back to the ranch. Our neighbour, who lived five miles away but he was still our nearest neighbour, came over to see what the 'dude' had bought. As the heifers were unloaded into our corrals they didn't seem nearly as fat as they had been only a few hours before. We had a set of scales too and I asked Elmer to run them on. I couldn't believe my eyes. The bloody things weighed only about 325 pounds instead of the 425 pounds they'd weighed before.

'Elmer, the scales must be wrong,' and I asked my neighbour if I could use his.

'Won't be necessary, young fella. I can tell by looking what they weigh. That's about right, between 300 and 350. Tell me, when were they brought into the corrals?'

'I don't know. They were already there when we arrived.'

'That's it then. They've pulled the usual trick they try on dudes. They bring the heifers in the day before and keep them off water. A couple of hours before you arrive they let them drink all they wanted and by that time they were real thirsty, so you've paid for about one hundred pounds of piss.'

Sheeit. Fifteen thousand dollars worth of pee. What would Jean say? But my troubles weren't over.

'Tell me, young fella, who did you buy them from? Think I recognize the brand.' I told him. 'Did he fake a heart attack when you were trading?'

'He didn't fake one, he almost had one, why?'

My neighbour started to laugh. 'His heart's stronger than yours or mine. He always does that when he's dealing with dudes.' Oh well, they say you learn by your mistakes, and I was in the process of learning.

The next day Elmer said we should drive the heifers out to the pasture chosen for them. We'd picked up a couple of cowboys in Silver City and they rounded up the very mixed bunch of horses grazing in the meadows. They came in all colours, palominos, paints, duns, liver chestnut, roan and even an Appaloosa. They cut out five of them with the Mexican advising us of the peculiarities of each: this one had a cold back, whatever that meant, that one was a kicker, the other had to have a nose twitch to be bridled, another was a head tosser, not one was just an ordinary, quiet, well-mannered horse. I learnt early on in the game that cowboys needed a challenge, and liked a difficult horse in order to show off their skill.

This cowboy wanted the quietest horse possible as my experience with the Western saddle was limited, to say the least. Elmer chose one for me that outwardly didn't seem to have too many killer instincts and we set off. The heifers, of course, had other ideas about where they wanted to go and I began to learn fairly soon that the cow is one of the stupidest animals on earth. You drive them along a nice easy path but they choose to tear off into a canyon or dive over a cliff, plunge through rough scrub, anywhere except the obvious trail. Eventually, after a lot of dashing about picking up the strays, we thankfully drove them through the fence and left them by the nearest waterhole.

On the way back one of the hired cowboys started showing off and managed to pull his horse over on top of him. He swore the animal was dangerous and he'd badly hurt his knee. I'd noticed this fellow limped a bit before he'd even mounted up but he put all the blame for his injured knee on Elmer for giving him a bad horse and said he was going to sue us. When we got back to the ranchhouse he limped over to his pick-up truck and left without a word. Elmer told me not to worry as all ranchers had insurance to cover them for such accidents and he'd get in touch with Bull Adams directly we got to a phone. When we eventually got through, Bull told us that he'd cancelled his insurance the day after he sold the ranch, thinking that we'd immediately take out a policy in the name of the new owner.

'Elmer, you're the manager, you're the one who's supposed to advise me, already you've allowed me to be hoodwinked by a phony heart attack, to pay for 100 pounds of piss at 30 cents a pound, and now I'm going to be sued by some goddamned phony crippled cowboy and I haven't any insurance.' I know my attack was unfair in a way as Elmer tried to justify his mistakes but I was already beginning to be a little disenchanted with this ranching bit.

But that evening, as I rode up the valley along the Gila river and inhaled that wonderful fresh air, so fresh I could almost taste it, and took in the beauty of the towering Ponderosa pine and the smaller but equally beautiful juniper and cedars, I knew that I'd made the right decision. Even the horse I was on seemed to sense that that evening ride was important to me as he never put a foot wrong, as much as to assure me that not all ranch horses were villains and that some, like him, were honest and trustworthy and for God's sake to relax and be thankful for what I had and not keep on thinking negatively. When I finally returned to the stables I was in a more positive frame of mind and I gave my horse an extra helping of oats in gratitude. So, asking Elmer to excuse my bad temper I left him in charge and flew back to L.A.

I had taken some photographs and Jean loved the look of our new acquisition but I didn't tell her anything about the mess-ups her 'dude' husband had made. She was working on her last film for Hughes, a potboiler called *Hilda Crane* and was not yet showing any signs of the approaching event. She would be in her fifth month when the film was completed so the cameraman had his time cut out masking that slightly protruding tummy.

Her gynaecologist told me that she was the most perfect patient he'd ever had, and I agreed with him. No morning sickness, no aches or pains, no wanting scrambled eggs with treacle at four in the morning, just that lovely contented glow that happily pregnant women seem to get. She would see me watching her anxiously when I thought she wasn't looking and smile at me. 'Don't worry, darling.' She knew of my experiences with Elspeth and would purr contentedly as I fussed over her when she got back from work. Vivienne, who was doing her hair on the film, had my instructions to see that Jean rested every possible moment at the studio and I saw that she rested at weekends and on her days off. In fact I was becoming a bore.

Bert Allenberg and his wife, and Spencer Tracy, were up at the house often and seemed as excited as we were at the coming event. I used to get rather jealous of all those hands feeling Jean's tummy to see if there was any movement. Spence entertained us with his stories of the films he'd made with Clark Gable.

'Did I tell you how Gable got his teeth knocked out?'

'No, Spence, tell us.'

'Well, we'd made about three films together and Clark would always get the girl. The girl would like me, of course, but goddamn Clark would always get her in the end. This was beginning to irritate the hell out of me. We had fights in practically all our films and I wasn't even allowed to win those. One evening we tried to finish off a fight sequence but there was one shot left over for the following morning, Gable taking a punch on the chin from me, off camera. I told them that I'd be goddamned if I was going to get up at crack of dawn just to stand off camera and have my fist pass in front of Gable's chin and told them to get someone else. They got a fighter, a real boxer. They stood him next to the camera and told him to throw a punch as Gable approached but to "pull" it an inch away from Gable's chin. Did he understand? Sure. Did he need a rehearsal? Hell, no. Okay. Camera, action and the boxer let one go, forgot to pull it and knocked Gable down. There was a stunned silence as Gable lay on the floor spitting out teeth. The boxer looked in horror at the movies' most valuable human being whom he'd just disfigured. He took off out of the studio, out of L.A. and some think out of the country. He was never seen again. Gable accused me of fixing the whole thing. I just told him he needed a new set of teeth anyway.' Actually Spence and Gable had been great friends and Spence secretly had hated his own unprofessionalism in not being there to deliver the punch.

One evening I came storming into the house and told Jean what Metro's latest idea was. 'They want me to play in a bloody stupid comedy called *The Little Hut* with Ava Gardner and David Niven. My part is a complete ass who's more interested in his dog than Ava. Imagine playing a straight man to David Niven with that bloody moustache.'

'What's the matter with David's moustache?' asked Jean placatingly.

'Well, he's always playing with it or twitching it on everybody else's lines. You can't win against Niven's moustache and, what's worse, they want to make the film in Rome. Rome, goddamnit. Another separation.'

'Now, just a minute, darling.' I could see Jean counting on her fingers. 'How long will it take?'

'Oh, about three to four months, I suppose.'

A smile came over Jean's face. 'Perfect. As long as it's not more than four months it's perfect.'

'What do you mean, perfect,' I howled. 'We'll be separated again. Separated at the most important time of our lives. The time of your pregnancy, the time you'll need me the most.'

'Angel, you know I love you, don't you. But please take that film. I can't wait to get you out of the house. I don't want you to see me getting fat and ugly. I don't want you worrying and fussing over me. Please, darling, go to Rome.'

I was flabbergasted. I'll never understand women. Just when I thought she'd need me most she didn't want me, and then of course I realized she was right. Always at the back of my mind was the thought of a miscarriage and I probably passed this fear on to her. So I agreed to do the film.

Rome in summer is one of the hottest cities in the world and Cinecittà Studios were not air-conditioned. On one occasion, some of the electricians on the gantry passed out and had to be lowered down to give them a chance to recover. Up there it must have been about 180 degrees. It was 140 degrees where we were and we thanked God that we worked most of the time in very scanty costumes, as the greater part of the film showed us running around a desert island in our underwear.

We had a lot of laughs on the film as David Niven is one of the most amusing companions in the world, in spite of that twitching moustache, and Ava was content as the attractive Walter Chiari, an Italian comedian who was playing with us in the film, had become her devoted slave. My old friend Bob Porter was once again with me, but this time in the more elevated position of assistant director.

Towards the end of the picture I'm afraid the restaurants and beauties of this glorious city were lost on me and I became a crashing bore to our nice director, Mark Robson, with my incessant enquiries about when the film was going to end. Naturally we were behind schedule and I was getting desperately worried that I wouldn't get back in time. Ava kidded me that I was behaving as if I were the one who was pregnant, but at last I was speeding on my way home. I burst into the house and stood in amazement as I saw Jean for the first time in four months. I had left a nicely rounded young beauty and now I was looking at a butterball. I couldn't even get my arms round her. How do women go through this nightmare? But of course I was quite wrong as Jean told me that, apart from our separation, these had been the happiest months of her life. Goddamnit, she should have been miserable without me.

I was just in time because a week later Jean calmly announced it was time to go to the hospital. 'Why?' I stupidly asked.

'Because it's started,' she replied with a smile.

'Started!' I shouted in panic. 'You mean you've started to have the baby? Well, for God's sake, what are you standing there for. Lie down, I'll fetch the doctor.'

'Don't be silly, there's plenty of time.'

I was shaking all over and Jean had to fetch me a drink. She had everything prepared and told me to get this bag and that suitcase and, holding on to my arm to steady me down, led me out to the car. Bessie was furious that she wasn't allowed to come and to shouts of good luck from Vivienne, Laura, our coloured cook and the 'nanny' who had spent the last week with us to get to know Jean, I shakily drove to the Cedars of Lebanon Hospital.

Of course I went to the wrong entrance and had to be guided round to the maternity ward, expecting the baby to pop out at any minute. At last Jean was tucked up in bed and Red Crone was in attendance, with my wife asking him for God's sake to give me something to calm me down. I was walking nervously up and down outside her room when Red came out and took me into the doctors' special quarters.

'You're not supposed to be here, but if you keep quiet nobody will say anything. It's going to be some time yet.' How right he was. Twelve hours later, poor Jean was still in labour with no sign of the baby. Christ, either they come too soon or don't come at all. I was becoming desperate. After eighteen hours, Red came in and told me that he thought Jean would have to have a Caesarean. 'She's just too small for the baby to come through. She's insisting on having a normal birth but I'm afraid that the strain is beginning to affect the baby. You'd better talk to her.'

I went in and saw my wife who'd been suffering for eighteen hours and wondered how women could be so brave.

'Darling, Red thinks you ought to have a Caesarean.'

'I'm not going to,' Jean panted as she clutched my hand. 'I'm going to have it normally. For once you're going to have a baby that came normally.'

I was in tears as I realized she'd been suffering like this for my sake, for me to get over my phobia about childbirth.

'Darling, I love you and I don't care how you have it as long as you're all right, but Red thinks it's beginning to affect the baby.'

Jean looked at me in panic. 'Oh, my God. I hadn't thought of that. Of course I'll have a Caesarean. Tell Red.' Ten minutes later Tracy Granger was born.

I was anxiously waiting outside the operating theatre when a nurse came out holding what looked like a plucked chicken up by its legs. 'This is your baby, Mr Granger. Look at the band on its leg.' I looked rather dazedly at a band which had been attached to my daughter's ankle with the words 'Female – Granger'. Apparently this was a necessary precaution as some mothers didn't like what they'd produced and thought that their babies had been switched. But why did the nurse have to hold my daughter up like that without giving me the chance to touch her? Apparently that was another rule. I might be infectious and could only hold my child when properly garbed in overalls and face mask. But I was more interested in Jean and thankfully watched her being wheeled out and put back to bed. She woosily looked up at me and asked: didn't I think our baby daughter was beautiful? Of course I told her that the 'plucked chicken' was the most beautiful child I'd ever seen and, with a contented smile, Jean went to sleep. Red assured me that everything had gone perfectly and that Jean would be up and about in a week.

The next day I asked the head nurse where I could find my baby and was led along to a glass screen and a nurse inside pointed to a tiny object in a cot among about thirty others. I didn't have to be told which one was mine. I'd have picked her out anywhere and I hadn't lied to Jean. She was the most beautiful baby I'd ever seen. Even the nurses agreed with me.

28

The children were home on holiday when Jean made her triumphal entry into the house proudly carrying Tracy. My two were absolutely thrilled with their new sister but Bessie hated her on sight. She snarled her resentment when Jean held out the baby for her approval and I had to grab her away or she would have bitten her.

There was another problem which became obvious that first evening. Our specially selected 'nanny' was an alcoholic. I hadn't noticed her addiction to the bottle when I'd first met her, as I'd been far too occupied with my very pregnant wife, but that first evening, when Jean had been tucked up in bed and Tracy put away in her cot, I paid a last visit to my sleeping daughter and caught the nanny knocking back a large glass of gin. When she went to the kitchen to get herself something to eat I made a quick search of her room and found the tell-tale bottles hidden away among her clothes. I had the bottles lined up in front of me when she came back and the usual denials and hysterics took place. In spite of pleas that she wouldn't touch another drop, I ordered her to pack up and leave. I couldn't tell Jean, as the doctor had warned me that she needed complete rest and no aggravations of any kind for the first week or two.

What was I to do? I looked down at the little thing sleeping in her cot and realized that she would need a bottle in a few hours as the doctor had decided Jean shouldn't breastfeed. I went to the kitchen where our much cherished Laura was preparing the kids' supper. Laura had come with our first Bel Air house, where she was working as the laundrywoman and had since become our cook. She was gentle, calm and soft spoken and Jean and I both adored her. I told her what I'd just done.

'Laura, you've been a mother, you know how to look after a baby. Would you look after Tracy? I'll do the cooking until we get someone else. Would you?' A lovely smile came over her face. 'Why, I'd just love to, Mr Granger,' and I knew I'd made the right decision. I'll never forget the look on Jean's face the next morning when Laura came in with Tracy and put her into her mother's arms. 'I'm the cook now, darling, Laura's the nanny and everything is just fine.' Jean was delighted that there wouldn't have to be a new person in our lives, and it all worked out beautifully.

But Bessie was something else. Our bed was her domain and when the baby was brought in to Jean, Bessie had to be locked outside or she would have bitten her. Later, when Jean was up and around, the same thing happened. Whenever Jean had Tracy in her arms, Bessie would go berserk and, in spite of all the cajoling and petting to show that she was still loved, she refused to be placated and Jean tearfully agreed that Bessie would have to go. I told her I was sure Elmer would look after her on the ranch and she could come back when Tracy was older.

Spencer Tracy was delighted with his god-daughter and gave her his own christening robe. Katie Hepburn gave her a pearl with the understanding that another would follow every year to make up a necklace by the time she was twenty-one. Sam and Mary Zimbalist and Bert and Mildred Allenburg were the other godparents, but the christening was constantly put off until we could get them all together, and in point of fact never actually took place.

When I went back to the ranch I took Bessie with me and Elmer promised he'd look after her. He had bad news about the crippled cowboy. Apparently this man had injured himself before and was looking for a chance to get some money and I was the sucker. My lawyer advised me to settle out of court as a jury would be sure to award a poor cowboy large damages against a 'rich' movie star. It cost us $30,000, but the lawyer calmed my rage by explaining that it would be tax deductible.

While I was there I joined the ten hired hands in the round-up of the elusive 200 steers. One here, another there, two miles apart, had to be collected and held in a temporary corral until a group could be gathered for the drive back to HQ.

On one occasion, having taken days to round up about twenty, we were making our way back when some idiot let off a loud Yippee! and the twenty steers were once more spread over miles of country. These weren't the gentle steers I was used to, these were wild animals.

My bottom was unaccustomed to hours of cowboying and after the third saddle sore I left them to it and went home. As soon as my bottom had healed and the children came home on holiday, I managed to tear Jean away from Tracy and we all made the trip back to the ranch. They loved it and, in spite of the tiring journey, were up early next morning and tucking into one of those ranch breakfasts. The air at that altitude gave us all enormous appetites and our cook was kept busy bringing in plate after plate of his fabulous hot biscuits.

Slim was an ex-cowpuncher of about seventy, never without a large 'chaw' of tobacco bulging his cheeks. He was too old to cowboy any more but loved the life so much he'd settled for being a cook. He still loved to ride and I had picked out a horse for him that in 'horse years' was older than he was and we loved to watch these oldsters arthritically cantering around the corrals on Slim's evening work-outs. I soon found out why his biscuits had a flavour all their own. One day I was watching him through a window, working the dough and saw him spit a stream of tobacco juice into the mixture.

'Slim, what the hell d'you think you're doing?' I yelled. He put a finger to his lips as he whispered, 'Shush, Mr Granger, don't you tell anyone, that's my secret.' I assured the old devil that his secret was safe with me but said that we'd prefer our biscuits straight, if he didn't mind.

One evening in front of a crackling fire Jean suddenly said, 'Darling, where are the schools? It's all right for your children, they're in boarding-school, but what about ours?' I wondered how many she was planning to have and then thought, Christ! The nearest day school was about sixty miles away in Silver City. 'I love the life but couldn't we find something nearer L.A. so that our friends can visit us? We'll never get anyone to come all this way.' Of course she was right. What a bloody idiot I'd been, but she was equally adamant that our children shouldn't be brought up in Hollywood.

We had a final barbecue out on the range, with me keeping a close eye on Slim while he made the biscuits, and Jean said a tearful goodbye to Bessie. Once back in Bel Air we felt claustrophobic after the vastness of New Mexico. We were conscious of smog, noise, the ugliness of the drive-ins, second-hand car lots, supermarkets, cars, cars, cars. I determined I'd find another place more suitable for Jean, nearer our work and our friends, with more amenities. I didn't mind roughing it but I didn't see why the hell my wife should.

Bert told me that the whispering Benny Thau wanted to see me. 'You'll never guess what it's about, Jim.' I hadn't realized that my seven-year contract was nearly up and Benny was offering me another. I should have been flattered as in 1957 very few studios were offering lucrative seven-year contracts but I turned it down. Bert agreed with my decision as he was sure I'd make far more money free-lancing, but warned me that Metro wouldn't give me anything interesting or important during my last year.

How right he was. My next epic was to be a Western, produced by Nicholas Nayfack, directed by Roy Rowland. This was nepotism squared. Nayfack's only claim to fame was that my old friend the lizard, Nicholas Schenck, was his uncle who made sure his fat, unprepossessing nephew got his name on a few films as producer. He couldn't produce a hard boiled egg but he had an office and made noises like an executive. Rowland was married to a sister of a brother married to a cousin of Louis B. Mayer, or something like that and I was conned into accepting Rowland's son as the juvenile lead. He'd never appeared in a film before and I don't think he's been seen since, but to keep everybody happy I said I thought it was a wonderful idea. I should have said no to the whole thing and spent my last year on suspension but that New Mexico ranch had to be paid for.

In this film I had to play a fast gun and was coached by an Indian called Lightfoot, who could do anything with a gun, fast draws, twirling it around his finger before flipping it back in its holster, back-hand draws, left-hand draws, shooting behind him, quite incredible. I'd never played a gunman before. I was built wrong. I had broad shoulders but not the snakehips necessary to wear the low-slung belt convincingly, so all this was new to me. You can't pull the trigger of a Western colt more than once without 'cocking it', so you have to 'fan' it. You cock the gun in the holster before drawing and firing, and Lightfoot thought it would be a good idea if I could do a 'double': cocking the gun in the holster with the right hand and, having fired, fanning it with the left. If done correctly this would have the effect of an almost simultaneous double shot. With an empty gun I became pretty efficient at this, but I was warned not to 'fan' until the gun had fired or I would get the sharp striking pin of the hammer through the palm of my hand. I practised for hours and photographers came to try and catch the speed of the double firing and were very impressed by this 'Limey's' dexterity. But that was with an empty gun. Later, when it was loaded with blanks I was glad the photographers weren't around.

I needed a 'cutting' horse for the film and told Elmer to find one for me. I was very proud when my own horse from my own ranch with my own brand appeared on the set. T – 4 – J: T for Tracy, and four J's for Jean, Jimmy, Jamie and Lindsay, whose second name was Jean. 'Sundown' came from the famous Pitchfork ranch in Texas and was the most intelligent animal I've ever seen. In the 'cutting' sequence, when I was showing my son how to 'cut' out a calf from its mother the whole crew were very impressed by my skill, but I did nothing, the horse did it all. I could ride him right up to the camera and he would hit his mark perfectly and not move. That is after the first take. The first time he hit his mark the camera started to roll and made a whirring sound. Sundown leapt three yards to his right and nearly threw me. I couldn't understand why my well-trained horse had disgraced me until Elmer explained. The whirring of the camera made Sundown think there was a rattlesnake around so he took off. I asked the cameraman to start up again and let Sundown realize that there was no danger and after that he was perfect, and probably the best thing in the film. The epic had been given the embarrassing title of *Gun Glory* and I was supposed to supply the glory.

The moment came for the first shoot-out. As he handed me the 'full charge' blanks, the prop man explained that they would be much more impressive, but warned me to take care as the flash could burn anyone within a three-yard radius. This was the first time I'd ever handled the gun loaded and I was already nervous while the scene was being lined up and my very experienced opponent took up his position opposite me. Naturally I had to beat him to the draw and, having seen him rehearse, knew I'd have to be damn fast. The whole crew with the extras, small part actors and the Hollywood wranglers were watching to see this Limey do his stuff. Action. Dialogue. My opponent went for his gun and I frantically cocked mine and in my anxiety fired it in the holster, the flash burning the whole side of my leg. The prop man had been right, that full charge was very impressive and very painful. My dresser gingerly eased my trousers off and

358

the doctor covered my burnt leg in some yellow muck and bandaged it.

Not wanting to hold up the film I pulled on another pair of trousers and, pretending that the whole thing was a joke, went for a second take with my confidence completely shattered. Once more I heard my cue, saw my opponent go for his gun and whipping mine out of the holster, 'fanned' before I fired and the sharp striker of the hammer went straight through my left palm. I stood there paralysed with the heavy revolver dangling, completely overcome with hysterics. So was everyone else. The prop man came up and, gently easing back the trigger, detached the gun from my hand. Again the doctor taped me up, trying to hide a smile, but I was beginning to think it wasn't so funny. Jesus, it looked so simple when Duke Wayne did it.

Lightfoot came up and calmed me down. 'Come on, Jim, you were perfect in rehearsal. Show them what you can do.'

'I already have, mate. Everybody loved it. I think we should make it a comedy.'

'No, come on, Jim, just forget about the blanks, pretend it's not loaded. Let's go.'

I took up my position once more and I went. Third time lucky. I drew and did that double shot quicker than I'd ever done it before and it was perfect, except that there was something wrong with the camera. A groan went up from everyone. Nobody believed I could do it again, myself included, and then I saw the look on Elmer's face. I couldn't shame him again. The doctor was looking at me anxiously as I think he was wondering what damage I was going to inflict on myself this time. I fooled them all and somehow managed to do it but it wasn't as fast as the one before. Nobody could have drawn that fast, not even Wayne.

The climax of this film involved a cattle stampede and the man who supplied the necessary five hundred animals was Ralph Wingfield from Nogales, Arizona. He knew that Jean and I had been married in Tucson and asked why I hadn't bought a ranch in that area. 'I was told it was too damned expensive.'

'It's sure not cheap but it's the finest grazing land in the West and I know of a couple of ranches that are up for sale. Why don't you come and stay with me and I'll show you round.' I promised him I would directly I had completed the film, provided I didn't shoot off a hand or a leg, as I had another 'quick draw' sequence to complete.

I fell off my horse a couple of times in the stampede without doing myself too much damage and the final shoot-out went off to the satisfaction of Lightfoot and the director, so heaving a sigh of relief I finally hung up my guns and went home. I thought I'd better stick to sword-fighting in future. I told Jean about Wingfield and with her blessing flew to Tucson, hired a car and once more made the trip down to the border town of Nogales.

Ralph Wingfield had a very nice 'spread' with the Santa Cruz river flowing through it, a charming home, presided over by his mother-in-law, a pretty wife and two sons. The country was completely different from New Mexico, with mesquite trees dotting the countryside in place of the ponderosa pine. It wasn't so savage and Ralph pointed out the different grasses that made the rangeland so valuable, blue and black gramma, side oats and curly mesquite.

'You can't go wrong here, Jim. We've got the best grazing land in the West and nearly all the ranches have bottom land along the river for a bit of farming. Come along, I'll show you a place I think you'll like.'

It was only a few miles from Nogales, right next to the Mexican border, belonging to an ex-state senator. It was small, about 1,800 acres, with a charming house, good grazing and 100 acres of farmland. I liked it enormously and the price of $150,000 wasn't too staggering as the owner was offering generous terms, but I had seen another ranch lying right next door. I asked Wingfield about it and was told it was much bigger and, naturally, much more expensive.

360

'Let's take a look, Ralph. I know I can't afford it, but let's take a look all the same', and with those words my doom was sealed.

This one was 10,000 acres of gently rolling hills, bordered by a mountain range with the Santa Cruz running right through it. All along the four miles of river towered gigantic cottonwoods and willows and I could see a marvellous house nestling among outbuildings and corrals. The owner was a charming lady, recently widowed and, as she showed me over the house, I knew that I just had to have it for Jean. There were rooms for my children, a suite for us, and an extra wing that could be transformed into a playroom and sleeping quarters for Laura and Tracy. There was even a guest house, a large swimming pool with changing rooms and a beautiful garden. My eye had immediately gone to the pine-panelled study and I could imagine my trophies on the walls.

Everything was perfect and of course we couldn't afford it. The asking price was $500,000, which included a herd of Santa Gertrudis cattle. There were six other houses belonging to the ranch scattered around and I noticed they were all connected to the electricity line that ran through the property. There was even a telephone. One and a half hours' flight from L.A. to Tucson, one hour's drive to the ranch, ten minutes from the town of Nogales, beautiful house with electricity and telephone, and by God there was even a little red schoolhouse right by the entrance. It was just what I'd been looking for and, although it was way beyond our means, I called Jean and asked her to meet me in Tucson.

We stayed once more at the Arizona Inn where we'd passed that crazy honeymoon and were given the same suite where I had disgraced myself by reading a book on our wedding night, but this time I made sure there were no books about. Next day I drove Jean down to the ranch and it was love at first sight. 'Oh darling, it's beautiful. We'd both have what we want. I'd have a lovely house and garden and you'd have your ranch. Can't we really afford it?' She looked at me pleadingly and I knew that somehow I was going to get this place for her.

'It would mean we'd have to work hard for five years, we couldn't pick and choose films and we'd have to sell the house in Hollywood. Are you sure you're willing to do all that?' Without a moment's hesitation Jean agreed and so the die was cast.

The owner couldn't bear the idea of the place going to a tough Texan cowman who had been negotiating for the property. Naturally, being a very rich man, he was trying to get it for $100,000 less than the asking price. I offered her the full amount, but explained that, although we had a big income we had very little capital, and would she accept $75,000 down and the rest over five years? She was sweet about it as she liked Jean and the thought of our children being brought up here, so we all made our way to her lawyer's office in Tucson. Just as the papers had been finalized the phone rang and the Texan was on the line, having heard that the ranch had been sold, and asked to speak to the new owner.

'Mr Granger, I was dealing on that ranch and I want it. Would you take a 100,000 dollars profit?' Here was a man who had been trying to get it for a 100,000 dollars less and was now offering a 100,000 dollars more. 'Jean, do you want a 100,000 dollar profit on the ranch?' I could see by the look on her face that she didn't. 'Sorry sir, we don't want to sell', and I hung up as he started asking me what price I would take. The fact that we'd already been offered a profit gave me a little more confidence as I was really terrified of the step I'd taken. We hadn't sold our house yet or the New Mexico ranch and we were using tax money for this purchase. I was waiting for the shit to hit the fan, and of course it did.

29

'I couldn't get you into *Quo Vardis* because you wouldn't sign a long-term contract and now I can't get you into *Ben-Hur*. Why couldn't you have been in touch with me before turning down Benny's offer? Where have you been?' I told my old friend Sam Zimbalist where I'd been and what I'd done.

'You need your head examined. You're an actor, not a rancher. What do you know about ranching?'

'Not a goddamned thing, Sam, but I'm learning. I'm sure as hell learning.'

Sam had apparently revived the old *Ben-Hur* classic that had starred Ramon Novarro so many years ago and had had me in mind for the lead, bless him. But now Metro weren't going to give me a plum part like that after I'd refused to sign on again.

'What are we going to do, Jim? I want you in that film.'

'I'm sorry, Sam, I really am. I'd have loved to have played that part and I could have done it, too.'

'Of course you could, you silly bastard, that's why I wanted to revive it.' He paused a moment. 'Now, Jim, don't get mad. Would you play the other part, the heavy, Messala?' I thought for a moment. Messala was a hell of a part, not the lead, certainly, but a hell of a part. 'Depends on who plays Hur, Sam. Who's playing it?'

'It's on offer to Brando. Metro are a bit scared about the size of the budget and Brando's hot at the moment, so he's first choice.'

'Okay, Sam. If Brando plays it, I'll play Messala.'

'Can I count on you, Jim? Messala's a damn important part.'

'Sure you can count on me. I said so, didn't I? When does it go?'

'Christ, not for ages. Next year. This is a big one and needs a lot of preparation.'

I left Sam's office thinking that at least I had one big one lined up. Then I went to see Bert and explained my position. 'I've got to keep working, Bert, doesn't matter what it is as long as it's not too crappy, but the money's got to keep coming in.' Bert assured me it wouldn't be too difficult and within a couple of months came up with a two-picture deal with Romulus Films, an English company operated by the Woolf Brothers. The first was a not too exciting cops and robbers thriller, to be made in England, and the second to be made nine months later, an exciting Eric Ambler story with parts for both Jean and myself.

After discussing it with Jean I told Bert to go ahead and sign. Shortly after, another offer came, *Harry Black and the Tiger*, to be made in India and England for Twentieth Century-Fox, which fitted in perfectly between the other two. I'd read the book and liked the story immensely and there was a chance that Deborah Kerr would play opposite me, so I signed up for that as well. I knew this meant we would be separated again but Jean understood it was necessary for our future, so that was four films over the next two years and I began to relax. I went up to New Mexico for the last time and arranged for Elmer to come down to Arizona and run that ranch, leaving Slim Salyer, a neighbouring ranch manager, in charge of the T4J.

The Arizona ranch was called the Yerba Bueno, Spanish for mint. It had been named by Father Kino in the eighteenth century when he was journeying to San Francisco and building missions along the way. This land had been part of Mexico in those days and he'd stopped at a spring which he'd named the Yerba Bueno, so naturally the ranch took that name. When I had time to study the deeds I was fascinated to find that most of the ranch was made up of

Spanish land grants dating back to the 1750s. I didn't like the Santa Gertrudis cattle, originating from the King Ranch and their famous bull, Monkey, as they were too Brahma for my liking and I wanted to change to the French Charolais. These were rare in America as, with the outbreak of foot and mouth in France, no more had been imported and the only source of supply came from the original herd that a Signor Pugibet had brought over thirty years before. Most of them were in Texas and if I wanted good stock that's the place I had to go.

Pete Lewis, my neighbour, married to a Spreckles sugar heiress, was also interested in Charolais, so together with Elmer Black we flew down to Weslaco, Texas, to visit the famous Turner Ranch. Fred Turner was one of the first to experiment with these wonderful cattle and had built up a famous herd but he had died and the place was now run by his widow, Pauline, who met us as we drove up to the property. She was flanked by two tough-looking Texans, who were her advisers, and we were led over to a corral containing about thirty females. I gave them a quick glance and saw that they were a pretty crappy lot. The Texans obviously thought that a 'fella from the fillums' wouldn't know his arse from a hole in the ground about cattle, but they'd made a mistake. I'd seen those famous Charolais when I motored through France and knew what they should look like and it certainly wasn't like this sorry bunch.

'Mrs Turner, if this is the best you have to offer, I won't waste any more of your time.' I turned to leave but was stopped by her herdsman.

'Now hold on, sir, we do have some others. Don't be in such an almighty hurry.' We eyed each other a moment.

'Mrs Turner, I want to buy an outstanding established herdsire, two young prospective herdsires and thirty top females, but I want to choose them myself. If you don't want that, just say so.'

There was a hurried discussion between the three and

eventually they agreed to show me everything there was. With Elmer and Pete we drove all over that huge ranch and trudged across enormous pastures writing down the numbers of the heifers that took our fancy. The herdsman groaned every time I made a note.

'Goddamn, Mr Granger, you're taking all the best.'

'That's what I'm aiming to do, so I hope you're right.'

Eventually we got back and I showed the list to Mrs Turner who, taking out the herdbook, checked the numbers against the pedigrees. With lots of 'Oh no, not that one', and 'Oh, I wouldn't sell that one for anything', we arrived at a list of thirty females and I asked the price. There was an exchange of glances and I was told that I could have the lot for the ridiculously low figure of $200,000. I said nothing although my stomach gave a lurch at this horrifying amount. We went into town and, during a good dinner, they gave me the usual bullshit about what a shrewd trader I was, but I could see them secretly rubbing their hands at my seeming acceptance of their outrageous demand. They were in for a shock but I let them enjoy their dinner.

The next day we went looking for the herdsire. I knew which one I wanted as he was already famous in the cattle magazines featuring Charolais. Argo Lin 245 came from the Pujibet line, a direct descendant of the champions in France and was primarily responsible for the quality of the Turner herd; this famous bull was therefore very necessary if I was to establish an accredited Charolais herd.

'I wouldn't sell that animal for a penny under $50,000,' Pauline stated firmly. I gave no reaction. 'Now about a couple of good young prospects...' I picked out two of the best yearlings offered me and was told they would be $10,000 each. I still gave no reaction. Pauline was looking a little worried as we walked back to the house. We sat down and sipped Bourbon and branch.

'Pauline, if I may call you that, and please call me Jimmy' (I thought I would try a little charm before I lowered the boom), 'I know that you're overcharging me about 50,000 on the heifers and 30,000 on the bulls but that's all right if you'll go along with my terms.' There was a shocked silence as they looked at me guiltily and wondered why I was being so affable. 'Now here's my offer. I'll pay you 50,000 dollars a year for five years, payable at the end of each year.'

I waited a moment for this to sink in. Then Pauline burst out, 'But that means you're getting them for no money down. For nothing.'

'Well, darling, not really for nothing. I'll go on a note for the payments and I'm sure if you check my yearly earnings you'll realize I'm good for it. That way you get a hell of a price for your cattle and I get a deal that I can handle, otherwise I'm afraid I've wasted your time, but that's trading, isn't it?'

After the bath I'd been made to take in New Mexico, I was determined I was going to get something my way for a change. I knew that as most of the Charolais were bred heifers I could amortize them over five years, so 90 per cent of the yearly instalments would be paid by Uncle Sam, tax deductible and perfectly legal. I left Pauline and her advisers looking slightly dazed as the 'fella from the fillums' drove off, following the truck containing some of their best stock and waving airily out of the car window. What a deal. No, two deals. I'd bought a half-million-dollar ranch and a quarter-of-a-million dollar herd of Charolais for $75,000 down. As long as we continued to work and our health held out there would be no problems but – no, I daren't think of the alternative.

The cream coats of the Charolais heifers looked wonderful against the green of the permanent pasture I'd prepared for them. Argo Lin strode majestically around in his private paddock, eyeing the young ladies in the distance and looking pityingly across at the two virgin bulls in their corral as much as to say 'you don't know what you're in for'. Neither did I. This purebred business wasn't as easy as I'd thought and soon I was to have a problem with our expensive herdsire. He 'stifled' himself serving some of the cows I'd bought from an entirely different herd for an 'outcross' and was crippled. He was never able to serve naturally again and it meant collecting sperm from him and artificially inseminating the waiting cows, a messy and complicated business.

In my innocence I'd thought that you bought some cows and some bulls and after selection from bloodlines, put the bull with the chosen cows. They mated and after about nine months you got a calf. Oh dear me, no. I never realized a bull could cripple himself making love, or that he could shoot blanks, in other words, be sterile. You didn't realize this until much later as he seemed to 'cover' the cows enthusiastically but of course nothing was happening and you'd wasted a breeding season. I hadn't realized that bulls could be 'queer', showing no interest in the opposite sex at all, that they could break their 'peckers' serving a cow, the cow in question moving at the wrong moment and that long instrument inside her would snap and the bull would be useless thereafter. I hadn't realized that cows could be barren, or 'shy breeders', that is, very difficult to settle, could constantly abort, could have deformed calves, could prolapse after delivery, could have the most incredible complications in giving birth or, having settled easily and given birth with no problems to superb calves, show their clumsiness by stepping on them. For someone with a complex about childbirth, bloodstock breeding wasn't the best chosen profession, but when things did go well, and a calf arrived that showed by its conformation that your breeding choice had paid off, the excitement and satisfaction made up for everything.

I had stopped off at San Antone on my way back from Mexico and bought a lot of pine ranch furniture for the house, including some marvellous handcarved Western figures playing different musical instruments around a chocolate-covered doughnut made up into a hanging light, with single figures on wall brackets. I couldn't resist them and soon they were installed in the bedroom and playroom so Tracy could go to sleep to the music of her own band.

Very little had to be done to the house, apart from decoration and furnishing and it was all looking spick and span when Jean arrived with her precious one-year-old toddler. She adored it all and was soon out in the garden showing everything to Tracy. I had seen a perfect place in front of the house and determined that when I'd finished the two films I'd think of a way of bringing water from the river to make a lake.

Jean had charmed two rich young bachelors into paying a good price for our Bel Air home and so our finances weren't quite so desperate. Elmer had moved into the ranch manager's house but little Bessie was left in New Mexico as Tracy was still too vulnerable. Thankfully there was nothing really important for me to do on the ranch apart from fattening up the rather depressing looking bunch of Santa Gertrudis so that I could sell them. We'd found a nice Filipino couple to run the house and Mexican help was in abundance from across the line so our new life couldn't have started off better.

I'd only been back a few days when I received a call from Steve Post, our business manager. 'Jim, you're going a bit overboard on feed for the New Mexico ranch, aren't you? I thought you were closing that operation down and trying to sell.'

'I don't know what you're talking about, Steve.'

'I've got colossal bills here for hay and oats, tons of it. Three thousand dollars worth.'

'What?' I shouted. 'There's got to be some mistake, Steve, I'll get back to you.'

I called Elmer over. 'What the hell's all this about tons of feed up in New Mexico?' I thought he looked a bit shifty and then he came out with an explanation.

'It's my fault, Jim. I shouldn't have trusted Slim Salyer.

The bastard's been ordering it and probably selling it off on the side. I'll fire him right away and get someone else.'

Oh Lord, and I'd liked Slim Salyer; I'd trusted him and now this. The next days were occupied with the exciting arrival of our first Charolais calves and I was riding quietly among my contented young ladies and basking in the peace of our home when the Filipino cook called out across the fields that I was urgently wanted on the phone. It was Slim Salyer. 'Mr Granger, I thought you trusted me. How could you fire me without giving me a chance to explain?'

'Okay, Slim, go ahead, explain.'

'Not over the phone. I'd sooner come down and see you.'

'Okay, come on down.'

I didn't say anything to Jean about the call and avoided Elmer, but I didn't get much sleep that night. Early next morning Slim turned up and, telling Jean to take Tracy for a drive, I took him into the study. 'Did Elmer see you arrive?'

'Don't think so,' Slim replied.

'All right. Tell me about it.'

It seemed that Elmer had a friend in Las Vegas named Benny Benyon, owner of The Silver Nugget, and Elmer had been his children's bodyguard, Benny seemingly being in trouble with the mob. My jaw dropped. Benyon had given Elmer seventy horses as a pay-off, or maybe to fatten them up for him on some deal or other. Anyway they'd arrived on the property and Slim had had instructions from Elmer to order that feed and look after them, saying he had my full approval.

'Do you know he also sold 5,000 dollars worth of yearlings? Did you know about that?' I just looked at him. I couldn't believe what I was hearing. 'I'll tell you something else. I don't think you know. He fired the old man, the cook Slim, found him drunk one night and fired him off the property.' This was the last straw. Slim, my old friend of the tobacco-flavoured biscuits.

'How could you let him do a thing like that?'

'Well, Mr Granger, Elmer was the boss and I couldn't get in touch with you.'

'You hire him right back, d'you hear? You tell him I'm sorry and ask him to forgive me.'

'Too late, Mr Granger. I got the word two days ago, he's dead. I think he died of a broken heart.'

I was looking out the window with the tears streaming down my face when Elmer came bursting in.

'Who told you to show up here? You're fired, Salyer, get the hell out.'

Now Slim was about six foot four and well-built and he slowly unwound himself out of his chair. 'If you'll put your gun away, I'll kick the shit out of you, you lousy crook.' The two men had forgotten about me as they glared at each other.

'Elmer, do you have a gun on you?'

'He always carries a gun, the chickenshit bastard. Go on, show it to the boss.'

'Elmer, come with me.' I wasn't feeling nearly as brave as I sounded when I went outside with him. 'All right, hand it over.'

Elmer took out an evil snubnosed .38 revolver. 'He's lying, Mr Granger, it's all lies.'

I took the gun away from him. 'Elmer, you know I didn't give permission for seventy horses to be housed on the ranch, or for the feed or for the sale of the yearlings. Why didn't you ask me? I thought we were friends. If you had a chance to make some money on those horses, why didn't you tell me?'

Elmer couldn't look me in the eye and I think he knew the game was up. I told him to go to his house and wait for me and went back inside. I apologized to Slim for the misunderstanding and reinstated him as my manager.

'What about Elmer? He ain't going to like that.'

'Elmer's not going to be with us any more.'

'Oh, I get it. See you, Mr Granger, and don't worry.

We're not all like that bastard,' and with that small consolation I returned to the ordeal of firing Elmer.

I told him I could have forgiven him for the horse bit and even the selling of the cattle but I could never forgive him for blaming it on to an innocent man and firing our defenceless old cook. Finally I told him to pack up and go. Elmer started to give halting explanations but I cut him short. 'One other thing. If you try anything with Bessie I'll take criminal action against you for selling those cows. I want Bessie back.'

He went out muttering that I'd regret what I was doing, that I wasn't giving him a fair chance. A couple of hours later, with his car and trailer loaded up with his personal belongings, he made a last appeal to me to give him another chance and, when I refused, he leant out of the window. 'You'll regret this, Granger. No Limey bastard can fire me and get away with it.' As I watched the car disappear I hoped it would be the last I ever saw of him. What a hope.

When Jean came back I told her that Elmer had left, but didn't give her all the details. We were lucky enough to find a married couple to take over and very soon Fred and Rose Voorhees moved into the vacated ranch manager's house. They were easterners and Fred was a farmer, a cattle man and a skilled catskinner, so at last I'd found someone I could be at ease with and who would become my good friend and stay with me until eventually I sold the ranch ten years later.

30

Much as I loved it, London seemed cold and bleak but in spite of seeing my mother, Elspeth and my friends, I was beginning to feel like a stranger. The film I had contracted to do for Romulus, *The Whole Truth,* was a run of the mill 'whodunnit', and I had the lovely Donna Reed playing opposite me with the suave George Sanders supplying the villainy. Our director went on to fame directing an oversized ape in the remake of *King Kong*. I'm sure he got on better with that mechanized gorilla than he did with us. He was peculiarly lacking in charm, to say the least.

Jack Clayton who, later, was to make a great name as director of *Room at the Top* was the co-producer and became a good friend. My old pal Bob Porter was again standing in for me as there was a 'kipper season' in the British film industry. Poor Bob should have been an assistant director or production manager but times being hard, stand-in was better than nothing. He had a problem, Christ, hadn't we all, which was that his sweet wife Nan had just had a baby whom he'd named Jamie after my son, and they had nowhere to live. Every free moment Bob and I would take off in the studio car and hunt for possible homes. We found one which was a dream: a nineteenth-century converted stables with a large garden and a greenhouse.

'Oh, Jim, what I could do with that garden; that's a perfect tree for a swing and there's a lovely kitchen for Nan, and...' he was in love with it the way I'd fallen for the ranch but, like me, he didn't have the money. The asking price was £3,000, a considerable sum in those days, but unlike my ranch owners they wouldn't take terms and wanted cash. Every other house we saw after that was an anti-climax and I knew Bob's heart was set on the dream cottage. It was underpriced and I was sure that, unless something was done quickly, it would be snapped up. I knew I should save every penny for our ranch, but I thought Jean would be sure to understand, so I bought the cottage in Bob's name and, taking the title deeds, put them in a fairly conspicuous place in the living-room.

'Bob, let's have another look at that cottage. Maybe there's a chance we can persuade them to take terms.'

'Oh no, Jim, don't let's look again. I love it so much I couldn't stand it.'

'Come on, Bob, let's have a look.' So we drove over and, pretending I'd just got the keys from the agents, we let ourselves in. I told Bob to have another look round the house to make sure it was what he wanted while I looked over the garden.

'Jim, you know it's what I want. There's no point having another look, it's perfect.'

'No, Bob, take a good look this time. Maybe it's got dry-rot or something.' I walked in the garden waiting for Bob to discover the title deeds.

'Jim – Jim – I don't understand. Look, there's a bit of paper with my name on it. What's it mean?'

'Let's see. It says here that the deeds to this home and adjoining garden are the sole property of one Robert Porter. It seems like you own the place, Bob.'

'Oh Jim, you didn't, did you?' There were tears in his eyes.

'Yes, I did, Bob, and gladly, but on one condition. You've got to call it "Tracy's Cottage".' So Bob, Nan and young Jamie Porter lived there happily for many years.

While I was in London I'd met Lord Brabourne, the producer of my next film, *Harry Black*, and was invited to spend the weekend in Kent. He was married to Lord Louis Mountbatten's daughter, Patricia, and I remember envying them their perfect life. They obviously adored each other, had a beautiful home with a magnificent park, lovely children and no money problems. How tragic that this happy life was to be shattered by some murdering madmen in a little Irish seaside resort during a family holiday many years later. After lunch, on that visit, John and Pat told me that I should feel very flattered as their snobbish butler had put on his frockcoat. 'He only does that for royalty, Jim, normally for lesser mortals he wears a jacket.' So Hollywood does have its advantages!

John told me that the locations in Southern India had been prepared a little earlier than originally planned owing to weather conditions and there would only be a few days' break between the two films. Jean and the baby had moved into a hotel apartment in L.A. as she found the ranch too lonely without me and no sooner had I got back than I was already packing to leave for another three months.

The day of my departure was awful. Jean became hysterical and told me she couldn't stand a marriage that meant continual separations and seemed entirely to forget our pledge that no matter what, we would accept any film we were offered.

'If you leave me now, I won't be there when you come back,' Jean told me tearfully. Oh, my God. Had all my plans for our life together on that ranch been just daydreaming? Had I taken on more than I could handle? If Jean felt like this then it was all for nothing. I was desperate as I explained I had to go, that I couldn't possibly let the company down at the last moment, even if I wanted to. Miserably I drove to the airport, thinking I'd probably blown my marriage and cursing myself for risking everything for that bloody ranch, which would mean nothing if we couldn't all be together to enjoy it.

My old friend Mike Wilding's marriage had broken up only the year before and Liz was now married to Mike Todd. I knew how utterly shattered Mike had been over the loss of his children as well as his wife and I didn't want to find myself in the same position.

As I was checking in at the ticket counter I was paged to go to the BOAC manager's office. Jean was on the phone. 'Oh, darling, I'm sorry. I didn't mean it. Of course you have to

go. You're doing it for us and I love you. Please forgive me.'
The manager was slightly shocked at the tough six footer
with tears streaming down his face murmuring endearments
into his phone. Well, sod him and whatever he thought.
Everything was all right again and the trip to India wasn't as
ghastly as it might have been.

The journey had to be broken in London and who should
be staying at the Dorchester but Sam Zimbalist. He'd left a
message at the desk for me to call him. 'Can you spare a
minute, Jim? I've got to talk to you.'

I went across to his suite and asked him what the hell he
was doing in London. 'Just on my way to Rome to fix up
studio space and look at some of the sets. This isn't a quickie
like you're doing. This is a big film we're going to make
together, but there's a slight problem.'

'Okay, I understand, Sam, they want Laurence Olivier to
play Messala.'

'Hell, no, that's not the problem, you're playing Messala,
but not with Brando. He won't or can't do it, so it's being
offered to Kirk Douglas. Is that okay with you?'

'Sam, I'm not casting the bloody picture. Of course it's
okay with me, he'll be great, almost as great as I would have
been.'

'Okay, wise guy, you know what I mean, will you play
Messala with Kirk?'

Christ, I'd forgotten. I was no longer under contract. I could
choose whether I played a part or not. It was a great feeling.
'Kirk-Schmirk. Sure I'll play Messala,' I said grandly.

'Now, Jim, you don't want to be separated from Jean, do
you. I was thinking she might like to play the girl. I know it's
not a starring part but at least you'd be together.'

Cunning devil. He knew he'd never get a star of Jean's
quality to play that part but, remembering her recent
outburst, I began to see that it wasn't such a bad idea.
'Okay, Sam, I'll talk to her when I get back, but you'd better
talk to Bert Allenberg first.'

'Right, Jim, that's great. We'll all have fun on the picture in Rome.'

Next morning I was on the plane to Bombay, accompanied by the leading lady, Barbara Rush. To my bitter disappointment Twentieth Century wouldn't release Deborah Kerr and I was lumbered with this lady who was a completely unknown quantity. The flight was pretty tedious, and not the best way to get to know someone who you're going to spend three months with, having taken my usual anti-airsick and sleeping pills I just wanted to sleep, whereas Miss Rush wanted to chatter and chatter she did, all the way.

At Bombay we changed to a smaller plane which took us to Mysore where we were met by his lordship, John Brabourne, and were driven to our camp in the jungle outside Bangalore.

I noticed that John started an animated conversation just as we entered the town and seemed to want to distract our attention. I looked round and noticed that the place seemed strangely deserted. When I remarked on this, John seemed slightly uneasy and his explanation of the lack of inhabitants was very unconvincing. 'All right, John, what's the problem, what's the real reason nobody's about?'

John became even more embarrassed but, after asking him to slow down, so that I could have a look around he eventually blurted out the truth. Just a short time before they'd arrived to set up this camp they'd discovered that there'd been a virulent outbreak of cholera. When I asked why that should affect our camp, located several miles away, John nervously admitted that our water had to be trucked in from the town well, that being the only supply for miles around. John also had to admit that there'd been some typhoid cases as well, but assured us that the water was strongly doctored with chlorine and other disinfectants so that we should have nothing to worry about.

He was right about the disinfectants as from then on we drank what seemed to be pure chlorine instead of tea and very little water was drunk in that camp. Cases of beer and Coca-Cola were quickly trucked in but it's amazing how you long for plain water when you can't get it. Apart from these minor inconveniences, our quarters were enchanting – the camp had been entirely built of bamboo. The producer, director and stars all had little bungalows, with the crew in tents. The cooks were Indian and all they knew how to serve was curry. Now, curry for dinner was bearable but curry for breakfast was pretty off-putting and, with my stomach, absolute death. I lived on baked beans and eggs. I'm exaggerating, of course, but my memories of that enchanting camp were smells of curry and chlorine.

My fellow actors, apart from the talkative Miss Rush, were Anthony Steele, formerly married to the blonde bombshell Anita Ekberg and one of the few really virile actors the British film industry had come up with, and a charming Indian star called I.S. Johar. He had to play my gun-bearer, close companion and friend and his lilting accent and marvellous hand gestures were a joy, and our obvious affection for each other played a big part in the success of the film.

The other star of the picture was a tiger and we were quickly shown where it was caged and suitable introductions were made. I was a little worried to see its attendant sported a large club studded with nails, holding it up rather menacingly as he led the tiger out of its cage. I thought this was supposed to be a tame animal, but India's idea of tame and ours were slightly different. If it wasn't actually trying to eat you, it was quite tame.

The second night in camp we discovered that the trainer of this ferocious-looking beast was keeping something else from us. We were kept awake by roars and gurgling grunts and next morning the local shikar pointed out the pugmarks of tigers that had been wandering through the flimsy camp. Tigers usually keep away from places inhabited by a large bunch of humans unless attracted by something very enticing and we had that something. Our tiger wasn't what it was supposed to be, it was a tigress and, what's more, she was in season. Like any cat, when a tigress is in season she calls to the male to come and accommodate her and that's why we'd had so many visitors. Our lady's cage was very quickly moved about three miles away but we could still hear the roars every night. Eventually she went out of season and we managed to get some sleep.

Our first location was among some rocks about half a mile from camp where an important part of the film had to be shot, showing me and Johar setting up a trap for the man-eating tiger in the script. I noticed our Indian help stepping very gingerly over the ground as they moved the equipment into place. They seemed to be looking for something and I asked Johar why they were walking like that? He too seemed rather nervous and was constantly looking around as we rehearsed. 'Oh my God, Jimmy my friend, you know what this place is called,' and he reeled off some gutteral singsong words.

'What does that mean,' I asked.

'Cobras' look-out,' Johar answered nervously. 'The cobras come out of their holes and sun themselves on the rocks. Not a good place, Jimmy, no, my God.' Jesus, cobras again. Carefully walking over to the director, a young South American called Hugo Fregonesse, I told him the good news. You've never seen an English crew move equipment so fast, and within about thirty seconds the place was left to the cobras.

The Maharajah of Mysore, an immensely fat man, had been a keen hunter in Africa and knew of the two outstanding trophies I had acquired there, the near world record buffalo and the Kerr Hartley rhino. He enquired if I would like to participate in a tiger hunt, this time not alone up a tree at night but with him and other hunters in line as a tiger would be driven towards us. I enthusiastically accepted the offer and told my good news to John, the producer. I thought he turned rather green as I excitedly discussed my plans for the hunt. That evening he came to my bungalow and, pouring himself a stiff whisky, nervously started to explain his problem.

'Jim, you've got a hell of a reputation for being knocked down by buffalo, chased by wild elephants [which had happened on my last African safari], charged by lionesses [also on that hunt], and treed by tigers. When I took out insurance for you on this picture I had to guarantee you wouldn't go in for any kind of hunting, so please, Jim, no tiger shoot or they'll cancel the policy.'

'John, I didn't guarantee anything, did I, and this is the chance of a lifetime to shoot with a Maharajah.'

'Jim, please, I'm asking you not to.'

I stared at him in disbelief and to my shame found myself crying with disappointment. But I couldn't help wondering what the insurance people would say if they knew that their highly insured star had already been exposed to cobras, cholera, typhoid and a very oversexed tigress.

While we were completing the interior scenes in London I received a call from Bert Allenberg. 'Now, Jimmy, I know Sam is a friend of yours. I know you've agreed to play Messala, but do you know who they've signed up for Hur? Not Marlon, not Douglas but Charlton Heston and I'm not letting you play second fiddle to him. I'm getting pretty fed up with this chopping and changing and anyway I wouldn't dream of letting Jean play the girl, it's a nothing part.' With that Bert hung up and I had to tell my old friend Sam that I wouldn't be available.

On my return to the States, Jean was just completing her film for Mervyn LeRoy, *Home before Dark*, which had locations in Boston. She told me of this very attractive senator who had wooed her with flowers and eventually ended up practically breaking down her bedroom door. 'Jimmy, he was so attractive and had such a lovely smile I nearly let him in.' She looked at me with a grin.

I didn't think it funny at all.

'Do you know his name by any chance?'

'Oh yes, he's a very important senator called John Kennedy.' I'd never heard of him.

At last we could go back to the ranch and have about three months to do what we liked. With the two films I'd just completed and Jean's two, we were fairly comfortably off.

Fred had begun working on my idea for a lake. The position I had chosen was thirty feet higher than the river, but two and a half miles upstream the river was sixty feet higher, so there was a fall of six inches in every 100 feet. This meant we had to engineer a ditch with a fall of only three inches in every hundred feet and that's pretty tight engineering. At one place, near the lake, we had to make a 150 foot cut, thirty feet deep, through the side of a hill to lay our pipes in and that had been the trickiest part of all. Like fools we'd filled in the cut to hold the pipes in position before trying it out to see if the grade was right. If it wasn't, it would mean bulldozing all that fill out and altering the pipes.

After what seemed like months of work the moment came to let the water from the river into our concrete ditch. With that slight gradient the water didn't seem to be moving at all and in different places even started to back up, but slowly and surely it flowed along that two and a half miles until it reached the pipe. We'd taken a bottle of Bourbon along intending to celebrate the completion, but we were already taking slugs out of it to celebrate minor successes with some tricky spots. By the time we reached the cut we were beginning to weave. The water, which had now quite a good head, flowed into the cut and disappeared. We both staggered over the hill and sat down by the exit. We seemed to sit there for ages without even a trickle showing, and Fred put his head into the pipe to see if he could hear anything. Nothing. We sat there gloomily. If the water didn't show soon we'd have to lay that pipe all over again and we consoled ourselves with another slug each. Suddenly I noticed a trickle. 'Fred, look, water!' We behaved as if we'd been lost in the desert dying of thirst as we scooped the water up and splashed each other. Soon it was coming in full flood and finding its way into the ten-acre hole we'd bulldozed, leaving a mound in the middle which would become Tracy's Island, and the thrill of seeing the water swirl on either side made us both let out yells of delight.

Jean came running out in surprise at the commotion coming from her normally quiet husband. 'What's going on?'

'Look, darling, look. It works. A lake!'

'What lake?' Jean wasn't entirely convinced as she looked at the two slightly pissed characters splashing around in about three inches of water, but I assured her that by morning she'd really see something.

I was up at about six with only a slight hangover, as I dragged Jean out of bed and we both rushed out to have a look. By God, it really was a lake. The water entirely surrounded the quarter acre island which at one end was only eight feet from the bank. I already had a little bridge prepared so, telling Fred to put it in position, the whole Granger and Voorhees families had their first breakfast on Tracy's Island with the mistress toddling around, anxiously followed by Laura to make sure she didn't fall in.

I'm afraid my joy was shortlived as first I received a call from Slim Salyer telling me that Elmer had called in at the ranch while he was in Silver City and taken Bessie and, second, I received a call from my lawyer in Tucson telling me that a completely mad sounding Elmer Black had been to see him and was threatening to kill me.

One moment he was describing me as the greatest guy in the world and the next he was cursing me as a cruel bastard who'd just thought up any excuse to fire him. The lawyer was very anxious and wanted to know if he should get on to the police. I told him not to worry as I thought Elmer was just blowing off steam and didn't really mean it.

The lawyer rang off, warning me to look out as he thought Elmer had become completely paranoid. I didn't worry too much about the threat but I did worry about Bessie. How could I get in touch with Elmer to ask him to give her back? I didn't have long to wait. One evening, while Jean and I were having a drink in my study, the phone rang and Jean, who didn't know what was going on, passed it over saying, 'It's Elmer, darling. I wonder what he wants.'

'Yes, Elmer?' I asked nervously.

'Hullo there, Jim. How's everything.' He sounded quite normal and very friendly.

'Fine, Elmer, fine. But what's this I hear about your conversation with my lawyer?' I signalled to Jean to leave me alone and she went out. 'I hear you want to kill me.'

'He's a liar, Jim. I never said anything of the sort.'

'Well, I'm glad to hear that. Now, Elmer, what about Bessie. You remember what I told you? If you don't hand her over I'll be forced to take action.'

'That's no problem, Jim. When I come back to work I'll bring her with me.'

'What d'you mean, Elmer, come back to work?' There was a silence.

'You mean you don't intend to have me back?'

'Elmer, are you out of your mind? Of course I'm not going to have you back. Our past friendship is the only reason you're not in jail.'

His whole attitude changed. 'Why, you bastard, you ain't never going to see Bessie again and you'd better look out for yourself and that kid of yours. I'll get you, Granger. I'll get you for sure.' The phone went dead.

I was sitting there stunned when Jean came back. 'What's the matter, darling. You look as white as a sheet. What's happened?'

'Oh nothing, just Elmer won't pay the money back he owes us, not to worry.' I poured us out another drink and Jean sat on my lap as she usually did. I loved holding her like that, with the fire going in the grate, looking out of the window at the lake and the trees that were just starting to be established round it: cottonwoods and willows: amazing how fast they grew if there was abundance of water. But that evening I was terrified. The lawyer had been right. Elmer was a psychopath and I was frankly scared of a man who had once been a gangster's bodyguard and seemed bent on killing me or, what was worse, threatening our daughter.

Next day I went into town and bought myself a .357 magnum revolver. I hid it behind the bottles in the bar. I still had that snub-nosed .38 I'd taken off Elmer, so I pushed that down the back of the padded seat of my favourite chair, and I waited.

My nerves were beginning to go. The thought of the vast amounts of money we owed, the constant problems of the ranch, the running of the house and worry about my next film were beginning to make me moody and short-tempered. I'm never too placid at the best of times but Jean and the kids were used to the sudden flare-ups that just as suddenly disappeared but now I became morose with worry and started to lose my confidence in what I'd undertaken.

The fact that some rancher had cheated me over the heifers, that the Charolais weren't increasing as quickly as hoped for, the sprinkler system that we'd installed was always giving trouble, these were the normal challenges for anyone as amateur as I had been when I started the venture. But I was learning, and I knew deep down that it could work eventually. The business with Elmer had been a kick in the stomach. I couldn't understand how someone I'd trusted, who had almost been a member of the family, could cheat and lie and then threaten to shoot me. That really got me down.

One day I suddenly said to Jean, 'Let's go into L.A. and tell Sam we'll do the picture. It doesn't matter if I'm supporting Charlton Heston and you're playing a lesser part. We'll all be together in Rome and the money's important.' Sam had rung up only a few weeks before, begging me to change my mind and it seemed so damned stupid to worry about billing and the size of the part. He was one of our best friends and this time I didn't think Bert had advised us properly. So, taking Fred Voorhees into my confidence, I told him to see that Tracy and Laura were always under his eye and for Rose and him to sleep in the house right next to their room. Something told me that Elmer wasn't after Tracy but me, so Jean and I flew to Hollywood. I told Bert what we planned to do and with his blessing called on Sam.

'Okay, you lucky man, you've got us both.' Willie Wyler, who was going to direct *Ben-Hur,* was in the office with Sam. There was a shocked silence and then Willie dashed out, shouting to Sam that he'd get on the phone right away.

'What's going on? We thought you'd be happy to see us.' Jean and I were rather crestfallen at our reception.

'You idiot, why didn't you say you'd do it last week? Metro has fixed Stephen Boyd and Haya Harareet.'

'Never heard of them,' I said cattily.

Sam ignored that and went on, 'Haya's no problem, as she's under contract to Metro, but Boyd's under contract to Twentieth and there's some big interstudio deal on. Anyway, Willie's on the phone now. We'll know soon.'

And we did. Twentieth wouldn't release Metro from the deal, and so Boyd played Messala and very good he was too, but that one week made so much difference to so many lives. It caused an unnecessary death and I think an unnecessary divorce, among other things. But none of us were to know that as we said goodbye to Willie and Sam and, wishing them luck, returned to the ranch.

Soon after, Jean got an offer to star in a costume blockbuster called *Spartacus,* with Kirk Douglas and Larry Olivier. She accepted and we moved back to the hotel apartment for her costume fittings and pre-production tests. Metro offered me a film with Gary Cooper, to be directed by Hitchcock and I was thrilled. I knew my part was very secondary to Coop's but that didn't matter a damn, Jean and I would be working in Hollywood at the same time. And then the bubble burst. Metro had decided to make the film in England. Another separation. In spite of my moodiness and general nervous state, Jean still didn't want another separation.

'You've just been away for seven months with only a week in between. I don't expect you to hang around here all the time while I work but at least you could come from the ranch at weekends and we could be together. I know you love the ranch and there's lots for you to do there and we do have that film together later on, so we shouldn't have to worry about money, should we?'

If only I hadn't listened. If only I'd gone and done that film in England things might have worked out differently. If only . . . So I refused the film and, after spending a few weeks with Jean to see her comfortably started in her work, kissed my girls goodbye and went back to the ranch. It was very lonely as Jamie and Lindsay were spending their holidays with Elspeth who had come over to live in America some time before to be near them, and without Tracy and Laura I was alone in the house. Thank God I was.

The New Mexico ranch had been on offer for some time and I'd had many visits from prospective buyers. They all seemed to think that they could get me to lower my price by running the place down – it's so far away – not much of a ranch house – fences in bad condition, too few watering places – pretty poor stock, etc. I was only asking the price I had paid which had been low, plus a normal valuation for the cattle. I hadn't even charged for that expensive 'pee'. Their constant knocking of that beautiful place infuriated me and I would tell them that, as it was so poor, I wouldn't dream of cheating them and showed them the door. When they started suggesting they might meet my terms I insisted it wasn't worth the money and they would go away completely bewildered. One day a knock came on the door and an obvious cattleman was standing there.

'Let me introduce myself, Mr Granger. My name's Degraftonreid and I think you own the most beautiful ranch in New Mexico. I'd like to buy it, sir.'

Well, that sure made a change. 'Come in, Mr Reid.'

'Degraftonreid, sir, one word; call me Eric, it's simpler.'

We went in and sat down and Eric started to extol the beauties of my ranch and, when told the price, admitted that it was very fair. 'There's one problem, Mr Granger. I'm a little short of cash at the moment.' Where had I heard that before? I started to grin as he explained that he could take over the remaining payments due to my old friend Bull Adams, but he would like time to pay me the rest.

'Yes, that seems fair, but how are you going to find the money?' I was thoroughly enjoying this and wondered if he'd be as persuasive as I'd been in the past.

'Well, it's like this, Mr Granger, if you could give me till October, I could round up the calves and, with the price I'd get, I could pay you out of that.'

By God, he'd gone one better than me. He was gambling on the price of beef at the end of the year and, if it went up, he'd be paying me with money from my own calves. He was a man after my own heart, a gambler and he was honest, he hadn't tried to bullshit me, he'd laid his cards on the table and I liked that. So Degraftonreid became the owner of the T4J with no money down but, unlike me, luck was with him as the price of beef soared and it meant he got the ranch for practically nothing.

During those quiet days with just Fred and Rose to keep me company, watching the Charolais bull calves develop as we prepared them for the end of year shows in Texas, I was sure I'd made the right decision in buying this ranch. I'd seen how my kids adored the life, with their own horses and their different chores to perform; Jean obviously loved her house and her special 'foolproof' horse that I'd found for her and was becoming an excellent horsewoman; Tracy, with her lovely playroom, gardens and even her own island, would obviously be happy growing up here and I, in spite of all the problems, loved it deeply. It wasn't going to be easy but with luck we'd make it. And then my new-found peace was shattered.

Elmer called and said he had to see me as someone else was trying to kill me, a fellow called Burris. He sounded sane and assured me that in spite of everything he had my safety at heart and insisted on seeing me to explain. I told him to come out right away, made sure the .38 was in its place in my chair and checked that the wicked looking .357 was behind the bottles on the bar.

Burris! I couldn't believe it. We'd had a little unpleasantness with him some time ago. He'd come to visit as he was the brother of Toodles Burris, my neighbour up in New Mexico, and told me how much he and his wife loved a house we had on the ranch near the entrance, two miles away from HQ. It was unoccupied and apparently without our knowing he'd been over it. He begged me to sell it to him with fifty acres and offered me $50,000. I told him that it was okay with me but I would have to discuss it with Jean as the place was half hers.

He had gone away very pleased but to my amazement Jean refused point blank. 'We don't want strangers so close. Please, darling, I'd much rather not.'

'Okay, Jeannie, if you don't want it, that's it', but I couldn't help smiling at Jean, who'd been brought up in Cricklewood where the houses are only separated by a few yards, considering a neighbour two miles away as being too close. When I'd phoned Burris and told him the news, he'd sounded very upset and had accused me of breaking my word, but I told him that was nonsense and he'd slammed down the phone. But surely he didn't want to kill me for that? I just couldn't believe it.

I heard Elmer's car crunching on the gravel and, as he knocked on the door, I gripped the gun behind me. 'Come on in, Elmer.' He came into the room and a strange feeling came over me as I looked at the scarred face of the man who had been my friend but who had since threatened to kill me.

'Got a gun on you?'

'Why hell no, Jim, of course not.' He turned round with his hands out and I could see that he was telling the truth.

'Well I have, Elmer, so no funny business.' I took out the .38 and showed him. I thought I could detect a look of fear in his eyes as he slowly sat opposite me. 'Now what's all this about Burris?' And he told me. It was incredible. He couldn't have been making it up, surely, he couldn't have invented the story.

He had run into Burris across the line in Nogales and heard from him how furious he was with me for double-crossing him about the house.

'I didn't doublecross him.'

'That's what he said, Jim, so listen, it gets better.' Burris had taken Elmer aside and told him he knew that Elmer had it in for me and taking out a packet of book matches, bent up two matches and said, 'That's what I'll give to have Granger knocked off', meaning two thousand dollars. That bit with the book matches had me convinced, nobody could have made that up. 'It's true Jim, I swear. Why don't you call him? You'll see.'

I dialled Burris's number. 'That you, Burris? Granger here. Elmer tells me you're mad at me about the house.'

'Well, Mr Granger, I sure was upset. Elmer will tell you.'

'I also hear you want to kill me. Is that right?' Burris laughed but said nothing. 'Why don't you come on out, Burris, and we'll talk about it.'

'Sure, Mr Granger, I'm on my way.'

I sat for a moment looking at Elmer, wondering if I wasn't dreaming. I just couldn't believe that a man was on his way out who had offered the man facing me money to have me killed.

I got up and took the .357 from behind the bottles and told

Elmer that in case of trouble I thought this might be more lethal. I sat down with the gun in my lap. 'I tell you Elmer, any funny moves when he comes in and I'll shoot you both.' Elmer sat there frozen, his face white as a sheet. I might not have been too good at a quick draw but he knew I was a crack shot, as we'd had competitions in our friendly days and I'd often outshot him. We waited in absolute silence. We heard the crunch of the car on the gravel and I took a firmer grip on the gun. There was a knock on the door and at my shout to come in Burris entered. He stood for a moment in shocked amazement as he saw me sitting there with the gun and then rather nervously put his hand inside his shirt front. Elmer leapt out of his chair and grabbed him.

'Put that gun away, you idiot. Granger's armed. Get out of here.' Elmer wrestled the frightened looking Burris out of the door. I had stood up and was pointing the gun and I swear if either had turned to come back I'd have shot them both. But Elmer had hustled Burris out to his car and I heard it take off. Elmer came back in. 'Hey, take it easy, pardner, put it away.'

I hadn't realized I was still pointing the gun straight at his stomach and I lowered it as I sank back trembling into my chair. 'The sonofabitch was going for a gun, you saw it, didn't you.' I had indeed, but I still couldn't believe it. Why should he have gone for his gun with me sitting there with one already in my hand? I marched across and dialled my friend Judge Hathaway.

The Hathaways were my good friends and neighbours and a very important family in Arizona. Bob Hathaway was a state senator; Greg, the eldest, was head of the Highway Patrol; Jim, whom I was now calling, was a judge and another was a colonel in the army. Good to have people like that as your friends and they one and all hated the man sitting opposite me who, as I found out later, had insulted their father.

Jim Hathaway came on the phone. I told him what had happened and he assured me that he'd have Burris picked up and would I come down to Nogales next morning to see him and prefer charges.

'All right, Elmer, what do I owe you? You obviously didn't do this for love.'

'Oh, hell, Jim, you know I really like you. We've had our differences' (you can say that again, I thought), 'but hell, I'll always be your friend.'

'What do you want, Elmer?'

'Well, now, you do have that stud.'

Elmer had always had his eye on a Poco Bueno stud I'd bought some time ago. Poco Bueno had been a champion cutting horse and his get were very valuable. I'd named this one Poco Tracy after my daughter. 'What about Bessie?'

'She's outback in the car.'

'Okay Elmer, give me Bessie and go collect the horse. But that's it. I don't ever want to see you again.'

Elmer wasn't able to argue as I still clutched that lethal weapon. I gave orders to Al, my herdsman, to help Elmer load the horse and in exchange took possession of a rather bedraggled Bessie.

Next morning I walked into Jim Hathaway's office and there was the ashen faced Burris in the charge of the town sheriff. Apparently they'd already heard his version and the true story was quite incredible. Burris had met Elmer across the line but the conversation had been entirely different. Burris had told Elmer how upset he was not to be able to buy that house and Elmer had asked him how much it would be worth if he could persuade me to sell. He'd intimated that he had something on me and there'd be no problem. Burris had offered two thousand dollars commission if the deal went through. My God, what a Machiavellian bastard Elmer was.

'But why did you go for your gun when you came in?'

'Hell, Mr Granger, I never carry a gun. I was going for my cigarettes. I always carry them inside my shirt.'

Jesus, I'd nearly shot a man for reaching for his cigarettes.

His story was absolutely believable and his reputation in the town far superior to the dubious Elmer Black's. They let the thoroughly frightened Burris go and Jim Hathaway suggested he and his brothers should all meet at my house that afternoon.

When I'd told my story, Greg, the head of the Highway Patrol, after a quiet conversation with the judge and the senator, went to the phone. 'Is that you, Emilio? Get out to the Granger ranch as soon as possible.' Greg then told me that Emilio was one of his toughest officers and would know exactly how to handle the situation. When he arrived, he turned out to be about five foot eight high and about the same width, and nearly crushed two of my fingers as he shook hands.

'Emilio, you know Elmer Black.'

'Sure do, Mr Hathaway.'

'Now, Emilio, listen carefully. Black's been giving our good friend and neighbour Mr Granger bad trouble. I mean really bad trouble. I want him out of the state, Emilio. Not out of the town, out of state. If he gives you any trouble you know what to do.'

Emilio saluted and, telling his boss it would be a pleasure, crushed my fingers again in another handshake and left. The brothers told me my troubles were over and to have complete confidence in Emilio. 'Supposing he refuses to leave?' I asked. I was told he'd better leave willingly or he'd leave in a pine box. Giving orders to my ranchhands that they were to report to me any signs of Elmer I nervously waited for news.

Four or five days later Emilio was on the phone to report that Elmer had 'done left town', as he put it and I invited him up to tell me what had happened. Over a Bourbon he gave me the story. 'He was staying in that motel he always uses and I parked my car right outside his cabin door. When he came out I gave him a look.' Emilio pulled his already frighteningly tough face into a horrible grimace. 'He went across to the coffee shop for his breakfast and I parked right outside. When he came out I gave him that look again. Then he went across the line where he's got a half-assed office and I parked right outside the door. After a few minutes he came out and I gave him that look again. He came up to me and said, "Are you following me, officer?" "I sure am, Black," I told him. "But why," he asked. "Because I'm going to kill you," I said. You should have seen his face, Mr Granger. You sure would have enjoyed it.' I could imagine. Highway patrolmen with their cars with flashing lights, rifles tucked over the windshield, .45 Colts on their hips, always gave me a scare when I was pulled over for speeding, but to have one tell me he was going to kill me would have given me a heart attack.

'Go on, Emilio, what happened then?'

'Well, Mr Granger, he asked why I was going to kill him. I told him I took orders from my boss Mr Hathaway and that he and his brothers were good friends of yours and that he'd been giving you trouble. "Now, Black," I said, "we don't want any more trouble for our friend Mr Granger, so if you don't leave Arizona now, and I mean now, I'm going to kill you." Of course I was only kidding, Mr Granger [I don't believe he was] but Black took the hint. He's done gone, Mr Granger. You ain't never going to see that sonofabitch again.' He was right. I never did. But what would I have done without my good friends the Hathaways.

I kept Bessie's return as a surprise and when Jean had finished her work on *Spartacus* and drove up to the house, she was met by a frenzied little bundle that jumped up into her arms. Jean, of course, was immediately in floods of tears and when she asked how I'd managed to get her back, I didn't tell her what it had cost me, and I didn't mean the horse. Luckily Bessie in her happiness at being reunited with her beloved mistress seemed to have completely got over her jealousy of Tracy, and the two of them became the best of friends.

31

Now that it was over I would like to be able to say that I became more relaxed and optimistic about our future, but the reverse was the case. I became suspicious and very demanding. I used to have nightmares about Elmer and in fact a lot of the joy had gone out of the challenge of ranching and breeding. I was obviously suffering a nervous reaction to all the troubles I'd been having. I hadn't really got over the strain of the Hughes years; the shock of Elmer's betrayal was the final straw and the effect made me irritable and short-tempered.

It must have been a difficult time for Jean to see her husband who, apparently having everything, never seemed really happy, laughing and joking less and not showing his love in a physical way.

Of course I still loved Jean. I loved my children and adored Tracy. I used to tell her stories at night, stories I invented about the inhabitants of her lake and island, Philip and Philomena the fish, Crafty the crane, Frightful the frog, Basher the bull, Flitter the fly, Slowly the slug and, naturally, Donald the duck and Gobble the goose. I made up all these creatures who used our lake and Tracy at three years old would correct me when I got the names wrong or left one out as I wove stories about their problems and encounters. I loved to hear her say grace before tucking in – naturally she'd inherited the Granger appetite – to see her say her prayers before story time. Of course there were moments of great happiness but in the small hours, with Jean sleeping peacefully beside me, I'd wonder if I'd taken on more than I could handle.

One day Howard Hawkes turned up and asked if he could

invite Duke Wayne and Ward Bond up to the ranch for lunch. They were working in the vicinity on a film called *Rio Bravo* and we were delighted to welcome them. Duke was amazed when I showed him over the ranch, the herd of purebred Charolais, the neat corrals, the show-barns, the lake, our farmland and the lovely house. 'Christ, Jim, I don't own anything like this and I earn three times as much as you. How did you do it?' I tried to explain the advantages of amortization, write-offs, expenses and how quite legally Uncle Sam paid ninety per cent for the first five years. He was fascinated so I introduced him to Ralph Wingfield and· that was the start of Duke going into the ranching business in a big way.

I was beginning to calm down a bit. Things were going smoothly on the ranch, I had told Jean about my ghastly experience with Elmer and she was very understanding, my young prospective herdsires were looking splendid and we all had great hopes of their success in the sales in Texas when another blow came. Christ, 1959 was not my year.

John Woolf of Romulus rang up to tell me that Jackie Clayton, who had been going to direct our film, had decided, after his success with the Oscar winning *Room at the Top,* to have a year off and therefore our film would have to be postponed. Oh Jesus, I'd been counting on that one. I rang Bert and told him for the love of God to get me another film right away. He said he would try, but starring parts in films were always booked six months ahead and things weren't too good in Hollywood anyway.

I waited anxiously and Bert eventually rang to tell me that there was absolutely nothing and I would have to wait until 1960, but he did say that Jean was wanted for *Elmer Gantry* which was to be made in a few months' time with Burt Lancaster. He had refused it before as he knew she was booked to do the Romulus film with me but now that it was cancelled, would she like to do it?

I felt so ashamed when I explained the situation to Jean

but she understood that we needed the money and accepted. It wasn't sufficient that I had made eighteen films to her twelve since we'd been married, that I'd earned much more up to that moment; those facts didn't help my feelings at all. The cancellation meant that I wouldn't have made a film for a year at a time when we desperately needed the money. I hated putting this responsibility on Jean's shoulders as I knew she would have loved the positions to have been reversed and had the chance to spend a year with her daughter on her lovely ranch. God, why hadn't I gone into Sam's office one week earlier? We would both have been in Rome now with Tracy, with lots of time off to enjoy that city together and earning big money. As I was thinking this and wondering how Sam was getting on without us, the phone rang. Jean saw the stricken look on my face. 'God, Jimmy, what's happened?'

'It's Sam. He's dead. He's just died of a heart attack in Rome.' Jean took the phone away from me as I couldn't speak and told Joe Cohn the production manager on the film that I'd call back. Sam, one of my two greatest friends, was dead. Why in God's name hadn't I been there?

When I was able I called back to find out the details. The film had been over schedule, the big boys from New York had constantly been on Sam's back, putting all the blame on him. Sam had been ill with worry and the strain had proved too much. Nobody there loved him enough to see that he rested, had a doctor. Maybe if I'd been there to insist that he took it easy...I started to blame myself. What did the importance of a part or billing matter where a friend's life was concerned.

Sam's body was flown back from Italy for burial and Jean and I joined his many friends who attended the funeral. I was one of the pallbearers and Sam being a very large man we had to struggle up the hill to the plot he'd picked out. Clark Gable muttered that he thought Sam had chosen this inaccessible spot on purpose but I'm afraid I didn't smile.

396

The funeral was a ghastly affair with Sam's wife, Mary, bravely holding up his old mother. Bert Allenberg was there amongst the many mourners and after it was over we all went on to the Hillcrest Country Club. I couldn't go in as I was completely shattered and told Bert that that was the last time I would ever attend the funeral of someone I loved. I just couldn't take it. Bert embraced me and told me not to worry as probably it would never happen again. I remember seeing his tall, handsome figure waving to us as we drove away. I was never to see him alive again.

We got back to the ranch and I tried to occupy myself in madly dashing about organizing the planting of crops, reconstructing the faulty sprinkler system, planning the building of new corrals, anything to keep my mind off Sam. I'd see my little daughter toddling about on her island and sadly think she'd never have that sweet man as her godfather.

Only two weeks later, while I was busy branding some new calves in the shute near the house, I heard Jean screaming for me. She was almost hysterical and all I could make out was something about the phone. I picked her up in my arms and raced inside. Putting her gently down on the couch I grabbed the dangling telephone. It was Mildred Allenberg to tell me that Bert had died that night. Oh no, not Bert, it couldn't be true. My two best friends dead within two weeks of each other. Instead of me comforting Mildred I heard her trying to comfort me. She was asking if Jean and I would come down for the 'Shiva' as she knew that Bert looked on us as part of his family. I told her that of course we'd be there and went to comfort Jean. She just couldn't take it in. Her own father had died when she was very young and Bert had been like another father to her from the moment she came to America nine years before. Strangely, I'd loved him like a father too and we both called him 'Pop' although he was only twelve years older than me. I don't know how we got through the next few days. The night before the funeral we sat with his family while Bert lay in his open coffin.

The synagogue was absolutely full for the service. He was a much loved man in a town that gave love very sparingly. Another close friend of his was Frank Sinatra who was openly sobbing as Jean tried to comfort him. Bert had proved a good friend to Frank when he was down and it took him a very long time to get over the loss. It took Jean and me very much longer, I'm afraid, in fact I never really did. Our beautiful ranch seemed desolate after those two desperate weeks and I couldn't bear the thought that my two friends would never see it. They had promised to come for a long weekend directly Sam got back from Rome and we had thought of asking Spence as well so that the long overdue christening of our daughter could take place.

Jean left to start work on *Elmer Gantry* and I was again left alone. My two children were in school and of course Tracy and Laura went to L.A. to be with Jean. As I wandered over the ranch and lived alone in that big empty house I nearly went out of my mind. If only I'd had a film to keep me occupied. It wasn't enough to see my young bulls loaded and on their way to the all-important shows in Dallas, Fort Worth and San Antone. I didn't really feel anything when my herdsman rang to tell me that our bulls had topped all the sales. It should have been great and encouraging news as it had proved that my choice of females and our breeding programme had been outstandingly successful but I really felt nothing. I knew deep down that it was all too late.

My visits to Jean in Beverly Hills were a disaster as I couldn't really take any interest in her stories about the film, the director or Burt Lancaster. I felt out of it and must have seemed completely uninterested in everything, herself included, but the film was nearly finished and soon she would be coming back. Then one evening when I called as usual from the ranch she told me she had agreed to do five more days on the picture for nothing. Nothing, at a time when we needed every penny we could both earn. We had an almighty row and I hung up on her. A few moments later Jean was on the phone telling me that she'd like a divorce. I told her that if that would make her happy it was all right with me.

I didn't mean it, of course, but I didn't think she meant it either. We were both suffering shock from the disasters of the last months and Jean was beginning to blame me for the ranch venture that was forcing us to work so often to fill that gaping maw of repayments. Of course her Hollywood 'friends' were dropping the poison of how could she stand having her husband enjoying himself while she worked her heart out, what did he know about ranching, that he was sure to lose everything, etc. Those trouble-making gossipers didn't know that I'd just had the biggest success any new breeder could possibly attain and that in only one more year with the new crop of calves that were already on the ground, most of our debts would be paid off. That kind of vicious talk hadn't helped but it had been a combination of things that had ruined our marriage; the nerve-racking strange wedding, the Hughes battle, the continuous separations, the bad timing of my turning down those films and the final blow, when we lost our two greatest friends.

Jean had made her shattering announcement early in December 1959 and I suddenly remembered that I'd promised Larry Olivier that he could spend Christmas with us. He had told me he wanted somewhere with peace and quiet where he could think things out. He knew about our ranch and I'd invited him to come and stay with us.

When Jean arrived back, having completed *Elmer Gantry,* I reminded her that Larry would soon be arriving and she agreed that we should behave as if nothing had happened. We didn't want to worry him with our problems at this crucial moment in his own life and so I found myself listening to Larry analysing his feelings about divorce.

He would go riding over the ranch all day and come back in the evening and tell us his thoughts. He still loved Vivien but had fallen in love with Joan Plowright. Vivien had given Larry a pretty hard time recently, but their twenty years together couldn't just be dismissed. Larry told us how absolutely miraculous his marriage had been for so many years but that during the last five he'd gone through hell with Vivien's illness and strange behaviour.

I had known them from the beginning when I had been that nervous young actor reading for the part with Vivien at the Gate Theatre in 1938. Only five years before I had experienced the horror of Vivien's nervous breakdown and realized the effect this must have had on him but I also knew how much Vivien adored him. We tried to advise but mostly listened as he reasoned things out aloud. I, of course, was inclined to advise against the divorce knowing what it would do to Vivien.

'Can you really be happy, Larry, knowing that you're making someone you love utterly miserable?'

'My God, Jimmy, why do you think I'm hesitating?'

Jean on the other hand was urging him to go ahead and marry his Joan if he really loved her, as no one should sacrifice their own happiness to protect the feelings of somebody else. I remember wondering at that moment if Jean had somebody else but quickly discarded this suspicion as she had already told me that there was no one.

That Christmas Day was one of the unhappiest I've ever spent. My children had no suspicion of the situation between 'Jeanniebags' and their father and of course my beloved Tracy, being just over three years old, was far too young to sense anything. I watched her as she excitedly opened her presents under the Christmas tree and miserably thought I would probably never see this happy family scene again. We'd bought Larry a watch and had it inscribed 'For darling Larry from J. & J.', and I believe he wears it to this day. And then I tried to think positively, that maybe Jean could be persuaded to change her mind and everything wasn't over yet.

The day before he was due to leave, Larry came and told us he'd reached a decision. I held my breath while I waited to hear what he would say, thinking that his decision might be the same as Jean's. He had decided to divorce Vivien. My heart sank as I saw the pleased look on Jean's face. Larry thanked us for our patience, advice and hospitality. He then said something I'll never forget. 'It was really seeing you two together, how much you loved each other, that made me decide I wanted that kind of happiness too.' Oh, my God, if he'd only known what had been going on in the privacy of our bedroom every night.

Larry married his Joan and became a happy family man. Vivien never recovered from the divorce. She knew that Larry had every reason to leave her and was quite right to take the step he had, but she loved and missed him until the day she died.

When my children went back to school after the holidays Jean returned to Beverly Hills with Tracy and Laura and once again I was alone on the ranch. One day, chasing a calf across a field, I twisted my already damaged right knee and was in agony. The doctor advised me to have an operation as apparently the cartilage had finally slipped out of place causing the swelling and pain. I went to the Cedars of Lebanon where only a few years before in another wing I had welcomed Tracy into our lives.

For this operation I had a spinal and the after-effect of this anaesthetic causes certain difficulties. The nurses were constantly insisting I should have a catheter to ease the situation but I strongly protested, saying that I had no special urge. I was irritated by their constant enquiries into this very personal procedure, suspecting that being females and having got a movie star into their clutches, they only wanted to see how he was built down there. Eventually I agreed to have it done but insisted on a male nurse, smiling at the disappointed looks on their faces.

The male nurse arrived and inserted an infected catheter. The result was horrific. My temperature would soar to 104° and then drop alarmingly. Apparently serious infection of the 'waterworks' is very hard to knock out and I was given very strong antibiotics. I could keep no food or fluids down and became so dehydrated that eventually I had to have fluids intravenously. Then I got a terrifying attack of hiccups, devastating hiccups that racked my body and continued nonstop for forty-eight hours. I lost twenty-five pounds in seven days.

Eventually I was moved into the rented house where I was looked after sympathetically by Jean and Laura, and little Tracy would come trotting in to chat with her crippled father. I was still on the very strong antibiotics when one morning I woke to find my hands so swollen I could hardly close them and had great difficulty in breathing. I told Jean I thought she ought to call the doctor as I was beginning to feel desperately ill and wasn't cheered by his reaction when he arrived. He took one look and muttering 'Jesus Christ' injected me with adrenalin. As I started to shake with the effect it had on my heart I heard him calling for an ambulance and, before slipping into unconsciousness, heard him say it was a matter of life and death. I woke up next morning in hospital, not knowing really what had happened, with Jean sitting beside my bed. Jean told me tearfully that I'd really frightened her as she thought I was going to die. I told her that that might have been the best solution but regretted the bitter remark when I saw the hurt look on her face.

'Darling, how can you say a thing like that. I still love you, it's just that I can't...' she broke into sobs as I told her I quite understood and that it was all my fault anyway. At that moment the doctor came in and told me that I was now completely out of danger but that it had been a near thing.

'You developed a massive allergy to the antibiotics. I've

never seen anything like it before. Your veins were collapsing and your lungs were filling with fluid. If I'd arrived half an hour later you'd have been dead. For Christ's sake be careful what antibiotics you take in future.'

After they'd left and I lay there dozing I suddenly remembered that far-off prediction made by Mrs Perryman, the fork she'd seen when I was forty-seven. If I survived that fork there would be another divorce and I would cross the sea again. She'd been so uncannily right in all her other predictions, why should she be wrong now? I was forty-seven that year and miserably realized I'd lost the battle over my marriage.

We decided that at all costs we must keep our proposed divorce secret because of the children. I had taken Elspeth into my confidence though she found it hard to believe as she'd thought we'd been so happy. She agreed to my suggestion that, if I would buy a house in England, she would look after Jamie and Lindsay as I was in no fit state to look after anyone or anything. Thank God she was still my very good friend and was sympathetic and understanding.

I had made up my mind to leave America as soon as possible as I couldn't face living on the ranch with all its memories and didn't want to work in Hollywood with the possibility of meeting Jean. I knew that would be as upsetting for her as for myself and decided to start a new life in Europe. The proposed divorce was to be a friendly one with no lawyers fighting over community property. Jean was generous and demanded nothing apart from custody of Tracy and told me she didn't want to do anything to force me to sell my beloved ranch. I tried to tell her that without my family the ranch was no longer 'beloved' but accepted the arrangement as being the sensible thing to do at the time.

We chose a Nogales lawyer who had been a friend of ours. He really couldn't understand why two people who obviously loved each other should want a divorce. 'You're always thinking of her when you discuss details and she's always thinking about you when she talks to me. Why in

God's name can't you patch it up?'

All I could say was, 'You don't understand.' How could anyone understand?

Jean had accepted an offer to appear with Cary Grant and Deborah Kerr in a film to be made in England. How strange that those two friends who had figured so prominently in my life should be with Jean at this particular moment, while I had accepted a film with John Wayne, so she'd be in England and I'd be in America. When these films were over and my two children settled with their mother, we would announce our divorce.

I helped Jean to pack for the last time and accompanied her, Tracy and Laura aboard the plane. As I watched it take off I hated those machines that had separated us so many times over the last ten years and were now taking my wife and daughter away from me for the last time. I knew I would probably see them again but it would never be the same. Jean would obviously find someone and I didn't see myself as the ex-husband always popping in to take his daughter away for weekends or holidays, that only confuses the child and upsets the new husband. Tracy would know that I loved her and I would always be there if she needed me but I didn't want to confuse that young life with divided loyalties. I hoped she wouldn't forget the stories of the lake with all its inhabitants too quickly but realized that of course she would. Three and a half isn't exactly the age to remember anything, myself included.

Henry Hathaway was the director of *North to Alaska* and in my first film for a year I nearly failed. He was a cigar-chewing, bullying kind of director who, although charming enough in his own home, became a monster directly he walked on to a set.

My first scene with Duke Wayne was a nightmare. I couldn't remember my lines. The more I 'fluffed' the more Hathaway glared and chewed on his bloody cigar. Duke was slightly bewildered by the behaviour of an actor who had starred in fifty films yet didn't seem capable of saying one line of dialogue. The truth was that I was terrified. I had lost all confidence and felt depressed and ill. No one knew what a strain I was under or of my broken marriage. They only knew that I was awful in the scene. I muttered that I had a touch of 'flu and, excusing myself, went to my dressing-room and took a belt of brandy and two tranquillizers. I had never taken a drink during work before and, knowing what a weak head I had, didn't know what the effect would be but it sure couldn't make me any worse than I already was. With my head starting to 'buzz', I walked out and took up my position, asking Duke to excuse me for holding him up. I nodded to the glowering director and sailed through the scene. By this time I didn't give a damn about anything and that's really the only attitude to have when working for Hathaway.

After only two weeks of work, Phil Kellog, who had taken over Bert Allenberg's position at the Morris office, phoned to tell me that Metro wanted me for two films in England after this one had been completed. He'd had my instructions not to accept any pictures to be made in Hollywood, so this worked out fine. Another week later, Phil was again on the phone to ask if I would be interested in two more pictures to be made in Italy, a blockbuster called *Sodom and Gomorrah* and a classic called *Gattopardo*. I accepted. Jesus, I was making a film with Wayne now and had four more lined up over the next eighteen months. Why couldn't this have happened last year? Everything might have been so different. Again that 'if only'.

Somehow I managed to get through the slapstick comedy with Wayne and returned to the ranch to make final arrangements for my long absence. I knew that I could leave everything in the hands of my friends the Voorheeses and warned them that I wasn't planning to return for at least three years, if then. I had put the property up for sale but knew that it would take a long time to move as it entailed a lot of money. There was a place on the ranch that we'd all named 'The Pimple', a hill overlooking the whole Santa Cruz valley with the headquarters, our house and the fields containing the grazing Charolais spread out below. I used to go up there with binoculars and watch our Mexican help work – more often not work – and they came to believe that I had occult powers when I would ask one of them why he had been sleeping under a Mesquite tree when he was supposed to be changing pipe. He had made sure I was nowhere around before he'd taken his siesta and couldn't understand how I knew. From up on The Pimple with powerful glasses I knew everything.

We had built a shelter up there, as in summer there was always a breeze, and with the clear air we could see fifty miles in every direction. We would picnic up there in the evenings and lie around on the cushioned seats enjoying the view of our spread. The children had all put their initials in the wet cement floor, together with Jean's and my own, and as I looked at them I realized we'd never all be up here together again, laughing and joking.

But in spite of all these gloomy thoughts I had to admit I was looking forward to going back to Europe. I longed to see London again and walk the streets where I'd spent my childhood, where I'd grown up. I longed to see my mother and sister and all my friends, to hear all those lovely English accents. In spite of the fact that I owned this ranch I was always expecting a Navajo Indian to come riding over the hills and tell me to get the hell off his land. Again I remembered Mrs Perryman's prediction. 'You'll cross the sea again and continue your success and later I see another marriage.'

I wondered what she'd look like. . .

Stewart Granger appeared in the following films

1938	*So This Is London*
1942–3	*Thursday's Child*
1943	*The Man in Grey*
1943	*The Lamp Still Burns*
1943	*Fanny by Gaslight*
1944	*Waterloo Road*
1944	*Love Story*
1944	*Madonna of the Seven Moons*
1945	*Caesar and Cleopatra*
1946	*Caravan*
1946	*The Magic Bow*
1947	*Captain Boycott*
1948	*Blanche Fury*
1948	*Saraband for Dead Lovers*
1949	*Woman Hater*
1949	*Adam and Evelyne*
1950	*King Solomon's Mines*
1951	*Soldiers Three*
1951	*The Light Touch*
1951	*Wild North*
1952	*Scaramouche*
1952	*The Prisoner of Zenda*
1953	*Young Bess*
1953	*Salome*
1954	*All the Brothers Were Valiant*
1954	*Beau Brummell*
1955	*Green Fire*
1955	*Moonfleet*

1955	*Footsteps in the Fog*
1956	*Bhowani Junction*
1956	*The Last Hunt*
1957	*The Little Hut*
1957	*Gun Glory*
1958	*The Whole Truth*
1958	*Harry Black*
1960	*North to Alaska*

Many other films followed, but they fall outside the time-limits of this book.

Acknowledgements

The publishers wish to thank the following for permission to reproduce stills from the listed films:

The Rank Organisation Ltd, for *The Man in Grey, Fanny by Gaslight, Love Story, Waterloo Road, Caravan, The Magic Bow* (all made by Gainsborough Studios), *Caesar and Cleopatra, Adam and Evelyne, Woman Hater*.

EMI Films, for *Saraband for Dead Lovers* (made by Ealing Studios).

MGM, for *King Solomon's Mines, The Light Touch, Soldiers Three, Scaramouche, Young Bess, The Wild North, The Prisoner of Zenda, Beau Brummell, Green Fire, Bhowani Junction, Gun Glory*.

Twentieth Century-Fox, for *Harry Black and the Tiger, North to Alaska*.

Index